Tensions in the struggle
for sexual minority
rights in Europe

Tensions in the struggle for sexual minority rights in Europe

Que[e]rying political practices

NICO J. BEGER

∼

Manchester University Press
Manchester and New York

distributed exclusively in the USA by Palgrave

Copyright © Nico J. Beger 2004

The right of Nico J. Beger to be identified as the author of this work has been asserted by him in accordance with the Copyright, Designs and Patents Act 1988.

Published by Manchester University Press
Oxford Road, Manchester M13 9NR, UK
and Room 400, 175 Fifth Avenue, New York, NY 10010, USA
www.manchesteruniversitypress.co.uk

Distributed exclusively in the USA by
Palgrave, 175 Fifth Avenue, New York NY 10010, USA

Distributed exclusively in Canada by
UBC Press, University of British Columbia, 2029 West Mall, Vancouver, BC, Canada V6T 1Z2

British Library Cataloguing-in-Publication Data
A catalogue record for this book is available from the British Library

Library of Congress Cataloging-in-Publication Data
A catalog record for this book is available from the Library of Congress

ISBN 13: 978 0 7190 6931 4

First published in hardback 2004 by Manchester University Press
This paperback edition first published 2009

Printed by Lightning Source

Contents

Preface	vii
Acknowledgements	viii
Introduction	1

Part I Theory and politics

1	European institutions: sexual rights lobbying	18
2	Queer theory and political practices	40
3	Mind the gap: hybrid relations of queer theory and political practice	59

Part II Rights

4	European strategies: human rights	78
5	Claiming protection: anti-discrimination	101
6	Gender identity and sexual orientation: legal rights politics	125
7	A process of recognition: European citizenship	145
8	Framing the debate: kinship	173

Part III Activists

9	The political activist: agency	202
	Afterword: tensions in the struggle for sexual minority rights	225
	Appendix	229
	Glossary	232
	Bibliography	235
	Index	249

To Mieke Bal and Kurt Krickler

and to all theorists and activists like them
so daring and outstanding in their field

Preface

This book is based on research conducted between 1997 and 2001. The core analysis uses mainly legal, political, and interview documents collected up until 2001, but the book has been updated with all necessary material up to August 2003.

A few of the interviews were conducted in German and some secondary sources are also quoted from German. For the convenience of the reader, I have translated them into English, unless a published translation exists, and indicated this after the quote.

I acknowledge permission to use texts that have, mostly in quite different versions, been published before. A merged version of Chapters 2, 5, and 6 has appeared as Beger (2002) 'Putting gender and sexuality on the agenda: queer theory and legal politics' in Reza Banakar and Max Travers (eds) *An Introduction to Law and Social Theory*. A version of Chapter 3 appeared as Beger (2001) 'Mind the gap: hybridity and the antagonistic relations of queer theory and gay/lesbian political practice' in Joyce Goggin and Sonja Neef (eds) *Travelling Concepts: Text, Subjectivity, and Hybridity*. A brief summary of the argumentation used in Chapter 4 appeared as Beger (1999) 'Gay and lesbian rights are human rights! Que(e)rying a political practice in Europe' in Amsterdam School of Cultural Analysis *Privacies. Yearbook 1999*. And an earlier version of Chapter 6 appeared as Beger (2000a) 'Queer readings of Europe: gender identity, sexual orientation and the (im)potency of rights politics at the European Court of Justice' *Social & Legal Studies* 9(2):251–72.

Acknowledgements

I gratefully acknowledge the financial support granted to me between 1997 and 2001 by the Heinrich Böll Foundation and the Amsterdam School of Cultural Analysis.

I am indebted to Bettine Menke at the European University, Viadrina, for giving this research a first home, but particularly to Mieke Bal at the Amsterdam School of Cultural Analysis, who has been a superb promoter, a brilliant teacher, and an extremely reliable source of personal support. Thanks also to my colleagues in her theory seminar for the sharing of knowledge and the astute critical engagement with theory.

Research in the field of gender and sexuality has one very rewarding side-effect: the international network of academics who are willing to communicate in a non-hierarchical manner and who offer support and astute help quickly and generously. I cannot acknowledge all of those by name who have been involved in reading various chapters or publication drafts, in discussing ideas, or organising academic events with me, but want to mention a few: Murat Aydemir, Sudeep Dasgupta, Antke Engel, Corinna Genschel, Joyce Goggin, Sabine Hark, Didi Hermann, Yolande Jansen, Jaap Kooijman, Alice Kuzniar, Karen Nairn, Baden Offord, Shane Phelan, Katrina Roen, Carl Stychin, Nigel Warner, Volker Woltersdorf, and Julie Wuthnow. Their comments have been invaluable and any failure on my part to mend what they identified as problematic is entirely my responsibility. I particularly want to express my gratitude to Baden Offord for personal and academic support right when it was needed most; to Katrina Roen, who has edited the whole book with amazing patience, skill, and speed amidst her own busy schedule; to Lars Jochimsen and Maik Heyne for generous technical help; and to Sheila Swatschek for her impressive critical skills just before the publication. I am grateful to the staff at Manchester University Press for believing in the project and being patient with me.

Besides academic support, this kind of research needed the support of the activists I researched. I am deeply indebted to all my interviewees for their time and trust, and to the many activists around Europe who invited me to stay on their sofas, cooked dinners, picked me up from train stations, and took me out to meet their networks. My colleagues on the executive board of ILGA-Europe have taught me a lot over the years about how to become an activist in a transnational network, able to speak, write, negotiate, moderate, fight, and knock on doors. Thanks for enduring joint work: Tiia Aarnipuu, Adrian Coman, Isabelle Cruette, Riccardo Gottardi, Tatjana Greif, Steffen Jensen, Kurt Krickler, Jackie Lewis, and Nigel Warner.

I must mention my parents for their immense generosity, Daniela Riess-Beger for ongoing support on so many levels, and Kirstie Murdoch, Melanie Keuthe, and

ACKNOWLEDGEMENTS

Sheila Swatschelk for their share in my life. But most importantly, a group of people around the globe and one greyhound have consented to endure me and this project – as the package deal. You know who you are, this book would not have been written without your love and support!

Introduction

Since the 1970s Europe has seen the rise of social movements fighting nationally and transnationally for participation rights in society. Gay, lesbian, bisexual, and transgender movements are one example. In addition – particularly in the wake of the AIDS crisis – sexuality has become central to modern politics. Academic theorists have increasingly paid attention to the epistemological and ontological roles gender and sexuality play in the creation and maintenance of political, social, and economic domains. However, in the daily process of arguing for and about rights, the centrality of those roles is mostly hidden from view in official institutional and movement discourses. This book seeks to investigate the practices of gay and lesbian rights and lobby politics in Europe and their open and hidden relations to binary and hierarchical orders of dominance. From the vantage point of critical queer theory I will examine political and legal texts to trace the centrality of gender and sexuality for the conditions of European political discourses.

Within Europe there are two supranational institutions at which rights are claimed: the European Union (EU) and the Council of Europe (CoE). As international political bodies, the EU and the CoE have – besides the economic role of the EU – a strong historical commitment to human rights, social integration, equality, and the overcoming of nationalistic prejudice. In fact, the concern for developing an inclusive European citizenship is becoming increasingly important in the political conceptualisation of the EU. Therefore, Europe – as institution and idea – has become one of the major stages on which the fight for rights is played out by those alleging discrimination and social exclusion. According to political scientists Margaret Keck and Kathryn Sikkink (1998:208), countries most vulnerable to pressure from advocacy and minority rights groups are those who care about their international image. This is generally true for the all Members of the EU and also of the CoE. Their institutions are susceptible to advocacy networks and, thus, have become an important target of achieving change. Yet, the pre-conditions and consequences of specifically European rights discourses have hardly been researched.

The conventions of identity-based rights politics dominate the field of minority movements and the official politics of governments in relation to issues of social justice, equality, and anti-discrimination. In the history of lesbian and gay movements, change of the status quo through reform – social and legal – has probably been the most successful rally point of mobilisation. The first phase related and relates usually to a de-criminalisation of homosexual (male) offences, age of consent, sodomy laws, and other coercive state practices, such as police harassment, disinclination to prosecute hate crimes, and rights of speech and assembly. The second phase was and is usually a shift from 'keeping the state off our backs' to a rights movement that demands partnership rights and positive re-enforcement in employment, as well as social and legal protection from all forms of discrimination. For European gay and lesbian movements today, both of these phases are still current in various regions of the geographic continent of Europe. None of these demands has become entirely obsolete in Europe. It was not until 1 August 2003 that the last law penalising relationships between people of the same sex in Europe was eliminated.

The achievement of reform in the social, legal, political, and economic domains of Europe is doing more than encouraging gays, lesbians, bisexuals, and transgender people to 'come out'. The struggle for these rights has promoted feelings of pride, self-worth, public subculture, and community identity. It has also produced a politicising process that facilitates public awareness, mobilisation, and the development of a specific gay, lesbian, and bisexual as well as transgender practice and theory. While this holds true, to my mind, unqualified praise of rights and reform is questionable without analysing the status quo of gender and sexuality as ordering principles. For lesbians and gay men, legal rights and lobby politics have, on the one hand, won rights of survival, expression, and social acceptance. On the other hand it is precisely those identity-based politics which have created problems for the inclusion and acceptance of alternative sexualities into a norm(ality) that is ultimately set up to signify and exclude difference.

In response to this, activists in the USA developed a form of queer politics in the early 1990s.[1] At the same time theorists in the field of sexuality and gender started to use poststructuralist thought to investigate the epistemological, ontological, legal, economic, and social conditions of identity-based rights politics and movements. The focus shifted away from challenges to political or legal rules and moved towards challenges of analytic categories and explanatory systems in politics. To be precise, they moved towards the way gender and sexuality are psychologically and socially realised and maintained in a hierarchical order in the first place. Following ideas coming from the field of literary and film studies, a substantial set of philosophical, sociological, political, and legal writings has arisen in the North American, British, and Australian/New Zealand context. Apart from some work about Great Britain, however, very little has been written about European national contexts and nothing at the transnational European level using a queer and poststructuralist approach. This book aims to fill some part of this gap.

The connection between theory and practice has been an issue at the forefront of gay, lesbian, bisexual, and transgender studies. With the advent and increasing dominance of queer theory as academic currency in the US, there is an apparent breakdown of that connection. Many scholars in feminist, lesbian, gay, bisexual, and transgender studies accuse writers in queer theory of rendering politics and the achievement of rights and equality an impossibility.[2] It is not my intention to re-examine this breakdown nor the merits of queer theory *qua* theory since this has been amply explored and debated.[3] What becomes clear from the literature is that letting go of legal rights and equality entirely will not do; but taking them for granted and as being unquestionable will not do either. What concerns me here, therefore, is an analysis from a queer theoretical perspective of the implications of doing politics and achieving rights or justice in the European context. In doing so I will add to a newly emerging body of literature that employs a queer theoretical analysis rather than merely perpetuating the polarised debate on queer theory's implications.

More precisely, I investigate the major themes through which gay and lesbian politics are argued, conceptualised, and staged in the European context by those who work and lobby for them. Relevant themes are, among others, anti-discrimination, human rights, marriage and family, social and economical participation, equality, and age of consent laws. The question posed is then how these themes impact upon some of the fundamental ordering principles of modern democratic societies: gender, kinship, citizenship, humanness, and the law. To address this question I investigate texts on several levels: firstly, political texts, such as parliamentary reports, resolutions, and speeches; secondly, court judgments and legislation drafted by the EU Commission; thirdly, statements, submissions, and programmes written by activists; and, fourthly, quotations from interviews conducted with activists who work at the European level. I focus on one advocacy network and NGO (non-governmental organisation), ILGA-Europe – the European region of the International Lesbian and Gay Association – which is the only lesbian, gay, bisexual, and transgender lobbyist officially accredited within the European structures.

While I focus primarily on the precise themes through which gay and lesbian rights are argued, it is also my aim to consider the history of European sexual rights lobbying, the complexity of the queer theoretical intervention into these political practices, and the difficulties of transfer between theory and politics. This has led me to divide the book into three parts. Part I will contribute to the lack of overviews over the European situation in terms of institutional and legal information and in terms of discussing queer theory's background and implications for Europe as well as the meaning of political practices. Part I also contributes to a necessary negotiation of the seeming impasse in the exchange between theory and political practice.

However, the second chapter of Part I already starts with the deployment of theoretical and political concepts, which is the theme of analysis that carries the reader through the longer Part II. In Part II, each chapter reviews a selection of documents and interviews for the systems and orders they draw upon. Five political concepts – or rights claims – are analysed in this respect: human rights, anti-discrimination, legal politics, citizenship, and kinship. These chapters focus on the organisational level of sexual rights claims. Part III follows the same type of analysis, but briefly foregrounds the individual level of activism and the concept of agency.

After Foucault, one could speak of a genealogical reading of the conditions that allow homosexuality to be staged the way it is in the European cultural context. This book will not create this genealogy itself, but use the substantial work already done in that field.[4] I depart from the understandings of those works to analyse how the main pre-conditions of gender and sexuality create the script for a European sexual politics drama and how a transnational political stage becomes the space for re-instalment and re-negotiation of these conditions. Thus, I aim to combine the analysis of practical politics with furthering theoretical thought on the gendered and sexual constitution of social and political relations. The texts analysed for this purpose operate on three levels: the personal narrative of activists, the written narrative of official texts of the movements petitioning European institutions, and the written narrative of official documents of the European institutions themselves.[5]

Through the engagement with this material and with queer theory as critical theory, I conclude that political practices engaged around gender and sexuality are simultaneously a re-inscription and a contestation of the laws and orders that govern two of the most decisive ordering principles of European cultures: gender and sexuality. The following critical analysis of gay and lesbian politics intends to develop the re-thinking of political rights discourses in a way that disrupts the logic of sexuality as a definable, natural core of humanity while emphasising the central role it plays within the political domain.

The term 'gay and lesbian' politics is used for the traditional legal rights and lobby politics I scrutinise. Yet, I am fully aware that these are not the only gay and lesbian politics in Europe. In fact, there are many different understandings of what involvement in the political means to different groups of activists, and their approaches to achieving change vary greatly. Gay and lesbian politics have ranged from visibility rallies, kiss-ins, or civil disobedience to traditional rights advocacy. The reason I focus on the latter is, firstly, that this is the kind of politics which has been most heavily criticised from a critical feminist, queer, or postcolonial viewpoint. The juxtaposition of theoretical critique and the struggle for rights is most obvious here and, thus, offers the best scope for examining the ruptures in both wherever they meet. Secondly, no other form of political activism has been so successful in mobilising large political debates over decades. This is not the case because rights politics is the only successful politics – whatever 'success' means in connection with the political – but because it fits into the dominant definition of the political. Rights politics for minorities fits the bill of those discourses with dominantly structure capitalist, parliamentary democracies throughout the world. Since it is important to understand those discourses in relation to their heavy dependence on systems of gender and sexuality, I chose to investigate the kinds of rights politics that find resonance in those discourses.

Throughout this book I focus on analysing lesbian and gay politics specifically, while strongly insisting on alliances with and inclusion of bisexuality and transgender issues.[6] This is because of the wealth of available documents and the long history of lesbian and gay lobbying. The issues of bisexuality and transgender would need to be addressed more specifically and thoroughly than possible within the scope of this book. Yet, any queer approach insists on the intrinsic connections between biological sex, gender identity, and sexualities. A queer approach could, thus, suggest an intrinsic connectedness of the issues and the use of umbrella terms. However, I have chosen simply to lump together 'lesbian', 'gay', 'bisexual', and 'transgender' – the infamous 'l/g/b/t' – by default since that would only add to the marginalisation and silencing that bisexuals and transgender people already encounter within gay and lesbian studies and political movements. Wherever I use the term 'l/g/b/t' I specifically mean to name them together.[7] It includes a clear awareness of the connecting issues involved and does not simply use 'queer' as a synonym for l/g/b/t, while actually talking about only lesbians and gays. In fact, 'queer' as an identity or group label is not used at all in this book, since I consider it an improper, vague, and contradictory usage of the term 'queer'. Wherever the politics I analyse is, in fact and reality, concerned only with lesbians and gay men I will use those terms, while insisting on a political and theoretical connection between homosexuality and gender identity as I explain in Chapter 6. The terminology is, thus, specific, and consciously chosen throughout the text.

Chapter outline

In the remainder of this introduction I will address some questions regarding the method employed in this book and my own relationship to the process of this research. Chapter 1 will start with providing the reader unfamiliar with all the details of European politics with the necessary background information to understand the later analysis. 'European institutions: sexual rights lobbying', it introduces the EU and the CoE, the history of gay, lesbian, and transgender rights politics at these institutions, and ILGA-Europe as a transnational advocacy network. Chapter 2, 'Queer theory and political practices', is a critical reflection on the character of theory and politics, the terms around which my inquiry is based. It develops a working definition of queer theory and of political practices, reflects on the transfer of queer theory to a European context, and sets out the theoretical principles to which this book adheres. The concept of meaning is engaged to understand how politics becomes effective practices.

The third chapter, 'Mind the gap: hybrid relations of queer theory and political practice',[8] concludes the first part of this book. It addresses a central theme of my initial involvement with this topic: the travelling between rights activism and theoretical critique. The apparent practice–theory gap that is usually opened in relation to the discussion of queer concepts is in urgent need of re-conceptualisation, and ultimate abandonment. I suggest a deployment of hybridity as an analytical concept to straddle this gap.

Theoretical and political concepts are the thread that also leads through the second part of this book. Chapter 4, 'European strategies: human rights',[9] focuses on a critical discussion of the central rights strategy used in Europe: human rights argumentation. I illustrate the centrality of human rights discourse in the European context and address the conditions, predicaments, and consequences of the claim 'Homosexual Rights are Human Rights'. The principles this claim calls upon, such as freedom, equality, integrity, and respectability, pose a crucial question when confronted with sexual rights. They imply cultural definitions of humanness and who is – or is not – included in those definitions.

Chapter 5, 'Claiming protection: anti-discrimination',[10] centres on an important theme of l/g/b/t rights struggles: discrimination and the fight for anti-discrimination legislation. The need for anti-discrimination measures has so far never been critically deconstructed. Yet, a careful exploration of the concrete implications of the discourse of discrimination illuminates tensions suggesting that the struggle for rights is only apparently unproblematic. I examine the way activists speak about discrimination and, thus, politically materialise and utilise the situation of lesbians and gay men in Europe. This incorporates themes and concepts – such as material change, ideological rewards, diversity, liberal legal equality, and the hegemony of the juridical – which can be read as problematic from a philosophical and a practical political view, albeit in a different way from each other.

The issue of legal rights and their implications is brought up again in Chapter 6. 'Gender identity and sexual orientation: legal rights politics'[11] will make use of the interpretation a queer theoretical reading offers for the fight for rights in courts. Through an emphasis on the simultaneity of regulation and disruption, the analysis of two important court cases at the European Court of Justice will allow me to problematise the hope for justice and equality in courtrooms.[12] The discussion of the cases necessitates critical reflection on the realm of law not as an all-powerful discourse, but as an important site for the constitution, consolidation, and regulation of sexuality. However, the cases also feature a high potential for disruption through their interconnection of gender and sexuality, gender identity and sexual orientation, and, subsequently, homosexual and transgender politics. This connection is a central tenet of queer thought and will be argued for from political, theoretical, and legal perspectives.

I then proceed to discuss another ordering principle of European politics, namely citizenship. Chapter 7, 'A process of recognition: European citizenship', points to the historical, political, and economic legacies implied in the call to European citizenship. This, once again, illuminates intricate complexities and tensions in the claim to citizenship, such as the ideology of nation states, transnationalism, a Eurocentric exclusion of the racial and ethnic other, or the economic focus of European citizenship. In principle the call to end a second-class citizen status necessarily involves recognition of the equal validity of lesbian and gay membership in the existing citizenship order. In fact, the process of recognition becomes the key to understanding the contradictory complexities of citizenship and the need to change the nature of citizenship claims.

The demand for equal citizenship is commonly assessed against the legal and social recognition gay and lesbian partnerships receive. In fact, marriage and the right to adoption, custody, or artificial insemination – in short, the right to be recognised as a family – are the central rallying point of European gay and lesbian rights struggles and also the greatest stumbling block. Chapter 8, 'Framing the debate: kinship', focuses on the condition of the political kinship debate in Europe. I argue that kinship is the frame within which the social being that forms the basis for the political sphere in European culture is created, shaped, and enacted. Using two specific examples, I analyse what kinship is presumed to be when discussed

INTRODUCTION 7

in the sphere of political institution. This analysis illuminates once more the apparent tensions between justifiable claims to family recognition and the problem that these claims contribute to reinstating heteronormativity as the overarching frame of any kinship debate. The concept of framing can increase our understanding of the relationship between political kinship debates and heteronormativity without reducing the one to the other.

The third part and final chapter, 'The political activist: agency', dares to make the leap from the organisational and institutional level to the individual level of the activists involved. The way the activists interviewed addressed their own possibilities of achieving change is not simple and straightforward. In fact, they highlight contradictions and complexities which can only be conceptualised and grasped if the theory of agency is re-thought and moved away from its connection to the so-called independent, free will of autonomous and coherent humanist subjects. Although the framework in which most activists locate their agency seems to be a liberal humanist framework, the way they actually express their agency already includes a re-thinking of that framework. After briefly introducing the terms of the academic debate on political agency, I trace the understandings of agency in the interviews and propose to interpret them within a poststructuralist frame of agency with regard to political practices. The afterword, 'Tensions in the struggle for sexual minority rights', concludes this study with a summary of the apparent tensions in the struggle for sexual minority rights in Europe and the many areas which still require research and to which this book could not make a contribution.

Through my reading of interviews and political texts, as well as gay and lesbian studies and queer writing, I have come to realise the risks involved in any attempt to come up with a definite characterisation of European political practices or l/g/b/t perspectives. The possibility of simultaneous assertion and rupture of the orders that maintain an exclusionary and discriminatory system of hierarchised binaries is present in all political practices. The task of critical analysis is to draw out the implications and pitfalls of political practice as well as their potential for rupture, which could, hopefully, subsequently be strengthened. Overall, I suggest that a theoretically informed queer and poststructuralist reading of political documents and interviews can contribute to an understanding of the conditions upon which politics of inclusion, participation, social justice, and equality rest.[13] It can illuminate how the paradigms of political discourses constitute, consolidate, and contest the meaning and cultural significance of gender and sexuality in modern, democratic, capitalist European societies. Before embarking on such a reading, however, the method I employ in my analysis and my own position in relation to the material investigated need to be clarified.

Method

This book offers a transdisciplinary theoretical analysis of the political practices of specific sexual politics. Throughout this book I will need to make use of strategies and principles from many disciplines, mainly from legal studies, philosophy, and political science. Insights from psychoanalysis, feminist theory, and cultural analysis are also utilised at several points. The nature of transdisciplinarity is certainly not to cover all classics and methods of each discipline and make the research fully sufficient inside every discipline touched.[14] Yet, sloppy scholarship disguised as a transdisciplinary approach is not the alternative to overcoming disciplinary presuppositions. Certain disciplinary presuppositions and methodical rules block the view to some more complex connections between cultural orders such as gender and sexuality. To analyse them in more detail, insights from different disciplines need to be used to grasp the connections. The analysis in this book, for example, could not have been done without understanding the principles of legal interpretation and how judgments are formulated. Yet, the legal analysis of the texts alone would not have allowed me to emphasise a rather philosophical approach to how sexuality and gender function underneath political concepts such as human rights.

Transdisciplinarity in this book is an encounter of different disciplines in a partial but deliberate exchange of premises and methodological possibilities. The borders of each discipline are taken to be porous. According to Mieke Bal (2001:2), such a definition of transdisciplinarity – in her case interdisciplinarity – is tenable only if it is accompanied by the development of a method that covers an understandable and arguable common ground. For Bal (2001:7), the study of theoretical concepts is the method that develops such common ground:

> It is around concepts that I see cultural analysis achieving a consensus comparable to the paradigmatic consistency that has kept the traditional disciplines vital, albeit, simultaneously, dogmatic. Rejecting dogmatism without sacrificing consistency is one way of improving the human *ambience* while increasing the intellectual yield. This is why I consider the discussion of concepts as an alternative methodological base for cultural studies or analysis.

In this book concepts play two roles: as theoretical concepts and as political themes. The former turns certain concepts – such as meaning, hybridity, framing, recognition, and indeed gender – into analytical tools which frame my reading of texts and produce, in turn, a frame within which certain complexities can be grasped. I follow Bal (2001:7-11) in understanding concepts to be programmatic and normative, developmental, bound to a tradition, more than tools, and perceptible to personal investment. If scrutinised carefully they can be seen to have travelled from the field in which they emerged, changing their meaning and the meaning of the insights in the field where they are newly employed. As political themes, concepts – such as human rights, the law, anti-discrimination, citizenship, or kinship – become the frames within which political practices are bundled for analysis. Here concepts are understood as themes that guide political action and dominate political discourses or orders. It is these concepts that rule the meaning of rights, equality, and justice. As political themes concepts are, yet again, signed and dated, changeable, programmatic, and normative.

INTRODUCTION   9

The concrete method with which both forms of concepts are brought to my research questions is the process of reading. According to Bal (1996:32), 'reading is an act of reception, of assigning meaning'. As a reader preoccupied with certain poststructuralist and feminist convictions about the cultural dominance of gender and sexuality, my assessment of political texts is an act of re-framing the words originally said in very specific formulae of, for example, judgments or parliamentary speeches. In general terms any viewing, listening, or reading is a way of framing, which, in turn, presents a 'constant semiotic activity, without which no cultural life can function' (Bal 1996:33).

Thus, the result, or the product, of my reading is a conclusion of propositional content: to identify underlying systems of dominance that I trace in the texts I analyse. I try to activate those texts and put them to work in relation to a specific way of interpreting political concepts as themes and of engaging theoretical concepts to understand the implications of these themes. This implies taking texts out of their proper context and departing from a strict analysis of them according to the rules of the discipline that usually assesses them in their specificity. It means transporting them into a frame of analysis they were not written for, but which one keeps sensing when listening to them without being allowed to view them under a conglomerate of different disciplinary insights. While reading is, according to Mieke Bal (1996:39), not an idiosyncratic act, it is definitely a subjective act. The way I read and analysed my material has a subjective connection to the way this research was initially designed.

The 'I' in the text

I came to this project with a specific interest in bridging the apparent gap between poststructuralist theory and political practice. I was fuelled by a careful fascination with the idea of Europe and the possibilities of overcoming nationalism into a wider cosmopolitan identification based on regions, diversity, and securing peace. Additionally, I was aware of my own desire for rights, particularly those rights that would help me secure a residence permit for my New Zealand partner in the EU. Yet, at the same time, I was deeply suspicious of the implied inclusion into a heteronormative system, which is the only inclusion these rights truly secure. In the course of the four years of this research project all of those motivations became troubling in themselves, partly because I became oblivious to them, partly because I began to find them naive, and partly because they were simply the wrong starting point for this project. However, to remain conscious of the conditions under which I started the project and under which I conducted the interviews and collected material, these conditions and my personal involvement in politics need to be at least mentioned here.

For reasons of my academic background and my initial interests in this topic, it seemed useful to combine an academic quest with political issues I felt passionate about and to involve myself in the very politics I was going to research. In the course of this research I worked in l/g/b/t politics in two directions: on the one hand for l/g/b/t rights groups mainly at European level and in Germany. On the other hand I have been involved in a project lasting several years – culminating in an international conference and a book – to discuss and evaluate queer theory for a German debate on democratic participation.

The European region of the International Lesbian and Gay Association became an important focus of concern and took up a large part of my time over the years. I am a member of the executive board and have represented ILGA-Europe on many occasions ranging from activist conferences to meetings with Parliamentarians, Ministers or Ambassadors, either in different European countries or at European institutions. Through their membership in ILGA-Europe, I have been able to get to know activist groups all over Europe – East and West – and groups that work independently from national contexts. ILGA-Europe's emphasis on joint work with other NGOs in the Platform of European Social NGOs also created the opportunity of work together with activists from other networks concerned with issues such as racism, disability, age, and gender equality. These experiences have shaped my thinking as significantly as my academic involvement in queer and feminist poststructuralist theory.

Since my political work tended to take over the lion's share of my time, it also became a significant part of my daily concern and the working relations with activists from all over Europe turned more often than not into cherished friendships. The meaning of international solidarity within the movement is surely illusory as long as it relies only on clear meanings of homosexual identities that all share. Yet, solidarity has been a concrete and practical resource for this book. In fact, this book would never have been written without the dinners, beds, car rides, knowledge transfers, e-mails, talks, and personal support that I have been given in many cities of Europe when travelling for ILGA-Europe and with my tape recorder for my research project. However, once the concrete writing process started this involvement – while having been an essential pre-condition for venturing into a critical analysis in the first place – also rendered itself problematic.

In some instances I lacked distance from my material as some of the political texts to be analysed were written by myself or I at least participated in their formulation. Distance and self-critique thus had to be analysed before I could even start writing an academic project. The 'I' in the text is consequently more than lip service to feminist research methodology acknowledging the non-existence of objectivity and positioning the researcher as subject of the text (Stanley 1990). My own presence in the writing is an integral part of this book, a necessity that cannot be escaped. However, being part of my own subject matter, as well as being the subject of it, is apparent not only through my political involvement, but also through the volatile academic status of researchers in the theory of gender and sexuality.

Coming to Europe, the university context in which I involved myself at the beginning made me notice the exclusion of anything relating to gender and sexual politics from the permitted academic theoretical rhetoric. It made me painfully aware that the challenges queer theory offers were not only directed to the kind of rights politics I was just getting involved in; they also offered a constant challenge to the kind of academic persona I permanently failed to present in the university context I was in. This only ceased to be a problem once I had changed to the Amsterdam School of Cultural Analysis, at which the intersections of critical theory and social practice are a legitimate academic pursuit. Overall, the journey of this book has been a journey of changing concerns, one of conflicts at all sides. My research created a critical stance that one cannot bring home fully anywhere – neither to my activist colleagues nor to my academic colleagues – but that remains interesting precisely because of this. My analysis in the following ultimately reflects on my own discomfort with the seeming contradictions of theory and political practice. It also reflects on my discomfort with the necessity to pretend there are such things as clearly describable sexual politics or a clearly distinguishable queer theory, none of which is ultimately possible. The process of writing this text was a process of constant negotiation among various claims, desires, and positions. I was often desperately trying to be a professional academic and a professional political activist at the same time. In the course of time, I have learned how to fail at both and accept that not as lack of achievement, but as a convincing sign for the impossibility of coherent, un-ruptured professional and personal identities. I want to emphasise that these contradictions are the main underlying theme throughout this book and I have not excluded myself and my work from the critical analysis I make, although only Chapter 3 deals with this issue explicitly. My sense of rupture also implies consequences for the relationship between me, the researcher, and one part of my material, the interviewees.

The researcher and the researched

I conducted interviews with gay and lesbian activists who hold some form of office in ILGA or are very active on the European stage, and with officials working for EU institutions, some, but not all, of whom are lesbian or gay themselves. All the interviews were guided by a question catalogue I had given the interviewees in advance and which was also used as guidance during the interview. After some test runs, I defined the type of interviews I conducted as problem-centred, narrative interviews (Witzel 1996), in which I try not to interrupt the flow of talking with questions in the beginning. In the second part of the interview I usually tried to cover the leftovers of the questions on the interview guide, if I felt larger question blocks had not been addressed at all. In nearly all oral interviews I contributed some of my own thoughts at the end, since nearly all interviewees wanted to know more about my research interests. These last sections of the interviews have not been used in the analysis since they are fairly structured by the ideas I voiced and to which the interviewees then responded.

The interviews were conducted mainly in English, but three preferred German, which is another language we shared. I subsequently translated the relevant quotations of these interviews into English and, thus, take full responsibility for the choice of words in these interviews. Since most interviewees are not English native speakers, I also corrected obvious grammatical mistakes in the quotations as long as that did not change the content. In principle, though, I retained both their sentence structure and their choice of words, as well as their way of writing in the case of the e-mail interviews. The interviews were conducted in two different ways, written via e-mail correspondence or tape recorded, and subsequently ordered according to themes. I did not produce full transcripts of all oral interviews, but rather chose to order their content according to themes and categories of analysis. I chose this method since it involved a repeated listening to the interview tapes that allowed me to discover different nuances each time. This is a rather unorthodox method closest to theme-related evaluation and problem-centred interviewing (Flick 1998; Witzel 1996), but has proven itself to be useful for my purposes.

Moreover, my focus is not a close narrative analysis of the interviews. Thus, I neither attempt to give an in-depth analysis of the narrative structure of the interviews, nor do I claim fully to represent the contents of what has been said. The interviews in my analysis function on the one hand as a means to gather facts otherwise not recorded or written down anywhere. On the other hand, they function as one way of investigating the precise workings of certain discourses employed as political practices. The interviews are, therefore, no more central to the analysis than the other documents used. This means that the reader will not be able to gain a full sense of the individual positioning and opinions of every interviewee, but will only meet the interviewees in small selected segments in some of the chapters. Only Chapter 9 offers an entirely interview-based analysis. Altogether I conducted fifteen interviews with sixteen people, four via e-mail and eleven audio-taped. Two of the interviews are not quoted in the text, but were an important part of the research process and a part of my analysis.

The particular relationships of power between myself and my interviewees in this research did not fit comfortably into the paradigms of feminist methodology. In general, feminist research methodology assumes the interview process to give voice to those who are powerless or marginalised, and, thus, emphasises power relations between the researcher and the researched (Gluck and Patai 1991). The interviewees could not be placed in the category of the dispossessed or marginalised very easily. Many of them have high-powered jobs with a good earning capacity. All take enough pride in their political work to deem it central, important, and empowering, including the interviewees from Eastern Europe. Thus, while these individuals were mostly, arguably, dispossessed of rights in relation to their sexual orientation, in many other ways most of them identify their lives as privileged. Although there are certainly differences of degree, this holds true for both groups of interviewees, activists and EU officials.

Therefore, my relation to the interviewees contained both the power assigned to academics who can proceed at liberty with the interview material and the power of those who have the practical knowledge and share it with a researcher. A slight feeling of superiority was occasionally suggested to me implicitly, a superiority of those who 'do' in contrast to those who merely 'think or report about it'. Being an activist myself made me 'one of us' or 'one of those who are discriminated'. Being an academic made me 'one of them', somebody not concerned with the practices of real change but merely with the privilege to do *l'art pour l'art*. The interviews are, therefore, products of our respective attempts to explain our agendas, express solidarity, create trust, and establish a relationship of knowledge transfer. The interview tapes are, arguably, a product of social process between the interviewees and me as well as between their respective understanding of politics and my theoretical concerns and political desires. Wherever I quote them this aspect should be kept in mind. Additionally, the choice of quotations is a political process in itself, a choice I made in relation to my analytical concerns and questions. I utilised them as illustration, contradiction, destabilisation, and re-affirmation of those concerns and questions. Thus, I do not claim to have represented each individual and his or her work adequately.

Finally, the issue of publication is not an easy one. None of the interviewees wanted to read a full transcript of the interviews, but all wished to see the specific quotations I would be using in my text if I wanted to quote them under their real name. All chose to be quoted under their real name. Not everybody liked the quotations chosen and surely not all will feel represented adequately in this book. Theoretically informed research, however, needs to be critical, and if I were to censor everything my fellow activists might feel criticised about, there would be little to no point in continuing a project such as this. On the other hand, I do not intend to ignore the concerns expressed or to engage in a less than respectful form of critical analysis.

In the course of this research I have subsequently utilised three primary devices to respond to the problematic of the researcher/researched relationship and the ethical and methodological problems any interview work always incurs. First I kept to my promise and sent the selected quotations to each individual. I did not promise to alter the words nor the choice of quotation, but I considered each question seriously and engaged in communication with the people concerned. I take full responsibility for the way each and every quotation is read and interpreted by me, acknowledging that there are many other ways of reading that same quotation and that any other interview process, for example another interviewer, might not have produced this very quotation at all. Second, I have kept a clear critical eye towards my own theoretical assumptions. I tried to be open at all times to the possibility that what I had considered problematic, such as, for example, unquestioned identity foundations, was in fact not claimed by activists in the first place. More than once I had to ask serious questions about the importance of certain queer critiques in the actual political practices in Europe. This related partly to the applicability of a queer academic critique deeply embedded in US–American culture to the European cultural context. This context is one in which queer is largely unknown to activists who often struggle against different barriers than in the US and who recall a different history of the movement they grew up in. Additionally, I always assumed that the critical reflexivity of the people I interviewed was at least as poignant as my own and we both shared an equally deep sense of the importance of tackling discrimination, hatred, and exclusion at their very roots. Third, and most importantly, I clearly position myself on both sides of the researcher/researched dichotomy. In this book I explicitly identify myself as both a critic and a critiqued person, an analyst and a person. What this means for my analysis will become clear in due course.

Notes

1 See Berlant and Freeman (1992) for an explanation of these queer street politics.
2 See, for example, Goldman (1996), Martin (1994), O'Driscoll (1996), and Savoy (1994).
3 See, for example, Berlant and Warner (1995), Berube and Escoffier (1991), Butler (1993), Cohen (1997), Currah (1997b), Duggan and Hunter (1995), Goldman (1996), Jagose (1996), Martin (1994), Namaste (1996a; 1996b), O'Driscoll (1996), Savoy (1994), Seidman (1995), and Warner (1993).
4 Such as the work of Michel Foucault, Judith Butler, Wendy Brown, David Halperin, Michael Warner, and Eve Kosofsky Sedgwick.
5 The material was collected from public and private archives, through work stays in Brussels and Strasbourg, through talking to activists and parliamentarians, and through the internet. The latter was used in several ways: e-mail information groups and newsletters; the e-mail network of the executive board of ILGA-Europe; the website of ILGA and ILGA-Europe, and the European Institutions and Courts. The internet has, thus, been a key method and locus of research. I have come to appreciate why the instrumentality of the internet as a research tool and a sphere of political action has gained credibility among political activists and among academic researchers in the 1990s. In particular, the internet presents a realm of investigation that implicates the interwoven character of research and political practice, which is also central to this book. Through three years of intensive research and collection of material, I gathered a great wealth of official documents, court cases, personal accounts, newspaper clippings, journals, and written conference reports. Gathering this large amount of material made it possible to gain a comprehensive overview of the actual happenings and practices, and, thus, was crucial for making the selective choices of material in each chapter.
6 Chapter 6, for example, is partly dedicated to the connection between homosexuality and transgender.
7 In the following I will shorten 'lesbian, gay, bisexual, and transgender' to 'l/g/b/t' since that has been established in official documents internationally and has become a commonly used term. 'Gay' and 'lesbian' will be spelled out and not shortened. All other terms and abbreviations are explained in the glossary.
8 A version of this chapter appeared as Beger (2001).
9 A brief summary of the argumentation used here appeared in Beger (1999).
10 Aspects of this chapter have been used in Beger (2002).
11 A version of this chapter appeared as Beger (2000a). Parts of this chapter also appear in Beger (2002).
12 *P v. S and Cornwall County Council* (1996); *Lisa Grant v South West Trains* (1998).
13 I want to emphasise that my usage of poststructuralist approaches is based on the feminist response to deconstruction. The term does not represent a political model of poststructuralism, but a politically re-thought theory challenged and informed by feminist and later queer readings of its own rules and assumptions.
14 Since my first university degrees were in the transdisciplinary field of feminist theory, the nature of transdisciplinarity has long been a concern of mine. It was Mieke Bal who, finally, made the concepts of transdisciplinarity and interdisciplinarity fully tenable for

me and developed a method with which some of its possible pitfalls can be avoided. However, Bal primarily utilises the term 'interdisciplinarity' rather than 'transdisciplinarity'. I employ the term 'trandisciplinarity' here, since 'interdisciplinarity' refers to the idea of reaching out to broaden and critically inform research issues one has formulated to some extent from one's disciplinary interest, which is always porous in its borders. Transdisciplinarity indicates a bit more that the initial research question never was designed out of any disciplinary interest in the first place, but already as something that arises out of questions, methods, texts, and academic traditions from many disciplines.

Part I
Theory and politics

1 European institutions: sexual rights lobbying

> We can identify the kinds of resources that make a campaign possible, such as information, leadership, and symbolic or material capital. And, we must consider the kinds of institutional structures, both domestic and international, that encourage or impede particular kinds of transnational activism.
>
> (Keck and Sikkink 1998:7)

> Recognising the fundamental pride that lesbians, gay men, bisexuals and transgendered people have in their sexual identities and orientation; Conscious that social and legal discrimination on the basis of sexuality is pervasive and that effective work against oppression calls for international solidarity; Seeking in ILGA an international organisation within which women of different political and personal choices (for example, separatism, feminism, orientation and identity) can work together; Concerned with the vulnerability of youth in a world that continues to practice so many forms of discrimination, the need for their protection from abuse and the goal of ensuring that young people experience both freedom and support as they develop their own sexualities and identities; Mindful of the impact of discrimination on the basis of sex, race, age, disability, economic status, national origin and ethnicity on lesbians, gay men, bisexuals and transgendered people, and the way in which such discrimination can exploit homophobia; Building on the work of previous generations who have struggled for equality and liberation; We approve this document as the Constitution of the International Lesbian and Gay Association.
>
> (Preamble of the ILGA world constitution)

Analysing European political practices is a complicated endeavour on a theoretical, a political and an institutional level. To follow the theoretical interpretations of political and legal texts I offer in the course of the following chapters, any reader not deeply involved in lobbying European institutions or working for them will wish to have a basic understanding of these institutions. This chapter will provide access to this understanding by explaining the difference between the two major European institutions – the Council of Europe and the European Union – by introducing ILGA-Europe as a European NGO and a transnational advocacy network, and by briefly summarising in a historical order the important political and legal events pertaining to lesbian, gay, and transgender rights on the European level.

During the twenty-four years of ILGA's existence the situation in which gay men, lesbians, bisexuals, and transgender people live in Europe has changed dramatically on a social, political, and economic, as well as a legal, level, and with regard to the movements. With specific regard to the success of legal rights struggles, a number of factors were involved. Firstly, the change of social climate that occurred after the de-criminalisation of homosexual (male) offences became so obvious that courts started to recognise this change. Secondly, a growing strength and sophistication of gay and lesbian legal activists developed, with more and more gay and lesbian lawyers practising and some former activists reaching high university positions in the UK, the Netherlands, and the Nordic countries. Thirdly, an increased visibility, vitality, and activism on the part of lesbian and gay communities infiltrated public and political knowledge generally in the nation-states and on an international level. Fourthly, the advent of positive human rights cases at the European Court of Human Rights from 1981 onwards and later in the European Union elevated sexual orientation into the realm of human rights.

Illustrating all elements of all four factors, even if reduced to legal matters only, would easily fill a whole book and more. Nevertheless, in this chapter I attempt to combine very different kinds of histories – the histories of international institutions, of a certain movement, of a lobby organisation, of political lobbying, and of legal rights. Since it can certainly not do full justice to any, it is intended to provide only the kind of factual knowledge that makes the understanding of the following theoretical analysis possible. The kinds of rights and politics described, therefore, are by no means the only forms of politics employed by gay men, lesbians, bisexuals, or transgender people throughout Europe.

I have divided the chapter into six sections. The first, very brief, one explains the difference between the Council of Europe and the European Union. The second provides detailed information on the European Union by going through its different institutions and later, in the third, listing the relevant rights pertaining to sexual orientation under each institution. The fourth section covers the Council of Europe, clarifying its overall structure and the important human rights cases for both sexual orientation and gender identity. The fifth section illustrates two examples of the lobby tactics and strategies employed by ILGA-Europe at the Council of Europe, the process of broadening Article 14 (discrimination) of the European Convention on Human Rights and the lobbying for a recommendation on homosexual rights in the Parliamentary Assembly. The history of lobbying at the European Union is much longer and less compounded and, therefore, too long for the purposes of exemplifying lobby strategies in this chapter. The sixth and last section gives a brief history of ILGA-Europe and explains the nature of the organisation as a transnational l/g/b/t activist network.

Council of Europe versus European Union

It is a fair estimation to say that the great majority of the 800 million people in Europe whose countries are members of the Council of Europe do have little understanding of the difference between the two existing European institutions, which are totally independent of each other. This is because of four confusing factors: the *proximity of space* – both the Council of Europe and the European Parliament of the EU are seated, at least partly, in Strasbourg, the *building* – the Parliamentary Assembly of the Council of Europe and the European Parliament shared the same building until recently, the *symbol* – the blue flag with yellow stars functions for both institutions although the Council of Europe has recently added a C into the ring of stars, and the *names* – European Council or Council of Europe? Committee of Ministers or Council of Ministers? The European Union has fifteen Member States until its enlargement to twenty-five in May 2004, which are all currently West European, and it is primarily an economic organisation, although in recent years it has increasingly become involved with human and social rights. The European Union is based in Brussels, but its Parliament also meets in Strasbourg and its Court is seated in Luxembourg. Approximately 370 million people are citizens of the European Union at the moment. The Council of Europe has forty-five Member States, covering more or less the whole of Europe. It is essentially a human rights organisation. Every Member State has signed the European Convention on Human Rights, which is enforced through the European Court of Human Rights, a supreme human rights court for Europe. All institutions of the Council of Europe are based in Strasbourg. Through the membership of their states, approximately 800 million people have the right to appeal to the European Court of Human Rights.

The European Union

What is known as the European Union today was founded in 1958, by means of the Treaty of Rome (European Economic Community or EEC), to establish a common market among its Member States. Two preceding treaties cleared the way for the Treaty of Rome: the European Coal and Steel Community (ECSC, 1952) and the European Atomic Energy Community (EURATOM, 1958). Subsequent treaties, the Single European Act (1987), the founding document of the European Community, the Treaty on European Union (Maastricht, 1993) and the Treaty of Amsterdam (1999) extended the scope of the European Union, so that it now has three *Pillars*, covering the following areas of activity: the *First Pillar* provides a common market based on the free movement of goods, persons, capital, and services, an economic and monetary union, and common policies and activities. Since the Treaty of Maastricht it includes an explicit European citizenship beyond the already existing direct voting rights to the European Parliament and since the Treaty of Amsterdam it includes asylum and immigration. The *Second Pillar* provides a common foreign and security policy based on the Treaty on European Union (Maastricht). And the *Third Pillar* manifests a police and judicial co-operation in criminal matters also based on the Treaty on European Union. The subsequent Treaty of Nice, which entered into force on 1 February 2003, changed some of the institutional balance of the EU and introduced qualified majority voting, but the whole pillar structure is likely to be abolished when the Intergovernmental Conference adopts the draft Constitution submitted by the Convention on the Future of Europe in July 2003.

The European Union is headed by one Member State rotating every six months and has three major institutions. The *Council of the European Union* – also known as the *Council of Ministers* – is the Union's main decision-making institution. It consists of the Ministers of the fifteen Member States responsible for the matters on the agenda, such as foreign affairs, justice, or agriculture. A Council of the heads of government, which is called the European Council and meets at least twice per annum, decides the Treaties of the Union. The meetings held with a view to amending the Treaties are called *Summits* and they are prepared by the *Intergovernmental Conferences*, which are important in terms of lobbying for the inclusion of certain new rights into forthcoming treaties. Many, but not all, decisions in the Council require unanimity and the future Constitutions provide for a lot more *qualified majority voting*.

The *European Commission*, an administrative body of permanently employed public servants from all member countries, initiates and drafts Community legislation, and implements, manages, and controls Community policies, programmes, and initiatives. The Commission administers the money of the European Union, which includes action programmes under which NGOs can obtain money for projects or for core funding. There are twenty *Commissioners*, who undertake to act in the interests of the Community as a whole, assisted by an administration, which is divided into different sections, called the *Directorates-General* (DG). For NGOs such as ILGA-Europe it is important to maintain good relations with individual officials in order to influence the drafting of legislation or obtain information on forthcoming action programmes quickly.

The *European Parliament* (EP) is the assembly of the directly elected representatives of the 370 million Union citizens. There are currently 626 Members of the European Parliament (MEPs) distributed between Member States in proportion to their population. They work together according to political groupings, not nationality. The Parliament's main functions are the following: it considers the Commission's proposals and is associated with the Council in the legislative process by means of various procedures – co-decision, co-operation, consultation; it has the power of supervision over the Union's activities through its confirmation of the appointment of the Commission and through the written and oral questions it can put to the Commission and the Council; it shares budgetary powers with the Council in voting on the annual budget and overseeing its implementation. These powers are important but distinctively less than those of national democratic Parliaments. Again, the new draft Constitution provides for further rights of the EP, particularly an extension of co-decision rights, yet it still does not make all laws subject to EP approval. Much of the work of the Parliament is done in its committees, which prepare reports on legislative proposals from the Commission and present them for debate by the full Parliament. The European Parliament can also form *intergroups* comprised of a certain number of MEPs from different political groups that are concerned with a specific issue. Since 1998 there has existed an intergroup concerned with 'Equal rights for lesbians and gay men'. ILGA-Europe enjoys consultative status to this intergroup and has in general very strong and long-standing ties to diverse MEPs and political groupings in the European Parliament.

The third institution is the *European Court of Justice* (ECJ), which is made up of fifteen judges appointed by agreement among the Member States. It has two principal functions: to check whether instruments of the European institutions and of governments are compatible with the Treaties, and, at the request of a national court, to pronounce on the interpretation or the validity of provisions contained in Union law. The Court of Justice has become an important tool in the struggle for equality rights in the Union.[1]

There are three types of binding legislation that can be adopted by the Union: Regulations, Directives, and Decisions. Regulations have direct effect, and apply in all Member States without the need for national legislation. Directives are binding on the Member States as to the results to be achieved, but leave the form and method to the discretion of the Member States while stipulating a time frame in which the Directive has to be implemented by the Member States. Directives must be implemented in national law in order to generate legal effect. Decisions are legally binding for those to whom they are addressed only. The Parliament, the Council, and the Commission can also adopt recommendations and resolutions, but these are not binding. The future Constitution will simplify the legal instruments basically distinguishing between laws and framework laws.

The European Union emphasises dialogue with the Social Partners and with NGO bodies. The social partners are employers and trade unions. The organisations recognised by the Commission for consultation within the *Social Dialogue* process are the ETUC (European Trade Union Confederation) for the trade unions, UNICE and CEEP respectively for the private- and public-sector employers. The *Platform of European Social Non-Governmental Organisations* brings together thirty-nine European NGOs, federations and networks, including ILGA-Europe. The Platform seeks to develop and strengthen a *Civil Dialogue* between European NGOs and the institutions of the European Union.

There are thirteen countries currently engaged in the process of accession to the European Union – Bulgaria, Cyprus, the Czech Republic, Estonia, Hungary, Latvia, Lithuania, Malta, Poland, Romania, the Slovak Republic, Slovenia, and Turkey. Ten will become members in May 2004 after many have successfully conducted a referendum on accession in 2003 and have satisfied the Copenhagen criteria, covering the following dimensions: the political – democracy, human rights, the rule of law and the protection of minorities, the economic – a functioning market economy, and the ability to resist competitive pressure in the internal market, and the full adoption of the Community legislation and regulations in various fields of community competence. Accession countries have to implement both the human rights standards of the Union, and all Union legislation, including that which is beneficial for lesbian, gay, bisexual, and transgender people. This means a considerable step forward in social rights in all accession countries, yet sexual orientation has caused problems for some countries. Poland, for example, tried to negotiate a specific opt-out from anti-discrimination for cultural and religious reasons in 2002, but was clearly rebuffed by the Commission. All accession countries were part of the Convention on the Future of Europe in 2002–03, which drafted a constitution for the EU, yet Romania, Bulgaria, and Turkey solely as observers.

Sexual orientation and the EU

Since the 1980s the European Union has become increasingly committed to the active promotion of human rights. Sexual orientation has by now become an established aspect of human rights considerations in the EU. After the Resolution and Report on 'Sexual Discrimination at the Workplace' (Squarcialupi Report) in 1984, the most decisive step in this direction was the so-called Roth Report, 'Equal Rights for Homosexuals and Lesbians in the EC' (A3-0028/94) in 1994 which included *inter alia* unequal age of consent, discrimination in employment or in the armed forces, the exclusion from marriage laws, the exclusion from adoption and custody, or the prohibition of public funds for lesbian and gay projects.[2] The European Parliament has since then included the issue of sexual orientation in all its annual human rights reports about the situation in the Union as well as in the rest of Europe. Depending on who the specific *rapporteur* is for the relevant report, ILGA-Europe may have to lobby more or less on the inclusion of all relevant issues from equal age of consent to discrimination and marriage laws in the draft human rights report. Yet, there have always been Nordic Left, Green, or Socialist MEPs willing to table amendments for inclusion during the debate on ILGA-Europe's request. The Parliament has also been instrumental in the process leading to the Directive on employment discrimination following Article 13 TEC introduced by the Amsterdam Treaty and in securing the inclusion of equality and anti-discrimination in the draft Constitution; in fact, the Parliament is the most reliable ally for European NGOs in the advancement of social rights.

The most significant manifestation of the commitment to anti-discrimination on the part of the European Union before the new Constitution is finalised was the inclusion of Article 13 through the Treaty of Amsterdam (1999) after much lobby work by NGOs during the preceding intergovernmental conference.[3] Article 13 empowered the Union as follows:

> Without prejudice to the other provisions of this Treaty and within the limits of the powers conferred by it upon the Community, the Council, acting unanimously on a proposal from the Commission and after consulting the European Parliament, may take appropriate action to combat discrimination based on sex, racial or ethnic origin, religion or belief, disability, age or sexual orientation.

This has led the Commission to put forward draft Directives during 2000: a horizontal Directive to combat racism in all areas of competency of the Union, a vertical Directive to combat all other grounds of Article 13 in employment only, and an action programme. ILGA-Europe, together with the Social Platform, has extensively lobbied the Commission to avoid splitting Article 13 into different Directives, but this effort was unsuccessful. ILGA-Europe was also unsuccessful in changing some of the problematic aspects of the draft Directive. In July 1999 the Commission published a discussion paper that split the discrimination grounds, which was officially criticised by the Social Platform in October 1999. On 25

November 1999 the Commission published the draft Directive. Because the unanimity rule in the Council could preclude success for a broad general Directive, the Commission considered racism to be the only safe ground to be covered beyond employment. While the anti-racism networks welcomed the Directive that became Union law on 29 June 2000 (Directive 200/43/EC), they joined the firm protest of the Platform against the split. The European Parliament supported the view of the Platform through statements from various intergroups concerned and officially on 11 July 2000 in the Joke Swiebel Report. Its social policy committee additionally demanded a duty that Member States report on the progress (PE 229.570/fin).

With regard to sexual orientation, the main problem during the lobby process became the freedom of religious employers to discriminate against homosexual employees, a freedom that was supported by many governments – particularly the UK – in the process of the expert group in September 2000. The Council passed the Employment Directive on 17 October 2000 (Directive 2000/78/EC), reaching a compromise after an initial veto by Ireland, which wished to strengthen religious rights pertaining to its specific historical situation.[4]

The Directive is a milestone celebrated by many NGOs, but it does include problematic aspects with regard to several grounds of discrimination. For sexual orientation these are the exclusion of benefits pertaining to marital status (s. 22), the definitions of discrimination (Art. 2), restrictions on third country nationals (Art. 3(2)), social security systems (Art. 3(3)), and the explicit right of churches to enforce genuine occupational requirements based on their ethos (Art. 4 (2)). Particularly the latter has led to some so-called anti-discrimination laws in Member States that now make it officially legal to discriminate openly on grounds of sexual orientation. Italy is a particularly worrisome case in this respect since July 2003,[5] but very few countries will translate the Framework Directive to the satisfaction of EU legal experts. Some of the highly problematic explanatory notes of the Commission on the difference between sexual orientation and sexual behaviour have not gained entry into the final Directive. I will offer a more detailed analysis of the draft Directive in Chapter 5.

The actual effect of this Directive will become truly apparent only once implementation in Members States and Accession Countries is complete. Most have only started the process, waiting until the last moment to implement, and it is very likely that a decisive number of states will not have implemented the Directive by the end of 2003. Some countries will go further than stipulated in both the Framework and the Race Directives, for example Belgium, Denmark, and The Netherlands, but some include exclusion rules for sexual orientation, for example the UK and Italy, or indeed exclude sexual orientation altogether from the planned laws, such as, for example Cyprus, Bulgaria, and Slovakia. The final results can be assessed only after the deadline and after the Commission's final assessment of implementation.

Another important consequence of Article 13 was the Action Programme passed that *inter alia* grants substantial funding to European NGOs – including ILGA-Europe – between 2001 and 2006. In December 2000, the Nice summit agreed an amendment to Article 13, which now allows a qualified majority of the Council under co-decision with the European Parliament to make decisions on anti-discrimination, yet unanimity is still required for all legal changes. This change is not likely to become relevant since the Article 13 Action Programme is already in place and runs until 2006, and in 2004 the new Constitution might bring in different legislation. The draft Constitution includes a horizontal article on anti-discrimination pertaining to the policies of the Union, but still requires unanimity for all anti-discrimination laws. This was one of the saddest losses during the Convention process, since unanimity with twenty-five Member States makes future anti-discrimination laws almost an impossibility, particularly since many accession governments openly oppose sexual orientation as grounds of discrimination. ILGA-Europe did not lobby the intergovernmental conference leading up to the Amsterdam Treaty extensively for the inclusion of gender identity. It did so, however, in the process of lobbying the anti-discrimination article for the Charter of Fundamental Rights.

All Member States of the EU are signatories to the European Convention on Human Rights. For decades that was seen to be enough protection of human rights for the EU. Since the Single European Act (1986), this attitude has changed, and European Union Treaties have contained more and more reference to fundamental and human rights in the Union. With the establishment of a European Union citizenship in 1993 – including the liberty to live and work in all Member States as well as passive and active voting rights to the European Parliament – it became clear that fundamental rights and non-discrimination needed to be dealt with explicitly in Union law to cope with the freedom of persons, goods, and services throughout the Union. To strengthen the support of the Union among its citizens, social rights needed to be strengthened and in 1995 the European Parliament demanded that the Council draft a catalogue of citizenship rights beyond the economic dimension.

Between 1995 and 1997 a *Commité des Sages* (committee of wise women and men) developed a catalogue, which asks the Union to include far-reaching non-discrimination laws in its Treaties. However, the Treaty of Amsterdam remained weak in terms of social rights and non-discrimination. The Commission, therefore, called another expert group under the leadership of Professor Spiros Simitis, who published a report in February 1999 – the Simitis Report – urging the Union again to agree on fundamental social rights in the Union before the Amsterdam Treaty was actually ratified. At the Summit of Cologne in June 1999, the Council finally agreed and initiated a drafting Convention made up of sixty representatives of the European Parliament, national Parliaments, and Member States, which published the draft in October 2000 after an exemplary transparent process of official consultation. The draft included the human rights guaranteed in the European Convention on Human Rights (ECHR), certain social rights, and those rights which pertain to EU citizens specifically, such as the free movement of workers. The Charter was signed by the Council at the Nice Summit on 7 and 8 December 2000 as a declaratory statement.

ILGA-Europe has engaged in lobby campaigns for this Charter since 1996 and made it one of its lobbying foci in 1999. ILGA-Europe submitted both a written and an oral submission to the convention during 2000 to argue for the inclusion of sexual orientation and gender identity in the non-discrimination clause, for a clause on the right to marry and found a family, and for adopting a language recognising the diversity of relationships in contemporary Europe. It also participated in the Social Platform and Trade Union (ETUC) activities on the Charter and supported the joint statements. The text of the Charter retains sexual orientation, but not gender identity, in the non-discrimination article (Art. 21). The article concerning the right to marry and found a family designates these issues as a matter for national legislation, and therefore excludes them from the scope of the Charter (Art. 9).

However, the European Charter of Fundamental Rights is the first international charter with a prohibition of discrimination and the only one that includes sexual orientation. Nevertheless, the critique of the restrictions in the Charter voiced by NGOs grew significantly among the members of the Social Platform and the trade unions. The protest focused on the fact that it drags behind the Social Charter of the Council of Europe (1996) and includes no rights to employment and minimal wages, to housing, to protection from poverty and social exclusion, to the right to strike, nor any reference to the rights of third country nationals legally resident in the Union. Instead, amusingly enough, it contains the right to freedom in business. This approach, however, changed during the Convention process on the future Constitution, when the danger of not having the Charter included in the draft at all led to a large NGO consensus that it should be included and its short-falls addressed in other parts of the draft Constitution. The Convention on the Future of Europe finally included the Charter after much concerted lobby effort inside and outside the Convention as Part II of the draft Constitution. Whether the IGC will leave in the final Constitution remains to be seen.

Other gains in the draft Constitution, in terms of sexual orientation, were the inclusion of equality among the values of the Union (Part I, Art. 2), anti-discrimination in the objectives (Part I, Art. 3), and the inclusion of a horizontal anti-discrimination articles concerning the policies of the Union (Part III, Art. 1a). As mentioned above, however, the anti-discrimination NGOs lost the battle for a change of the unanimity rule for anti-discrimination legislation in Part III, Art. 5. There is still no mention of gender identity anywhere in the text.[6] This second Convention, brought to life at the Laeken summit to make the Union capable of enlargement, was again a decisive step forward in terms of democratic decision-making and transparency regarding Treaty change, although its process and composition, and particularly its outcome, has many significant weaknesses identified by NGOs.[7]

The years 2002 and 2003 were probably the busiest lobby years for ILGA-Europe in the EU to date, since, besides the Convention on the Future of Europe, a wealth of Directives and regulations with significant impact on sexual orientation and gender identity were and are in the making. The main focus is still on the Directive on

Freedom of Movement for EU citizens (COM (2001) 257), which, it is to be hoped, will include the rights of non-married partners to move freely. The definition of 'family' also plays an important role here. ILGA-Europe published a legal position paper on this question, which also pertains to quite a few Directives in relation to third country nationals' rights: there are new Directives on asylum (COM (2001) 181; COM (2001) 447; COM (2002) 326), refugee status and qualification (COM (2001) 501; COM (2002) 326), and family re-unification (COM (2002) 225). Additionally, a Regulation on the EU Staff Regulations (COM (2002) 213) also included work on the recognition of gay and lesbian employees. For all of these Regulations and Directives, ILGA-Europe lobbied the European Parliament and Commission continuously, with considerable effort, and the EU wide network was mobilised to lobby the Council during decision-making stages. Many demands of ILGA-Europe were included by the European Parliament, some adopted by the Commission, and almost all Council decisions are still pending.[8] There was also some very restricted work on the two new Gender Directives to include gender identity under sex discrimination, in both cases unsuccessful to date.

The European Court of Justice has heard several important cases on sexual orientation and gender identity, some of which are discussed in detail or are at least mentioned in Chapter 6. The two main cases are *Grant v. South West Trains Ltd* (C-249/96 ECR) and *P v. S and Cornwall County Council* (C-13/94 ECR) dealing with sexual orientation and gender identity respectively. Both will be discussed at length in chapter six. Another important case is *D v. Council of the European Union* (T-264/97) dealing with sexual orientation and employment conditions at the EU commission. While *P v. S* was successful, both *Grant* and *D v. Council of the European Union* failed. In the aftermath of the implementation of the Employment Directive at national level, more success at the ECJ is to be expected in the future. On 10 June 2003, the opinion delivered by Advocate General Ruiz-Jarabo in Case C-117/01, *KB* v. *The National Health Service Pensions Agency and the Secretary of State for Health*, concludes that national rules which, by not allowing transsexuals to marry, deny them entitlement to a widow's or widower's pension are contrary to Community law. The judgment in this case was passed in favour of transsexual rights in January 2004.

The Council of Europe

The Council of Europe was founded in 1949, in the aftermath of World War II. Its main role is to strengthen democracy, human rights, and the rule of law throughout its Member States. Today, it has forty-five Member States, covering a population of 800 million people, extending from Vladivostock to Lisbon, and from Istanbul to Helsinki. Its most important instrument is the European Convention on Human Rights (ECHR), to which all forty-five Member States subscribe. This establishes the basic fundamental human rights that are applicable all across Europe. Individuals are allowed to bring cases against their government with respect to possible violations of the Convention.

The main institutions of the Council of Europe are the following: firstly, there is the *Committee of Ministers*, which is made up of the Ministers of Foreign Affairs of the forty-five Member States. It is the main political decision-making body and decides on the official broadening of the Convention or its additional Protocols. Secondly, there is the *Parliamentary Assembly of the Council of Europe (PACE)*, which is a deliberative body, made up of 626 representatives and 18 observers from the Parliaments of the Member States. Each delegation's composition reflects that of its Parliament of origin. The Parliamentary Assembly holds four week-long plenary sessions a year and while it is divided into national delegations it works in political groupings across nationality. Its debates on a wide range of social issues and its recommendations to the Committee of Ministers have been at the root of many of the Council of Europe's achievements. The Assembly plays a key role in the accession process for new members and in monitoring compliance with undertakings entered into.

The *European Court of Human Rights* is the third institution of importance. It is made up of one judge from each of the forty-five Member States, makes judgments with respect to possible violations of the European Convention on Human Rights. Where the Court finds that a particular government is in violation of the Convention, that government is obliged to take corrective action. Judgments of the Court, which establish a general principle with respect to one country, should, in theory, be acted on by other countries, which are similarly in violation of the Convention. However, in such cases, the government in question may fail to take the necessary action. The Court has no judicial powers to force Member States to act on its judgments, but the moral and political pressure is fairly high on many levels, and, thus, the judgments do often have an immediate effect.[9] Until five years ago, a separate body, the European Commission on Human Rights, first reviewed cases under the European Convention. In 1998 the functions of the Commission were taken over by the Court, as part of a reorganisation of the latter.

The Council of Europe has an accredited NGO body in different NGO groupings – such as human rights, social rights, gender equality, and civil society. ILGA-Europe enjoys official consultative status with the Council of Europe as of 15 January 1998 and started its work there in September 1998. Its first application dates back to 1989, and was rejected in 1990 because ILGA-World's activities were not 'directly related to the present work programme of the Council of Europe' (letter of refusal by the Council of Europe to ILGA). The re-application was launched in 1995.

The European Convention on Human Rights has been of great significance in promoting lesbian, gay, and transgender rights since the 1980s. With regard to homosexuality, the first successful case, *Dudgeon v. UK*, occurred in 1981. It declared the criminalisation of homosexuality in Northern Ireland a breach of the Convention under Article 8 (privacy), but not under Article 14 (discrimination). Similar cases followed for Ireland (*Norris*, 1988), and for Cyprus (*Modinos*, 1993).[10] In 1997, the European Commission on Human Rights found that the UK's discriminatory age of consent violated the Convention (*Sutherland*, 1997, discussed in Chapter 4). It was not until the end of 2000 that the UK lifted the unequal age of consent, since the House of Lords blocked several previous attempts launched by the Labour government in the wake of the Commission's opinion.

The year 1999 featured three important judgments of the Court, which found that the UK had violated the Convention with its ban on lesbians and gays in the armed forces (*Lustig-Prean and Beckett v. United Kingdom*, and *Smith and Grady v. United Kingdom*) and the Lisbon High Court's discriminatory treatment of a gay father in a custody case (*Salgueiro Da Silva Mouta C. v. Portugal*) also violated the Convention. All three cases are interesting for the comparative statements made in them. *Lustig-Prean and Beckett v. United Kingdom*, and *Smith and Grady v. United Kingdom* compare sexual orientation discrimination with discrimination based on race:

> [T]o the extent that they represent a predisposed bias on the part of a heterosexual majority against a homosexual minority, these negative attitudes cannot, of themselves, be considered by the Court to amount to sufficient justification for the interferences ..., any more than similar negative attitudes towards those of a different race, origin or colour.

Salgueiro Da Silva Mouta C. v. Portugal then declared distinctions based solely on the sexual orientation of a person to be intolerable according to the Convention and directly comparable to religious discrimination (*Hoffmann* case): 'It must therefore be concluded, in the light of what precedes, that the [Lisbon] Court of Appeal drew a distinction dictated by considerations relating to the applicant's sexual orientation, a distinction that cannot be tolerated according to the Convention.' (See, *mutatis mutandis*, the *Hoffmann* judgment referred to above, p. 60, § 36.)

Both these statements are important progress in international human rights law, which were taken further, in July 2000, in *ADT v. United Kingdom*. Here the Court found that the UK's discriminatory privacy laws were a violation of the Convention. This latter case broadened the applicability of privacy laws beyond the *Dudgeon* case for the first time.

On 26 February 2002 a case specifically adopted by ILGA-Europe and worked through by one, its legal experts, *Frette v. France*, on the adoption rights of a single gay father, was lost by a slim majority (4 to 3) despite very hopeful proceedings. The time was not yet ripe for human rights protection of gay parents. The Court considered the right of a State to apply rules against gay men and lesbians as admissible since opinions diverge about this issue, there is not enough research to prove that gay fathers are not detrimental to a child's development, and the low number of adoptable children also made restrictions permissible. However, the minority opinion presents important steps forward in terms of the recognition of lesbian and gay parents. On 9 January 2003, unequal ages of consent were once and for all made contrary to the European Convention on Human Rights after decades of lobbying and after almost all European countries had changed their laws in this respect, including Austria, which pre-empted the judgments in *L and V v. Austria*, and *SL v. Austria* by half a year.

And, finally, on 24 July 2003, there was a positive judgment on succession to rent contracts after the death of a same-sex partner in *Karner v. Austria*. This case was also officially adopted by ILGA-Europe and the Court mentioned ILGA-Europe's submission in the 7:1 judgment. The case is a milestone in gay and lesbian legal rights lobbying, since it does not come after the law has been changed in almost all Member States, but affects thirty-three Member States who do not grant equal rights to unmarried partners of the same sex. The implications of this case are potentially very far reaching for the future. On 1 August 2003 Armenia became the last country in the Council of Europe, to scrap the penalisation of same-sex relationships from its penal code, while seven countries retain discriminatory provisions in the criminal law (Albania, Bulgaria, Greece, Ireland, Portugal, Serbia/Montenegro, and the United Kingdom), and thirty-three do not provide legal recognition for same-sex partners.

In relation to transgender issues, seven cases have been heard in full, plus nine which were heard by the Commission on Human Rights only. Five cases gained specific significance:[11] *B v. France* (1992) on the change of gender on national identity cards (won), *XYZ v. United Kingdom* (1997), dealing with the acceptance of a female-to-male transsexual's rights to fatherhood (lost); *Sheffield and Horsham v. United Kingdom* (1998), dealing with the UK's refusal to issue a new birth certificate to a British transsexual woman living in the Netherlands (lost), and finally, in 2002, *Christine Goodwin v. United Kingdom*, where a transsexual woman having undergone gender re-assignment is legally still recognised as a man in the UK and therefore has to pay National Insurance contributions until the age of 65 (won). Had her gender identity been recognised by the UK she would, like women in general, cease to pay National Insurance contributions when she turned 60. This case has now finally led to a law change being underway in the UK in 2003 that will make changed birth certificates available and will also grant fatherhood status to transsexual men whose female partners conceived via artificial insemination as attempted in *XYZ*. 2003 also finally saw *van Kück v. Germany* won ensuring health insurance coverage for gender reassignment.

Lobbying examples at the Council of Europe

The anti-discrimination provisions set out in Article 14 of the European Convention on Human Rights, under which the successful cases have been won, have a significant weakness: protection from discrimination is provided only with regard to 'the enjoyment of the other rights and freedoms' in the Convention. There is no general right to freedom from discrimination, leaving any discrimination not related to one of the rights in the Convention unprotected. In March 1998 the Committee of Ministers of the Council of Europe initiated the development of an optional Protocol 12 to the Convention with a view to remedying this deficiency. If ratified successfully in Member States, this will represent the first extension to the Convention's anti-discrimination provisions in its fifty-year history.

ILGA-Europe has used the opportunity presented by this event to mount a major campaign to have sexual orientation and gender identity included in the list of prohibited grounds of discrimination included in the draft Protocol. In May 1999 ILGA-Europe made two professionally prepared legal submissions, arguing first sexual orientation and later gender identity to the Intergovernmental Steering Committee on Human Rights. However, when the Committee of Ministers published its proposed draft of the Protocol 12 in August 1999, ILGA-Europe's recommendations had been ignored. Following publication, the draft Protocol 12 was referred to the Parliamentary Assembly for its opinion. ILGA-Europe immediately contacted the *rapporteur* for the Assembly, Senator Erik Jurgens of The Netherlands, and proposed to him the inclusion of both sexual orientation and gender identity. He was supportive of the inclusion of the former.

His reasoning, as expressed in the wording of the Opinion (Opinion No. 206 (2000)) was unequivocal: '[the Assembly] believes that the enumeration of grounds in Article 14 is, without being exhaustive, meant to list forms of discrimination which it regards as being especially odious. Consequently the ground "sexual orientation" should be added'. The Assembly debated the Opinion on 26 January 2000. The great majority of speakers were substantially in favour of the inclusion of sexual orientation in the draft Protocol. Yet, an attempt to delete sexual orientation from the Opinion was only narrowly defeated: opponents of gay rights had remained silent, hoping that the apparent absence of opposition would lead its supporters to leave the Assembly. Prior to the debate ILGA-Europe had written to more than 300 parliamentarians providing additional information in support of the Opinion, urging them to be present for the debate, and phoning many to ensure their presence right before the debate.

The Opinion was then forwarded to the Steering Committee on Human Rights for its response. ILGA-Europe took this opportunity to make a second submission to the Steering Committee. Despite these efforts, the Opinion of the Parliamentary Assembly was rejected, and in June 2000 the Committee of Ministers adopted the text of Protocol 12 unamended.[12] Although the objective of ILGA-Europe's campaign was not achieved, the fact that the Parliamentary Assembly had voted in support of the inclusion of sexual orientation was an important statement of support for lesbian and gay rights. Another significant success was the passing of two recommendations in the Parliamentary Assembly of the Council of Europe, one on asylum and migration[13] – passed in June 2000 – and one on the situation of gay men and lesbians in Europe – passed in September 2000. Reports and recommendations of the PACE are not legally binding on Member States, but such documents are often resources the ECHR draws upon in its opinions. Both were initiated, lobbied, written, and fought through from beginning to end by ILGA-Europe's volunteer board members. I will concentrate on the latter.[14]

The Report and Recommendation on the *Situation of Gay men and Lesbians in Europe* (Doc. 1474) was prepared for the Legal Affairs and Human Rights

Committee by a Spanish Socialist Member of Parliament, Ms María del Carmen Calleja, after initiation by ILGA-Europe in June 1999. In September 1999 the Secretariat of the Parliamentary Assembly sent out questionnaires to all Member States, which were prepared by ILGA-Europe. In preparation for the Report an all-day hearing on a large range of subjects was held before the Sub-Committee on Human Rights of the Assembly in Paris on 14 October 1999. ILGA-Europe prepared this hearing in the background providing most of the information, selecting almost all experts, and providing help for speech preparation. It also provided evidence in the form of a thirty-page survey of discrimination in Europe as a draft report. The hearing raised a lot of interest and the fact that sexual orientation framed a whole day for the Sub-Committee was a milestone in itself. After much internal debate, ILGA-Europe suggested the recommendations should stop at registered partnership and not include adoption rights, since it had good evidence to fear that adoption would loose the whole recommendation.

In spite of this the secretary of the Committee in charge of drafting the final report included adoption in the recommendation, but left out a number of other important aspects on which ILGA-Europe had insisted. With the *rapporteur* leaving the Assembly in spring of 2000, it seemed as if ILGA-Europe's chances of influencing the report were vanishing. The role of *rapporteur* was taken over by a Hungarian Socialist Member of Parliament, Mr Csaba Tabajdi, and the final report was published in June 2000 including the sentence 'The Assembly is pleased to note that some countries have [recognised] ... even the right to adopt children', which caused a significant stir among conservatives. ILGA-Europe – in order to safeguard the whole recommendation, but a little ironically – helped initiate changes through amendments and the reference to adoption was deleted with a 63 per cent majority.

The Assembly debated the Recommendation on 30 June 2000. Although the great majority of speeches were very supportive, opponents of the Recommendation succeeded in postponing the vote until the September 2000 session of the Assembly, on the basis that insufficient parliamentarians were present for there to be a quorum.[15] However, the final Report and Recommendation was finally passed with 77 per cent, and covers a whole range of discrimination experienced by lesbians and gay men in Europe, putting forward proposals for tackling this both at the level of Member States and at the level of the Council of Europe.[16] In the course of the process ILGA-Europe wrote to around 300 members of the Assembly and co-ordinated a lobbying campaign by its members at national level, and by other networks, including the Amnesty International Group for l/g/b/t concerns, the International Lesbian and Gay Youth Organisation, and the European Gay and Lesbian Sports Federation.

On 21 September 2001 the process of this recommendation came to a close with the Committee of Ministers of the Council of Europe issuing a statement regretting that discrimination and violence against homosexuals still occur in Europe, and acknowledging that progress in ending discrimination is still needed in Member States' domestic law and practice. In their reply the Committee of Ministers advised their agreement to several of the eleven recommendations, but did not state which. This lack of clarity almost certainly reflects disagreements between Member States on certain of the recommendations, particularly those relating to the age of consent and registered partnership. However, the Committee chose to emphasise the need for measures in the areas of education and professional training 'to combat homophobic attitudes in certain specific circles'. Previously, the Committee had once on its own accord referred to the need for anti-discrimination measures on ground of – *inter alia* – sexual orientation with regard to access to higher education (R 98, 3) in March 1998.

The International Lesbian and Gay Association

ILGA-Europe's development as a European lobby NGO is framed by the historical formation of an international lesbian and gay political movement in Europe. The first international conferences on sexual equality after the efforts of the *Wissenschaftlich-Humanitäres Komittee* in Germany in the late nineteenth to early twentieth century were sponsored by the Dutch Group COC between 1951 and 1958. While these conferences were called 'international', they did not in fact have a large international participation, but gathered together professionals and gays and lesbians aiming to make homosexuality legitimate within society (Quan 1994:6). The next international conference of gays and lesbians was organised by the Scottish Minorities Group in 1974, which reached, however, no consensus to form an international organisation (Quan 1994:6). It was four years later, after preparatory links between the Dutch organisation COC and the English Campaign for Homosexual Equality (CHE), that an international workshop was held in Coventry, UK, in August 1978, as part of the CHE's annual conference. Thirty men from fourteen countries were present and agreed upon a Founding Declaration for the International Gay Association, IGA. IGA became ILGA in 1986 and gave itself a constitution in 1981 in Turin. Up until then, participation was primarily European with some North Americans.[17]

The ILGA was established as a federation of grass roots organisations. Today there are approximately 400 groups in over 70 countries of the world. ILGA was not supposed to take decisions on behalf of its members, but instead only act as an umbrella organisation to support member groups through information circulation and co-ordination of political actions. Until the second half of the 1990s the means by which ILGA fulfilled its aim to fight all types of discrimination and towards the liberation of lesbian women and gay men was to gather and distribute information, to unite movements, and to aid political lobbying and actions. Its strategies were to hold conferences, launch actions, and facilitate twinning projects and information exchanges – such as a bulletin, books, or EU sponsored projects resulting in publications. While major decisions can only be decided upon by members during the annual conferences, the management of ILGA between conferences used to be done by the Secretariat's Committee and is today done by an executive board and two Secretaries-General. Originally, the secretariats functioned only to co-ordinate the exchange of information and international action projects. In 1986, the two leadership positions of Secretary-General were designated. Since then, the Secretariat's Committee has moved more towards a Directive role, and this was enshrined in the Constitution at the 1990 Stockholm conference.[18]

ILGA used to be an organisation for gay men, lesbians, and bisexuals. Since the Rio conference in 1995 its mandate also covers transgender people. This addition was put into the draft of a new constitution by Andy Quan, full-time employee of ILGA at the time. It remained unchallenged – despite traditional opposition to the inclusion of transgender issues by many European member groups – because the Latin American context in which the conference was held was favourable to the combination of homosexuality and transgender issues.[19] ILGA has undertaken a regionalisation process, defining six regions – broadly corresponding to the defined continents – with independent organisational structures. In December 1996, ILGA-Europe became the first of these regional associations to be formally established with its own constitution and its own executive board led by two co-chairs elected at the annual ILGA-Europe regional conference. ILGA-Europe is registered – as is ILGA-World – as a non-profit international association under Belgian law. Its head office as well as ILGA-World's head office is in Brussels. Since its constitution is modelled on the world constitution, it is also a l/g/b/t organisation.

Up until 1999, ILGA-Europe had not lobbied for transgender rights at all. The first step in taking up the issue was to release a second submission on gender identity to the broadening process of Article 14 of the European Convention on Human Rights. Gender identity was taken up for the second time during the process of lobbying the Charter of Fundamental Rights of the European Union. In both instances ILGA-Europe was unsuccessful in including gender identity. The Bucharest conference in October 2000 explicitly included transgender issues for the first time into the work programme for the executive board and demanded attention to an increase in transgender membership in ILGA and representation at conferences.

The office established in 2001 under EU funding cannot include work on gender identity since the Commission regulations explicitly exclude it from the Action Programme from which ILGA-Europe receives funding. The position papers and legal expertise generally include transgender issues[20], and occasionally bisexual issues, but the transgender work of ILGA-Europe remains weak. The board has now founded an official working group on transgender and is in the process of securing funding for employment in this field. Bisexuality has until now not received equivalent attention. The executive board commissioned a policy paper on bisexuality in 2002 and is in the process of establishing work in this area, but progress is slow.

ILGA has so far, with a few exceptions, depended on volunteer work of dedicated activists willing to invest their time, energy, and money into the organisation and its causes. ILGA-World has occasionally had a full-time employee, depending on short-term funding, and ILGA-Europe is as of 2001 co-financed by the European Union with first two full-time employees and by 2003 four, including an executive director. By 2004 there should be up to six employees in the Brussels office and three in an East European office outside the EU. Up until this moment ILGA-World still is and ILGA-Europe has until three years ago been a very poor organisations with only their membership fees available and often unable to even pay the travel expenses incurred by their board members. The large majority of work in ILGA-World and ILGA-Europe is done via the internet, which has revolutionised the amount of work ILGA activists can donate to their cause.

In its twenty-four years of existence, ILGA's most notable achievements have included many different successes. One is surely the hosting of conferences on all continents of this world ranging from very small participation to hundreds of people attending. Convincing Amnesty International to accept persons imprisoned for their homosexuality as 'prisoners of conscience' was another major achievement. The successful lobbying at the European Union and the consultative status with the Council of Europe, as well as contributing to the World Health Organisation's decision to stop considering homosexuality a disease are considered milestones. Additionally, the official recognition by the United Nation's ECOSOC in 1993 as consultative NGO is important to ILGA. This accreditation was suspended, though, through a homophobic attack by conservative US senator Jesse Helms. He convinced the US Senate in January 1994 not to pay its 118 million dollar debt to the UN as long as the UN recognised paedophile organisations such as ILGA.

ILGA had indeed three member organisations that called themselves paedophile from the time of the early 1980s, in which all gay organisations could become members of ILGA without screening. The most prominent organisation was NAMBLA – North American Man Boy Love Association – which ILGA expelled at its 1994 conference in New York alongside the other two.[21] Although ILGA's constitution explicitly supports the UN charter on the rights of children – groups or individuals advocating paedophilia can, therefore, no longer be members of ILGA – its consultative status to the UN has not been re-instituted to date in spite of good working contacts over the years with the High Commissioner on Human Rights. As late as 2002, despite of much lobby effort, Spain pulled out of an already reached majority, and ILGA was denied consultative at the UN status once more.

Since 1994, ILGA has clearly become a rights-centred lobby organisation promoting human rights discourse rather than a discourse advocating sexual liberation and radical politics. In terms of movement history this is a break with the traditions of the gay liberation movement in the 1970s in Europe and North America in favour of a civil rights and law reform approach that centralises, at least in Europe, on human rights discourse. A long-time ILGA activist, Lisa Power, commented that 'in the 80s, ILGA was purely a solidarity movement. Since then it has moved a long way to become an effective human-rights lobby' (Quan 1994:22). This move is mirrored in its membership. The most influential member groups of ILGA-Europe are the large national rights groups engaged in lobby politics, such as COC in the Netherlands, RFSL in Sweden, LBL in Denmark, Stonewall in the UK, and newly formed Eastern European groups such as ACCEPT in Romania.

Important players and information distributors in ILGA-Europe are also the trade union groups, such as UNISON from the UK, and staff organisations, such as EGALITE, representing gay and lesbian employees of the European institutions.[22]

ILGA incorporates a mixture of movement history in its own understandings of itself as an organisation and in its activities. Since its inception, its character has developed from an information network of grass roots groups throughout the world in which decisions can only be taken at the conferences, to a professionally run, internationally accredited NGO with an executive board that has powers of decision – though only on the mandate of the work programme approved at the annual conference. ILGA-Europe does not set any claim to representing the European lesbian, gay, bisexual, and transgender movements, it does not even claim to speak for all its own member groups at the same time. However, it does claim a mandate from its member groups to focus on certain rights issues and promote its own definitions of gay, lesbian, bisexual, and transgender rights as goals to be achieved. In those definitions, issues of discrimination and violation are connected to the living situations of gay men, lesbians, bisexuals, and transgender people in Europe. ILGA-Europe, thus, does partake in representational politics based on conceptions of sexual and gender identity, even though its own institutional interpretations of these identities and of representational politics are not clear cut and have historically never been stringent.

Considering ILGA-World's and ILGA-Europe's history and their working strategies of lobby politics at international institutions, ILGA as an organisation can usefully be defined as a transnational advocacy network. According to Margaret Keck and Kathryn Sikkink, transnational advocacy networks have four things in common: 'the centrality of values or principled ideas, the belief that individuals can make a difference, the creative use of information, and the employment by non-governmental actors of sophisticated political strategies in targeting their campaigns' (1998:2). ILGA-Europe mobilises competent actors – from lawyers to academics to professional administrators and rights activists – bound together by at least the idea of shared values, a common discourse, and intensive exchanges of information and services. As a network ILGA-Europe managed to strategically mobilise information about the living conditions of gay men, lesbians, bisexuals, and transgender people to help create new issues and categories and to persuade, pressure, and gain leverage over much more powerful organisations and governments (1998:2). According to Keck and Sikkink, advocacy networks normally involve a small number of expert activists that often define themselves against the background of a larger movement (1998:204). Yet, a characteristic of transnational advocacy networks is also that their issues are unlikely to sustain mass mobilisation. ILGA defines itself against the background of a large worldwide movement that manages to create mass mobilisation at least once a year in huge pride marches all over the world. However, ILGA or ILGA-Europe themselves are unlikely to ever sustain any mass mobilisation for a specific issue they are campaigning for.

Strategically speaking, therefore, ILGA-Europe uses two kinds of facts to argue its aims and make its issues more real: technical facts – such as legal or procedural facts – and dramatic testimony of discrimination – most prominently issues involving bodily harm and equality. The mobilisation of shame through attacking double standards in the interpretation of fundamental rights is an important strategy. The immediate goals of ILGA-Europe are the same as those defined by Keck and Sikkink for advocacy networks: issue creation, influence on the discursive positions of states and institutional procedure as well as policy change and change in state behaviour (1998:25). Keck and Sikkink, however, differentiate advocacy networks from NGOs: the latter are seen to only form part of networks. Considering the mixed organisational history of ILGA, I would suggest that ILGA-Europe is both a transnational advocacy network and a professionalised NGO all in one. Since ILGA-Europe defines itself as a European NGO, I will continue to use the term 'NGO' throughout this book, while keeping in mind that ILGA-Europe also fits what has in recent political science been termed advocacy network. In line with Keck and Sikkink I define ILGA – and particularly ILGA-Europe, which is the focus of this book – as a group of activists who try to

> frame issues in ways that make them fit into particular institutional venues and that make them resonate with broader publics, use information and symbols to reinforce their claims, identify appropriate targets, seek leverage over more powerful actors to influence their targets, and try to make institutions accountable in their practices to the norms they claim to uphold. (1998:201)

In this endeavour the network as an actor derives a great deal of its effectiveness from the network as structure, within which ideas are formulated, reformulated, tested, and negotiated (1998:207). This combination also accounts for the mixture of levels that need to be addressed throughout this book.

While I predominantly analyse discourses on an organisational level, the interconnection between individual agents/activists and the network occasionally necessitates a leap in the analysis from the organisational level to individual psycho-social processes of gender and sexuality wherever the persuasive power of rights and equality discourses is addressed. This is the case for the theoretical analysis in several instances in this book.

Notes

1 The EU has four more institutions, which have so far not been relevant to the topics of this book, but will be mentioned at least: the Court of Auditors, the Economic and Social Committee, the Committee of the Regions, and the European Ombudsman.
2 For a comprehensive analysis of the political processes of and the press responses to the Roth Report, see Thomas F. Kramer (1997). Claudia Roth, a Bavarian Green MEP, was ex-communicated by the Pope for her role in this report, which became her 'personal claim to fame' (Claudia Roth in conversation with the author, September 2000).
3 The lobby process started in May 1996 after a resolution of the European Parliament. Until the summit on 18 June 1997, Article 13 (originally Art. 6) was changed several times, sexual orientation was included in the drafts at different stages by the Irish, Italian, and Austrian governments. The Dutch presidency cut the reference to age, sexual orientation,

social origin, and disability in February 1997. Through an indiscretion the draft was put on the internet and ILGA-Europe, together with Dutch organisations and Members of the European Parliament, forced the Dutch government to change the draft again. See *Lambda Nachrichten* 23 (1) 2001:39 for further explanation.
4 Northern Ireland received a specific section in the directive that limits the applicability of the directive in terms of religion with regard to teachers and the police force.
5 In fact, the new Italian law can only be titled a 'discrimination law' and Italian NGOs, with much support from the European NGO level, are up in arms against it.
6 There has been no lobby effort by ILGA-Europe to have gender identity included.
7 For an overall assessment of the Convention by all four NGO sectors – environment, social, development, human rights – see the documents of the Civil Society Contact Group and the act4europe campaign (www.act4europe.org).
8 To list all results in detail would go beyond the scope of this chapter. ILGA-Europe maintains a comprehensive website with several overview documents on the results of the lobby processes (www.ilga-europe.org).
9 The case of Cyprus, for example, is interesting here. Cyprus changed its ban on homosexuality in 1998 according to a European Convention on Human Rights judgment (*Modinos*), but the changes where not satisfactory to the CoE, which pressured Cyprus to enact further changes in 2000. The EU considered those demands in its own processes of accession and, thus, increased pressure. The UK and Romania have been similarly pressured in relation to sexual orientation, successfully in both cases. The UK has also succumbed to pressure by the ECHR on the legal recognition of gender reassignment in July 2003 and Austria pre-empted the ECHR judgment on unequal age of consent by half a year, when the positive outcome became foreseeable.
10 For a comprehensive analysis of human rights cases under the ECHR until 1996, see Heinze (1995), Kane (1992), Kimble (1992), and Wintemute (1996).
11 The others are: *Van Oosterwijck* (1980), *Rees v. United Kingdom* (1986), and *Lossey* (1990). All cases are available on the website of Press for Change (www.pfc.org) an important lobby organisation in the UK.
12 However, an explanatory note is appended to this article which states that 'other grounds' can be interpreted to include sexual orientation.
13 Recommendation and Report *On the Situation of Lesbian/Gay Couples with regard to Asylum and Migration* (Doc. 1470, 2000).
14 The Parliamentary Assembly had previously passed a number of Recommendations supporting lesbian and gay rights. The 1981 *Report on Discrimination against Homosexuals* (Doc. 4755, Voogd Report), the Recommendation 924 (1981) on discrimination against homosexuals, and the resolution 756 (1981) on discrimination against homosexuals. The Parliamentary Assembly also issued a written declaration (No. 227, Doc. 6779) on homosexuals' rights in the new democracies in 1993. This has led to de-criminalisation of homosexuality becoming a pre-condition for accession to the Council of Europe.
15 It is interesting to note that the debate was scheduled on a Friday morning of the Parliamentary session. Quorum votes are in general uncommon since there is always a poor turnout of parliamentarians on Friday mornings. Many supporters left the Assembly before the vote since the debate was overwhelmingly positive. It seemed as if the scheduling on Friday morning as well as the late call for a quorum by a Polish Conservative Parliamentarian was a deliberate homophobic attempt to defeat the resolution.
16 These include: making sexual orientation a prohibited ground for discrimination in their national legislation; the repeal of all laws making homosexual acts between consenting adults liable to criminal prosecution, and the release of anyone imprisoned

under such laws; the application of the same minimum age of consent for homosexual and heterosexual acts; ensuring equal treatment with regard to employment; adopting legislation which makes provision for registered partnership for same-sex couples. It also repeats the Assembly's call to the Committee of Ministers to add sexual orientation to the grounds of discrimination prohibited by the European Convention on Human Rights, and calls for the terms of reference of the European Commission against Racism and Intolerance (ECRI) to be extended to cover homophobia.
17 This information is taken from an interview with Nigel Warner and from the archived conference papers of the early IGA conferences.
18 Information provided by Nigel Warner (interview, February/1998), and Michiel Odijk and Jan Willem de Jong (interview, February/1998).
19 Information obtained from Andy Quan in an e-mail exchange in 1998.
20 The term 'transgender' within ILGA-Europe is currently used for people whose gender identity and/or gender expression differs from the sex they were assigned at birth. The term may include, but is not limited to: transsexual, intersex people, cross-dressers, and other gender variant people. There is a clear awareness that issues pertaining to intersex people in particular might be very specific and incomparable to issues pertaining to transsexual people. Gender identity is understood as the individual's gender concept of self, not necessarily dependent on the sex they were assigned at birth. Gender identity concerns every human being and it is not only a binary concept of either male or female (ILGA-Europe transgender working group, May 2003).
21 See Quan (1994) for a precise analysis of this process in ILGA and the debate that preceded it.
22 EGALITE – Equality for Gays and Lesbians in the European Institutions – used to be an important source of information for ILGA-Europe, since its members are professionals everywhere in the European institutions, ranging from interpreters to administrators to court employees. It has ceased its political work in recent years.

2 Queer theory and political practices

> Social movements are collective efforts by socially and politically subordinated people to challenge the conditions and assumptions of their lives. Collective action becomes a 'movement' when participants refuse to accept the boundaries of established institutional rules and routinized roles ... While traditional definitions usually focus on movement challenges to political structures, economic arrangements, and institutional rules, social movements – perhaps especially contemporary ones – also take on established cultural codes and social identities ... The seeming contradictoriness of movement activity ... challenges not only political systems and cultural status quos but also many of our explanatory frameworks and analytic categories.
> (Marcy Darnovsky, Barbara Epstein and Richard Flacks 1995:vii)

This book takes the terms 'theory' and 'politics' as its starting point for inquiry. Since both are only seemingly self-evident, but actually very much undefined and unclear, their meanings are at best tentatively defined here. First I will concentrate on theory, more particularly queer theory and poststructuralism. This section is not intended as an exhaustive overview of the literature on queer theory. It rather tries to explicate the term and get a grip on the way in which the term is used in the following chapters. I will, then, move into defining and explaining the kinds of politics I investigate as political practices. The concept of meaning is engaged to understand how politics become effective practices. Both – queer theory and political practices – are deployed to understand certain aspects of political change and social movements, in this case the European lesbian and gay movements' struggle for rights.

Queer theory in Europe

'Queer' is an old and also quite recent phenomenon in l/g/b/t contexts. It has been a slang term for homosexuals while also being used as a form of homophobic abuse. Since about 1990 'queer' has become an umbrella term for all sorts of things: a substitute for 'gay' and 'lesbian', a descriptive term for all unruly sexualities, the hip title, noun, verb, or adjective for everything in relation to gays, lesbians, bisexuals, and transsexuals, for example, journals, parties, demonstrations, politics. It is fundamentally connected to AIDS activism and has become the infamous name of the ACT-UP spin-off QUEER NATION as well.[1] While being all these things, 'queer' has also turned into the brand name for numerous new academic theories and practices of writing (Warner 1992:18). The queer community is, so to speak, an oxymoronic community of difference (Duggan 1992:19). The term carries with it an excess of meanings, which it can never fully recognise or fulfil. Alongside this abundance of meaning, it is also a profoundly Anglo-American term that has become common currency in many international l/g/b/t cultures without ever taking on board all its Anglo–American contents, while at the same time being enriched by new meanings in different language contexts.

Queer ranges from a new group identity to a form of marketing l/g/b/t events to a radically different form of political activism or to a body of highly theoretical academic writing. By the beginning of the twenty-first century, it seemed as if the layers of complication in attempting to define queer as a political or a theoretical concept will not end; the more the term spreads, the more it becomes *something*, the less anybody can define it. However, for the sake of clarity, the usage of the term 'queer' in an academic context should not be left unexplained. 'Queer' is used in this book only to demarcate a specific form of theoretical thinking that has political implications. It is not used to describe an identity, a subculture, or a specific form of radical activism. The latter is not my subject of investigation, for reasons I explained in the introduction and for reasons to which I will return later in this chapter. The former two I simply do not subscribe to, for several reasons.

David Halperin summarised the aspect of queer identity in the following way: 'There is nothing in particular to which it necessarily refers, it is an identity without an essence' (Halperin 1995:62). I would maintain, however, that queer as an identity makes little sense whatsoever, even if queer is understood to reach far beyond gay, lesbian, bisexual, and transgender communities. In common language use throughout Europe, 'queer' has become a substitute term for 'gay' and 'lesbian', and sometimes it functions as the umbrella term for the l/g/b/t connection. While I firmly believe in the connection between gay and lesbian issues and transgender issues, I see no need to assign a new identity to that connection. A new identity suggests a form of sameness that has already been de-stabilised for gay men or lesbians as a group from the vantage point of gender, race, class, or culture. Experience in Europe shows that the label 'queer' as an identity more often than not only functions as a substitute for 'gay'. Used in that way, it marginalises lesbians once again, and does not even consider bisexuals or transgender people, nor is it capable of addressing the intersections among homosexuality, gender, race, and class. While I hesitantly and with a constant sense of trouble continue to use the terms 'gay men' and 'lesbians' throughout this book – since they continuously carry political relevancy in the context under investigation here – I never use 'queer' as an identification for a group of people.

As for the theoretical aspect of queer, Michael Warner once called queer theory 'a largely intuitive and half-articulate theory' (Warner 1992:19) that, for him and Lauren Berlant, barely existed in 1995 (Berlant and Warner 1995:343). Indeed, the first time it was used academically was in 1991 by Teresa de Lauretis in the infamous issue of *Differences: A Journal of Feminist Cultural Studies*. There, she defined queer as 'an agency of social process whose mode of functioning is both interactive and yet resistant, both participatory and yet distinct, claiming at once equality and difference, demanding political representation while insisting on its material and historical specificity' (de Lauretis 1991:iii). The most common denominator of queer theory since then is its transgressive moment in relation to regimes of the normal and its insistence on de-stabilising all seemingly natural categories of sex and gender, such as fixed homosexual identities or biological gender identities. But that is probably already all that has been agreed upon in the literature around queer theory.[2] According to Eric Savoy (1994:133), queer theory is a portable toolbox that contains a well-known array of binarised category explosives. Moreover, queer labels are a performative disruption of the very concept of identity itself. Overall, I find Linda Nicholson and Steven Seidman's (1995:18) description of queer theory a useful summary:

> queer theory shifts the center of analysis from viewing homosexuality as a minority identity to a cultural figure. The hetero/homo binary is imagined, parallel to the masculine/feminine trope, as a symbolic code structured into the texts of daily life, from popular culture. ... to disciplinary knowledges, law, therapeutic practices, criminal justice, and state policies. It frames the way we know and organize personal and social experience, with the effect of reproducing heteronormativity. Queer theory aims to expose the operation of the hetero/homo code in the center of society and to contribute to destabilizing its operation.

Concepts of queer, thus, are at their best where they defy definition and where they concentrate on disruptions of the normal – the normal being male, heterosexual, white, bourgeois, but also normal business in the academy or taken-for-granted gay and lesbian identity politics. The way queer theory is used in this book is no summary, nor is it exhaustive in all aspects of queer terminology, nor indeed in itself an attempt to find proper answers and objects of research or dissolve all objections. Queer theory has no stable referential content and pragmatic force. Wanting to demarcate queer theory entirely from any of its many meanings would be an attempt to normalise and define something that destroys itself in definition. And as Judith Butler (1994:21) pointedly remarked in this respect, 'normalising the queer would be, after all, its sad finish'. However, I do adhere to a set of assumptions that can be called queer theory. While reading political texts through a queer-theoretical glass, I follow Nicholson and Seidman's path of assuming gender and sexuality to be a binary, hierarchised structure firmly embedded in European political orders. In fact, gender and sexuality are assumed to be a decisive frame of all political orders under investigation here. Although these assumptions have been thoroughly argued by feminist researchers over decades, they are not self-evident to the extent that they need no clarification in this context.

Provisionally, queer theory could be characterised as framed by poststructuralism, or postmodernism. As such, it works from the vantage point of discourse as the meaning-creating system, which pre-exists and, consequently, shapes and signifies the formation of subject positions, identity, and, indeed, reality. Queer theory, thus, maps an unstable, non-essentialist, non-transparent or -coherent, and anti-humanist understanding of sexuality and gender identity. Queer theory is fundamentally a critique of identity. Accordingly, queer as a theory emerged out of 'access to the post-structuralist theorisation of identity as provisional and contingent, coupled with a growing awareness of the limitations of identity categories in terms of political representation' (Jagose 1996:77).

Poststructuralism itself is not a monolithic bloc or a fixed school of thought either, but a re-definable and fluid set of understandings, a practice and process of theorising.

> Rather, 'post-structuralism' indicates a field of critical practices that cannot be totalized and that, therefore, interrogates the formative and exclusionary power of dis-course in the construction of sexual difference. This interrogation does not take for granted the meanings of any terms or analytic categories, including its own ... Poststructuralism is not, strictly speaking, a position, but rather a critical interrogation of the exclusionary operations by which 'positions' are established. (Butler and Scott 1992:xiii–xiv)

Consequently, poststructuralist critiques are not new in themselves, they draw on what has been discursively produced about identities. They, thus, form an identity critique in the sense of de-stabilising the one most naturalised cultural category each of us inhabits: the sense of oneself as being *something*, belonging to a certain defined group, in fact, the very sense of human existence *as something*. And that something is in its primary principle male or female, gender is the first category each human is assigned at birth.[3] Gender is very obviously a central mark of being human.

While certain identities remain central, it is their naturalness that is brought into question. Queer theory emphasises that there is no such thing as a universal identity. According to Madan Sarup (1996:73), every person's identity is a site of struggle between conflicting discourses. He maintains that 'discourses emerge and function as a means of struggle, and, at the same time, a series of controls master and constrain discourses. And in the struggle of discourses, not only words change their meanings, but identities also'. Sarup draws – as does queer theory in general – on a Foucaldian concept of discourse that led to the disruption of natural, universal identities. Joan Scott (1988:254) summarised this concept of discourse as 'any system – strictly verbal or other – through which meaning is constructed and cultural practices organized and by which accordingly, people represent and understand their world, including who they are and how they relate to others'. According to Scott, the analysis of discourse then provides a starting point for conceptualising how social relations are understood, how they work, how they are institutionalised and how collective identities are established. This is an understanding of discourse as the fundamental place in which social relations are formed, defined, and contested. Individual subjectivity and identity are located and constructed in culturally, socially, and historically specific ways in discourse.

Individuals do not create or contest meaning as unified, autonomous subjects from an essential human core, but always from already being positioned in several discourses. This does not mean that discourses are constructed outside of actual relations and then placed on passive individuals. The meanings constructed by discourses are in fact created, used, and contested by all participants who are in different ways located in them. Even members of strongly marginalised groups are not simply passive recipients of a dominant discursive meaning about them. In fact, queer challenges the story of marginalisation as a weak trope even if it produces a story of struggle and oppression itself. Queer theory moves instead into the central production site of cultures and asserts centrality for the queer subject.[4]

However, this does not mean that all individuals have the same access to influencing the establishment of meanings that become dominant. For gays, lesbians, bisexuals, and transgender people it is crucial to understand that, while we actively participate in the constitution of discursive meaning, the organisation of social relations extends beyond individuals. Therefore, while, for example, white women are actively involved in relations and practices, their interpretation of events has not got the same power of influence for creating dominant meaning as white men's. And further, the discrepancies in access to social space and power do not always provide the possibilities for creating non-dominant interpretations in the first place. This understanding is based, yet again, on the Foucaldian concept of power. According to David Evans (1993:11), Foucault's concept of power is

> an all pervasive, normative, and positive presence, internalised by and thus creating, the subject. Indeed, the subject seems not to exist outside of immanent patterns of normative knowledge derived from language, objects and practices, i.e. discourses. 'Subjectivity' in the Foucaldian sense is always discursive, it refers to general subject positions, conceived as empty spaces or functions occupied by particular individuals in the pronouncement of specific statements. We are what we learn, internalise and reproduce as knowledge and the language through which it is understood. We are subjects of the power immanently installed in that knowledge.

As Michel Foucault elaborated extensively in his *History of Sexuality*, *The Archaeology of Knowledge*, and *Discipline and Punish*, his theory of power was simultaneously a definition of how the subject comes into being as, foremost, a sexual subject, who considers sexuality the most essential, but hidden secret of its being. According to Foucault (1980:154), European history shows how the sexual subject of modern societies was constructed out of an obsessive pursuit of ever greater knowledge about the subject's innermost selves – its bio-power – a secret to be discovered everywhere. Gender and sexuality became the most pervasive form of identification in modern regimes, a fact which – ironically – apparently evades discursive interpretation through its stringent claim to eternal truth. The history of sexuality, in consequence, became a subject of academic research, largely through the circulation of Foucault's work by feminists and gay and lesbian authors (Duggan 1992:22). It is the insight into the centrality of sexuality for the creation of subjectivity that makes queer theory challenge 'the regime of sexuality itself, that is, the knowledges that construct the self as sexual and that assume heterosexuality and homosexuality as categories marking the truth of sexual selves' (Seidman 1996:12). The same insight is the reason why 'queer theory aspires to transform homosexual theory into a general social theory or one standpoint from which to analyze social dynamics' (Seidman 1996:13).

This aspiration is intended as a critical intervention into heteronormativity. 'Heteronormativity' is a central term within queer theory.[5] It is based upon understanding sexuality as more than just the effect of cultural or discursive practice or merely the product of ideology or institutions. Rather, sexuality is 'a regulatory apparatus that spans the organization of social life in the modern world and that works in concert with other social totalities – capitalism, patriarchy, colonialism' (Hennessy 1995:70). As a regulatory apparatus, sexuality is not universal and equally valued in all its expressions, but it functionalises heterosexuality to occupy the centre of human sexuality and gender relations. Through thematising heteronormativity rather than heterosexuality, queer theory uncovers the institutional powers of certain discourses that organise more than just the sexual (Genschel 1996:528). According to Corinna Genschel (1996:529), queer analysis is directed against those systems of thought and those institutions which insist on the naturalness, the binding nature, and the pre-condition of heterosexuality, just as feminists have shown how terms such as morality, rationality, or the public sphere are deeply dependent on gender. Thus, it is the normative ordering force of (hetero)sexuality, which comes under critique, not practices of heterosexuality *per se*. This marks queer theory's distance from any notions of essential gayness or lesbianism.

Some of the best research in gender and sexuality has demonstrated how normative discourses interpellate individuals into hegemonic social orders that produce gendered subjects and the trajectory of their desire. These studies show how discursive technologies inlay into psyche and corporeal reality the structures of corporeal rules – such as proper and improper gender identity – and linguistic options that together limit the social register upon which social space for speech and self-identification is based. The rules and features of human identity – foremost gender, sexuality, and race – compose the personal grammar that every subject has, and this grammar, unperceived, migrates with persons as they enter and transgress public and intimate spheres, orienting their expectations and demands. Rights struggles are a form of public demand in which the rules of gender and sexuality are prominent and easily traceable. It is one of the reasons that traditional rights and lobby politics make such suitable material for tracing the conditions and the nature of the political (sexual) subject endowed with human rights in European democracies.

Discourses compete with each other for the authority to establish dominant meanings or dominant forms of subjectivity, and, consequently, to present themselves as truthful, proven knowledge. Power imbalances in dichotomies such as male/female, white/black, heterosexual/homosexual are symptoms of a continuing struggle for dominance. They rest on establishing oppositions and exclusions. However, the existence of dominant discourses always include the existence of non-dominant discourses that constantly challenge and contest what is dominant knowledge. Therefore, there are always different meanings or subject positions available at any given time. The institutionalisation of heterosexuality as the only sexuality must, thus, logically always already fail, as it needs to create its own exclusions to maintain itself.[6] Politically speaking, however, the failure of logical coherence does not defuse patterns and relations of power that hold political regimes together. Even though gays, lesbians, bisexuals, and transgender people are excluded from centres of cultural production, they are not free to invent their own meanings independent from existing social relations (Walkowitz et al. 1989:30). They are, moreover, constantly participating in the active construction of dominant and contested meanings.

Hence, the examination of competing political discourses and of particular individuals' and groups' participation in the creation, affirmation, or contestation of actual social and material relations on the official political stage, is an investigation into the very conditions of the social and the political *per se*. According to a queer approach, it is the task of political activism potentially to utilise such theoretical examination to make the incoherence of the dominant order speakable, known and eventually intolerable, so that change can begin. Queer theory always has an intrinsic political aspect to itself. According to Mark Blasius (1998:668), queer theory is 'an active engagement through thought with the vicissitudes of lived experience – theory, to paraphrase Nietzsche, is an expression of a will to power – rather than solely commentary on text'.

There is no high queer theory whose conditions remain stable while politics are analysed through it. Rather, the combination of the terms 'queer' and 'theory' in academia since the early 1990s, expresses a clear will to academic power, renders central what is deemed marginal and questions the stability of knowledge productions that are contained in the normative binary gender order. This explains again why queer theory is a project of de-stabilisation, of questioning and of unmasking the regimes of the normal rather than the heterosexual without claiming to stand objectively outside. That project includes normal business in what counts as academic theory (Warner 1992:18).

Thus, queer theory cannot remain aloof from that which it observes. The sovereign epistemic agent, i.e. the theorist, cannot assume an autonomous position as a master of the social, cultural, economic, or political relations theoretically analysed. Although queer theory has an ambiguous relationship to gay and lesbian activism at the best of times, it roots itself firmly in a political vision of change and challenge to the status quo. Queer theory produces knowledge that is central to living. Lauren Berlant and Michael Warner (1995:348) answered the 'sixty-four thousand dollar' question about what queer theory teaches us with respect to political change in exactly that vein: 'Sometimes the question of what queer theory teaches us about *x* is not about politics in the usual sense but about personal survival. Like feminist, African-American, Latina/Latino, and other minority projects, queer work strikes its readers as knowledge central to living.' Queer theory cannot be thought without a connection to the world outside of theory – theory and the political form an inseparable bond, although it is precisely that bond which is questioned the most by critics of queer theory.[7]

This bond requests the acknowledgement that queer theory has arisen at a specific time in a specific cultural and political location of the United States of America.[8] To target queer theories' critiques precisely and fairly in a European transnational context, the specific locations of European gay and lesbian politics are to be taken into consideration. The most important difference is the dominance of the human rights discourse in European political discourse. Chapter 4 is entirely dedicated to an analysis of human rights discourse. Yet, beyond paying attention to the specificity of human rights argumentation, queer theory needs to calibrate itself slightly in the encounter with a few other cultural and historical conditions of gay and lesbian politics, for example, the connection to leftist political culture, the lack of a dominant Christian Right, the different AIDS history, and the transnational character of national difference in Europe. None of these differences is as central as the dominance of the human rights discourse. Yet, to complicate the way in which queer theoretical critique is formulated in the European context, these differences need to be acknowledged.

European movements for equality and social justice, whether they are about women or sexual minorities, have a strong history of alliances and loyalties with leftist ideologies (Hekma *et al.* 1995:31). The fact that most European countries have a parliamentary system of proportional representation, which includes left-wing political representation, provides a different political culture compared with the US. This includes, for example, the reduced impact of the anti-communism hysteria the US experienced after World War II. Being left and socialist did not and does not imply a total marginalisation of oneself in political and economic life. It is potentially part of the legitimate political landscape and the diversity of left-wing cultures provided a differentiated home for differentiated forms of lesbian, gay, bisexual, and transgender politics. The alliances with left-wing movements and the non-existence of a black civil rights movement account for a different history in modelling lesbian and gay liberation: different in the sense that there is a lesser need to unify one movement with one form of strategy. The different degrees of assimilation or of identity politics can find advocates within a part of the mainstream political landscape. The connection between the Left and issues of gender and sexuality is not unproblematic, but it is a decisive factor that shapes European gay and lesbian political culture.[9]

Additionally, the polarisation of gay and lesbian movements into an assimilationist wing and a more radical left-wing – each trying to focus on fighting the Christian Right's backlash in different ways (Epstein 1999:64–76) – has not occurred in Europe to the same extent as in the US.[10] The absence of the Christian Right backlash makes for a very important difference in the discourse of survival, threat, and rights in Western Europe in general. The late 1990s and the early 2000s sparked a few significant political debates about gay and lesbian partnership rights and in some countries – for example in Germany and in France – conservatives and Catholics staged major homophobic campaigns. Yet, sexuality does not carry the same general political significance as in the US – sex and sexuality lack the central significance in everyday politics that the Monica Lewinsky affair brought to the forefront so vividly. Even if gay and lesbian partnership rights spark homophobic campaigns, these campaigns are nothing compared with the open xenophobia displayed by politicians standing anywhere right from the very left. Multiculturalism and access to European citizenship is likely to be the most central rally cry of everyday political debate throughout Western Europe.[11] Whereas queer critiques reflect the polarisation into two radically different responses to the political needs in countering the Christian Right backlash, the absence of the Christian Right backlash in Western Europe can potentially deprive the queer critiques of some of their legibility.

Some of queer theory's lack of legibility in the European context is also because of the difference in the history of the AIDS crisis. Queer theory and politics are strongly rooted in the specific US American setting of the AIDS crisis (Genschel 1997:88–90). Questions of the connection between race, homophobia, and public health care suddenly became an issue that concerned white gay men. The deep-rooted critique of normative structures that underlie different forms of exclusion and marginalisation was a new and much-needed insight that the AIDS crisis provoked. The social and historical implications of the AIDS epidemic were, however, slightly different in Europe. Neither is the anti-gay backlash in relation to AIDS entirely comparable – since it was never as harsh as the anti-gay response of the US government – nor were the consequences of the AIDS experience in European welfare and interventionist systems the same (Annets and Thompson 1992:228–31). The existence of public health care systems all over Europe, for example, made a significant difference to the way the shock of AIDS was experienced. Discussion of health care, sexual politics, and welfare ideologies were not new to gay and lesbian activists in Europe, but were a fairly well rehearsed ground in most Western European countries. The sense of newness that queer carried in the US, in its move to politicise an epidemic, is not shared in the same way by gay men and lesbians in Europe.[12]

Minoritising approaches have been valuable in legitimising homosexuality and in gaining some rights of recognition not only in the US (Nicholson and Seidman 1995:17), but also in the European context (Adam, Duyvendak and Krouwel 1999:7). They served as symbolic resources for the successful efforts in community building all over the world in the 1970s, 1980s, and 1990s. (1999:1–2) Yet, while for the US context the quasi-ethnic or cultural minority became pivotal (Epstein 1999:32), the discourses deployed for rights in each European national context added their own historical trajectory for the mobilisation of l/g/b/t movements. Thus, when approaching Europe as a cultural and political context, one has to talk about the intricate connections of discourses of national difference and of transnational solidarity or identity.

A few interesting examples of particularities can be named. Firstly, France. forced activists to speak a language of egalitarianism rather than minority, since strong discourses of nationality – and the importance of being French first – hinder the articulation of gay identity as a distinct minority.[13] Secondly, some national European movements have never depended much on identity. This is particularly the case within lesbian activism, for lesbian activism across Europe has a strong and long history of questioning clear identifications to a much higher degree than gay male activism has (Llamas and Vila 1999). Thirdly, northern European countries in particular experienced an early separation of commercial subculture and the political movement (Duyvendak 1996:433). There is, therefore, more of a split between what seems to be apolitical culture and formalised movement (Adam, Duyvendak, and Krouwel 1999:9). Fourthly, in the Southern European context, as well as in the Eastern European context, desire and non-politicised identities overall dominate the subcultures – as far as they can find public space to exist – and resemble aspects of 'Western communities' (1999:9). However, looking more closely at the specific post-Communist setting, one can see significant diversity again. In Romania the argument of minority and ethnicity is the only available and politically successful discourse on gay and lesbian identity (Long 1999:245–6). The Czech Republic employs citizenship and reference to the parliamentary structure of the state as its discourse (1999:249–50). Hungary displays a strange combination of granting legal rights to a weak movement that is denied official recognition (1999:253), whereas in Poland, rights discourses connect to a long national history of tolerance and democracy.[14]

It is a truism to state that gay and lesbian political practices in Europe depend on the cultural and regional differences in such things as the meaning of sexuality, sex-gender systems, the development of civil society, and organised religion. What is of interest for the pan-European context, however, are the ways in which 'transnational diffusion is an important facilitating condition' (Adam, Duyvendak, and Krouwel 1999:24) for the development of a sense of identifiable European gay and lesbian politics, which ILGA-Europe purports to exist in its European rhetoric. Queer theory's attention to cultural specificity and the precise workings of structural marginalisation makes it a powerful tool for analysis as long as it indeed becomes more legible for European activists and their particular movement histories. Yet, since queer theory demands that its practitioners position themselves clearly with respect to their object of investigation – a stance queer theory adopted from feminist methodology – there is nothing that prevents changes of focus. There is no one and only valid form of queer theory.

Queer theory demands from its practitioners a self-understanding that is constituted at the intersection of an intersubjective understanding of the hegemony of social reality and an intersubjective understanding of oneself (Bal 1991:31). Yet, the obvious partiality of all participants involved – from the analyst to the analysed to the reader of the analysis and the representatives of political institutions and courts – is a crucial insight that can be gained from queer analysis *and* from political practices for rights. What queer theory brings into the focus of critique is what a careful interpretation of political practices could well reveal by itself. Queer theory's insights are to some extent only the result of problems that arose within the realm of the political before anybody coined the term 'queer'. Queer theory's political ambitions, and its connections between theory and its subject of analysis, make it a critical theory, according to four characteristics Mieke Bal (1991:35) identified.

Firstly, in queer theory – as in critical theory – the subject is seriously studied, situated, and made explicit. Secondly, all action – whether that is theoretical analysis or activism – is clearly oriented by interests and this interest is neither denied nor hidden behind seeming impartiality and academic objectivity. Thirdly, queer theory is normative. Not as a set of normative propositions and a normative corpus of analysis, but 'by describing its corpus by means of definitional concepts' and allowing, thus, 'for a normative analysis of the corpus' (Bal 1991:35). Queer theory derives its norms explicitly from systematic reflection of an epistemological order and describes its corpus of analysis through definitional concepts such as heteronormativity. It renders itself plausible and transmissible as a critical tool through precise interdisciplinary methodologies (Bal 1991:27) and becomes, fourthly, at different stages comparative, so as to allow disciplinary and political challenge. As a critical theory, queer theory has – just as its sisters feminism and postcolonial theory – a clear commitment to politics and change, an anti-hegemonic and anti-oppression stance (Weston 1998:145). Yet, despite professing to have the political at its core, queer theory more often than not fails to define exactly what politics or the political mean.

Political practices

Politics and the political are an aporia (Hark 1996:144). We discuss politics, speak about political movements, of political rights or minority politics without demarcating the political differences the term 'politics' or the political entails. Contemporary Western nomenclature commonly derives 'politics from the Greek '*polis*' and '*politeia*', emphasising the human capacity to constitute a particular mode of communal life through generating boundaries, rules, morality, habits, institutions, and law. It emphasises the human capacity actively to produce an order, a world of meaning that results in institutions, social control, and processes of change. The term 'politics' also acknowledges the existence of power, the necessity to maintain it and disperse it, circulate it, and assess its effects. It, thus, clearly draws on human agency.

Departing from this conception, two aspects have to be added to the concept of the political when considering a poststructuralist mode of thinking: politics are also a) discursive and b) a performative way of producing meaning. The former is clearer than the latter in this respect. A discursive understanding of politics emphasises its dependency on language as the site at which politics, as practice, are possible in the first place, created, challenged and subsequently enacted. All meaning attached to politics or to the political is necessarily discursive. This means that discourses are constructive of reality, of the social, political, economic, and legal order we live in. This view does not deny any extra-discursive material reality. Rather, it suggests that the meanings we attribute to that which we perceive to be real are discursively constructing that reality – given that we cannot interpret reality outside of meaning-constructing discursive frameworks.

With respect to the realm of the political, the performative – a term introduced in the philosophy of language by J. L. Austin but strongly associated with Judith Butler's philosophy of gender – is to be distinguished from representation, which presents another aspect of the political.[15] To represent homosexuals as an identity group or as people with a common life-style choice – which has political consequences and is, thus, worthy of the formation of a political movement – is often understood to be at the centre of lesbian and gay politics. Representational claims are deeply problematic in that they pretend to mirror adequately a reality that is true for all members of the group, as if they are speaking for someone. Representation is a part of the political practices I analyse in this book and it has been critiqued substantially before. However, it is the aspect of performative meaning production in political practices that is the site of interest for the analytical definition of 'political practices' here.

Political practices aim to take part in the definition of legal, social, and economic relations. They do so by producing meaning about a certain situation they wish to change or maintain or find solutions for. Political practices are an interpretative act. They claim to know what the problem is, what causes it, and how it can be mended. Thus, they need to be culturally and politically intelligible, the meaning they produce needs to be understandable. The requirement of intelligibility in this sense does not mean that no new meaning can be produced. It does imply that any new meaning needs to be fitted to the political institution and the political discourse in which it is presented.

Judith Butler defines performativity as citationality (1993:12–16). Something is cited and re-cited as stemming from the seemingly natural origin, which in fact never existed, but is an invention of the process of citation.[16] Political practices need to participate in citing or reiterating the norms or the sets of norms that define the political realm and legal or moral orders from which that realm gains its existential authority. These regulatory orders are not timeless structures, but historical and revisable forms of intelligibility. Speaking about a group in that sense is not to be understood as a theatrical performance, but as a derivative action, an action that cites the conditions of authority to speak about that group.[17] Within the concept of the performative, politics is understood as reiterative and citational practices that are strictly connected to power and not in any external relation to the oppositions of power in our societies. Strategies of power and who gets what, when, and how are, thus, still central to this concept of politics.

Such a concept of politics could surely contain manifold political practices. Queer theory would suggest political practices, for example, at the level of styles, of visible disruptions of normality, of civil disobedience, or of utterances that perform the marginal, such as displaying unclear gender appearances. Why, then, analyse a purely traditional form of political lobby practice? Why analyse court judgments, EU Directives, or parliamentary resolutions which often only re-establish heteronormative foundations of social, political, legal, and economic structures?

Additionally to what I have said in the introduction, the answer to this question relates to desire as a political category: the desire for rights and the never-ending fascination terms such as 'equality' carry even for those consciously identified as queer. Accepting legal equality as true equality will not do; but ignoring the desire for legal equality will not do either.

Certain forms of political practice set themselves up for dominance and, in the popular conception of politics, are accepted uncritically as politics *per se*. Their narration is the canon of politics and meaning about the political is always in one way or another mirrored against that canon. Radical queer politics, for example, often publicise itself as explicit non-participation in the traditional political canon and, thereby, once more cites it as dominant. Government lobby politics forms the main focus of the queer critiques, which, in turn, renders it central within the queer vein of thought yet again. For reasons of hegemonic power, government politics, lobbying, law reforms, and anti-discrimination legislation remain the focal point for the formation of most organisations that root themselves in a movement. Critical as that might be, it still is worth analysing since the conditions of these gay and lesbian politics need to be exposed in order ultimately to make critical political practice a powerful tool of changing hegemonic orders. Maintaining sight of the centrality of power relations in politics is made possible, I would argue, by a deployment of the concept of meaning for the definition of political practices.

If political practices are performative ways to produce meaning, then meaning as a concept gains centrality for the political. The biology of meaning, to borrow Jerome Bruner's (1990:69) term, is a foundational aspect of the political. Bruner derives the human capacity to communal life from the capacity to produce meaning and the capacity of the child to learn the language of meaning production.[18] Meaning production is a narrative process and it needs human action, a sequential order, reference to the canonical, and something like a narrator (1990:77). This narrative process is strongly demarcated by the tool kits of culture that equip us with the traditions of telling and interpreting. Logos, narrative, and cultural practice are inseparable (1990:80–1). In short, 'a right story is one that connects your version through mitigation with the canonical version' (1990:86). Children learn that the degree to which a story is convincing is the degree to which they master the canonical and they learn how to deceive in order to make their stories fit.[19] The clue of Bruner's biology of meaning is that our sense of the canonical or the normative is nourished in narrative, but the same accounts for the breach and the exception. This means that deviance, the non-fitting aspect of a story is the central moment that – according to Bruner – sparks narrative. It is the only thing that actually produces new meaning in its attempt to become the new canonical. And it is ultimately the capacity to see and recognise the non-canonical that makes us 'fit for culture' (1990:97).

Transporting Bruner's fitness for culture into a fitness for politics would imply that l/g/b/t lobby practices contain on the one hand an advantageous point of departure in that they are to some extent necessarily deviant. The protection of homosexual rights as human rights, for example, clashes with some of the fundamental discourses on humanness that define human sexuality as heterosexual normality. On the other hand, l/g/b/t lobby practices need to master the politically dominant discourse so that they remain intelligible within the political institution that grants rights, such as courts or parliaments. The point of deviance is, thus, purposely masked in a narration that fits the right story of, for example, human rights. In consequence, any political practice contains reiteration and rupture of norms at the same time.

The production of meaning in political practices is, therefore, not simple. It is more than an author's or a group of authors' intentional argument for challenge and change. The political text – written document and oral testimony – produces meaning on several plural levels. In relation to the critique of identity and politics of representation central to queer theory, this insight has significant consequences. While, for example, the political act does not necessarily need to claim a pre-existing identity or – to say it with Nietzsche – while acknowledging that the deed creates the doer, the claim to an authority to speak more often than not seems to need an identity upon which it rests. ILGA-Europe, in this case, can never – and I doubt it would even want to – represent *the* European movement. But a movement is claimed to exist in lobby politics insofar as individual people build their political practices upon a performance of identity that creates the fantasy of commonality and subsequent solidarity with many others. A fantasy that is by no means unreal, but that can never fulfil its own promise of sufficiently describing the lived experiences of many. The complexity and contradictions with regard to identity as a political tool evident in lobby documents and personal accounts are, however, not simply naive or essentialist.

On the one hand, there are always dangerous aspects to political representation. Mainly, the claim to speak on behalf of a group, which is assumed to be homogenous for the purpose of legal recognition, is normatising. It implies that there is a political progress from which all could benefit. This is illusionary given the huge diversity of life-styles and intricate connections between many exclusionary identification factors, such as gender (identity), class, age, or race among ILGA-Europe's constituency. In order to be representable, a group has to be homogenised as an abstract totality that wants rights and fits the conditions of those rights. Any political practice that speaks of a group is, by definition, reductive of diversity and potentially normative.

On the other hand, the outcome of identity politics is not a given. Unexamined assumptions about what activists actually believe can prove to be an academic fallacy. The arguments used in documents and oral statements towards rights-granting institutions are clearly a deployment of tactics, a political strategy. They do not present the complex nature of sexual identities that, for example, all my interviewed activists were aware of and upon which they create a sense of community among each other. In the practices of politics, the term 'identity' is, in general, specific to describing a group, however phantasmatic those commonalities might be. Identity is in that respect more often linked to minority and group commonalties than to subjectivity or psychic constitution, even though that is rarely clarified and often formulated ambiguously. As a political strategy, certain deployments of identity could address the need for structural social change beyond rights for a homogenised minority. What is significant in that is the relationship any concept of identity has to the political discourse in which it is employed. In the human rights discourse, for example, there remains a need to deploy an identity that can be ascribed rights by virtue of that identity being considered human and therefore having an intrinsic value worthy of protection (Offord 1999a:281). Through understanding politics as a citational and performative production of meaning, contradictory aspects of single political actions or texts can be conceptualised. Such understanding positions strategies of power and the crucial reality of who gets what, when, and how as an intrinsic aspect of the meanings that political practices are capable of producing.

This understanding of meaning is also the reason why I prefer to speak of 'political practices' in this book rather than simply politics. I wish to emphasise the political realm as a space in which discursivity and the performative production of meaning play a role. Handling terminology in this way will help to escape a total negation of representational politics as adequate, fair, or just to the reality of lived sexual and gender life-styles which the queer critiques seem ultimately to suggest. Understood as practices, politics permanently exposes its contingency and, thus, makes space for the existence of realities that do not fit neatly into identity categories prescribed by the regime of the heteronormative gender binary. Or as Sabine Hark (Hark 1996:146) formulates: "'A politics of politics"… would be a politics conscious of its own contingency and not making it disappear, and would in its creation of reality leave room for other creations of reality' (translation mine).

Political practices can be consciously contingent when they are also understood as a set of argumentative practices. The tool and strategy of producing meaning is an argument. Every political practice contains an argument for or against something and, in general, every political practice is oriented towards achieving something. Part of what is involved in analysing what activists mean by what they say or write is not just a review of the expressed content but a recognition of what implicit discourses they are drawing on in order to say something by means of argumentation structure. Lobby documents, court judgments, or parliamentary texts are based on the assumption that political and legal processes are democratic and adhere to an ideal of communication in which all participants are seen as rational agents who are sincerely interested in resolving an argument and in accepting mediation. Political argumentation is in its ideal built on seeking resolution, not mere acquiescence or settlement. The political text is employed to create a social problem-solving process via argumentation; it becomes the means by which controlled change is democratically institutionalised. A discourse of ideal political process is, thus, one of the discourses ILGA-Europe's political practices implicitly draw upon. Many others will be traced in the course of this book.

Frans van Eemeren, Rob Grootendorst, Sally Jackson, and Scott Jacobs (1993) developed a theory of argumentation suitable for explaining the ideal political process to which rights politics in Europe implicitly adhere. Van Eemeren *et al.* (1993:14) firmly maintain that the structure of argumentation, the requirements of justification, and the need for argumentation itself are all adapted to the contexts in which opposition, objections, doubts, and counterclaims arise. Argumentation is, thus, functionalised. Yet, it is also externalised – distinguishing reasoning and argumentation – socialised – as an interactive not an individual process – and dialectified – the conditions under which rational judgement can take place are taken into account (1993:11–15). A speech act of argumentation pursues a communicative aspect aimed at achieving an interactional effect of accepting (1993:55). The commitment to being legible within the traditions of certain political institutions can, thus, be assumed to be a strategy aimed at achieving the acceptance of a claim, or of a legal right.

Within an ideal model of political process, the acceptance or rejection of a claim to rights should be determined by what objective grounds there are for belief or disbelief in it (1993:114). Activists conduct argumentation with attention to the practical consequences of their speech, orienting themselves towards a resolution of the dispute they initiated. Yet, they make an orientation to resolution of dispute subordinate to the reporting of their reality, in this case a reality of discrimination. Although compromise occurs regularly in the negotiation of, for example, new legal rights, the argumentative structure of the political argument is geared at reporting a seeming totality of reality and wanting a seeming totality of rights. There are definite limits to compromising the original aim of gaining what was defined as full rights. This original aim is argumentatively set up as objective grounds, but in practicality as standing against the objective grounds of the other party to the dispute. Although the ideal of political process pretends there is one objectivity only, political practice clearly affirms many objectivities. The ideal political process and the practicalities of politics are connected in argumentation, but they are nevertheless contradictory in nature.

Following this elaboration, a tentative attempt at defining politics could look like this: political relations are one of the existing discursive and material orders through which people are constituted as subjects of a state and a society and through which they, in turn, are engaged in the re-constitution of several discursive orders, such as, for example, gender, kinship, or citizenship. This engagement takes the form of political practices. These practices reflect the power existing in the relevant discursive order and they are active producers of meaning. As such, they need to remain politically intelligible and are taken from an already existing array of practices commonly used within the relevant political system. As subjects in politics, we are subjugated to the requirement of ordering social relations. Social relations are understood as the wider relations of a community comprising individuals, but also classifications of individuals as groups. The requirement to order social relations needs to be understood as a discursive tradition upon which Western–Christian knowledge production rests. Engaging in politics is, then, a discursive – and therefore not an autonomous and independent – act of understanding how we became the political subjects we think we are. It is not a chain of necessity relentlessly linking the past with the present, but an active participation in competing sets of narratives that are already or are being rendered open to contestation by that very political act. Therefore, the potential of human agency – although understood to be discursive – remains an essential part of the access to politics as clear will to change and to regulate, distribute, and participate in power. Analysing political practices in Europe is, then, a task that draws out the contingencies of political practices and their constitutive aspect in relation to the political subject.

Conclusion

From the perspective of queer theory, sexual politics as political practices are, thus, intrinsically connected to challenge and change. Not in the radical sense of a revolution that will in the future create a material reality congruent with the experiences of a group, but in the sense of rendering perceived experience politically audible. The experiences upon which political acts are apparently grounded are actually the ones made available by the political act. The political practices that individuals perform are constitutive of the experiences said to pre-exist the politics; constitutive of the very identity upon which individuals or groups rest their status as political subjects. Through being constitutive of the political subject, political acts certainly also constitute something: they open up forms of discursive agency that entail the claim to an authority to speak on behalf of a group or an issue. The meaning-creating character of politics is the means through which challenge and change can become an aim of politics and through which material realities, such as actual change, can be obtained. The combination of queer theory and political practices does not designate a deterministic fate of failure for political and social change.

However, in order to achieve its aim, a political practice must adhere to an intersubjectively or institutionally acceptable discussion procedure. That procedure must be negotiated against a substantive background that is taken for granted (Van Eemeren *et al.* 1993:171). Argumentation in political practices, therefore, is to be analysed not only in terms of its success in gaining assent for a right, but also in terms of the background of the procedures by which the assent is gained. The background may be evaluated by participants in political processes in 'ways that are tied to the practices of a particular social group sharing certain values and background assumptions, and that what merits assent is itself subject to argumentative scrutiny' (1993:22). Part of the task of a queer theoretical reading of political practices is to select and codify that pre-existing system of relevancy.

Yet, analytic reading itself always takes place in terms of a theoretical framework that concentrates on certain aspects of the discourse to the exclusion of other aspects. It reconstructs an argument actively and highlights various features of a political process to the exclusion of other features (1993:38). Reading reflects the particular interests of the analyst as much as it reflects the argumentation and its implicit adherence to ordering discourses. Taking this condition seriously, a queer analytic reconstruction strives towards remaining justifiable methodically, empirically, culturally, politically, and theoretically. Not in any objective and truthful sense of justifiability, but in making the frames it places around political and social conditions explicit, contingent, and changeable. The applicability of queer theory to the analysis of political practices is not sought in the translation of theory into a bundle of instructions and prohibitions. It presents a form of critiquing the rules and procedures to which political practices in Europe are forced to adhere, it points out the fallacies implied in this obligation, and it highlights opportunities for disrupting seemingly fixed orders.

Notes

1 ACT-UP is an activist group founded in the US, campaigning for radical AIDS politics. It has become famous for explicitly addressing sexuality and race in relation to AIDS. ACT-UP has sister groups in different European countries. Queer Nation was a split-off group that formed itself, in the US only, in response to the marginalisation of gay men in ACT-UP.
2 See, for example, Blasius (1998:669), Butler (1993:229), Hennessy (1995:34), Jagose (1996:131–2), Nicholson and Seidman (1995:18), Seidman (1993:130–2 and 1996:9), or Warner (1993:xxvi).
3 Wherever that is not possible – such as in the case of intersexuals – clear gender assignment is forced into existence through mutilating operations and compulsory hormone treatment in all European countries.
4 Although – if one looks at this claim a bit more closely – slogans such as 'we are here, we are queer and we designed everything you are wearing' is probably less a belief than a hope for centrality.
5 Heteronormativity is discussed at length in Chapter 8.
6 This line of thought is one of the fundamental arguments Judith Butler made in *Gender Trouble* (1990).
7 There exists an extensive body of literature on the critique of queer theory. The oppositions between queer theory and its critiques are discussed in Chapter 3.
8 John D'Emillio (1983) argues that US gay politics were overwhelmingly oriented to civil rights with the aim of social assimilation. The predominance of this political strategy is summarised aptly by Epstein (1999:32), when he points to the development of 'a clearly demarcated social group with a fixed ethniclike [sic] identity' in the formation durable organisations that promote a liberal agenda. Epstein mentions three debates that were initiated in the US to counter such an approach to gay and lesbian politics: debates of identity and difference, debates of desire, and public/private debates (Epstein 1999:32–3). Queer critiques, according to Epstein (1999:64), participate in these debates 'as a reminder that, for many, the goal of the politics of sexuality was not assimilation but confrontation' and that the mainstream movement is 'incapable of aggregating the diverse interests of all those on behalf of whom it purported to speak'.
9 For an analysis of the problems of that connection in the European context, see Hekma *et al.* (1995). For the US American context, see Rosemary Hennessy (1994).
10 This statement is generalised. In Britain, for example, OutRage as a more radical, queer organisation was founded partly to counter Stonewall's assimilationist tendencies. Particularly in Germany, lesbian groups explicitly counter politics of inclusion that are said to be perpetuated by the Lesben und Schwulenverband Deutschland (LSVD). For

reasons of this opposition, very few lesbians responded, in early 1999, to the call for broadening the SVD into LSVD as a joint national organisation.

11 The generalisation of this statement cannot so easily be conferred onto the Eastern and south-eastern European context in which religiously marked national identities are re-erected. In some places, such as Romania and Poland, sexuality plays a more open role in political discourse. The economic poverty and zest of these countries to enter the EU often makes Eastern European people themselves the target of the ethnic exclusion countries such as Germany promote so heavily.

12 This is admittedly a generalisation again that only explains certain responses to queer, but does not do justice to the significant difference in the national settings with regard to the AIDS crisis. Different European countries produced very different levels of politicisation with regard to AIDS. French and Spanish movements, for example, had to encounter more homophobia than the Netherlands and, therefore, politicised their responses in a stronger way. See, for an elaboration on this comparison Duyvendak (1996). Spain and France had chapters of ACT-UP strongly modelled on the radical politics of ACT-UP in the US. See, for further analysis, in the case of Spain Ricardo Llamas and Fefa Vila (1999) and in the case of France Olivier Fillieule and Jan Willem Duyvendak (1999). The Dutch government supported AIDS prevention by the gay community financially from the beginning and, thus, produced a climate of national consent that is unmatched in the world. See Schuyf and Krouwel (1999) as well as Duyvendak (1996) for further elaboration.

13 This condition accounts for a specifically strong connection between French nationalism, xenophobia, and homophobia. See Fillieule and Duyvendak (1999:189-90) as well as Seidman (1995) for further elaboration.

14 Long (1999:253) qualifies his description of the Hungarian situation by explaining that rights of common law partnership rained on the gay and lesbian movement from above, while gay and lesbian organisations were long denied official registration or acknowledgement.

15 Butler uses the word 'performative' to describe how the body provides a surface upon which various acts and gestures accrue gendered meanings. What she, thus, calls corporeal signification reveals that gender does not appeal to an ontological essence granted by nature. Rather, the belief in the naturalness is an illusion that depends on performative acts (Butler 1990:136).

16 Butler's context here is gender and the naturalness of bodies as gendered bodies.

17 This approach would include the consequences of Roland Barthes' (1986) notion of the death of the author. The political activist is not the fully intentional producer of a political practice or a text, but the practice or the text has a life of its own and the process of reading a political action is more important than the intentions of the authors.

18 He (1990:75) illustrates this via the language development of infants and young children, a learning process that eventually enables them to master and manage meaning production.

19 There is an amusing implication hidden in Bruner's argument here, which is the idea that the canonical arises out of learning how to lie. For Eco (1976:10), in fact, this capacity to lie defines signs.

3 Mind the gap: hybrid relations of queer theory and political practice

> The homosexual and the postmodernist have been sleeping together a lot lately. And yet, as with much intercourse, the experience has been less than fully pleasurable.
>
> (Gregory Bredbeck 1993:254)

Critiquing the rules and procedures to which political practices in Europe are forced to adhere is no task that has nothing to lose. Queer theory has not been welcomed by all feminist and lesbian or gay theorists nor by all l/g/b/t activists. Its criticism, on the contrary, is often understood as an attack on the achievements of activists and researchers; an attack on what they hold to be essentially necessary and real in their personal lives and their political or academic work. Many see a gaping abyss between theoretical queer concerns and the real-life practice of achieving political change. Queer theory is portrayed mainly as an abstracted way of fetishising discourse, as despising empirical research, as confusing the social and the individual as well as language and lived identity, and as substituting the verbal for the political.[1] With the birth of queer theory, another of the well-known theory–practice gaps, debated before in feminism and anti-racist work, was born. The serious dispute over queer theory's merits and dangers takes over a large part of the academic literature on queer theory and its political applicability. Lisa Duggan (1992:19) once pointedly summarised this debate:

> In its most clichéd formulations, this controversy is presented in one of two ways: Valiant and dedicated activists working to get civil rights for gay and lesbian people are being undermined by a bunch of obscure, arcane, jargon-ridden academics bent on 'deconstructing' the gay community before it even comes into full visibility, or: Theoretically informed writers at the cutting edge of the political horizon are being bashed by anti-intellectual activists who cling – naively – to the discursive categories of their oppressors.

The theory–practice gap Duggan describes in its clichéd formulations has in parts surely become a kind of annoying re-iteration and continuing with its oppositional stances is not of interest in this book. However, the implications of this gap have – willingly and unwillingly – become a dominant conflict in my own work, which is characterised by contradictory and conflictual manoeuvres. Manoeuvres within and between traditional rights politics for sexual minorities at a transnational level and the fundamental challenges queer theory – to which I subscribe as an academic – fires at precisely those politics. The theory–practice gap cannot be ignored, neither from the academic nor from the activist side. Thus, I want to pay attention to 'mind the gap' in two stages.

First, three personal stories will be used as anecdotal indications for the necessity to re-theorise the apparent contradictions of queer theory and gay and lesbian political practice. The influences of queer theory and its blurring of gender and sexual boundaries are visible almost exclusively at the level of style rather than politics. Many queer theorists remain substantially wary of any politics of recognition that assume the modern constitutional state – or, in the case of the EU, a state-like institution – and its legal system as the privileged site of political action. It is at this point that the apparent rift between 'practical politics for rights' and 'academic critique' is continuously shaped. Second, I will suggest a deployment of the concept of hybridity as an analytical tool to straddle this gap. Three elements of hybridity are particularly helpful in this respect: antagonistic relations, dialogism, and desire. I ascribe a particular importance to desire as the decisive term that designates both sexual identities and the claim to rights.

Queer theories' political (im)potency

The following three stories are accounts of a personal 'changing of hats'. They exemplify what keeps drawing me and many others back to thinking about the gap between theory and politics. The stories do not serve as conclusive data, but merely illustrate how telling stories as a theorist while simultaneously theorising as an activist has to become a permanent process of dialogisation. A dialogisation that remains – in Bakhtin's words – an intentional hybrid, a contestatory, conflictual political, and ontological setting.

Story I

On an exceptionally warm and sunny Saturday in February 1998, I sat on the wrong side of the window in a meeting room of the lesbian and gay community in Brussels, attending a board meeting of ILGA-Europe. There was excitement in the room: we received 35,000 Euro from the European Commission to write a report on the situation of lesbians and gay men in the fifteen Member States of the EU.[2] The political aim was to liaise with other social NGOs to mainstream the broad spectrum of lesbian and gay issues, as a matter of equal participation in civil society and in EU policy. The task of drafting the main chapter outlining the arguments fell to me as the young academic in the room. This task lasted several months and turned out to be complicated: there was a clear agreed political goal of arguing the lack of full civic participation beyond simple rights of status. Yet, there was not much time for fundamental critiques and questions about the sense and consequence of a strongly identity-based political argument that remained central. In the course of time, the board also had an argument about the mentioning of transsexual and transgender people, which I had included in the draft along with the explicit goal of helping to create a truly multicultural and ethnically diverse Europe. The latter remained; the former was deleted. Overall, the result seemed somewhat tenable to me but flaunted many of the fundamental problems at the heart of my theoretical concerns.

Story II

Early October 1998. Berlin hosts the first academic conference on queer theory and politics. The conference is held just a week after the Green Party entered into a new coalition government for the first time and announced new citizenship rights – which have since then failed – and some form of partnership bill for homosexual couples – which became law in 2001. The conference featured many renowned American scholars. The organising team's main goal was to create space for long overdue debates. Debates on how gay and lesbian rights – and the movements to obtain those rights – have to be critically viewed for their involvement in re-inscribing and re-iterating a legal and cultural system that was invented to exclude homosexuality in the first place. In her lecture, Sabine Hark, a German queer theorist and member of the organising team, used the main chapter of the EU report to illustrate what is at stake in essentialising identities to form a group that can claim rights. She, thus, accused me, as one of the authors of the ILGA-Europe report, of doing precisely what I had set out not to do: of essentialising identity politics. Wearing the hat of a member of the conference's organising team, in addition to being another speaker and having put a year's worth of 'blood, sweat, and tears' into this project, I could not help but agree with her analysis.

Story III

While we were busy critiquing politics based solely on inclusion into heteronormative normality, we were, in turn, critiqued for our seeming oblivion to the real struggles in the real world. Four days before the conference, we invited Lisa Duggan to a public lecture organised for the press. On the second day of the conference we received full-page coverage in the largest German left-wing newspaper, the *TAZ*. This press coverage brought to the forefront the conflict of interests in gay and lesbian rights politics. It also brought to the forefront the enormous threat that queer theory in general – and a femme lesbian professor from New York in particular – apparently poses to what could now, with the new left-wing government, be achieved. The reporter of the *TAZ* (10–11 October 1998:ix) wrote:

> queer theory is losing its sight for the really important things: the difference between subtle discrimination – like a hateful glance – and repression – for example the threat of death penalty in Afghanistan ... questions of rights and the law, as the possibility to democratic influence are not of interest to queer theorists ... queer theory carries no relevancy in the political fight currently happening in Bonn around the new coalition treaty. (translation mine)

When I finally approached the sentence 'Many young women – is one still allowed to call them lesbians? – came dressed in garçon style, dedicating themselves with boyish eyes entirely to their groupie culture' (*TAZ*, 12 October 1998:22), I decided to end my readership of this paper. There was a clear conflict of interest being played out here. All of a sudden, a group of young lesbians in suits became deeply threatening to a renowned white, gay journalist in Berlin. How do these stories picture the dilemma at stake in queer theory's practical political (im)potency and how might the concept of hybridity be relevant in relation to the theory–practice gap illustrated through these stories?

These three experiences raise mixed feelings in me: I felt defeat at not being able to articulate my sense of what is important in gaining rights. I also felt defeat at not being able to write a political piece that reflects my critical queer concerns. And I felt anger at the sleight of hand and overt sexism with which our attempts at discussing queer theoretical implications for Europe were received in a newspaper that prides itself on being supportive of gay and lesbian rights. Clearly, the *TAZ* response highlights the fears of acknowledging the limits of gay and lesbian political agendas based on civil and human rights strategies. The conference was searching for a political direction and agenda that does not focus on the integration into dominant structures but instead seeks to transform the basic fabric and hierarchies that allow systems of oppression to persist and operate effectively. Yet, whatever is said, the queer theoretical critique continues to be received as standing in opposition or in contrast to the aims of the real political fight. Or worse, in opposition to the enormously brave people who dedicated their lives to fighting for fundamental human rights, such as some of my colleagues in ILGA-Europe.

Queer critiques have argued that civil rights do not change the social order in dramatic ways – they change only the privileges of the group asserting those rights. Hence, civil rights strategies do not challenge the moral and anti-sexual underpinning of homophobia, because homophobia does not exhaust itself in a lack of full civil equality. Rather, homophobia and heterosexism arise from the nature and construction of the political, legal, economic, sexual, racial and family systems within which we live (Urvashi Vaid 1995:183). 'Thus, a theoretical and political project which aims exclusively to normalise homosexuality and to legitimate homosexuality as social minority does not challenge a social regime which perpetuates the production of subjects and social worlds organised and regulated by the heterosexual/homosexual binary' (Seidman 1995:126). Many theorists also claim that gay and lesbian movements have been based on ethnic or essentialist politics in which clear categories of collective identities are necessary for successful resistance and political gain.[3]

From the vantage point of a queer or poststructuralist mode of thinking, identity-based rights campaigns are, thus, the creation of a phantasmatic political and social space, in which sexual object choice becomes the master category of self and self-identification. The question is whether or not the re-creation of such a master category inevitably and always engages in re-inscribing the fundamental conditions of exclusion. Whether identity-based rights campaigns are the ultimate victory of normatising regimes or can be strategically deployed at times to expose the instability of sexual difference can only be answered at the specific locations where those campaigns are staged.

The main chapter of the EU report – as a practical political piece – is an attempt at capturing the many differences among all those who might be called lesbian or gay and the many levels of exclusions they face on the grounds of their sexual and life-style choices. The report clearly undertakes to broaden the issues, create connections, and pull lesbians and gay men out of the specific interest group corner into the ranks of the majority of people in Europe who face social exclusion because of one or several aspects of their nature, role, or choices. Yet, in spite of all efforts to the contrary, gay men and lesbians as a somehow fixed category loom large over the argumentation. An example of the type of argumentation used is the following:

> In the context of this report, it is irrelevant whether homosexuality is 'caused' by biological factors, socialisation, or choice: the fact is that there is always a decisive number of people in every society who are sexually and socially attracted to members of their own sex. According to the advocate general of the Court of Justice of the European Communities, Michael B. Elmer, the estimated number in the EU is 35 million (Case C–249/96). Sexual orientation is one of the many human diversities that simply exist as a matter of fact. This impacts on how the vision of pluralistic and democratic European societies is argued, lobbied, and enforced; it impacts on all programmes that try to integrate difference, ensure human rights for all people, and attack social injustice … Gay men and lesbians have already reached some of their goals towards equality and social justice, but there remains much to be done. The focus should not, however, be solely on existing discrimination and difference of lesbians and gay men as a group by themselves, but on the ways in which different aspects of the social, economical, and political realm interrelate with issues of sexual orientation, and the importance of the inclusion of lesbian/gay issues in the civil and social dialogues and in the agendas of all NGOs. In this sense, ILGA-Europe sees gay men and lesbians not as a discreet, insular minority, different from the rest of society, but focuses on the many different social positions gay men and lesbians occupy while being part of all walks of society. This can be achieved through an identification of the specific ways gay men and lesbians relate to their social, political and economical environment and an acknowledgement of homosexuality as a factor that potentially hinders their equal participation in some aspects of society, and prevents them from obtaining full social and legal citizenship. (ILGA-Europe 1998:15)

The fragment contains important common political arguments. Queer theory maintains that identities are constructed precisely where politics are staged, whereas most rights organisations are built on the belief that they represent something that exists prior to their own formation. Diverse sexual orientation is portrayed as a fact of human nature in the excerpt quoted. No matter what discourses on biology or socialisation say, there remains a factual truth expressed in numbers. The final acknowledgement of that truth, according to the argument, necessarily leads to a change in the vision of democratic European societies. This argumentation is based on a claim to truth, but it is not necessarily based on the representation of an identity group. Sexual orientation can be many things beyond fixed identities. It includes an emphasis on sets of practices and it is not necessarily connected to homosexuality or heterosexuality as clearly distinguishable, opposite, and fixed. Yet, the terminology leaps from homosexuality and a clear number of a population group, to sexual orientation and from there to lesbians and gay men. Through this leap, sexual orientation, as human nature functions as the proof for the existence of a population group that is denied rights and whose rights can be described in their complex relations to gender, class, economic, racial, and social difference.

The argumentation contains a political representation of a complex issue in which many inequalities intersect. There is no explicit claim to represent an actual group in this quotation nor anywhere else in the introduction to the report. In fact, the text (1998:14) explicitly recognises that sexual identity does not amount to a coherent gay identity shared across Europe. Nevertheless, a clear group, albeit diverse, features as an entity describable through an identity category. That group is presumed to exist prior to the political movement's formation. The political argument claims to make visible and politically deployable what has apparently been there before: 'Sexual orientation is one of the many human diversities that simply exists as a matter of fact' is happily followed by 'Gay men and lesbians have already reached some of their goals towards equality and social justice'.[4] Despite all efforts to make the issue of social exclusion complex with regard to other forms of oppression, the language employed continues the fiction of the possibility to describe what all gay men and lesbians share – namely a fixed sexual orientation that is not the norm.

Admittedly my – and probably ILGA-Europe's – operative logic in walking the corridors of high power is an assumed homology between experience, interest, identity, and politics. In this logic, the homosexual act leads to an experience of exclusion, the act or at least the experience of exclusion forms an identity, which, in turn, creates a shared interest and a movement that acts on the different aspects of this shared interest. Politics is, then, one form of publicly expressing interest, an argumentative externalisation of a social problem-solving process.[5] Clearly, a movement is not one organisation or one particular interest group. According to Ron Eyerman and Andrew Jamison (1991:55), a movement is 'more like a cognitive territory, a new conceptual space that is filled by dynamic interaction between different groups and organizations'. They continue:

> And although movements usually involve the creation of organizations or the renovation of institutions, it is important not to mistake the one for the other. Organizations can be thought of as vehicles or instruments for carrying or transporting or even producing the movement's meaning. But the meaning, we hasten to add, should not be reduced to the medium. The meaning, or core identity, is rather the cognitive space that the movement creates, a space for new kinds of ideas and relationships to develop.[6]

ILGA-Europe is an organisation that carries, transports, and produces meaning about European gay and lesbian movements. At its core, the meaning ILGA-Europe produces refers to a homology between experience, interest, identity, and politics. While none of my interviewees claimed to be able to actually speak for – and therefore do not assume to represent – all lesbians and gay men in Europe, they do claim to represent issues of inequality and justice. They have a clear sense of the existence of a movement prior to their taking up these issues.[7] This operative logic finds expression in the formulations quoted above. Through these formulations, identity re-enters the stage via the back door. Not as a fixed and describable essence of gayness, but as a handrail along which sexual experience, discrimination, sexual and social community, and political interest become expressible. The contents of the gay and lesbian movement and homosexual identity are, thus, created at the very instance of argumentation practice in politics.

The leap in the EU report from sexual orientation to gay men and lesbians as a social group – which was the focus of the critique voiced by Sabine Hark (1998:14) – is not the only way identity re-enters in a critical way. The problem is also the way that leap takes part in manifesting other categories of oppression and exclusion as describable identity groups. The fact that lesbians and gay men as a group remain politically identifiable in the argumentation implies the existence of other clearly distinct groups, such as racial minorities or transsexuals. Although the aim was to find joint ground with other social NGOs and to connect the issues of discrimination applicable to the respective constituencies, the maintenance of the logic of homology produced the scope for the debate among the executive board about the inclusion of transgender people and a multicultural Europe. In consequence this logic also produced the scope for the compromise of deleting the former and include the latter. The problem of gay identity in that logic is not so much that we mistakenly *believe* in our self-namings. It is rather that we believe in the promise of inalienable rights assigned to those namings. These rights seem to accrue once our status as political subjects is secured. (Patton 1995:23) Hence, we miss the point that clear collective categories are often an obstacle to resistance and change.

Most activists on the European stage are not actually guilty of inscribing fixed identity categories. As Cindy Patton (1993:166) remarks, 'deconstructionists may believe in the imputed essentialist identities, much more than those in the political sphere who are purported to have them'. Yet, to let go of identity entirely seems to destroy the base principle of the political argument most commonly and successfully deployed. The back door entry of identity remains a crucial crutch. Therefore, a sense of threat and annoyance at the impracticability of the queer critique arises alongside the agreement that the basis of domination and control rests in the power invested in certain identity categories and in the idea that bounded categories are not to be transgressed (Cohen 1997:481). This simultaneity features in my illustrated troubles with my 'changing hats'.

The logic of the queer critique still vies with the logic of shoring up all those oppressed to demand the recognition of their actual lives. It vies with the logic of commonality between people who work for equality, freedom, and social justice, for the right to make choices, and to have access to the social and financial means to exercise a wide range of democratic choices. Although I have just analysed the problematic aspects of the political text I drafted myself, I still feel I could switch hats and argue for every sentence in the report's introduction. So, on the one hand, the critique outlined above does little in terms of practical advice about how to take on regulatory institutions, such as the law, governments, or education, which continue to enforce the heterosexual gender binary. The critique does not do justice to the degree in which presenting a group that claims rights can be both a necessary and a fulfilling strategy of survival. On the other hand, my piece in the EU report does little to challenge the principle of heteronormativity and the rigid binary gender system. It substantially fails to do justice to the fundamental interconnectedness among different discourses of marginalisation, such as transgender, race, and disability. In my work, each logic is somehow true and none is fully tenable. Hence, the challenge is not to determine which position is true, better, or more successful, but to cope with the fact that both logics make sense.

Thus, the conflict at stake – or my own re-opening of the theory–practice gap – should be conceptualised as a productive procedure: a productive procedure in the sense of reconnecting a critique of identity to the actual political forces that make collective identity necessary and meaningful. This reconnection needs to occur at the same time as a move to reconnect the particular necessity to render our lives intelligible through creating categories of belonging to the analysis of the damaging effects of buying entry tickets into the world of the privileged (Gamson 1996:411). Although entry tickets to regulated partnerships, for example, might be obtainable, only a few will get to use them. They won't be valid for anybody whose life-style choices disrupt a clear sense of gender identity or monogamous coupledom.

At the heart of what one could call queer theory's political (im)potency is the simultaneity of different workings of oppression, exclusion, and marginalisation. On the one hand, oppression, exclusion, and marginalisation stem from the binary gender structure and the pretended natural pre-script of sexed bodies. On the other hand, they stem from the already established institutions with whom we somehow have to negotiate, whether we want to or not (1996:412). The former makes de-stabilising categories a smart strategy the latter needs bounded categories in order to remain intelligible and smart (1996:413). Could ILGA-Europe, as an NGO with official consultative status to transnational institutions, develop a repertoire of political argumentation able to cope with the simultaneous workings of oppression, exclusion, and marginalisation? When does a quasi-ethnic identity manoeuvre reach out to de-stabilise its own implications and when does a deconstructionist tactic effectively help a gay transsexual win his custody case?

Asking these questions brings to the surface a residue of dissatisfaction with this analysis. While being intellectually satisfying and important, the recognition of paradoxes – here the validity of both the critique and the success of identity politics – is too often the point at which we stop analysing. Such a recognition of paradoxes acknowledges that the 'lesbian and gay faith in the authenticity or even political efficacy of identity categories and the queer suspension of all such classifications energise each other, offering in the 1990s – and who can say beyond? – the ambivalent reassurance of an unimaginable future' (Jagose 1996:132). Yet, the recognition of paradoxes alone does not explain how that energising takes effect. It also does not put an end to the constant re-opening of a theory–practice gap among activists and among academics, which blocks an engagement that takes the queer critique to heart and works with it.

Rather, I want to suggest that this energising could be understood as a fertile – but hopefully non-normative – intercourse, and its offspring is a hybrid in the classical sense. There is no path out of the theory–practice dynamic I set out to examine, only a path into it. In my attempts to probe the possibilities of going beyond the recognition of paradoxes I want to re-visit the concept of hybridity as one possible path into the dynamic set out above. Three of the many possible aspects of hybridity seem intriguing in their ability conceptually to handle or dissolve the gap: antagonistic relations, the dialogic unmasking of the normative, and desire.

Straddling the gap: hybridity

The concept of hybridity has become an important category in gay and lesbian studies. Originally stemming from biology – where it referred to offspring of two different species – and historically connoting the considered-to-be-infertile offspring between a slave and a white master, hybridity has been taken up – in spite of its racist history – as an analytical concept in many disciplines. As an analytical concept it has travelled more or less successfully from theorists of language and race or ethnicity to theorists concerned with sexual identity and homosexuality. Within the deployment of hybridity in gay and lesbian studies the focus usually rests on subjectivity, i.e. the construction of sexually non-normative subjectivities in a diasporic and dialogic existence relative to the dominance and hegemony of heteronormative discourse. Inspired by Michail Bakhtin's, Stuart Hall's, and Homi Bhabha's usage of hybridity, theorists in the field of gay and lesbian studies have deployed concepts such as mimicry, performativity, and discursive constructedness to understand the formation of gay subjectivity, resistance, challenge, and change. Queer theory is probably the most persuasive, in-depth, and articulated branch of the field that engages in the explicit, or implicit, mobilisation of hybridity as an analytical concept.

A recent assessment of hybridity in the field has been undertaken by Alan Sinfield in *Gay and After* in 1998. Sinfield is critical of any concept of hybridity that simply transfers it out of its relations to race and ethnicity. The connection of hybridity to the diaspora and the diasporic experience as it comes out of postcolonial studies is not simply applicable to any homosexual experience. There is no imaginary place homosexuals originate from and kinship is not the transmitter of gayness. Nevertheless, in relation to where most l/g/b/t people come from, the creation of the family substitute subculture is indeed a form of diaspora in a hegemonic heteronormative society. Sinfield (1998:30–1) summarises:

> The hybridity of our subcultures derives not from the loss of even a mythical unity, but from the difficulty we experience in envisioning ourselves beyond

the framework of normative heterosexism – the *straightgeist* – as Nicholson Baker calls it, on the model of *zeitgeist* ... It is a kind of reverse diaspora that makes our subcultures hybrid.

The concept of hybridity, though, remains a mixed blessing for Sinfield when he re-considers Homi Bhabha's concept of hybridity as the third space that gives rise to something new (1998:32). According to Sinfield, Bhabha's and – more directly relevant – Judith Butler's cases of mimicry play back or imitate colonial discourse or gender norms and, in turn, disclose the precariousness of the authority of those discourses.[8] Yet, both are not taking into account the factors of power and resistance to the extent necessary in facing the gender and race hegemony. Sinfield (1998:34) contends that 'hybridity has to be addressed not in the abstract, but as a social practice' and he warns that 'Hybridisation may be a necessary tactic, but it has to be pursued with determination and suspicion (of straightgeist influence). Certainly its political impetus cannot be taken for granted as some theorists seem to be saying' (Sinfield 1998:37). Sinfield gives the assessment of hybridity as analytical concept a common twist here. He opens a gap between the radical queer anti-essentialist critique and the practice of politics focused on what can be realistically achieved politically.[9] Although hybridity functions as another stabiliser of the gap between queer theory and politics yet again, it can alternatively be deployed as a concept that remedies the re-iteration of that very gap.

As my stories at the beginning of this chapter illustrate, it often seems as if queer theory and gay and lesbian rights politics are entirely antagonistic to each other, even if that apparent antagonism is complex. Yet, antagonistic relations do not necessarily present a deadlock. They can be the very aspect that progresses critique and practice. Antagonistic relations are a central aspect of understanding political practice as a hybrid articulation. However, in this respect, hybridity cannot function as a 'closed system in which elements given distinct, diametrical identities clash, and definitely resolve their contrast in the (re)production of a 'higher unity' external to them' (Becquer and Gatti 1991:70).

Marcos Becquer and Jose Gatti suggest that the two elements that form a hybrid – in their case European and African symbolic systems – are antagonistic to each other.[10] Antagonism here avoids the impression that the product is compared of two essential distinct parent elements into a new-born, but independent and distinct new entity. What forms the hybrid, to them, are not contradictory elements that can be joined at any level, but elements which are in antagonistic relations and which 'thereby expand the logics of struggle' (1991:72). What emerges is never a unity at peace, but a creature that is marked by internal struggle. Substituting the term 'hybridity' with 'syncretism', for historical reasons, Becquer and Gatti (1991:74) conclude that hybrid 'relations are, in this sense, traversed by a double movement of both alliance and critique'.

Queer theory could as such bring its alliance – its clear commitment to politics and social change – and its critique – its fundamental destabilisation of essentialist assumptions or its open address of desire – to human rights based work, supporting and questioning it simultaneously. As a syncretic or hybrid articulation, the mixture of queer theory and gay and lesbian rights politics becomes a radicalisation of the impossibility of the search for definite political practices and rights. The mixture becomes a radicalisation of the logic of struggle, internally for the dangers and successes of representational politics, and externally for the most productive disruption of the gender binary and the heteronormative structure of European democratic societies. It seems, therefore, not useful to talk about an unresolved conflict, but rather about a fertilisation that encompasses the antagonistic relations of what can become critical queer political practice. The gap is, thus, straddled not by re-iterating it each time political practices are theoretically analysed, but by understanding antagonism to be the very factor that renders such analysis fruitful.

In antagonistic relations to each other, critique and practice also relate dialogically and retain the power to unmask and destabilise hegemonic discourses. This task of unmasking authoritative discourse, of unmasking hegemonic statutes of truth is what inspired Mikhail Bakhtin to first introduce the concept of hybridity into linguistics. In his *Discourse and the Novel*, Bakhtin (1986:667) connects the hegemony of certain cultural–ideological discourses to the hybrid nature of language:

> A common unitary language is a system of linguistic norms. But these norms ... (are) forces that struggle to overcome the heteroglossia of language, forces that unite and centralize verbal–ideological thought ... Thus a unitary language gives expression to forces working toward concrete verbal and ideological unification and centralization, which develop in the vital connection with the processes of sociopolitical cultural centralization.

'Heteroglossia' in Bakhtin refers to the conflict between official and unofficial discourses within national languages, but also to the micro-linguistic level: every utterance contains conflictual traces of different meanings. Because heteroglossia is present in all utterances, speech and discourse are always hybrid; they foreground the clash of antagonistic social forces (1986:668–70). Dialogism is, then, the characteristic epistemological mode of a world dominated by heteroglossia, where there is a constant interaction between meanings (1986:669).

> The word in living conversation is directly, blatantly, oriented toward a future answer-word: it provokes an answer, anticipates it and structures itself in the answer's direction ... Responsive understanding is a fundamental force, one that participates in the formulation of discourse, and it is moreover an *active* understanding, one that discourse senses as resistance or support enriching the discourse. (1986:672)

Bakhtin (1986:671) posits an internal dialogic imperative of words, as the world of language pre-exists any human inhabitant of it. This view of the pre-existence of language is crucial for poststructuralist thought.

Words, practices, and political relations always undergo dialogisation; they become relativised, de-privileged, aware of competing definitions. Only at the point where a discourse sets itself up as authoritative, absolute, and true does it become undialogised for Bakhtin; or better – to speak with Judith Butler (1990:72-8) – does it *seem* undialogised. In fact, all authoritative discourse always already contains its own contestation by the very processes with which it sets itself up as truth. Although Bakhtin's writing is clearly connected to a theory of the novel, Graham Pechy (1989:54) points out that 'there is nothing in the concept of dialogism that prevents us from using it to explain the organisation of hegemony itself'. As such, the concept of dialogism can easily travel over and into the theory–practice gap.

As utterances, both identity-based rights argumentation and queer critiques are geared towards an answer structure, carry their contestation in themselves, albeit not necessarily in reply to each other. While the queer critiques usually take representational identity-based politics as their opposite, organisations involved in those politics gear their discourse less towards academic theory than to what is perceived as the rights-granting majority or to institutions. However, that is not a hindrance to a dialogic engagement between theory and political practice, since ultimately both practices aim at eliminating structures of oppression and exclusion in relation to sexuality and gender. My efforts in coping with my 'changing hats', then, become an intentional semantic hybrid in Bakhtin's sense: a semantic hybrid that is inevitably internally dialogic and distinct from organic hybrids (Bakhtin 1986:674–5). Two points of view are mixed, but set against each other dialogically.

Whereas in organic hybridity there is a merging and fusing into a new and independent product, language, or world view, intentional hybridity retains the different points of view or objects in a conflictual structure that remains energetic and open-ended.[11] Bakhtin's intentional hybridity intervenes in the re-iteration of the gap as a form of subversion, translation, or transformation. In its dialogical structure, hybridity offers a permanent sense of interrogation, of unmasking, and of the fundamental priority of discourse as the site of the staging of politics and the articulation of theory. Hybridisation as queer political chaos does not produce a new theory that faithfully reflects practical political necessity or a political activism that faithfully reflects the conditions of queer theory. It is rather closer to Butler's restless, playful, interstitial performativity: a radical heterogeneity, discontinuity, the permanent revolution of the meaning of sexuality as a marker of identity and subsequent social, political, or economical rights. Yet, not only queer theory produces that restless, playful, interstitial performativity: the political practices of rights politics carry the potential to do the same.

Revolutionising the meaning of sexuality within the political practices of European lesbian and gay rights lobbying foremost entails a centralising and re-conceptualisation of desire as the motor for sexual identity formation and for rights argumentation. Within the history of the concept of hybridity, desire played an important role. Theories of race in the nineteenth century – settling on the impossibility or possibility of hybridity – focused explicitly on sexuality and fertility: 'theories of race were also covert theories of desire' (Young 1995:9). The term 'hybridity' is surely problematic in its call on the history of racism, in its connotation of the pure origin of the two things that are joined (Becquer and Gatti 1991:66) and in its reference to parents and offspring, which potentially re-inforces a heteroessentialism of sexuality (1991:68). However, its connection to language and sexuality, hence, to a theory of desire, sheds an intriguing light on some aspects of the theory–practice gap: the relations between the desire for rights – for a social belonging – and the desire for the expression of sexualities and gender identities in a heteronormative social, economic and political world.

The operative basis for my involvement in ILGA-Europe six years ago was a clear leftover desire for equality in its mainstream humanist sense, as equality before the law. It was a desire that is intrinsically fuelled by some form of acceptance of the hegemony of the juridical as measurement of whether *we* – who express deviant sexual or gender desires – are allowed to belong to the citizenship of the European Union. Both desires – the desire for the expression of one's sexuality and gender *and* the desire for equal rights – are involved in all political practices for rights. Desire wields power over the perception of the homosexual experience and over the formulation of rights politics.

The so-called homosexual experience in and of itself is already a critical concept for two reasons: first, experience is not a transparent, true, and objective mirror of a reality structured by an essential identity, but rather in itself already a discursive event that produces identities and realities.[12] Second, the so-called homosexual experience of homophobia and heterosexism that leads to the claim for rights is a ruptured experience that does not allow any one conclusion to be drawn from it. Even within essentialist definitions of gay identity, the reports on daily homosexual experiences acknowledge contradictory elements in relation to what the meaning of gayness entails in the different social relations in which each human lives. Equality before the law can obviously never accommodate all those relations; it remains a fantasy never to be fulfilled.

Nevertheless, the re-entry of identity through the back door in rights argumentation hinges on a belief that gay and lesbian experience is describable and that rights can accommodate that experience. It appears as if the definition of a certain sexual desire as a marker of discrimination needs to rest on a clearly identifiable group that shares the same experience. In turn, it is that same group which expresses a desire for rights through their struggles to obtain equality. Thus, apparently both forms of desire are involved in all political practices employed in a fight for rights for lesbians, gay men, bisexuals, and transgender people. Additionally, there is a third desire involved when queer theory comes onto the plan: the desire to grapple with the ruptured experiences in many different social relations that are not captured by identity politics. By placing sexuality into the centre of European knowledge production, queer theory also places desire in the centre of epistemology. Desire, therefore, fuels both mainstream rights politics and queer theoretical critique.

The previous argument, however, involves a shift: a shift from sexual desire to political desire, or to the desire for rights. The connection I establish in this respect is not self-evident; it only works within an understanding of desire that is discursive rather than a psychological reality eternally fixed by the rules and laws of gender formation. In this respect, desire cannot be understood as the uncontainable psychic nature of an individual that bursts through cultural constraints. Instead, desire is an outcome of the productive qualities of discourses made available in discursive practices.[13] As Bronwyn Davies (1990b:501) writes:

> But I argue here that desire is spoken into existence, it is shaped through discursive and interactive practices, through the symbolic and the semiotic. Desires are constituted through the narratives and storylines, the metaphors, the very language and patterns of existence through which we are 'interpellated' into the social world.

In Davies' concept of desire, unconscious processes take a significant part in the constitution of desire. Davies criticises the juxtaposition of an unconscious desire and a conscious agency, and, hence, the oppositional character of that which is conscious and that which is unconscious (1991:44). It is crucial to understand that – given the fact that gender matrices constitute a major part of our dominant discourses – desire is constituted in gendered identities. Desire is, therefore, never independent from the regulatory practices of the dominant dualisms of male/female, or heterosexuality/homosexuality through which we construct a sense of personhood. This sense of personhood, in turn, is the basis upon which people can claim membership to the realm of democratic rights. A queer or poststructuralist understanding of the concept of personhood emphasises that the desire to be something and act as something originates in discourses rather than essential selves. In this sense, desire functions as a fundamental signifier of what constitutes people as lesbian, gay, bisexual, or transgendered and, thus, belonging to a minority *and* as persons that can and do claim rights which are denied them. In the case of lesbian and gay politics, the desire to have rights others apparently have is an active positioning of oneself in relation to discourses of democratic rights and simultaneously to discourses of sexual desire.

The positioning of selves in discourses is, in this context, understood as a process of locating selves in conversations and written texts in which participants interactively assign meanings to their identities and experiences. As such, participants can position themselves as reflexive expressions of past experiences or culturally dominant interpretations, and they are simultaneously positioned by what others say about them. Although we can actively participate in our positioning, the process of positioning is not assumed to be necessarily intentional or fully coherent, nor consciously recognisable. Also, any active positioning depends on the capacity to take oneself up as a person, consciously or unconsciously, which is possible only through discursive practices.[14]

Discursive practices are ways in which people produce social and psychological realities through engaging in – or refusing repetitions of – certain practices (Davies and Harré 1990:45). Discourses provide practices that regulate the intelligibility of identities and through their repetition or disruption we take ourselves up as participants and producers of those discourses. Through engaging in discursive practices people appropriate as their own the desires that are made relevant in the discourses to which the regulatory practices belong. Desire is, thus, relevant for the expression of sexuality and subsequent formation of a homosexual identity upon which rights are apparently claimed. It is also relevant for the expression of being a human or a citizen endowed with rights. Any analysis of rights politics needs to centralise desire as the motor of taking oneself up as a person belonging to a community in law or in social and political orders. Claiming rights becomes an appropriation of the desire made relevant in the discourses of participation and citizenship, which are – among others – based on the regulatory practices of a gender order. In turn, it is this gender order which functions as the *only* available field in relation to which sexual desire and the desire to belong to a gender can be formed.

Hence the connection between sexual desire and the desire for rights. And hence also the central role desire needs to play in a critical analysis of l/g/b/t politics. Naming the conditions of desire – understood as the central motor of any sexual identity *and* of the constitution of oneself as a person entitled to rights – and centralising it in the formation of the political is a path towards tackling some of the contradictions and troubles the queer critique has raised. An analysis of desire brings to the fore the contradiction of sexual identity as such and troubles any idea of a subsequent erection of rights claims based on an *a priori* existing group. Additionally, such an analysis also addresses the point at which, as Antke Engel (2001: 354) identifies, queer theory occasionally becomes problematic: when it primarily turns gender and sexuality into a function of constituting the subject and brings the subordinating and exploitative effects of gender and sexuality and the actual political change too far out of sight.

Considering sexual identity as a basis for the political is to some extent a 'productive contradiction in terms' (Butler 1997b:104). According to Butler (1997b:103), identity is formed through a prohibition on some dimension of the very sexuality it is said to describe. She continues that any formation of the subject – including the rights-bearing citizen – requires a sexuality founded on the prohibition of a certain desire, which at the same time forms that sexuality and the subject that is said to bear it. Thus, any political practices that firmly ground themselves in clear and fixed sexual identities will prolong a contradiction in terms into the political without being able to utilise the productive sides of this contradiction. To expose those contradictions as productive is a necessary task that becomes accessible only when and where desire is centralised as the site at which the transition from sexuality and gender to effective political practice occurs. I contend that it is also for this reason that queer theory needs to centralise desire beyond affirming the sexualisation of the public and the ways all humans are gendered and sexualised at every moment in which they interact.

Desire beyond the gender binary could be said to rest at the heart of queer theory and the desire for rights at the heart of European gay and lesbian politics. To marry the two, to hybridise them, means to relate the sexual and the political through desire. This becomes a relation that functions in various ways, which grants access to seeing the multiple effects of displacements, intensification, reorientation, and modification of sexuality and gender in the performance of political practice. I contend that the conflictual energy and open-endedness of hybridity is, arguably, a way into the conflict, a stirrup into the saddle of the theory–practice gap analysed above. Conceptualising hybridity, as I have, offers a contestatory activity, a politicised setting up of epistemological differences against each other dialogically. The crucial effect of hybridisation is the political moment at which, within a single discourse, one meaning of an utterance unmasks the other, a point at which the authority of any discourse is undone, questioned, de-stabilised. Engaging in theory and political activism is not a process of merging but one of dialogisation: a dialogisation of differences in the operative logic of theory and politics set critically against each other. To be fruitful, these differences need to be two simultaneous phases of the same movement, which constantly overlap and mingle. Or, to put it differently: my multiple hats shall be left in a state of *coitus interruptus*, with the memory and tease of a process and not the assurance and smugness of orgasm.[15]

Conclusion

Having said all this, however, does not grant a final peace to the conflicts that arise out of my wearing two hats. This argument only ends a destructive analysis of this conflict. It ends an analysis that re-creates an insurmountable gap between theory and practice and that precludes all applicability of queer theory to the practicalities of rights politics in Europe. Conflicts between theory and political practice are not new. What the queer critique foregrounds is the fact that the line between normative and non-normative has ceased simply to run along the heterosexual–homosexual divide. The cutting edges of that line are a zigzag and they continuously move with the changing conditions of modernity. After all, the fact that the location of this line is not so obvious any more is possibly the grandest success of the gay and lesbian movements in obtaining visibility, acceptance, and tolerance.

To those seeking legal equality and social justice in the existing order, queer theory need not pose any threat, but presents an acknowledgement of their successes: eventually, inclusion will be gained, homosexuality will cease to be the primary factor of radical exclusion as long as it does not challenge the fundamental order of human relations which remains heteronormative. Queer theory simply foretells the breaking apart of what was formerly a group characterised by solidarity into new affiliations around different rally-points than homosexual identity. It foretells the eruption of new gaps along non-identitarian subjectivities or along the hierarchised binary gender divide that rests beneath questions of sexual orientation. Queer theory addresses those troubled by leaving the heterosexual order unchallenged. As a historical moment the poststructuralist feminist and queer critiques form something like an epistemic break in the conception of gender and sexuality. They are neither new nor old and the gap they currently produce might not remain an issue of concern in the future when certain rights have been gained and when movements evolve into other movements along different issues.

Why, then – I might ask rhetorically – should we mind the gap in the first place? What dangers await us if we don't? What desires could be fulfilled through the free fall? Tampering with the signs that prohibit entry into formerly unknown spaces is after all what gay liberation used to be about. So while the unsexy tin voice of the London Tube continues to warn us 'Mind the gap!', no stop requires one to exit through it once and for all, and no gap prevents us from applying critical modes of reading to the predicaments of staging rights politics. In short, I suggest a deployment of queer theory as one mode of reading political reality for the purpose of putting desire back on the agenda, centralising it by understanding the formative power it wields over the claim to rights and over the subject formation of activists as agents of change, which I discuss at the end of this book. Yet, the applicability of queer theory as a mode of reading remains context-specific. Any form of applicability needs to include a critical examination of queer thought in a European context that centres so fundamentally on universal human rights as a political rally-point.

Notes

1 Many different concerns are raised in the academic debate. They mainly run along three themes. Firstly, queer theory's abstract and highly academic discourse uncannily appeared at a point in time at which gays and lesbians had won positions from which to speak. The deconstructive manoeuvres of queer theory erase affirmative standpoints for gayness, do not incorporate a belief in the future, and dismantle gay studies in academia (Derbyshire 1994:39–45; Savoy 1994:131–8; Walters 1996:839). Secondly, queer theory is often accused of erasing lesbians and transgender people yet again, of becoming the universalised voice of the white gay man again and of hierarchising deviance (Penn 1995:34–9; Walters 1996:846; Guess 1995:23). Queer theory's separation and mixture of sexuality and gender is mostly identified as a reason for this erasure (Martin 1994:107–8). And, thirdly, the cancellation of identity, while being simultaneously fixated on identity (Guess 1995:35), reduces gay men and lesbians to dispensable fashion victims and focuses on art and style above the political (Savoy 1994:134; Abelove 1995:48). Hennessy (1995:31) adds that the visibility of sexual identity is often a matter of commodification. A subjectivity that is primarily sexual – as in queer theory – erases the intersections of sexuality with class, gender, and racial histories and fetishises commodity (Hennessy 1995:34/52). While these three themes are recurring features of most critical stances towards queer theory, there are distinctive differences among the authors named here. Their accounts range from trashing the queer project to serious critical engagement and close reading of queer texts.
2 The booklet that emerged out of this project is called *Equality for Lesbians and Gay Men. A Relevant Issue in the Civil and Social Dialogue*. It is available in print in English, German, French, and Spanish and on the website of ILGA-Europe.
3 See, for an elaboration on this, among others, Cohen (1997), Epstein (1999), Gamson (1996), Seidman (1993, 1995), Sinfield (1998), or Warner (1993).
4 Gay identity is not the only pre-existing category here either. The European, as the entity to whom citizenship rights are granted, is another unproblematised category.

5 See my explanation on argumentation theory according to van Eemeren *et al.* (1993) in Chapter 2.
6 Plummer (1995:141) adds another important feature to the theory of social movements: to 'maintain vitality, all successful social movements must remain in conflict and struggle. Once conflict ceases, movements are prone to co-optation by the dominant order, becoming institutionalised or even ceasing function. They need to be moved on through contestation, schism, and conflict: without these, they become static, wither, and often die'.
7 I will analyse the conceptualisation of identity apparent in the interviews more specifically in relation to agency in Chapter 9.
8 Butler illustrates her point through a description of drag and butch/femme cultures. She sheds new light on the relation between imitation and the so-called original. In imitating gender, drag, for example, implicitly reveals the imitative structure of gender itself, as well as its contingency (1990:137). The mimicry favoured by both Bhabha and Butler is not a narcissistic identification that will ultimately deny subjectivity and agency to the marginal subject, but is rather used as the 'gaze of otherness ... where the observer becomes the observed and "partial" representation rearticulates the whole notion of *identity* and alienates it from essence' (Bhabha 1984:129).
9 To be fair, Sinfield is himself a strong critic of essentialism and gay ethnicity arguments. However, he unwittingly re-opens the typical theory–practice gap in his assessment of hybridity.
10 Becquer and Gatti (1991:69) prefer syncretism instead of hybridity as the better term to emphasise heterogeneity. In fact, one of the central tenets of their paper argues against hybridity and for syncretism. This argument rests on the aim of defeating hybridity's racist history. I will not engage in the distinction of these terms here since I deploy the term 'hybridity' in a way that is cut loose from the debate about its history. This is, admittedly, a slightly de-contextualised appropriation of the term that focuses only on some aspects of hybridity as a theoretical concept.
11 The term 'intentional' is problematic in that it often connotes an independent author outside of discourse. What is meant here, however, is an intentional or better aware creation of antagonistic relations. An intentional hybrid is a form of relation that exposes its own origin, remains conscious of its contingency and is intentional in the sense that the contradictions that emerge are part and parcel of the aim from the outset.
12 See, for a critical investigation of the concept of experience, Scott (1991) and my own elaboration in relation to historiography in Beger (1997).
13 I have explained the following in more detail elsewhere (Beger 1997).
14 In relation to sexuality and desire, Teresa de Lauretis (1994:293) emphasises that both belong to the realm of fantasy 'which trespasses beyond the couch, beyond the bedroom, into the public spaces of representation. Thus the public representation of lesbianism, including most importantly lesbian discursive and performative practices, can be an equally effective discourse, yielding 'multiple effects of displacements, intensification, reorientation, and modification of desire itself' (Foucault). Desire is, thus, subjected to the conditions of fantasy and to the conditions of the imaginable realm in which discursive boundaries are effective but also transgressable (1994:284). De Lauretis' formulations are another more psychoanalytic way of explaining what Bronwyn Davies calls the process of positioning.
15 Bredbeck (1993) has formulated this in relation to postmodernism and homosexuality.

Part II
Rights

4 European strategies: human rights

> Indeed human rights, viewed at the universal level, bring us face-to-face with the most challenging dialectical conflict ever: between 'identity' and 'otherness', between 'myself' and 'others'. They teach us in a direct, straightforward manner that we are at the same time identical and different.
> (Boutros Boutros-Ghali 1994:7)

> The human rights activist, therefore, ... cannot help but represent the actuality of the human condition and respond in a language that posits unity (interconnectedness) in diversity (pluralism).
> (Baden Offord 1999a:64)

On 18 November 1998, Queer Planet – an international l/g/b/t e-mail network – published the following report, which has since then been repeated in newspapers around the world:

> During a talk at a US American university, Desmond Tutu, the famous South African Anglican Bishop, talked about what his priorities are now that South Africans are beginning to heal from apartheid. When a student asked Tutu what injustice he would most want to reverse, he gave a surprising answer. 'Will you give me two?' he said with a grin. First, Tutu called on world leaders to forgive the mounting debts owed by developing nations. Then he said the persecution of homosexuals is as unjust as apartheid. 'Sexual orientation is just like race', Tutu said. 'People do not decide to be gay any more than they decide to be black or white', he said. Tutu condemned the killing of Matthew Shepard in Wyoming in October 1998. 'For me it's a matter of human rights and a deeply theological issue', Tutu said. 'I believe they are as much God's children as anyone ... I can't be part of a scheme for clobbering them'. (Desmond Tutu, 17 November 1998, quoted in Queer Planet, 17 November 1998).

In choosing homosexuals' right not to be persecuted as a primary human right, Desmond Tutu rocked the international lesbian and gay community. His comment was astonishing, unexpected, and impressive and it was celebrated extensively in much of the gay and lesbian national and international press. Hearing one of the most prominent human rights advocates in the world cite sexual orientation as a human right on par with race seems to corroborate the long deployment of human rights in arguments for justice, equality, and freedom for gay men and lesbians.

Within the transnational European context, in particular, human rights are the argumentational strategy most central to lesbian and gay lobby politics. Human rights are a pivotal discourse of the European supranational institutions – the

European Union and the Council of Europe – which draw much of their identity from building Europe as a peaceful post-war unity that secures the protection of fundamental rights. In fact, the human rights discourse may be the most dominant discourse of rights in Europe. Therefore, it warrants close investigation as a political practice. The aim of this chapter is to present such an investigation through a critical reading of ILGA-Europe's EU Action Plan, ILGA-World's Human Rights Manifesto, interview material, and the 1997 *Euan Sutherland v. United Kingdom* case (European Commission of Human Rights).

The first section of this chapter will examine the arguments and obstacles of homosexual rights as human rights. Traditional human rights discourse places emphasis on the individual as the bearer of rights *qua* her or his human status. Freedom, equality, recognition, and integrity are the features through which human rights are argued and that fuel the belief in human progress with regard to the respect for fundamental rights. Human rights literature that considers sexual orientation tends to name several steps necessary for the successful inclusion of lesbians and gay men into the dominant human rights discourse. While naturally a bit more elaborated, the human rights logic behind the academic arguments is principally the same as the one employed by activists. From a critical queer perspective, the fact that human rights violations on the ground of sexuality continue to occur, and are rarely named or accepted as such, begs for a more fundamental interrogation of human rights discourse and why human rights have historically not been applied to people with non-normative sexualities.

The second section of the chapter will undertake such interrogation of the problematic history of human rights. Through its reference to a humanist concept of personhood, the widely argued exclusion of women in the conceptualisation of rights has implications for human rights relating to sexual orientation. Human rights are individuated rights. This potentially precludes an examination of those structures that produce and maintain human rights violation in the first place. I will argue that human rights grant a freedom and an equality deeply dependent on notions of humanness that exclude homosexuality; the respectability and recognition they promise are paradoxical to homosexuality. Finally, I will show that behind the seemingly universal human identity and rights that apply to individuals, sexual identity as a marker of political group formation is legally and politically re-introduced. I conclude that the only territory truly negotiated in human rights discourse is the territory of humanity. As long as the stakes of humanity are not openly designated as the territory of negotiation, human rights will continue to burden those they actually seek to liberate with an identity of injury and suffering.

Homosexual rights as human rights

Rights argumentation in lesbian and gay political practice is primarily based – either explicitly or implicitly – on the discourse of human rights. The focus rests on sexual rights as intrinsic rights asserted for gays and lesbians by virtue of fully acknowledging their humanity. The discourses on European unity in general draw heavily on human rights discourses. The connection between unity and similarity, cultural difference, and human rights is also not rare in academic thought on citizenship and the European Union. Jürgen Habermas gives a prominent example of this:

> In a future Federal Republic of European States, the same legal principles would also have to be interpreted from the vantage point of different national traditions and histories. One's own national tradition will, in each case, have to be appropriated in such a manner that it is related to and relativized by the vantage points of other national cultures. It must be connected with the overlapping consensus of a common supranationally shared political culture of the European Community. Particularist anchoring *of this sort* would in no way impair the universalist meaning of popular sovereignty and human rights. (Habermas 1992:7)

For Habermas, the common denominator for Europeanness is the universalist meaning of human rights, which stands above and beyond national traditions as the supranationally shared political culture. The dominant human rights discourse Habermas refers to does not defy nationalism, nor does it question Europe as a project comprised of national virtues, which are joint by European cultural heritage. In fact, Habermas' vision of human rights is profoundly connected to the official rights rhetoric of the European institutions.

Both the Council of Europe and the European Union were, among other things, built on the idea of uniting former enemies in Europe and protecting human rights in perpetuity.[1] Building Europe as a peaceful unity that secures the protection of human rights is part of the mission statement of all European institutions.[2] So far, the EU is not a legal personality able to sign the European Convention on Human Rights, but the draft Constitution allows for this step to be taken. In order to cope with the complexities of freedom of movement and European citizenship, the EU has, however, created a Charter of Fundamental Rights – which contains important human rights – that was declared in December 2000. This Charter is not legally binding until the new Constitution is ratified, which includes the Charter as Part II of the draft so far. The rhetoric of the EU is heavily influenced by human rights discourse. Since 1994, the annual Human Rights Reports of the European Parliament – concerning Member States of the EU – mention homosexuality or sexual orientation discrimination as a violation of human rights.[3]

The European Parliament usually referred to unequal ages of consent, non-provision of partnership rights, social, economic, and legal insecurity, equal treatment of EU employees by the European institutions, the treatment of lesbian and gay prisoners, and homophobic violence. The violation of human rights within the EU is a contentious item in the EU Parliament, but human rights rhetoric appears on a very regular basis and is considered pivotal to all MEPs and parties. Considering the dominance of human rights in much of the official political and ideological rhetoric on Europe, the predictable recourse to human rights strategies in European gay and lesbian political practice is not astonishing. The argumentation for rights when approaching the EU – and obviously the Council of

Europe – necessarily draws on human rights as the remedy to that which has been denied to lesbians and gay men in Europe.

The political stance of ILGA-World is put most succinctly in the phrase 'Lesbian and gay rights are human rights'. In this phrase, ILGA draws upon human rights language inscribed in the UDHR – Universal Declaration of Human Rights – and Boutros Boutros-Ghali's exhortation of 'all human rights for all people' (ILGA 1998: 3-4). ILGA-Europe, in turn, mentions human rights specifically in almost all political argumentation and in its activity reports. The interviews I conducted with ILGA-Europe activists bring to the forefront the predominance of human rights argumentation in European gay and lesbian political practices as well.[4] The human rights issue *is* the grand narrative of activists on the European stage.[5]

During 1998, ILGA-World carried out a great deal of human rights activism. This activity included a human rights manifesto called 'The Rights of Lesbians and Gays are Human Rights' and culminated in an official meeting with Mary Robinson – the UN High Commissioner on human rights. The ILGA 98 Manifesto – celebrating ILGA's 20th anniversary and the 50th anniversary of the Universal Declaration of Human Rights – states:

> Mankind has been able to abolish slavery and establish certain basic rights of women in almost all parts of the world. We have developed democratic institutions and civil societies. Respect for human rights and fundamental freedoms is the condition for successful social and political life in all societies. We must recognize equality and respect diversity. On the 50th anniversary of the Universal Declaration of Human Rights, we bear witness to the strengthening concern of peoples and societies for human rights. A fundamental part of human rights in our time is the recognition of the right of individuals to develop their personalities, identities and sexuality, free from coercion or discrimination. We condemn the discrimination and oppression that continues in many States, including criminal sanctions and even the death penalty. In solidarity with ILGA, we demand full equality before the law for gay men, lesbians, bisexuals and transgendered persons. We demand the end of criminal penalties. We seek laws prohibiting discrimination. We demand the full and equal recognition of relationships. We look forward to the inclusion of equality rights, irrespective of sexual orientation, in national laws and international human rights instruments. Together we can all make a better life for each other and for future generations. Gay and lesbian rights are human rights!

Similarly, the European Action plan of ILGA-Europe, which has been presented personally to each Commissioner by ILGA-Europe and EGALITE between 1997 and 1998, takes its starting point from a human rights argument:

> The basic aim of the International Lesbian and Gay Association (ILGA) and of its 400 member associations is to work for the liberation of lesbians and gays from legal, social, cultural and economic discrimination … The assumptions

underlying this aim are the equality of all citizens, one of the fundamental principles of Community law, and the right not to be discriminated against on the basis of sexual orientation, *a basic right of all human beings.* (ILGA-Europe Action Plan 1997 – emphasis mine).

The EU Action Plan clearly declares that the right not to be discriminated against and the right to live one's sexual orientation freely are basic rights of all human beings.[6] Given the confidence with which just statements are asserted and the centrality of the human rights discourse in the official rhetoric of European institutions, it is reasonable to ask questions about the precise historical conditions and concepts upon which the claim 'Homosexual Rights are Human Rights' is based. The excerpts quoted above shed light on the dominant human rights discourse in Europe and show how that discourse is brought to bear on sexual orientation.

The first aspect evident is a strong belief in human progress. Boutros Boutros-Ghali (1994:8–9) once suggested that the 1990s signal that human rights have become core considerations for the international community and all peoples of this world.[7] He considers this to be a major success in the consciousness of humanity. The ILGA Manifesto taps into this belief in progress in its first four lines: after humankind has finally abolished slavery, the world will now realise that progress demands the recognition of sexual rights as human rights as well. Evidence for this progress is located in the development of democratic institutions, of civil societies, and of respect for diversity. In short, there is no future successful social and political life without respect for human rights and fundamental freedoms according to the Manifesto.

The belief in progress and development is part of the history of human rights and of their intrinsic reference to morality, hope, and authority (Evans 1998:4). Tony Evans (1998:12) argues in this respect that 'human rights are the outcome of power relations' and 'in the current era all issues must be subordinated to the imperatives of globalization'. Through the extinction of the socialist human rights project, the US approach of extending freedoms only to those who do not challenge the free market principles or resist the imperative of liberal processes for economic growth and development has become dominant in global human rights discourse (1998:12). International human rights discourse increasingly turns to the language of democracy rather than individual freedoms, following the logic that, if capitalist democracies are installed, human rights will automatically follow (1998:13). ILGA's Manifesto – drawing on this historical context in which human rights are situated in the 1990s – turns to using the language of democracy. In its first three lines, the Manifesto praises progress in social and political life of capitalist democracies as benchmarks for human rights.

Academically speaking, human rights are said to 'imply the amelioration of human life, that is, its improvement and its protection' (Offord 1999a:50). A. Belden Fields and Wolf-Dieter Narr (1992:5–6) identify four values that ensure and promote the amelioration of human life: the longing for freedom, social recognition, equality relative to the social context in which people live, and integrity. 'Freedom' in this sense needs to be understood in terms of what is felt to be lacking in the given social and historical context. This includes all forms of marginalisation and social exclusion as well as physical freedom from torture and coercion. It includes freedom to engage in free choices and freedom from discrimination, the latter being the principle claim upon which ILGA(-Europe) rests its human rights position. The Manifesto asserts freedom of discrimination with the words 'a fundamental part of human rights in our time is the recognition of the right of individuals to develop their personalities, identities and sexuality, free from coercion or discrimination' (lines 7–9). The Action Plan names freedom from discrimination, a basic human right that is connected to the principle of equality, which the Manifesto features as well in line 11.

According to Fields and Narr (1992:6), the claim to equality is a strategy of opening up space in which previously accepted historical structures of inequality become the focus of a struggle for social reconstruction. Putting sexual orientation assertively on the agenda of what matters in rights of choice manifested in human rights (Manifesto, lines 8–9) is an act of struggling for a new social order in which previously accepted inequalities – such as homosexuality as unnatural illness – are now considered unjust. The recognition of this injustice is expressed in the demand for legal recognition, which both quotations include. The need for recognition stems from the insight that any sense of self-worth depends upon recognition and respect from others (1992:6). When the Manifesto claims that 'a fundamental part of human rights in our time is the recognition of the right of individuals to develop their personalities, identities and sexuality, free from coercion or discrimination' (lines 7–9), then recognition of personal choice and of existing injustice is clearly made a social process that depends on the willingness of others to acknowledge sexual orientation as a diverse feature of human nature.

Equality will be achieved only when discrimination on the grounds of sexual orientation is commonly considered a clear violation of human rights and when gay men and lesbians are liberated 'from legal, social, cultural and economical discrimination' (Action Plan, lines 2–3). Yet, freedom from coercion and discrimination grants more than only recognition. It grants integrity of one's body and social relations. Integrity relates to the belief that personal lives 'constitute something true, something whole, something valid for themselves and for others with whom they interact' (Fields and Narr 1992:6). Human rights language is fundamentally built on the notion of integrity, which is affirmed in Article 1 of the Universal Declaration of Human Rights: 'All human beings are born free and equal in dignity and rights. They are endowed with reason and conscience and should act towards one another in a spirit of brotherhood.' [sic!]

These features of human rights language – the belief in progress, freedom, equality, recognition and integrity – are not only presented in written and official political statements, but are also a strong part of why and how activists centralise human rights discourse in their work. Additionally, the emphasis on individuals rather than groups and the accrediting of rights to people by virtue of their humanness in human rights discourse frames the approaches activists take to these features of human rights argumentation. To my initial question in the interview guideline 'What are the most successful strategies and arguments in your work?' Outi Ojala (March 1998) – MEP and President of the intergroup 'Equality for Lesbians and Gay Men' at the time – immediately responded with 'it is very easy to say: it is the question of human rights. The whole idea why I am working for lesbian and gay rights is that they must have human rights'. Ojala not only centralises the human rights discourse as an important political strategy, but also as her personal motivation for her courageous involvement in the issue over years transnationally and nationally in Finland, while she, herself, does not identify as lesbian. She justifies this focus with:

> It is a question of every person having the same right to decide on her or his sexuality and sexual behaviour. It is a private question, but the right for equal treatment has to be the same independent of what is your sexual orientation ... people have to face the question of what it means to be gay or lesbian, what the discriminatory elements are in daily life ... the reason I struggle for gay and lesbian rights is the human rights question, and I am also very involved in other minority rights questions ... for the same reason.

Implicit in her words is a strong emphasis on individuality. She speaks of rights for gay men and lesbians, not emphasising their group status as such, but rather their individual right to choice. Choice is portrayed as a right that heterosexual people exercise in the same way and a right to which every human person should have access. This individualisation of rights is a strong feature of the classical human rights discourse. Jack Donelly (1984:410) asserts in this respect: 'Human rights are inherently "individualistic"; they are rights held by individuals in relation to, even against, the state and society'. According to Donelly, human rights are held equally by all against the state, which limits the state's legitimate range of actions and requires positive protections against predictable economic, social, and political contingencies (1984:416). Individualised rights are 'a seemingly natural and necessary response to typically modern threats to human dignity, to basic human values, traditional and modern alike' (1984:416). Human rights are, thus, rights that every person has by virtue of being human.

Adrian Coman – Executive Director of ACCEPT in Romania and member of ILGA-Europe's executive board at the time – concludes that sexual rights as human rights are best argued 'by underlining the need for sexual rights that also apply to straight people' (Adrian Coman, e-mail interview, June 1999). Coman implicitly refers to sexual orientation in the human rights context as the assertion of an immutable status; everybody has a sexual orientation, and a choice at the same time. It is, therefore, applicable to all human beings who have a right to respect in relation to the pursuit of their happiness and health. Tatjana Greif (e-mail interview, January 2000) – Slovenian lesbian activist and member of ILGA-Europe's executive board – also formulates this applicability to the whole of society:

> The crucial thing is the concept of individual civil and human rights. Instead of talking about different minorities, the struggle for any socially marginalised group and individual rights is the wise strategy, I think. Women are certainly no minority, but they are, similarly as g/l, socially marginalised and discriminated against. The struggle for legal equality, individual rights, and free choice, also the freedom of sexuality, can benefit all people and the society in general.

For Greif, individual human rights are a way out of the problem of minority politics she identified as problematic at another point of the interview. Sexual freedom is a choice that benefits society beyond minority groups. Her, Coman's, and Ojala's points also imply the usefulness of a concept of consciousness-raising about sexuality as a marker of humanness, which will eventually lead to the reduction of human rights violations on grounds of sexual orientation.

A significant part of any consciousness-raising is the belief in progress: once people have been made aware of human rights violations, progress towards securing human rights can be made. This approach also carries the hope of abolishing the prejudiced belief that non-heterosexual behaviour is either sinful, sick, or a perverse crime. As Adrian Coman (e-mail interview, June 1999) said: 'On the long term, gay and lesbian people will achieve equality, respect and even the protection of public authorities in a world that becomes every day more and more politically correct.' Coman and Ojala vividly present the belief in progress as an important aspect of human rights argumentation. This belief proclaims that if human rights are taken seriously in just the way they already exist, equality, freedom, recognition, and integrity will be a logical consequence.

Within the common logic of European human rights discourse, this conclusion makes sense and presents a good political strategy. It is in principle also not far from what most lesbian and gay scholarship offers in its analysis of the situation and in its proposal for finally establishing sexual rights as human rights. The literature identifies four primary obstacles for the recognition of homosexual rights internationally. Firstly, it mentions the crisis of sexuality in the twentieth century, including the development of Western concepts of sexual identity and the fact that gay liberation has started to perturb notions of one true fixed human sexuality.[8] Secondly, it names the widespread criminal laws against homosexual acts.[9] Thirdly, there is the lack of international gay and lesbian co-ordination that is focused and coherent.[10] And, finally, it mentions the fact that so many states would block any move to acknowledge the human rights of homosexuals.[11] Most writers argue that all those obstacles can be tackled within traditional human rights discourse one way or the other, deploying concepts of equality and human nature.

Beyond those four obstacles, several steps are needed, according to the literature, to ensure homosexual rights *intrinsic* to the traditional human rights discourse. These steps are argued within a logic that does not necessarily problematise the historical principles and contexts of human rights discourse, but puts existing human rights laws and argumentation to work. Firstly, gay men and lesbians have to be rendered human, the traditional 'process of de-humanisation' – as Offord

(1997 1999a/b) calls it – has to be stopped.[12] Secondly, sexual orientation needs to be presented as a central part of human identity similar to ethnicity and gender. In this respect, the choice to live what is a clear and unchangeable part of one's human identity is declared a human right. Unchangeable status and choice become the central turning point of maintaining integrity (Wintemute 1995:17).

Thirdly, sexual rights are declared universal. Cultural relativism – such as denying the relevance of human rights in certain cultural traditions – is considered a homophobic instrument of denying the existence of people who – across cultures and eras – transgress gender or have sexual relations with people of their own sex.[13] Fourthly, equality before the law is paramount to the concept of freedom, a freedom to choose one's association freely. Equality and protection by the law cannot wait for the majority to accept homosexuals as worthy of protection; they are fundamental rights that need to be enforced by human rights instruments, such as courts, human rights conventions, and governments. Fifthly, the way forward in lobbying and filing cases would be either by arguing that sexual orientation is already part of existing human rights instruments[14] or by explicitly including sexual orientation in all new amendments.[15]

Yet, even in the twenty-first century, none of these steps is easily argued or given credibility within courtrooms and at intergovernmental meetings that decide on human rights instruments, nor can they be considered already achieved or very successful anywhere in the world. As Amnesty International, the International Lesbian and Gay Human Rights Commission, and ILGA have shown extensively, homosexuals throughout the world are more often than not demonised, killed, violated, socially excluded, and forced to lead closeted lives. Human rights statutes from America to Africa and Europe to Asia do not apply to lesbians and gay men. Northern and Western Europe is perhaps the territory with the least explicit brutality against homosexuals besides New Zealand, Australia, and Canada. Homosexuality continues to be an internationally contentious issue to the extent that so far – short of the new EU Constitution – no internationally enforceable human rights covenant includes sexual orientation and any attempt to include comprehensive rights at international assemblies has at the utmost been partially successful.[16] The international community does not generally recognise homosexual rights as a valid dimension in international human rights law (Hagland 1997:357). Yet, as I have shown, the human rights rhetoric remains the most important instrument of political change, political mobilisation, change of public opinion, and increase of self-worth among lesbian and gay activists. Hence, both the dominance of human rights discourse in European activism and the reality of terrible human rights violations of sexually or gender deviant people all over the world indicate the need for a more critical examination of the staging of human rights discourses.

There are more fundamental obstacles to the inclusion of gay men and lesbians into human rights discourse than activists and most gay and lesbian human rights literature appear to see. The main argumentative features of gay and lesbian human rights activism – the belief in progress, freedom, equality, self-worth, and respect(ability) implied in the concept of integrity, and choice in relation to sexual identity – warrant a closer analysis. After all, they are fundamentally built on human rights as rights of individuals who have a concept of humanness conferred on them. This concept of humanness is far from being natural, objective, and universal: it is a historical product that heavily relies on binary and normative structures, and, thus, presents an important field where interrogation is paramount. It is this history, I argue, that forms the actual substantial obstacle to the inclusion of non-normative sexualities and gender identities in concepts of human rights. Human rights are more complex than they might appear and some of their conditions are critical at the best of times. In fact, their conditions can be paradoxical at times, as Baden Offord (1999a:57) aptly summarises:

> From all this it can be seen that the concept of human rights is paradoxical even – at once dynamic and changing as well as monolithic and derivative. It challenges the role and meaning of the individual, community and state, what defines the human being. It is a concept that is constantly contested, deployed and utilised as much under its universalist umbrella as it is galvanised and reinterpreted by local terrain. A crucial reason why the concept of human rights is difficult is that while it brings up many important theoretical and abstract issues it also involves immediate problems demanding concrete responses that are faced by people every day in all parts of the world. The dilemma between theory and practice, therefore, is foregrounded in human rights discourse.

Interrogating human rights

There is no doubt that human rights discourse has become entrenched in the consciousness of people all over the world. There is also no doubt that human rights conventions and political rhetoric have been an important response to the immense violence and suffering inflicted along lines of race, religion, gender, sexual orientation, and disability in the twentieth century. In fact, human rights still form the dominant humanist response to the Holocaust, which is often interpreted as humanism's utter demise. Yet, humanism as well as the French and the American Revolutions are the denominators of the historical background against which the human rights discourse is pitched (Evans 1998:4).

The sovereignty of the individual – historically ascribed only to white men – to exercise power and rule is a significant base concept of humanism. Humanism invented a set of sovereignties: the soul – ruling the body, but subjected to God; consciousness – sovereign to judge, but bound to truth; the individual – titular control of personal rights, subjected to the laws of nature and society; and basic freedom (Foucault 1977:221). Human rights are shaped by the history of humanism as the philosophical foundation of Western civilisation and 'by the impact of the modern state – social isolation, order, identity, and the unending and insatiable lust for individualized profit which is the central motive of modern capitalism' (Fields and Narr 1992:52). In fact, the right to property and the exercise of power over this property is not only the base principle of capitalism, but also of the concept of citizens' participation rights after the French Revolution.[17] In the course of time, human rights discourse as well as citizenship discourse has become deeply implicated by liberal, Western democratic and capitalist ideology, and it adheres to a language of morality that has its roots in a gendered and racialised European epistemology.

To summarise the problem briefly: the central obstacle to homosexual rights as human rights rests on the Eurocentric, masculinist, heteronormative, and racialised base upon which human rights have developed.[18] What matters in this context is that human rights imply a sexualised conceptualisation of personhood connected to desire as the primary motor for identification and for rights. Political human rights discourse is strongly rooted in a liberal humanist framework of the individual endowed with intrinsic rights and coherent personhood (Peterson and Parisi 1998:138).

Mary Poovey (1992) has convincingly argued that women were not included in the construction of the liberal humanist person endowed with rights in the first place. According to her, the basic assumption of liberal humanist metaphysics is that every subject has a core that precedes social or linguistic coding. This core is the ground for a personhood that rests in the capacity to reason, the capacity to moral judgment, and agency (1992:241). Moreover, this core precedes the endowment of human rights to every human being thus constituted. However, considering, after Lacan, the constitutive character of language itself, this core of human personhood does not, in fact, precede language, but is created and institutionalised by it (Salecl 1993:463). According to feminist and queer poststructuralist thought, the continuity and coherence of the person is actually created and maintained by 'regulatory practices of gender formation' (Butler 1990:16). As Poovey (1992:242) notes: 'the appearance of a coherent "core" within the "person" is not the reflection of something essential that is really there, but merely the *effect* of a set of social institutions that differentiate between people on the basis of a binary system of coherent genders.'

According to Judith Butler (1990:145), all rules that are connected to the ability to assert an intelligible 'I' in liberal humanist discourse are fundamentally connected to gender hierarchies and compulsory heterosexuality. In addition, the concept of liberal humanist personhood – built on a differential structure of coherent gender – can only be granted to women in relation to the personhood of man (Salecl 1993:450; Peterson and Parisi 1998:132). In the course of the late nineteenth and the first half of the twentieth century, Western women gained political access to personhood only on their claims to equality and sameness to men, who were the norm in the creation of liberal humanist discourses.[19] In terms of human rights discourse, women are only able to have humanness conferred on them when they are positioned as autonomous, coherent, unified persons, in their sameness to men. 'Human rights are in actuality men's rights' (Peterson and Parisi 1998:132).

Following on from this feminist insight, it can be argued that homosexuals and bisexuals face a dilemma similar to that of women. Sexuality is deeply entrenched in the binary gender structure, which remains central to why and how heterosexuality is set up as the only natural, desirable, and morally promotable form of human sexuality. Spike Peterson and Laura Parisi (1998:141) argue that human rights discourse is predicated upon both gender hierarchies and exclusion of abnormal sexualities. To them (1998:133), human rights are based on what they call heterosexism. The normalisation and reproduction of binary gender identities are inextricable from the normalisation of heterosexism, which is inextricable from Western State making and its concomitant ideological productions, of which human rights are a significant part (1998:137).

To Peterson and Parisi (1998:142–55), rights concerning sexuality and gender are mostly privatised and, thus, remain outside the space of human rights protection in all three existing generations of rights: civil and political liberties are based on public male citizenship; economic, social and cultural rights disregard unpaid work and cultural oppression; and collective group rights discussed for the future often inscribe hierarchies as cultural rights. They (1998:145) also argue that the narrow construction of the family is a successful means of excluding homosexuals from imperatives of love and affection. Thus, kinship rules, which negate homosexuality, demonstrate 'a process of de-humanisation in relation to non-normative sexualities' (Offord 1999a:76). The binary gender structure marks out the borders and limits of what is considered natural and truly human. The invention of the idea of the human is also strongly connected to the history of rights as a process of capitalist individuation. Even attempts of producing a 'Bill of Gender Rights' that explicitly tries to mend the gendered nature of human rights in the context of transgender does not escape re-naturalisation and subordination of other rights aspect, as Antke Engel (2000) has shown in her queer reading of transgender human rights.

To reiterate, human rights are strongly rooted in a liberal humanist framework of the individual endowed with intrinsic rights and coherent personhood. They draw on a history of humanist sovereignty of the individual set against the State, which means they emerged both as protection against arbitrary abuse and as a mode of securing and naturalising dominant forms of power, such as property or the family (Foucault 1977:221–30). Rights functioned as a modality of what Foucault termed 'biopower'. Through that double manoeuvre rights discourses in the nineteenth century were also an instrument of masking the social power of institutions by de-politicising those structures that maintain inequalities and particular possibilities to violation. The process of de-politicising is a process achieved through individualisation.

Wendy Brown (1995) – drawing on a close reading of Karl Marx's essay 'On the Jewish Question' – convincingly problematises an individualisation of rights within a universalist idiom that masks precisely those structures that are maintained to exclude and negate rights, thus, re-inventing an identity that is continuously presented as injured. To Brown (1995:110), liberal rights guarantee that we will be equally abstracted from the social powers that constitute our existence and equally de-contextualised from the unequal conditions of our lives. Yet, not only do rights equally abstract, and, thus, mask, unequal relations, they also take part in forming the political individual said to precede the claiming of rights:

Marx is again underscoring how certain modalities of social and economic domination are less eliminated than *depoliticized* by the political revolutions heralding formal equality, although these modalities are transformed in the process, losing their formal representation in the state as estates. At the same time, Marx is seeking to articulate the extent to which the modern *individual* is produced by and through, indeed *as*, this depoliticization and in the image of it. He is proffering a political genealogy of the sovereign individual, whose crucial site of production is the depoliticization of social relations. (1995:112)

The historical emergence of *rights of man*, therefore, naturalises and entrenches specific social powers, which set up difference or exclusion and socially stratify individuals as members of a group (1995:113). Given that human rights claims are made to protect historically and contextually marginalised and violated identities, one needs to ask whether the universalist idiom of human rights that focuses on the individual's rights is not part and parcel of re-subordinating through re-naturalising precisely those identities it seeks to emancipate by allowing their expression.

Homosexual rights as human rights proclaim the expression of an injured identity and promise to defend individuals. They promise to give homosexuals a sphere of bodily integrity and privacy, and to announce personhood and membership in human communities. However, human rights as political practice and strategy only ask for rights without assessing how human rights operate politically in the wider culture they take part in re-creating. This would suggest that, in effect, activists who deploy human rights potentially walk into their battle unarmed since they are fighting at the wrong front. They are subjugated to the crippling effects of those forces that designate humanity and deem non-normative sexualities as unworthy of that very humanity.

Human rights as the dominant political practice in Europe need to ask after the relationship between the promise of progress and the functioning of individualisation processes that mask – via de-politicising – the historical power relations and definitions of humanness, which ensure the workings of gender, sexuality, class, and racial hierarchies. The precise working of heteronormative structures – whose abolition should, after all, be the explicit focus of lesbian and gay political practices – cannot be tackled through the emphasis on the individual's humanity. Rather, the opposite is the case: claiming human rights without questioning its recourse to individualisation masks the very structures that ensure the workings of heteronormativity. This process is visible not only in the individualist predicament and the implication of historically problematic concepts of humanness, but also in the other features upon which human rights draw that are mentioned above: freedom, equality, recognition, and integrity. Let me demonstrate this through some interview excerpts and the decision of the European Commission on Human Rights in the *Euan Sutherland* case, as an example of the dominant legal human rights discourse. *Euan Sutherland* was the first successful case on unequal age of consent.

In *Euan Sutherland* a 17-year-old British male claimed discrimination within the ECHR on the ground of the unequal age of consent for gay sex – namely 18 – in comparison with that for heterosexual and lesbian consensual sex, which is set at 16 in the UK. His case was declared admissible by the European Commission of Human Rights on 1 July 1997 under Article 8 – the right to privacy – and Article 14 – the rights to freedom from discrimination.[20] The Commission ruled that the unequal age of consent in the UK violated the Convention and offered the UK government time to change the law before the case was referred to the Court. The Labour government in Britain tried to introduce changes, but the reform was blocked in the House of Lords for years. The unequal age of consent was finally repealed in December 2000. What the judgment in *Euan Sutherland* illustrates vividly is the difficult double bind the concept of freedom – as a human rights strategy and measurement – produces:

> The Commission recalls that Article 14 of the Convention affords protection against discrimination that is, treating differently persons in relevantly similar situations without due justification... In particular, a difference of treatment is discriminatory, for the purposes of Article 14, if it 'has no objective and reasonable justification', that is if it does not pursue a 'legitimate' aim or if there is no 'reasonable relationship of proportionality between the means employed and the aim sought to be realised'. Moreover the Contracting States enjoy a certain margin of appreciation in assessing whether and to what extent differences in otherwise similar situations justify different treatment. (para. 48) ...
>
> The Commission notes that it is not contested that the applicant, as a young man of 17 years of age who wished to enter into and maintain sexual relations with a male friend of the same age, was in a 'relevantly similar situation' to a young man of the same age who wished to enter into and maintain sexual relations with a female friend of the same age. (para. 52)
>
> ... the Commission is unable to accept that it is a proportionate response to the need for protection to expose to criminal sanctions not only the older man who engages in homosexual acts with a person under the age of 18 but the young man himself who is claimed to be in need of such protection. (para. 64)
>
> As to the second ground relied on – society's claimed entitlement to indicate disapproval of homosexual conduct and its preference for a heterosexual lifestyle – the Commission cannot constitute an objective or reasonable justification for inequality of treatment under the criminal law. (para.65)

Freedom figures most centrally in human rights language. The ECHR's proper name is the Convention for the Protection of Human Rights and Fundamental Freedoms. Wherever human rights are argued by ILGA-Europe, freedom – usually freedom from discrimination – is the issue around which the argument revolves. Freedom, in this respect, may take one of two forms: a) a positive freedom *to do* something, for example, freedom to marry or pursue one's own happiness, and b) a negative freedom as freedom *from* something, most prominently from discrimination on various grounds. Both forms of freedom are debated in the excerpts quoted above: the freedom to engage in homosexual acts at the age of 17 and the freedom from criminal persecution. The right to freedom is granted in principle, yet not actually conferred onto the identity that is violated. Homosexual identity is not mentioned as worthy of protection *per se*.

Three questions bind themselves to both parts of freedom. Firstly, the court considers whether enough similarity to heterosexuals can be established that defies the need for protection against harmful sexual acts. Secondly, the court discusses whether there exists a justification for punishing those who are said to be in need of protection. And thirdly, the court reflects on whether society's view on homosexuality can, in the 1990s, still justify discrimination in the name of protecting morals. However, Euan Sutherland's freedom to act and his freedom from criminal persecution remain two different issues. Criminal persecution is regarded as against human rights, i.e. the right to privacy is now considered higher than the State's right to protect morals. Yet, that does not imply the freedom to sexual choice as a fundamental aspect of what makes Euan Sutherland a human, a person endowed with rights. His right to act homosexually is not directly affirmed, only the similarity to heterosexual acts at age 17.

Homosexuality is not a central marker of Euan Sutherland's humanness. The court defines it only as an aspect of his right to private life and no longer regards homosexuality as a justification of inequality in criminal law. Yet, homosexuality is not considered an intrinsic marker of the personhood that precedes personal freedom. It is not Sutherland's sexual humanness that is protected. In fact, sexual freedom remains disconnected from personal freedom. This means that what constitutes a person in principle is above (or beneath?) her or his sexuality. Sex, or better the rights to engage in sexual relations of one's choice, is not a crucial aspect of personhood, of that which renders us human it is a secondary aspect to be respected, but not centralised.

This split between sexual freedom and personal freedom is an important aspect of the way in which human rights strategies mask and de-politicise the centrality of sexuality and gender. Activists who utilise human rights discourse surely do not deny the importance of sexuality as a marker of whether or not a person is allowed to have rights or make equal choices. Yet, to make sense in courtrooms, the personal freedom of the individual is often stressed more since it fits into the concept of personhood, which underpins human rights discourse. Marion Oprel (February 1998) – co-president of EGALITE – formulates this succinctly: 'I fully agree that sexual rights are human rights ... Personally I vote for personal freedom as a strategy ... Individual freedom is higher on my list of priorities than sexual freedom'. One could interpret Oprel's move as a strategy to render sexuality unimportant for the definition of humanness that would imply sameness and equality between heterosexuals and homosexuals.

However, even interpreted as such, this strategy perpetuates an illusion. It perpetuates the illusion that equality of all humans can be achieved irrespective of gender and sexuality all the while ignoring the centrality that gender and sexuality have in the historical development of human rights discourses. It is this illusion that continues to deny freedom and equality to those who are considered outside the norm, whose choices and acts are not accepted as a human right even if they are protected from harsh discrimination. The concept of freedom in dominant European human rights discourse remains a freedom fraught with inequality and with a hierarchised norm that precedes the formation of any human status. In consequence, the concept of equality that is linked to that kind of freedom remains at the most equality in spite of difference.

Freedom from discrimination is predominantly considered an issue of equality. In fact, equality ranges on the same level as freedom. Kurt Krickler (February 1998) – Co-Chair of ILGA-Europe – combines equality with discrimination in talking about human rights: 'For me human rights are a question of equality, they are central in anti-discrimination.' In this logic, equality needs anti-discrimination measures to be achieved as more or less simple strategies to counter the actual lived inequality produced by normative structures in societies. Thus, equality in human rights emphasises inclusion into legal rights and privileges. Hannele Lehtikuusi (e-mail interview, July 1998) – Finnish ILGA-Europe activist – for example, combines equality with freedom and with the relationship of the individual to the state and citizenship in society:

> The question is in the field of ethics. Equal treatment of citizens is a human right – as I understand the responsibilities of a modern state. If all citizens are equal, sexual orientation is not a character that should make a person unequal – the state has to take care of its citizens' rights and protect this principle as firmly as any other human right issue.

Here the language of democracy and citizenship gains entry into human rights discourse. Civil rights are simply declared human rights, a matter of participation in a modern state. The concept of equality in human rights connects states' responsibilities towards their citizens with the transnational idiom 'all human rights for all human people'. Equality in human rights rhetoric calls on the history of the human subject in relation to the state and on citizens' rights. This history is a history of comparisons.

As stated above, it has been widely argued by feminists that women only gained the right to vote by proving their sameness to men. In the claim to equality in human rights such history of comparison continues to take effect as a comparison of the homosexual minority to the assumed heterosexual majority that grants rights of inclusion. The European Human Rights Commission in *Euan Sutherland* did not consider the right of society to hold negative views against homosexuals a justifiable reason for unequal legal treatment. Yet, the justifiability of those views in principle is not tackled. 'Society' in the excerpt of the judgment above remains an assumed heterosexual formation that can grant equality to those who are different if – and only if – they can prove enough *human sameness*.

The call for equality participates in an historical circle of substituting actual lived inequalities with abstract representative identities, abstract conceptual subjects said to be formally free and equal human beings. In fact, calling for equality is a process of abstraction. It declares the subject equal – a free human being – and abstracts that formal equality from the power structures that create the inequality and the subject in the first place. In the process of abstraction, the concept of equality re-subordinates precisely those it is said to liberate through an idealist disavowal of the discursive structures and material constituents of humanness that constrain freedom and equality (Brown 1995:106). Without breaking the circle of individualisation that solicits a de-politicisation of hierarchised structures – which, in turn, ground the *raison d'être* of powerful exclusionary institutions such as the family and of the right of states to govern, legislate and deploy force – equality in human rights discourse remains ambiguous for l/g/b/t politics. The universality of the modern state, heralded as the guarantor of equality in Lehtikuusi's ideal of human rights, is premised upon that which it pretends to transcend and requires the maintenance of that which human rights strategies seek to abolish. Equality granted by the modern state is blinded by what much of post-Marxist and feminist research on the state has identified as problematic: the state is invested in maintaining and stratifying – via naturalising – social and economic powers. Modern states legitimise themselves as neutral and universal representative of people, thereby disguising the actual powers that are constitutive of civil society and the state.[21]

Granting human rights, fundamental rights, and citizenship rights was – among other things – a historical process of legitimising the sovereignty of states after the natural order of kings was rejected in favour of a new order in which people are sovereign through democratic citizenship. The authority of civil governments from then on depended on the moral claims to securing human rights besides defining modern citizenship rights. In fact the legal systems of modern European states are pitched against the background of a fundamental rights catalogue that adheres to the ideology of human rights. Therefore, the human rights discourse ranges among the most respectable political strategies available in European political culture. Human rights discourse presents a recognition that seemingly not only assures rights, but will also help to support self-worth and respect for individuals. Recognition and self-worth feature in political practices around human rights besides equality and freedom. Peter Ashman (May 1998) – founding member of ILGA, lawyer, and Director of the European Human Rights Foundation – connects human rights to recognition by society as well as to equality and integrity:

> There was this perspective that people are basically behaving in a criminal way, leading illegal as well as immoral lifestyles. And this had all sorts of knock-on effects on the way of life, culture, work ... Once that had gone, once there was equality then people would have the confidence to express themselves to live their lives, not to worry about losing their jobs ... Society's attitude would, hmm, I don't say would change, from negative to positive or something, but the institutional negativity would go ... Law influences the way people see their lives ... once you conceive that people have rights, of course, then rights are, well, human rights in particular they are indivisible, so if you are entitled to one lot of rights as a human being then you are entitled to the lot. And that includes not being discriminated against. There is sort of a relentless logic about that which people are loath to accept, but which you then have to keep pushing for.

Ashman emphasises a common human rights logic, which seems to be supported by historical development. For example, he explains that while police forces all over Europe used to raid gay bars, nowadays most of them offer protection schemes for lesbians and gay men. The right to bodily integrity is seen as the factor that changed the attitude of police forces. Human rights – or legal rights in general – do not radically change society according to Ashman, but they influence the sense of self-worth individuals can develop. Society is changed as a consequence of more proud self-assertion of gay men and lesbians. Yet again, rights are accrued by virtue of being human; if one is granted one set of rights one should gain the lot since they are indivisible. The rise in recognition and self-worth does not imply that sexual choices are considered any more natural than they were before. What changes is the broadening of the circle of those that can be argued into the category 'human', including their allegedly abnormal sexual preference. The definition of the category 'human' itself, however, remains intact in principle. Yet, human rights discourse not only promotes self-worth, it also grants respectability and acceptance, which belong to the process of recognition.

Hein Verkerk (May 1998) – Dutch activist and employee of the European Parliament – centralises the human rights rhetoric as a rhetoric of respectability:[22]

> Raising it as a human rights issue is part of that demand for respect and respectability of people, human rights is almost a world wide consensus and raising the gay lesbian issue as a human rights issue – which I think it is – has to do with the fact that the gay/lesbian community wants to be, wants to have some respectability. In that sense it is useful to raise it as human rights.

Verkerk's mention of respectability in the context of political practices based on human rights brings an important aspect into sight. Human rights are respectable, they are accepted by most politicians as valid and they confer respectability upon those who are officially acknowledged to have suffered from human rights violations. Respectability serves as a focal point of what is deemed successful in lobby politics. What is respectable in political culture is pivotal in the selection of strategies. The more closely a political association is connected to the impartiality of human rights, the greater becomes its clout of political influence and public respect. Yet, the connection of respectability and homosexuality is – even at the best of times – unstable.

Organisations such as Amnesty International (AI) enjoy a reputation for impartiality. They refer to human rights as a focus on the principle of protection from fundamental violations of human dignity above political partiality. How important a sense of respectability is in AI's understanding of itself is mirrored in the endless internal debate on whether homosexuality can be properly included in AI's mandate. AI only officially integrated sexual orientation work into its research, campaigns, actions, and publications in 1997 after a decade of being lobbied. Yet, it could not change its statute for years since homosexuality was considered too contentious internationally and, thus, potentially threatening AI's respectability and integrity and, therefore, its livelihood.[23]

The internal debate of Amnesty International highlights two aspects of respectability. On the one hand it emphasises how respectability is a pivotal measure for what political arguments are acceptable. On the other hand the AI debate highlights that homosexuality is fundamentally at odds with respectability. The focus on human rights is strongly linked to its high respectability in mainstream society in Europe. In short, it seems that if one can argue sexual orientation as a fundamental human right, that argument raises the hope of 'no defeat possible', since who can defy human rights in Europe? Yet the sense of moral respectability that the official recognition of human rights violations entails also perpetuates norms of respectability. While homosexuality might be protected from discrimination, it will surely never enter the pantheon of those sexual choices that are considered be on a moral high ground and a part of European culture.

Human rights are bound to European historical conditions in which gender and sexuality function in a heteronormative way. Since every norm needs to exclude its opposite in order to set up and maintain itself as the norm, homosexuality will have to remain non-normative. Thus, the respectability of human rights creates a paradox in relation to homosexuality. While human rights assure a sense of self-worth and integrity for the gay and lesbian subject and communities, they are also part and parcel of the political culture that continues to stigmatise homosexuality. The respectability of homosexual rights as human rights – emphasised by Hein Verkerk – is bought at the price of gaining inclusion without challenging the structures that produce and maintain exclusion. What is considered truly human will never truly include homosexuality, although all human rights treaties might indeed one day protect sexual orientation.

Beyond this paradox, the issue of respectability complicates human rights even further. Self-respect, respectability, and integrity through human rights rest on the assumption that a sense of self can only be acquired via recognition by others. If human rights are quite centrally about the means of survival, then it is the recognition of one's rights by others that makes survival possible.[24] In the human rights discourse, social survival is guaranteed by the access to choices in the pursuit of happiness and by the access to self-worth and integrity. Peter Ashman (May 1998) formulates this pointedly: 'It [human rights] includes the idea to express, to seek happiness and that includes sexual happiness in love ... this argument was bought by the European Court of Human Rights.' Yet the pursuit of happiness presumes a certain subjectivity and the capability and permission to speak a coherent 'I'. In relation to sexuality, this subjectivity has in the past hundred years been channelled by sexual identity, i.e. the possibility of appellation into being a homosexual and expressing a sense of self in the label 'gay' or 'lesbian'. Respectability is gained through yet another affirmation of fixed identity.

European human rights lobbying entails the fight for recognition of discrimination based on sexual orientation, as Outi Ojala emphasises, and for recognition as the means of creating and maintaining a sense of self and self-worth, as Peter Ashman and Hein Verkerk elaborate. This entails two assumptions: on the one hand sexual orientation and lesbian and gay identities are equated. Sexual orientation – basically a description of sexual object choice and sexual act – thus becomes the sign of an identity immediately followed by a shared legal, social, and economic discrimination. Identity is once more rooted in the seemingly natural body and its desires. In consequence, human rights are more often than not based on *who we are* rather than on *what we do*. On the other hand, human rights rhetoric claims that difference should not matter: equal rights for all. Human rights are a strategy that not only respect diversity, but potentially declare it a human principle (Offord 1999a).

At first, it seems that diversity as human principle refutes stable identity markers; identity politics seems less prominent in transnational human rights centred contexts than in national civil rights centred contexts. Human rights discourses do not seem to need concepts of stable gay identity, since they offer humanness as the base upon which rights are claimed. Adrian Coman (e-mail interview, June 1999), for example, answers to a question about the importance of identity in politics that it is not the political sphere, which creates a necessity for identity, but the quest for community and subculture. The ultimate aim in politics would be to render identity unnecessary, because a general human identity is accepted to apply to homosexuals too. Specific mention of homosexual identity in politics is a necessary evil with an expiry date imprinted on it:

> The quest for a gay and lesbian culture/subculture, therefore for a gay and lesbian identity, is incredibly increasing. It has almost become an aim in itself. I think that the concept of a 'human identity' should first be brought into both politics and in our lives with less hypocrisy. If that works, we may NOT need to refer to particular groups.

In Adrian Coman's human rights argumentation one would, thus, presumably find humanness as the decisive factor that qualifies access to rights. Gay identity is not considered stable and the belief 'that most of the minorities have diversity and multiplicity inside of them' – as Hannele Lehtikuusi (e-mail interview, July 1998) formulates it – is clearly a part of human rights argumentation launched by European gay and lesbian activists. Yet, to reach the political aim of equality it seems necessary and unavoidable to present homosexual identity as an aspect of humanness. A 'human identity without hypocrisy' is an identity upon which fundamental rights of survival can be based. These fundamental rights include rights of sexual choice and *then* homosexuals will eventually cease to be a specific group since their personal and community integrity is secured. There will clearly be no freedom, equality, or recognition without first ensuring the personal, physical, and psychological integrity of lesbians and gay men.

Integrity in human rights, consequently, demands that homosexuality is respected as a true, whole, and valid form of human sexuality for every individual and in all social relations in which people interact. The principle of integrity affirms the possibility of finding one's true sexual identity behind one's human identity. Gaining integrity *burdens* people with an identity in granting the chance to demarcate personal and community spaces as part of the legitimate human territory.[25]

Humanness, thus, becomes in itself an identity category, something composed of diverse human choices and relations, which are bounded by the territory of humanity. In human rights rhetoric, humanness forms the basis for any recognition of an 'I', it presents the psychic and social possibility of relations with others, and it describes commonalities in species, character, and value among all humans. Any rights that have historically been built upon shared human identity are a consequence of designating the definitional category humanity. Yet, humanity is a composite territory, fecund in meaning, and contestable vis-à-vis history and context.

Conclusion

Through its firm connection to the concept of individuated humanness, the dominant European human rights discourse is based on and maintains historical exclusion of gay men and lesbians. Human rights discourse presents major stumbling stones on the way to establishing fundamental rights for non-normative sexualities. This conclusion would seem to suggest that human rights strategies are only a problematic form of identity politics yet again, too paradoxical to promise significant change. That is, however, not the point at which my critical analysis of human rights discourse is aiming. Rather, I want to suggest an active deployment of the composite, fecund, and contestable character of any politically invoked concept of humanity. This would imply consciously burdening non-normative sexualities with a human identity, i.e. letting go of the idea of sexual identity as liberation and recognising human identity as a very temporary political strategy. A strategy that is intelligible in institutional political discourse, but that needs to be positioned as a means to an end.

Political practices that deploy human rights in that sense make explicit rather than implicit the reliance on the problematic history of humanity, freedom, equality, recognition, respectability, and integrity. That history is interpreted as something that does not liberate but burdens those who suffer most under human rights violation in the world: women, l/g/b/t people, and ethnically or racially persecuted groups. The equality and the freedom European human rights statutes hopefully grant in the near future can be a positive change in the daily living conditions of millions of people in Europe. Yet, the only territory truly negotiated in human rights discourse is the territory of humanity. The way activists position themselves in relation to this territory is already differentiated, but ought to be made more explicit. For as long as the stakes of humanity are not openly designated as the territory of negotiation, human rights will continue to burden those they actually seek to liberate.

Notes

1 See Bischoff (1994), Jacobs *et al.* (1992), and Weidenfeld and Jung (1994) for further elaboration on this history.
2 See for this the websites of the EU on citizens' rights (www.europa.eu.int/abc/cit1-en.htm) and the Council of Europe (www.coe.fr/eng/present/index.htm).

3 For example, 1994 (A4-0223/96), 1995 (A4-0112/97), 1996(A4-0034/98), 1997 (A4-0468/98), 1998-99 (A5-0050/2000) and continuously since then.
4 In the response to the question, which areas of discrimination are of most concern to them, legal equality was nearly always at the top of the list and equality was – with very few exceptions – connected to basic issues of human rights.
5 The widespread use and impact of human rights instruments and argumentation for sexual orientation – or rather the limited success of these instruments – have been widely analysed in different cultural, national, and global contexts. See, for example, Hagland (1997), Heinze (1995), Garkawe (1997), Offord (1997, 1999a, 1999b), Offord and Cantrell (1999), Morgan (1995), Richards 1988, LaViolette and Whitworth (1994), LaViolette (1997), and Wintemute (1995, 1996).
6 The latter formulation was also used in ILGA-Europe's submission towards the EU Human Rights Agenda in the year 2000.
7 He did this in the face of several Asian countries expressing their rejection of Western human rights that place preference on the individual above the community.
8 See Morgan (1995, 1996), La Violette and Whitworth (1994).
9 See the comprehensive country overview on ILGA-World's website (www.ilga.org).
10 See Sanders (1993).
11 See Sanders (1993), Wintemute (1995), and Heinze (1995).
12 Offord refers to the fact that homosexuality is mostly declared an unacceptable dimension of humanity as a process of de-humanisation. He argues (1999a:72-7) comprehensively that human rights discourse reveals a stark omission of and silence on homosexuality. Homosexuals are deviant to the degree that their homosexuality is not considered properly human but a perverse diversion. Bunch (1995:12) develops a similar argument in relation to lesbians. She maintains that any exclusion of any group, on whatever grounds, always involves cultural definitions of that group as less than fully human.
13 In the course of the 1990s an increasing number of the so-called Asian tiger states – those with growing economic power – voiced their distance from international human rights invoking the fundamental difference of Asian culture that values the need of the community above the need of the individual. For further elaboration on a quite extensive academic debate on cultural relativism in gay and lesbian studies, see Altman (1997), Heinze (1995), Garkawe (1997), and Offord (1999a).
14 This fact was established in the 31 March 1994 decision of the United Nations Human Rights Committee in *Toonen v. Australia* (UNHR Committee Doc. No. CCPR/C/50/D/488/1992) para. 8.1, when it decided that sexual orientation discrimination was included in the meaning of discrimination on grounds of sex in Article 26 of that Convention.
15 See Robert Wintemute (1996) and Eric Heinze (1995). Both arguments have their merits. I will argue in Chapter 6, however, that the inclusion of sexual orientation discrimination under sex discrimination is preferable from a queer point of view. ILGA-Europe has decided to move forward via arguing for a specific mentioning of sexual orientation and gender identity in all forthcoming treaties and laws.
16 The difficulty of debating issues of rights internationally was vividly shown at the Beijing world women's conference, where women's sexual rights were excluded. See Charlotte Bunch and Susan Fried (1996) for an assessment of the Beijing process. However, in 2003 Brasil introduced a UN resolution entitled 'Human Rights and sexual orientation' (E/CN.4/2003/L.92) which has so far been blocked in the Assembly, because Spain pulled out of an alliance for favourable states. If ever adopted, it will be a milestone in the international human rights field.

17 This is a point originally emphasised by Karl Marx ([1843]1969) in his essay 'On the Jewish Question'. He ([1843]1969:366) called human rights the rights of the bourgeois private property owners. Civil rights are to him the means of the political state for maintaining human rights within the bourgeois society.
18 This has been argued by Bunch (1995), Flynn (1996), Offord and Cantrell (1999), Offord (1999a and 1999b), Peterson and Parisi (1998), Poovey (1992), and Stychin (1998). The issue of Eurocentrism and racial foundations of rights concepts will be part of Chapter 7's discussion of citizenship. Stychin (1998) gives a convincing account of both issues in relation to nationalism, rights, and homosexuality.
19 There exists an extensive body of feminist literature on this statement. See, for an overview over the feminist reasoning behind this statement, Bunch (1995), Peterson and Parisi (1998), and Salecl (1993).
20 Article 8 of the ECHR reads: 'Everyone has the right to respect for his [sic] private and family life, his home and his correspondence. There shall be no interference by a public authority with the exercise of this right except such as is in accordance with the law and is necessary in a democratic society in the interest of national security, public safety, or the economic well-being of the country, for the prevention of disorder or crime, for the protection of health or morals, or for the protection of the rights and freedoms of others.' Article 14 of the ECHR is no prohibition of discrimination *per se*, but simply refers to discrimination with regard to the enjoyments of other rights guaranteed in the ECHR. It reads: 'The enjoyment of the rights and freedoms set forth in this Convention shall be secured without discrimination on any grounds such as sex, race, colour, language, religion, political or other opinion, national or social origin, association with a national minority, property, birth or other status.'
21 See Armstrong (1992), DuPlessis (1992), and Pringle and Watson (1992) for a more elaborated explanation of this thought.
22 Asked what the most successful strategies are, though, Verkerk contended that human rights are not the most central argumentation. To him, simple everyday matters of administration, employment laws etc. matter and go beyond the more principled argument of human rights. He, thus, decentralised human rights discourse just after centralising it in the context of how basic rights are argued.
23 Capetown ICM 12–19 December 1997. The gay and lesbian workgroups of AI had already collected extensive material between 1991 and 1997. See AI press release of 18 December 1997 and the lobby campaigns started by the International Lesbian and Gay Human Rights Commission in 1998. See also Queer Planet. 17 March 1998.
24 The process of recognition is an interesting aspect that could be analysed further here. I will, however, pick up the concept of recognition in relation to citizenship in Chapter 7.
25 To describe gay identity in human rights as a necessary burden is an idea of Offord (1999a).

5 Claiming protection: anti-discrimination

> It is said that human conditions do not exist until they are named: but they are not named until they are noticed, and they are hardly ever noticed until their existence becomes a matter of concern, of active search and creative/ defensive efforts.
>
> (Zygmunt Baumann 1996:49)

> If rights thus codify even as they may slightly mitigate certain modalities of subordination or exclusion, it behoves radical democrats not simply to proliferate rights but to explore the historically and culturally specific ground of the demand for them.
>
> (Wendy Brown 1995:12)

The previous chapter illustrated human rights as composite and contestable territory. The apparent objectivity and universal applicability of human rights was challenged and human rights argumentation in lesbian and gay rights struggles put to the test of its own premises. One central aspect of the claim for human rights is freedom from discrimination. Throughout the world, marginalised groups base their claim to rights on their effort to render the harsh discrimination against them visible and to obtain protection against such discrimination. Therefore, the demand for anti-discrimination legislation is a crucial part of rights struggles. It is a part of rights struggles that is generally acceptable even to those critical of mainstream rights politics. The implications of anti-discrimination discourse are taken for granted and are rarely analysed. In fact, anti-discrimination claims are probably the only rights claims that have not been substantially deconstructed by queer theorists so far. In the following, I will offer a theoretically and politically critical reflection on speaking about discrimination and on the discourse of anti-discrimination legislation as a tool to combat violations, injustice, and threats.

Rights have historically been distinguished into civil, political, and social rights. Civil rights are commonly understood to mean liberal negative rights that protect the private legal subject against illegal infringement of the state on her or his individual freedom and property. Political rights historically refer to the rights of political participation that enable the active citizen to take part in the democratic processes of opinion and will formation, and social rights secure for the client of the welfare state a minimum of social security (Habermas 1992:10). On a structural level, rights can be divided into two types: firstly, negative rights as freedom *from* something – for example persecution – establishing inhibitions of official powers and prerogatives; secondly, positive rights as freedom *to do or have* something – for example the right to marry or to adopt.

In a political context strongly attached to human rights discourses; both structural forms are central. Considering the fact that human rights were a historical response to the modern power of states and to horrific events such as genocide, the attempt to protect the individual against society and the state – and, thus, to secure his or her negative rights – is more significant. Human rights present minimum guarantees of basic personal dignity and are essential guarantees of individual autonomy (Donelly 1984:417). Besides a set of individual protection rights – such as the right to life, liberty, and integrity of the person – it has historically been important to ensure equality irrespective of status and identities – such as race, gender, religion, age, disability and now sometimes sexual orientation and gender identity. These negative rights function as *a protection from* infringement and have politically been more widely accepted as inalienable and universal than most positive rights have been. Historically, freedom from discrimination has been established more quickly than any right to act differently from the norm.

Anti-discrimination rights as a shield against abuse are among the first minority rights to be established within the European Union. The importance of anti-discrimination was established for the first time in the 1994 White Paper on Social Policy, which recognised that the EU could not achieve its aim of integration, common market, and freedom of movement without providing a guarantee for people against fear of discrimination. The Treaty of Maastricht (1993) prepared the ground for a formal decision on this and the Treaty of Amsterdam (1999) finally ensured anti-discrimination for the first time through Article 13 TEC. Indeed, the largest success of European NGOs concerned with minority rights lobbying has been the establishment of precisely this Article 13 through the Amsterdam Treaty. An Employment Directive covering sexual orientation was formally adopted in October 2000. Additionally, Article 21 of the Charter of Fundamental Rights signed in December 2000 promises to grant a more far-reaching anti-discrimination prohibition, and the draft Constitution of July 2003 adds anti-discrimination to the objectives of Union and a horizontal article relating to the policies of the Union.[1]

This chapter begins with a reading of the legal consequences of the first successful inclusion of sexual orientation into an international Treaty's anti-discrimination section by the Treaty of Amsterdam, which came into force on 1 May 1999: the Council Directive establishing a general Framework for equal treatment in employment and occupation (2000/78/EC). I will critically examine the legal conditions of the drafting process of the Directive and point to the intrinsic problems of discrimination rights for gay men and lesbians apparent in this Directive. This is followed by an examination of the way in which ILGA-Europe speaks about discrimination and, thus, politically materialises and utilises the situation of lesbians and gay men in Europe.[2] I draw out the themes and concepts upon which anti-discrimination as a political practice is based and argue why anti-discrimination is tainted with many implicit problems. Those problems will be addressed in a more philosophical manner in Part III, which ends with a reflection on the theoretical and political demands this analysis bequests on future political argumentation for anti-discrimination legislation.

Article 13 and the Framework Directive: an example of anti-discrimination legislation

Since the mid-1990s the EU institutions have developed some dynamism with respect to anti-discrimination. Many NGOs, supported by the European Parliament, lobbied for years to extend the existing anti-discrimination focus on sex and nationality. Finally, in 1997, in the Amsterdam Treaty, the Member States agreed to amend the Treaty of the European Community, with Article 13 stating:

> Without prejudice to the other provisions of this Treaty and within the limits of the powers conferred by it upon the Community, the Council, acting unanimously on a proposal from the Commission and after consulting the European Parliament, may take appropriate action to combat discrimination based on sex, racial or ethnic origin, religion or belief, disability, age or sexual orientation.

This rather weak formulation was nevertheless celebrated as a victory by NGOs and the Commission acted on the momentum faster than is usual.[3] In April 1998 it announced the launch of a broad debate on the use of Article 13 in its Social Action Programme 1998-2000. At the Second European Social Policy Forum in June 1998 considerable pressure was exerted on DG v. – the directorate general responsible for social affairs – by individual NGOs, the Platform of European Social NGOs, and the European Trade Union Confederation (ETUC). The Commission then launched a consultation conference in Vienna, in December 1998; culminating in the publication of the Commission's anti-discrimination package on 25 November 1999.

This package was characterised by three central elements. First, a 'proposal for a Council Directive establishing a general Framework for equal treatment in employment and occupation'.[4] This Directive prohibits employment discrimination on the grounds of racial or ethnic origin, religion or belief, age, disability or sexual orientation. Second, a 'proposal for a Council Directive implementing equal treatment between persons irrespective of racial or ethnic origin'.[5] This Directive has the objective of prohibiting racial discrimination in employment, social protection, education and access to goods and services. And third, a 'proposal for a Council Decision establishing a Community Action Programme to combat discrimination, 2001–2006'.[6] This action programme seeks to combat discrimination on grounds of racial or ethnic origin, religion or belief, age, disability or sexual orientation through non-legislative avenues. In particular, funding was provided for activities to develop understanding of issues related to discrimination, to promote exchange of information and good practice, and to 'disseminate the values and practices underlying the fight against discrimination'.[7] The reduction to employment for all forms of discrimination apart from race and ethnicity was heavily criticised by NGOs, the European Parliament, and the Committee of the Regions of Europe. Yet, the Council of Ministers adopted the 'Race Directive' in June 2000 (2000/43/EC) and the 'Employment Directive' (2000/78/EC) as well as the 'Action Programme' in November 2000 without taking this critique into consideration.

In the following I will scrutinise the Employment Directive in its relevance to sexual orientation.[8] I also use parts of the draft published by the Commission since it contains an explanatory section, written by the Commission, justifying the proposal to the Council and these explanations are at times relevant to understand the current logic behind anti-discrimination legislation in the EU.

The actual effect of this Directive will only become apparent once implementation in Members States and Accession Countries is complete. Most have only started the process, waiting until the last moment to implement, and it is very likely that a decisive number of states will not have implemented the Directive by the end of 2003. Some countries will go further than stipulated in both the Framework and the Race Directive, for example Belgium, Denmark, and the Netherlands, but some include exclusion rules for sexual orientation, for example the UK and Italy, the latter being particularly homophobic, or indeed exclude sexual orientation altogether from the planned laws, such as Cyprus, Bulgaria, Slovakia. The final results can only be assessed after the deadline and after the Commission's final assessment of implementation. ILGA-Europe keeps a regularly updated overview on its website. The Directive covers third country nationals in terms of discrimination in employment, but explicitly excludes discrimination on grounds of nationality, as well as entry, residence, and access to employment rules for third country nationals in the Member States. What is of interest with respect to the theoretical discussion in this chapter, however, is the definition of discrimination that forms an integral part of the Directive.

Article 1 of the Directive states that the Directive shall help putting into effect the principle of equal treatment by combating discrimination on the 'grounds of racial or ethnic origin, religion or belief, disability, age or sexual orientation'. There is no further definition provided for any of the grounds in the draft of the Commission, but, in its commentary on Article 1, the Commission's draft Directive states that 'a clear dividing line should be drawn between sexual orientation, which is covered by this proposal, and sexual behaviour which is not'.[9] The most likely explanation for this commentary is to assume a concern that a ban on sexual orientation discrimination could extend to cover all forms of sexual behaviour, most notably sexual abuse. This concern is worrisome since nothing in the Directive calls into question criminal law, which clearly and rightly penalises sexual abuse. No anti-discrimination legislation could, thus, truly cover a criminal offence without abolishing it. It seems as if this is another instance where perceived public opinion was taken into account as a precautionary measure against a non-existing ghost: the traditional connection between paedophilia and gay male sexuality.[10] The formulation is, thus, potentially open to a homophobic interpretation during the implementation process, since the EU process that leads to a Directive is not always disregarded implementation.

More to the point, though, the formulation insists on naming a necessary lesbian or gay identity. It refers to sexual orientation rather than merely to sexual behaviour as a pre-condition for access to protection. Sexual orientation is equated with an identity. The term becomes a clear marker of personality, an unchangeable aspect of a person's character, rather than a chosen behaviour that does not necessarily materialise an identity. In consequence it will presumably be difficult to obtain protection if a person does not proclaim a firm sexual orientation for himself or herself, but rather the right to sexual choices. Indeed some planned national laws, such as those in Germany, are planning to use the term 'sexual identity', which makes matters even worse by mixing sexual orientation, gender identity, and gender. Here is a clear instance of the legal proliferation of fixed minority identities, which, in turn, make equality a critical concept as was argued in the previous chapter. The issue of sexual orientation as gay and lesbian identity as a distinctive marker of difference permeates the whole Directive.

The Directive sets out to define unlawful discrimination in three dimensions: direct discrimination, indirect discrimination, and harassment. Article 2(2)(a) states 'direct discrimination shall be taken to occur where one person is treated less favourably than another is, has been or would be treated in a comparable situation, on any of the grounds referred to in Art. 1'. In practice, this formulation will mean that the establishment of sexual orientation discrimination requires a comparison between the treatment of gay men, bisexuals; or lesbians, and the treatment accorded to heterosexuals. There is no provision for a distinction between sexual orientation and homosexual or bisexual identity. The Directive stipulates two exceptions to this total ban on direct discrimination: genuine occupational requirements and positive action schemes.[11] The former allows religious employers to discriminate on grounds of religion and against gay men, bisexuals, and lesbians. The latter is meant to allow affirmative action to take place.

Indirect discrimination is defined in Article 2(2)(b) of the Directive, which states:

> indirect discrimination shall be taken to occur where an apparently neutral provision, criterion or practice would put persons having a particular religion or belief, a particular disability, a particular age, or a particular sexual orientation at a particular disadvantage compared with other persons unless: (i) that provision, criterion or practice is objectively justified by a legitimate aim and the means of achieving that aim are appropriate and necessary, or ...'[12]

This is progressive in comparison with the 1976 Directive on gender discrimination that demands proof of a substantially higher proportion of women or men to be affected and, thus, involves the necessity of statistical data, which would be highly contentious in the case of sexual orientation at the best of times. Here the onus is only to prove that something is liable to adversely affect a person. The draft still contained a reference to groups of persons which extended the scope slightly to protection of a group to which a person can be ascribed or to which s/he ascribes herself or himself (Bell 2001:7)[13]. Additionally, the Directive proposes a ban on harassment, which it also defines broadly.

'Harassment, according to Article 2(3), is behaviour 'with the purpose or effect of violating the dignity of a person and of creating an intimidating, hostile, degrading, humiliating or offensive environment'. This could imply that not only direct harassment – such as promotion in exchange for sexual favours – will be potentially in breach of the Directive, but any behaviour which damages the working environment (Bell 2001:8). Legally speaking, this is a strong article, but with regard to sexual orientation it contains a glitch: what are the standards used to determine whether certain actions create a hostile environment? It is to be expected that courts will draw on the standards a so-called reasonable person would be likely to have rather than on the perception of the victim (Bell 2001:8).

The Directive does meet several of the central NGO demands voiced during the lobby campaign in the section on enforcement and in the final provisions. Firstly NGOs' legal standing to bring cases on behalf of a complainant, with the latter's approval (Art. 9(2)). In practical terms, this can allow lesbian and gay organisations to act legally on behalf of an individual victim of discrimination. It also permits trade unions to represent individuals in discrimination cases. Article 14 additionally establishes dialogue with NGOs to promote the principle of equal treatment. Secondly, the Directive includes a provision for a shift in the burden of proof where the complainant establishes 'facts from which it may be presumed that there has been direct or indirect discrimination' (Art. 10(1)). And thirdly, victimisation of complainants is forbidden (Art. 11) and the penalties for violations of the Directive must be 'effective, proportionate and dissuasive' (Art. 17). The provisions of enforcement are promising and take into account the difficulties of individuals with respect to carrying a complaint through to courts. To a large extent, they cover the demands made by NGOs.

The problems I have raised so far could have been accounted for in a re-drafting of the Directive or will be accounted for in a progressive development in the judgments to come. What is of theoretical and political interest beyond this point, however, is to ask another series of questions: questions that relate to the principle nature of anti-discrimination rights within a political field in which the juridical is a hegemonic and definitional site of equality, politics, rights, and difference. The Employment Directive is a result of many years of lobby work and a change in political climate. To understand the problems of this first pan-European result, the language of discrimination employed by activists has to be scrutinised further.

Speaking about discrimination: implicit problems

On Wednesday, 26 January 2000, parliamentarians from across Europe voted to recommend that sexual orientation be added to the list of prohibited grounds of discrimination in a new legal instrument designed to strengthen the anti-discrimination provisions of the European Convention on Human Rights. This historic development took place during the review by the Parliamentary Assembly of the Council of Europe of a draft protocol put forward by the Council's governing body – the Committee of Ministers – with the intention of making good the shortcomings in the existing anti-discrimination provisions of the Convention.[14] The vote was a result of extensive lobbying efforts within the

Council of Europe and by ILGA-Europe, which submitted a legal request for sexual orientation and gender identity to be included in the revision of Article 14 ECHR.[15] The vote in the Parliamentary Assembly of the Council of Europe occurred at the same time as the publication of a discrimination report by ILGA-Europe, originally designed as part of a motion for resolution tabled by Social Democratic Parliamentarians. Together with the ILGA-Europe Equality report for the EU (1998), this report to the Legal Affairs and Human Rights Committee, published on 16 February 2000, forms a comprehensive overview of the legal and social situation of lesbians and gay men in Europe.[16] All these documents submitted to the European institutions are written in the conceptual language of discrimination.

With the discrimination report ILGA-Europe tried to argue that 'discrimination against lesbian, gay and bisexual persons remains endemic and extremely serious' (Rex Wockner, International News, 13 March 2000). The report to the Legal Affairs and Human Rights Committee alleges severe discrimination and illustrates this allegation with literature, research and statistics. It covers discrimination in the following areas:

1 sexual offences law – including age of consent and terminology used in sexual offences law;
2 freedom of expression and association;
3 the classification of homosexuality as an illness;
4 the police's use of beatings and torture in custody, their general harassment of the lesbian, gay and bisexual community, acts of extortion and blackmail, and police lists of lesbian, gay and bisexual persons;
5 support for sexual orientation discrimination by some religious leaders;
6 hate crimes and other abuses by private parties;
7 violence;
8 countries in which lesbian, gay and bisexual communities do not exist;
9 lesbian invisibility;
10 young gays, bisexuals, and lesbians;
11 employment discrimination through denying access to jobs and promotional opportunities, as well as harassment;
12 the denial of parenting rights;
13 the legal recognition of same-sex relationships.

Additionally, the report asserts evidence of a world-wide trend towards recognising lesbian and gay rights as fundamental human rights in areas such as international and national law, anti-discrimination legislation, and legal recognition of same-sex couples.

The allegation of specific, but widespread, forms of discrimination that persist throughout Europe is usually followed by a set of recommendations that always include the claim to legally binding anti-discrimination measures. The discrimination report to the Legal Affairs and Human Rights Committee reads in its introduction:

> On the threshold of a new millennium it is manifestly necessary that the Parliamentary Assembly again assert the right of lesbian, gay and bisexual persons to freedom from discrimination as an expression of the fundamental principle of equality and recommends actions to governments and the Council of Europe that could help finally bring to an end hundreds of years of persecution and intolerance.

The formulation 'to end hundreds of years of persecution and intolerance' 'on the threshold of a new millennium' makes use of the successful shift of boundaries within legal liberal constructions of homosexuality. In Europe the gay and lesbian movement has achieved a conceptual move 'from the "deviant and dangerous offender", to the "minority" subject of human rights protection, to the "spousal" recipient of social benefits previously available only to heterosexual couples' (Herman 1994:8).

The wish to 'end hundreds of years of persecution and intolerance' and the address to equality as a fundamental principle of the identity of the Council of Europe is clearly an appeal to liberal legal ideology. The discourse of liberal legal equality in European democracies inhabits an authoritative dominance within European institutions to the extent of excluding or marginalising other possible concepts of equality from debate. This liberal legal ideology of equality – strongly bound to the principle of human rights – produces a consensus within which lesbian and gay equality is defined and permitted to some extent. Legal equality for lesbians, gay men, bisexuals, and transgender people has become imaginable and achievable in the assumed consensus about what is realistically possible in Europe politics.

The appeal to the liberal legal tradition of European institutions in political practices that utilise a language of discrimination is firmly connected to a hope of progress and future change. 'On the threshold of a new millennium' hundreds of years of discrimination can be ended through anti-discrimination legislation. This quest for anti-discrimination legislation is premised upon a particular understanding of society: namely that it contains a variety of diverse minority-like populations, each of which suffers a kind of antiquated prejudice no longer tolerable in liberal democracies. The state or the pan-European institution then acts as a neutral protector, facilitating the eradication of what is seen to be *individual* aberrations through the passage and enforcement of anti-discrimination measures. Legal scholar Morris Kaplan (1997a:43) points to this logic of hope in his justification for anti-discrimination legislation in spite of the queer critique he opposes:

> The underlying rationale of the anti-discrimination provisions of civil rights legislation is the recognition that formal legal equality is inadequate to provide for equal citizenship under conditions of popular hostility and pervasive social inequality. It is precisely the intensity and extent of the prejudice against homosexuality that justifies the claims of lesbian and gay citizens to protection against discrimination.

The hope Kaplan expresses – namely that a long-existent prejudice can be countered by a legal prohibition – is also typically evident in ILGA-Europe's argument. The submission on the extension of Article 14 ECHR, with regard to gender identity, exemplifies this: 'It is only by adding to Article 14 that there will be no discrimination based on gender identity that nation states will be obligated to initiate some steps towards addressing this contradiction and the other legal anomalies that transgender and transsexual people face.' Here, the changes to an anti-discrimination article only valid within the bounds of the rights granted in the ECHR are made significant in the struggle to better the actual living conditions of a specific minority group. The hope of progress and change, which forms the central theme of arguments for anti-discrimination legislation, is based on a set of concrete visions of change. The law and the state are addressed as the most significant agents of political and social change. This address affirms the political hegemony of the juridical. The logic of hope, then, runs approximately like this: through anti-discrimination legislation, the hegemony of the juridical in European political culture will assure equal treatment and, thus, reap ideological rewards and material change for those suffering from discrimination. Let me examine the steps of this logic one by one.

When I speak of the juridical here, I mean to imply the discursive structure of social–legal regulation: everything that belongs to the discursive institutional processes of regulating and maintaining power over societies as sets of social networks. This includes concrete practices of institutions such as the law and the legal arena.[17] The latter contains law-making bodies, courts, lawyers, and legal documents, as well as the discursive order of legality in parliamentary democracies in Europe. The juridical adds the ideological and discursive structures that assign power and truth to these institutions and maintain their rank of superior opinion. The juridical is, therefore, more than the written law and more than the practices of courtrooms: it extends into the political and into the way individuals understand themselves as members of a social community, as well as into the mechanisms, the histories, the predicaments, and the workings of rights within democracies. The law itself is structured in its very existence by this ideological support from the juridical. There exists a certain historically singular access of the law to defining powers and the power to speak with physical consequence through Judeo–Christian culture and enlightenment (Cover 1986:1611).

However, the rules of the juridical are a historical fact not a philosophical absolute nor a tangible entity. They are a discursive relational and contextual practice that takes shape in opposition to whatever is locally and ideologically conceived as the public and as the political. In European cultures the juridical ideologically grants liberal freedom, fitted to an economic order in which property and personhood are not equally distributed, and this freedom is conveyed by rights against arbitrary state power on one side and against anarchic civil society or property theft on the other (Brown 1995:6).

Through the address to the state and the law, the juridical becomes yet again the dominant and central discursive site to speak effectively about discrimination as political capital and the site to receive alleviation. This dominance is maintained by the institutional prerogative concerning speech and silence. The law can serve to command speech and to preserve the ontological comforts of silence (Goldberg-Hiller 1998:521). The power to apply both tactics, that of speech and that of silence, is a power that those who speak within the legal arena receive through the historical hegemony of the juridical in the politics of modern democracies. Both these tactics are the means to draw important distinctions between courts and the public. That has significance for the question whether discrimination is acceptable, indeed whether it exists as a recognisable structure at all, and whether the dominance of the definitional power of the juridical, and thus its political hegemony, can be maintained or not.

To adopt Robert Cover's approach (1986:1611), this means that any legal interpretation is not only practical, but is a practice in itself in that the institutional context – and Foucault might add, the historical claim to ultimate truth that characterises the law – ties the language act of practical understanding to the physical acts of others in a predictable, though not logically necessary way. The power and violence of the word (Cover) spoken, or not spoken within law-making institutions and courtrooms, is the essence of maintaining the prerogative of political definition. Any political practice that addresses the law – that speaks and claims consequential speech to be made on somebody's behalf – needs to locate itself somewhere within the juridical and its hegemonic discourses of institutional power and intelligible difference. No political practice can remain outside the hegemony of the juridical if it wants to address law.

The legal arena, as one significant part of the juridical, is in that climate an obvious target of political negotiation about difference. In European cultures and modern democracies, the law functions as assurance of individual and property rights as well as ordering the duties of social belonging. For this reason 'lesbian and gay rights movements, from their inception, have engaged in legal struggle partly on the basis of what changes in legal provision *signify* more generally' (Herman 1994:4). Herman names the defeat of bigotry and the moral majority, safety to come out, feelings of self-worth, citizenship, and community identity as themes that are seen to be influenced by legal changes. The legal arena is, thus, said to provide a space for negotiating which differences are genuine and, hence, acceptable reasons for differentiation in treatment.

The logic of hope and change is, therefore, seemingly a realistic logic in the European political climate. The hegemony of the juridical promises that equal treatment in law will reap rewards on an ideological and a material level. This promise is part of how the juridical is maintained as hegemonic. The first step the logic of hope and change takes is to assure equal treatment in law. In order to make discrimination visible and understood as such, comparisons are needed. In legal discourse, discrimination occurs where one person who does not share one particular feature is treated unfavourably, all other aspects being the same. The establishment of discrimination in that respect features numbers and personal testimony as the most common political practice of writing and speaking. Both the Article 14 submissions and the discrimination report utilise exactly that technique in their substantial referencing of court cases and research. Each evidence of discrimination is supported as much as possible by a combination of personal witness, reviews of mainstream human rights organisations, academic assessment, existing judgments, and statistical proof. Discrimination is rendered factual in that it contains a truth claim. That truth claim is maintained through a reference to the principle of equality and the seemingly agreed-upon common sense judgement about what differentiation should be acceptable and what differentiation should not.

That gay men, lesbians, bisexuals, and transgender people are discriminated against is established as a political fact by the kind of discourses rights organisations use in their political practices. What becomes utilisable in the political arena is, thus, not necessarily what is actually experienced. Or to say it differently, experiences of discrimination are closely bound in their possibility of recognition to the possibilities of turning them into political capital. Or to give it yet another twist: the very existence of mainstream lobby organisations, such as ILGA-Europe, actually facilitates the possibilities of recognition of discrimination. This is a similar argument to the identity critique of queer theory analysed in Chapter 3. Whereas ILGA-Europe politically claims to represent a pre-existing group with a certain describable identity, in fact, it participates in the very production of this group as a *group*. ILGA-Europe's representation of discrimination in Europe does not simply describe the existing reality out there, but is productive of that very reality. This does *not* mean that ILGA-Europe invents discrimination or that the reported discrimination is unreal. Nothing could be further from my argument. Yet, turning an accumulation of descriptions of discrimination into a cohesive understandable political practice is creative of the way in which discrimination is voiced and embedded in political discourses. Consequently, discrimination is experienced as politically negotiable only with reference to equality as the base theme of liberal political and legal discourses.

The equality promised to accrue from anti-discrimination legislation is said to grant a specific ideological reward: it is hoped adversely to influence the acceptability of homophobia. This ideological effect is central to political practices that utilise a language of discrimination to render injustice and inequality visible. Hence, in order to call something discrimination – and to turn it into political capital and claim anti-discrimination rights – political practices have to be embedded within discourses of common sense. They have to be tailored to the dominant liberal legal ideology of equality, with regard to what is acceptable and what is not. To identify what is acceptable, social movement activists who enter a public debate on sexuality – legal or otherwise – 'engage in a process of self-censorship whereby the movement's internal politics are deliberately transformed and rendered compatible with the perceived prevailing social climate' (Herman 1994:6). Indeed, the anti-discrimination report arguably taps into a perceived prevailing social climate:

> The London pub bombing[18] was preceded by similar attacks on the city's Afro–Caribbean and Bangladeshi communities, emphasising the many similarities between racism and homophobia. However, there is one big difference:

for many people homophobia remains *respectable*. Statements and actions that would be unthinkable in respect of [sic] ethnic or religious minorities are commonplace with regard to the lesbian, gay and bisexual minority. Some governments or parliaments deliberately maintain discriminatory legislation, while some religious leaders oppose gay rights in terms that can only be described as inflammatory.

The idea of bringing up the issue of acceptability in the introduction to the discrimination report makes this usually implicit tailoring explicit. Any talk of discrimination is held up against liberal political, social, and legal discourses of acceptability in equal treatment. Discrimination is not acceptable for racial minorities, thus, it should not be acceptable for sexual minorities. While homophobia and racism have aspects in common, the assumed consensus about the non-acceptability of racism and the existence of anti-discrimination legislation in the area of race institutes a difference between racism and homophobia. The formulation of this passage was debated within the executive board since some regarded its implications of hierarchising forms of oppression as problematic. The argument partakes in inventing a certain social and political reality that does not actually exist even in the Member States of the EU.

While, for example, in Great Britain anti-racist discourses carry a certain modest political weight in mainstream political discourse, in countries such as Germany racism and xenophobia are a perfectly acceptable mainstream political discourse. In fact, the xenophobia blatantly evident is in general much worse than any homophobia ever displayed by politicians or by the Catholic Church. Asserting the non-acceptability of racism as agreed ground could be viewed as an affirmative act that now aims to elevate homosexuality to the same high moral ground racial protection should have. Yet that logic – besides being obviously problematic – does not actually argue facts, but argues perceived perception.

This leads me to conclude that the task of arguing discrimination can be successful only if it fits the generally perceived social and political climate. The ideological reward anti-discrimination legislation promises is to fit homosexuality – and potentially transgenderism – into the *perceived* social and political climate. Activists search out the most successful argument to address the audience with a minimum compromise on their own actual political thought.[19] Speaking about discrimination with reference to gross injustices, such as physical harm and significant employment disadvantages, fits the climate of modern democracies. Hence, it is ultimately the perception of the social and political climate that defines what can progress and what cannot and this explains, in turn, why certain equalities are more easily achieved than others. Self-censorship with respect to perception is, therefore, an important aspect of ILGA-Europe's daily business. What is seen to be manageable within a perceived political reality is the decisive factor for any decision on argumentation strategy.[20]

Yet, this is so on both sides of the fence. European politicians and judges persistently talk about a perceived consensus about homosexuality within European societies irrespective of whether they support claims to rights or want to keep the status quo.[21] Homosexuality is portrayed as either 'now widely accepted' or 'generally considered to be morally wrong by the majority of the population'. The discrimination report anticipates such reference to society's opinion. It appeals to European institutions to act as a civil protection shield so that gays and lesbians will become protected despite the fact that conservative, homophobic segments of society oppose such a move. If that protection is not granted, the significance of discrimination will continue to be severe:

> The discrimination described in this report affects almost all aspects of the lives of lesbians and gays: many have homophobia instilled into them in childhood before they have even recognised their own sexuality, leading to self-hatred, isolation, difficulty in self-acceptance, and in some cases, suicide attempts; many hide their sexual orientation throughout their life, 'living a lie', with profound negative consequences for their self-esteem and happiness; and for many, legal discrimination, whether in the criminal law or in the recognition of their relationships, contributes to a sense of alienation and exclusion.

The assumption behind this formulation is that anti-discrimination legislation would protect the public announcement of a life-style and, thus, give self-confidence, sovereignty as a participating citizen, and a sense of equal belonging, as well as an identification with the social movements that have already worked to achieve those rights.[22] The change of law is considered to have direct influence on everyday life in that under certain circumstances victims of discrimination have access to the courts to challenge injustice and access to legal recognition formerly denied. Eventually, this access will persuade the majority of the population to accept that discrimination is no longer acceptable. Anti-discrimination argumentation has a tinge of education: teaching the nations respect, forcing them to acknowledge and protect individual expression. In consequence, gay men and lesbians will gain material equality on a social, individual, and economic level.

Considering the rules that are necessitated in speaking about discrimination and the demand for anti-discrimination legislation, the political territory of anti-discrimination features contradictions. This fact does not escape the ILGA-Europe documents: they proclaim a certain political territory as won – namely the liberal democratic ideology of equality in the European institutions – and at the same time demand the fulfilment of the equality promise, thus fully acknowledging that the territory is not won entirely. For example, it is not yet won with respect to the hate speech many churches actively pursue, or with regard to the fact that severe discrimination persists. Thus, ILGA-Europe holds liberalism to its own promises. This is a conscious and clear tactic that permeates the utilisation of discrimination as political practice. Yet, within this logic, anti-discrimination rights are obviously problematic or at least a location from which questions arise.

The centrality of the legal arena – and in consequence the support for the political hegemony of the juridical inherent in anti-discrimination claims – raises a few problems: considering the power of the word in legal practice; it is not enough to simply say that rights are self-affirming and consider their ideological consequence unproblematic. Anti-discrimination legislation affirms a homosexual self and it speaks on behalf of that self. Yet, that homosexual self is a historical construct born out of the late nineteenth century, and it is not something to be celebrated unquestioningly.[23] Within anti-discrimination discourse the homosexual subject is permanently re-created as a discriminated subject. The effect of anti-discrimination legislation is up for definition within the constitutive power of the law and remains subjugated to the dominant liberal discourses of equality and freedom only.

Consequently, the mentioned problems inherent in political speech about discrimination should be scrutinised further with respect to the need in anti-discrimination politics continuously to create a subject of discrimination, a historical subject in possession of an identity that is at least temporarily injured. The implicit problems of anti-discrimination also warrant scrutiny towards the way in which the law is productive in maintaining a circle of heteronormative desire and in hiding its own involvement in the perpetuation of discrimination in the first place. Such further analysis will allow us to formulate different political and theoretical demands in the realm of anti-discrimination measures. To do so, I will return to some aspects of Article 13 of the Employment Directive.

Analysing the problems: political and theoretical demands on anti-discrimination

The definition of discrimination as occurring when 'one person is treated less favourably than another is, has been or would be treated in a comparable situation' on grounds of that person's sexual orientation – or any other ground for that matter – defines eligibility for a right. Protection is accorded to those who are directly or indirectly disadvantaged or harassed in comparison with those presumed to be in the possession of all available rights by virtue of belonging to the majority or the presumed average normality. This intrinsic and unavoidable comparison not only involves a normatising move – what normality functions as reference point? – but also necessitates the location of a discriminated subject. The language of anti-discrimination assigns a non-agentic position to those historically injured. Anti-discrimination necessitates a self-definition compatible with pre-existing concepts of identity.[24] It continues to imply a homogenous minority population. In the logic of anti-discrimination there has always been and will always be a majority of heterosexuals and a minority of homosexuals. This carries a danger Didi Herman (1994:44) identified for the Canadian human rights charter:

> representing lesbians and gay men as an immutable minority may restrict rather than broaden social understandings of sexuality. Lesbians and gay men are granted legitimacy, not on the basis that there might be something problematic with gender roles and sexual hierarchies, but on the basis that they constitute a fixed group of 'others' who need and deserve protection.

The permanent recreation of a fixed group of others has an effect on discrimination: as I argued above, the protection granted participates in re-establishing, as injured or discriminate, the very individual subject that it seeks to protect. Anti-discrimination involves a permanent leap in logic from identity as a marker of a group to the individual subject as a historically injured subject. Sexual orientation – legally established in the Employment Directive as an identity, not as a behaviour – becomes a protected subjectivity, but also a subjectivity presumed to be established prior to the event of discrimination. The discriminated subject in legal interpretation is a historical and discursive product of the two basic actions available in the political domain: telling and listening. The telling of discrimination – significantly bound to the possibility of experience – and the listening to those stories, as well as the telling of legal rules with regards to the acceptability of this discrimination are productive of a subjectivity and of the group to which that subject apparently belongs. Legal discourse demands that subjectivity be pre-established in order to make discrimination intelligible.

Yet, in the course of telling the story, this subjectivity is, in fact, invented for the first time as an injured subjectivity said to be the marker of membership to the identity group that is protected.[25] The rules of the juridical come to constitute the subject by offering the possibility of locating oneself within them and, thus, becoming intelligible within the order that permeates the understanding of the political in a hegemonic way. So, paradoxically, legislation that makes the subject free to tell her or his story independent or in spite of the allegedly objective outside world – in which prejudice prevails – adheres at the same time to those orders that design that world as eternally structured by difference.

This interpretation connects the formation of a discriminated subject with the concept of experience. Experience is a strong element invoked for the ability to speak about discrimination. The discriminated subject is not merely a human individual, but more a position at which different discourses intersect: those of individuality and those of membership in social groups. In that understanding, the rules of legal and political intelligibility can be productive of the experience of discrimination an individual expresses. According to Joan Scott (1991:779), it is 'not individuals who have experiences but subjects who are constituted through experience'. The experience of homosexuality is a historical and discursive event resulting from intersections between cultural meanings of homosexuality, from the availability of discourses that make homosexuality speakable, and from individual relations. Thus, homosexual experience is at once an interpretation of an alleged reality and in need of interpretation (1991:797). The language of anti-discrimination legislation is one way of interpreting an experience that already is an interpretation of a perceived historical reality, namely that of discrimination.

Activists lobby actively for protection rights and, thus, present themselves as agentic. However, the game of legal anti-discrimination is one that grants protection to victims who need the law to protect them from outdated but unfortunately widespread prejudice against which they have no weapons themselves. Hence, the language of anti-discrimination assigns a non-agentic position to those historically injured. Dorothy Smith's (1987:32) feminist image of the gender hierarchy as a ball game is applicable here:

> It is like a game in which there are more presences than players. Some are engaged in tossing a ball between them; others are consigned to the role of audience and supporter, who pick up the ball if it is dropped and pass it back to the players. They support, facilitate, encourage but their action does not become part of the play.[26]

A member of a discriminated group becomes a presence in anti-discrimination: the injustice is heard and accepted as real. Yet, the ball tossing, in deciding what constitutes discrimination, which groups are affected, and what qualifies an individual for membership in that group – for example, sexual orientation and not sexual behaviour – does not include the victim of discrimination as equal player. Social movements lobby for anti-discrimination legislation actively, but that action does not give them definitional power in the game of meaning production about discrimination. In short, the general heteronormative structure of the political game contradicts anti-discrimination ideals.

This means that the intersection between discrimination as a political practice for rights and the dominance of the juridical in the domain of rights remain locked in a circle that offers no real remedy to the actual structure of discrimination. This detrimental circle is kept in place because of three processes: firstly, because of the production of subjectivities within a logic of identity as group membership, secondly, because of the investment into discrimination of the law itself, and thirdly, because of the finite list of grounds in anti-discrimination legislation.

With regard to the first process, Renata Salecl (1993) offers in the context of women's human rights a reading of Lacan that can partly be deployed here. She connects rights and demand through distinguishing need, demand, and desire in legal rights (1993:456).[27]

> When put into words, a need becomes articulated in the symbolic order. At this moment, we start to perceive it as a *demand* – as a demand to the Other to satisfy the need. On the level of demand the subject asks the Other for a specific object (the child, for example, wants food) which is supposed to fulfill a need, but by articulating this need as a demand the subject also asks the Other for its love (by demanding food the child also demands love and attention from the mother). The object of demand thus becomes the subject's means of attaining this other goal – the attention or love of the Other. At this point the third element of the triad, *desire*, emerges: desire arises as the excess of demand over need, as something in every demand that cannot be reduced to a need. As Lacan argues: 'desire is neither the appetite for satisfaction, nor the demand for love, but the difference that results from the subtraction of the first from the second'.

Taking the aspects of psychoanalytic thought offered by Salecl's reading of Lacan to the intersection of individual subjectivity, identity as marker for a group, and political practices employed to demand anti-discrimination rights, the following logic can be applied.

Individuals obtain anti-discrimination rights as a substitute for a fundamental, if implicit, prohibition: the discriminatory history of sexual and gender minority groups is an effect of normatising heterosexuality in a binary gender hierarchy. It is also an effect of creating a true, natural, and biologically essential way of being a gender and of being sexual.[28] Anti-discrimination rights express a need *and* a demand for full acceptance and value within society. They express the hope of defeating homophobia, as I have shown above. Yet, obtaining rights actually prevents the full and equal acceptance that is sought after, since equality, acceptance, and value with regard to gender and sexuality are defined by the prohibition of homosexuality, in this instance expressed through the heteronormative structure of the law.[29] Anti-discrimination rights function as a substitute for something fundamental that all 'out' members of the designated minority group have indeed lost: the freedom from subjugation under the hegemony of the binary gender hierarchy which essentially connects sexual and gender identity choices to essentialised sexed bodies.

As a substitute these rights surely fulfil a need – and as such they have a real effect – but they do not actually fulfil the demand for substantial equality and acceptance. This means, as Salecl (1993:458) puts it, that it appears as if 'rights are not so much linked to demand as they are to desire: they are akin to that surplus of demand over need because of which demand always remains unfulfilled'. A poststructuralist concept of desire, as I argued in Chapter 3, fundamentally connects the desire for rights with the desire to express non-normative gender and sexual practices. Desire – understood as discursive rather than a psychological reality eternally fixed by the rules and laws of gender formation – functions as a fundamental signifier of what constitutes people as deviant or belonging to a minority *and* as persons that can and do claim rights that are denied them.

Claiming rights becomes an appropriation of the desire made relevant in the discourses of participation and citizenship, which are among others based on the regulatory practices of a binary gender order. It is this gender order that, in turn, functions as the *only* available field in which sexual desire and the desire to belong to a gender can be formed. Thus, beyond Salecl's Lacanian approach, the Foucaldian insight that social structures produce individuals as personal subjects, as social subjects, and as subject of the law is relevant. Naming the conditions of desire – understood as the central motor of any sexual identity *and* of the constitution of oneself as a person entitled to rights – is a possible answer to the crucial question of how anti-discrimination rights remain locked in a problematic that cannot be resolved intrinsic to official rights discourses. Beyond desire, there are, however, two further possible answers to this question.

Firstly, anti-discrimination legislation is also a move to hide the power and involvement of political institutions and the law itself in the establishment and persistence of discrimination. In the definitional, procedural, and remedy sections of the EU Commission's draft Directive on discrimination in employment, for example, individual persons are reduced to observable social attributes and practices, and consequentially assigned membership to an identifiable identity group. These attributes and practices are defined empirically and positivistically as if their existence were intrinsic and factual, rather than effects of discursive and institutional power. Yet, it is institutional power that connects sexual and gender identities to natural, essential bodies and their desires. Definitions of discrimination additionally participate in positivist definitions of persons as their attributes and practices and, thus, fundamentally invest into a logic of fixed group identity. When these definitions are written into law, they ensure that those people describable according to them will now, through them, become regulated as members of a group: a group that has historically suffered severe prosecution from the institution that now re-defines it.

In consequence, anti-discrimination rights call on the state as the neutral arbiter of discrimination and, hence, on the agency that institutionalises heterosexual legal privileges in the first place and that has historically been the persecutor of homosexual desire. Granting anti-discrimination protection is, thus, also a convenient way of hiding that involvement. One could go as far as considering whether anti-discrimination rights are not a perfect instance of the way in which the language of recognition is also the language of historical discrimination. Or how the articulation of political demands in a language bound to the context of liberal legal discourses can become a vehicle of subordination by re-establishing the discriminated group identity as an identity in need of protection without addressing the structural aspects of Euro-Christian thought through which that difference was produced. Anti-discrimination language has so far not included an emphasis on the 'processes of differentiation' (Scott 1997:24); it leaves us in the dark as to why difference in sexual behaviour has any influence on the construction of our subjectivity, our political identities, our social relations, or why that difference is meaningful at all.

Secondly, another answer to the question of why anti-discrimination remains problematic is the tendency in the European institutions to create a limited list of grounds for discrimination claims. Activists call this the shopping list of anti-discrimination. These lists necessitate the continual challenging of themselves in order to accommodate more and more minorities. ILGA-Europe, for example, will be faced with the task of ensuring the inclusion of gender identity in the future. More importantly, however, these lists cannot deal with two fundamental aspects of the existing structures of discrimination: firstly, the emergence of new social groups and political alliances along lines of affiliation disconnected from ascribable identities. Secondly, they cannot deal with the structural interconnection of different kinds of discriminations, such as the intersections of racism, sexism, and homophobia, and the intrinsic bonds of the binary gender hierarchy to heteronormativity.

Legal regimes, in general, produce and enshrine fragmented identities. People are forced to compartmentalise their complex subjectivities in order to make a claim (Herman 1994:46). Considering Renata Salecl's approach to rights again, the discourse of anti-discrimination presents a fantasy scenario. In this scenario society and the individual are perceived as a whole; a non-split entity that can be rationally organised to accommodate certain differences in a non-conflictual manner if we only believe in the promise of equality (1993:459). Yet, in the existing language of the law the subject can never be satisfied in its desire to regain the fundamental social loss that has forced her or him into a minority subjectivity. There will always remain a gap between positive, written anti-discrimination law and the universal idea of equality.

Having said this much about the problem of anti-discrimination, it obviously remains necessary to ask what political consequences this critical analysis has to offer. The language of discrimination and demands for anti-discrimination legislation will continue to be crucial in political practices as long as lesbians, gay men, bisexuals, and transgender people suffer from discrimination in European societies. What political and theoretical demands can, then, be made on anti-discrimination claims as political practice? The argument I have presented in this chapter does not imply that the acts of discrimination gay men, lesbians, bisexual, and transgender people experience almost daily are not harmful; they are, but the reason that certain acts are experienced as harmful is not universal and ahistorical, but culturally and historically specific. It is that specificity which needs to be addressed if anti-discrimination measures are to have actual impact beyond individual acknowledgement of harm. I want to argue that this insight declares anti-discrimination legislation a primarily political terrain, not a legal one. This means that legal change needs to be discussed in the wider terrain of the political and the juridical and not reduced to simply adding sexual orientation and gender identity to existing anti-discrimination articles.

Dealing with anti-discrimination in the realm of specific laws only is likely to add a manifestation of harm and discrimination as a natural burden to certain identities such as blackness, forms of femininity, homosexuality, and disability. The effects are similar to those I discussed with regard to human rights. It is not enough to reduce anti-discrimination to the existence of treaties and laws, as some gay and lesbian scholars suggest.[30] The politics of anti-discrimination need to address the concern that law in European cultures features the double bind of inclusion and exclusion. Anti-discrimination rights, thus, are to be dealt with as potential problems.

The effects of anti-discrimination rights are not only complex in their problematic, but also in the positive hope they present. As I argued above, there is a clear value ideal attached to anti-discrimination rights apart from the indisputable material effects they might have for individuals. Nevertheless, that value is not considered an objective gain of actual equality; it is crucial to put it to work. The political potency of anti-discrimination rights, then, lies not in their concrete content, but in their idealism. According to Wendy Brown (1995:134), the value of the ideology of equal rights lies in a revelation of the limits of equality and political emancipation in the discursive struggles that surround it. The decisive potential is here that the parameters of the discursive struggle entered into with every discrimination claim are negotiated rather than secured in advance and that the outcome is never fully guaranteed (Brown 1995:134). In consequence, anti-discrimination can be understood as a political and a theoretical discourse that consequently has theoretical and political demands made on it.

On a theoretical level, the relationship of anti-discrimination to identity – its promise to address a social harm that is itself constitutive of the discriminated identity – presents a contradiction in which difference is needed to conceptualise discrimination. Without clearly addressing this contradiction from the perspective of the discriminated, anti-discrimination strategies forfeit any capacity to analyse the basic structures of suffering. Hence, critical strategies need to be found that scrutinise the different forms of power the project of anti-discrimination is flanked by on all sides: the powers against which it is demanded – prejudice, legal disadvantages, institutional abuse – and the power a discriminated subject must claim to enact itself. Effective anti-discrimination measures deal with the powers that situate, constrain, and produce subjects as well as with the power entailed in taking up political agency in the claim for protection. They find ways to deal with the historical 'processes of differentiation' (Scott 1997:24). The defeat of homophobia cannot remain a goal that can actually be achieved, but political practices form a permanent struggle against heteronormative structures.

The demand I propose to make on anti-discrimination strategies from a theoretical perspective is, thus, to go beyond the discrimination logic into a questioning of the parameters of difference. In a Derridian sense of differance, this would imply staging difference politically as a diversity stemming from the Latin *differere* – to move or see apart from, to defer – rather than as discrimination and hierarchy as in the Latin *discrimere* – to differentiate. An injurious past cannot be compensated for unless a necessarily discriminated identity ceases to be invested in it. Yet, identity cannot cease to be invested in the past without giving up essentialist identities as such, giving up the economy of hurt minorities and investing into the address of structures and ideological systems such as gender and sexuality themselves (Brown 1995:73).

On a practical level, scholars such as Sabine Hark (1998:17) urge us not to confuse the sphere of the political with the sphere of the legal when we are trying to address the contradictions of legal rights in their protective and regulative aspects. Rights are not the same as equality; legal recognition is not emancipation. While I agree with this standpoint and with the necessity of questioning the dream of redemption by the law among rights activists, the contrary would seem to be an applicable way forward as well: addressing the political of the juridical – and law as the order under its auspices – making the realm of the law an intensively political realm whose inner life is up for negotiation whenever groups or individuals claim rights, whenever court cases are heard, whenever laws are lobbied and decided. Using the law and anti-discrimination only makes sense when it is accompanied by a political fight over their democratic 'hardware and system configuration' with the aim of creating spaces in which prescribed forms of being can be constantly questioned.

This view maintains the language of discrimination as an acceptable political strategy, but with a different goal: the challenge of heteronorm(ality). The necessary comparison intrinsic to discrimination argumentation brings definitions of the normal into the public, spoken realm. It presents the opportunity actively to allow or disallow certain comparisons and to present difference. Words and strategies in the formulation of discrimination do not necessarily have an inherent meaning. While there are surely dominant meanings with more power in courtrooms and legislative bodies, struggles between social movements are precisely over the power to interpret social relations (Herman 1994:64). In fact, anti-discrimination is also a process of historical interpretation that needs to be pursued actively. Acts of interpretation could be picked up much more consciously than they have been to date.

This implies a change with regard to political argumentation. Political practices, then, move from arguing the existence of a sexual difference minority to arguing a political opposition to the dominance of heteronormativity. Occasionally, that shift might simply cause a slight change of wording. Even so, a change in wording is important. Claiming anti-discrimination as a political opposition renders the project of protection against discrimination a continuing debate on normative gender and sexuality regimes, rather than a benevolent protection for a weak, passive minority. The wording needs to emphasise that human beings as an entity or a group do not have prescribed fundamental protection rights, but that no one remains without rights of protection. Universalising norms according to which differentiating is reasonable means creating exceptions and deviations from the norm. Thus, a poststructuralist approach to protection rights could be based on the claim that no one should remain without anti-discriminations rights. This has the consequence that nobody can universally possess them and, thus, constitute the normal majority *not* in need of protection.

Conclusion

As it is high time to develop a more critical approach to anti-discrimination, and given the hegemony of the juridical in most spaces of politics, the realm of the law cannot be discarded from a queer theoretical point of view. In fact, just the opposite is the case: it needs to be examined carefully. According to the logic emphasised here, what happens through political practices that engage with juridical discourses cannot be solely normatising and reductive either. All political practices – in one way or another – already engage in negotiation about the political and in the preconditions of what can be conceptualised and granted as rights, although there is much scope for development in this respect. A similar insight prompts many theorists in critical legal studies to remain convinced that traditional rights do have some value. Carl Stychin (1998:198) is one of them:

> I remain convinced that the struggle for the inclusion of 'out' gays and lesbians in the United States military, and the fight for same-sex marriage rights, *could* be discursively deployed to re-imagine these central national institutions, and by extension, the ways in which the nation state has been gendered and sexualised.

While that re-imagination remains doubtful – as Stychin (2001) himself acknowledges elsewhere – it would indeed be worthwhile to explore the possibilities of specific legal strategies in this respect. In the following chapter I will investigate two court cases at the European Court of Justice that argue discrimination on grounds of sex to apply to transsexuals and to lesbians. This strategy – although only partly successful – potentially troubles the binary gender structure as the base of discrimination and challenges the now dominant listing of grounds in anti-discrimination articles.

Notes

1 See Chapter 1 for a detailed explanation.
2 I use, as instances of ILGA-Europe's approach to anti-discrimination, its discrimination report to the Council of Europe in early 2000 and its submissions to include sexual orientation and gender identity in the broadening of Article 14 of the European Convention on Human Rights in 1999.
3 See Flynn (1999) and Waddington (1999) for further legal interpretation of Article 13 itself.
4 COM (1999) 565, 25.11.1999.
5 COM (1999) 566, 25.11.1999.
6 COM (1999) 567, 25.11.1999.
7 Article 3.
8 I am grateful to Mark Bell for summarising the consequences of the draft Directives from a legal point of view for the ILGA-Europe executive board. The following paragraphs are strongly informed by his analysis in the legal aspects of the first drafts published by the Commission.
9 COM (1999) 565, 25.11.1999. The Commission published two versions of this draft, one in October and one in November 1999. It only clarified the two different versions in February 2000. The October draft does not contain this explanatory note. ILGA-Europe inquired on this aspect and it seems that some pressure by Austrian Catholic bishops has fuelled this restriction.
10 This connection is a traditional homophobic argument and denies the fact that most sexual abuse is of heterosexual nature and occurs between an adult and a child known to each other. In fact, 'paedophilia' as a term is so heavily linked to a history of prejudice against gay men that I prefer the term 'sexual abuse' since that term names what the issue actually concerns not sexual behaviour or sexual orientation, but abuse.
11 A further set of exceptions is provided in Articles 5 and 6 of the Directive, but only in relation to disability and age respectively. By mid-2003, genuine occupational requirements have already become a way of institutionalising sexual orientation discrimination in some new national laws, for example in Italy, the UK, and in the German draft.
12 The article continues to specify rules on disability.
13 One example of indirect discrimination could be employers' dress codes, where, for example, a woman might find that certain skirts and blouses offensively foreground a sexuality she does not wish to foreground. For an analysis of this, see Paul Skidmore (1999:509).
14 Draft Protocol 12. This parliamentary decision did not mean that sexual orientation was actually added. Draft Protocol 12 was signed in November 2000 without sexual orientation. See Chapter 1 for an elaboration on the process.

15 The submission on gender identity, however, was unsuccessful. Legal experts within ILGA-Europe consider this to be for two reasons: (1) the fact that almost no legislation in the whole world includes specific reference to gender identity – so the Council of Europe, as a rather conservative organisation, is unlikely to take a lead in this and (2) the fact that transgendered people are a very small minority: the argument about not having an endless number of rather small minorities specially mentioned in the list of grounds and of leaving some to be defined under 'other status' comes into play. I am grateful to Robert Wintemute and Nigel Warner for this assessment.
16 *Equality for Lesbians and Gay Men. A Relevant Issue in the Civil and Social Dialogue*; Report to the Legal Affairs and Human Rights Committee of the Parliamentary Assembly of the Council of Europe as a Contribution to the Preparation of its Report and Recommendations on the Situation of Lesbians and Gays in the Member States of the Council of Europe, Motion for a Resolution (Doc. 8319).
17 When I speak about the 'law' in the following, I do not imply the psychoanalytic use of this term.
18 A homophobic bomb attack on a gay pub, in London in April 1999, that killed three and left dozens maimed.
19 This actual political thought, however, is often not formulated specifically among the leading activists but is rather assumed to be agreed in its content.
20 Vaid (1995) devotes a whole chapter (Chapter 5) to arguing how political lobbying in professional organisations necessarily means the adoption of system-intrinsic political practices. There exists a logic of political structure withdrawn from individual agency or the individual wish to be as radical as possible. According to Vaid, this logic impregnates lobby work, and nobody can totally resist it.
21 The apparent agreement of society about homosexuality is in fact mentioned in one way or the other in every court case that has been heard so far before the European Court of Human Rights and before the European Court of Justice.
22 See Chapter 4 for an analysis of the interview material in this respect.
23 As a historical product of the nineteenth century, the homosexual self is located in medical and psychoanalytic as well as religious and early political movement discourses. This early cultural development of homosexual identity was not simple and clear cut, but subject to a differentiated debate, for example, between Magnus Hirschfeld and Karl-Heinrich Ulrichs. A more precise analysis can be found in Vicinius (1993, 1994), Stanton (1992), and Stümke (1989).
24 Butler (1997a:43–71) elaborates this point through establishing a connection between hurt, a history of discrimination, and identities in her critical analysis of hate speech legislation.
25 This approach is informed by a poststructuralist understanding of the subject and subjectivity. See, for a general introduction to this concept, for example, Weedon (1987). More specifically, Davies (1997:272) shows how 'the humanist self is so convincingly achieved, and goes on being achieved, through the inscription of humanist discourses on the one who is always already a subject ... and who manages indeed to become what will always already have been'.
26 Dorothy Smith works within Marxist feminist theory and would probably not subscribe to the kind of analysis I put forward with this image.
27 I want to emphasise that the following is a critical engagement with Salecl's work and not with Lacan's directly. Hence, I do not claim to offer any comprehensive understanding of Lacanian thought here. Psychoanalytic theory of subject production is taken into consideration only in a very marginal way at the intersection lines of subjectivity and group identity, since I am interested in political practices and not in the

complicated processes of the production of individual homosexual identity by themselves.
28 Much research has been conducted on the historical processes of this. See for further information Bech (1997), Boswell (1990), Bristow (1997), Bullough (1990), and Butler (1990).
29 See, for an explanation of this, Bower (1997), Halley (1993), Morgan (1995), and Stychin (1995). I also wish to emphasise again that the term 'law' here does not refer to the 'Law of the Father' in Lacanian thought.
30 Kaplan (1997a:45), for example, suggests in an attempt to counter theoretical queer identity critique: 'When a citizen believes that she has been unfairly treated in a relevant way, she may exercise her rights under the law to challenge the treatment as discriminatory. No one is obliged to do so; the definition of protected classes does not construct personal or political identities but rather than treating her in terms of her individual character and qualities. The objectionable construction of identity in cases of discrimination results from a social history of subordinating and stigmatizing specific groups, not from the laws designed to remedy such effects.'

6 Gender identity and sexual orientation: legal rights politics

> the law remains a powerful (but not 'all powerful') too in the constitution and regulation of identities, as well as in their repression. In the end, the law is an arena which demands and warrants social struggle, for despite the frequent failures of the past, it can prove to be (sometimes unintentionally) one mechanism for social/sexual change.
>
> (Carl Stychin 1995:156)

The law is an important site of struggle in activism for rights. Yet, it is also a site to which political participation and rights have often been reduced and which, in turn, presents a nearly hegemonic signifier of what is understood to be the political, liberation, progress, and success in the history of lesbian and gay rights struggles. Law is more than the texts of treaties, Directives and codes. Through its reference to the juridical it includes the discursive logic of ordering social, economical and political relations and of what subjects and societies *are* before the law. The questions of how the juridical maintains its hegemonic position in the field of civil and individual rights, and how dominant forms of political practices are so inextricably interwoven with the juridical, are questions I explored in Chapter 5. In this chapter I will investigate some specific instances of legal politics as production sites of gendered and sexual meaning.

Since the early 1970s, great achievements have been seen in lesbian and gay legal politics in Europe, from de-criminalisation and anti-discrimination legislation to registered partnership. These rights are indeed powerful insignia. They often feature as final justice for those historically considered to be subjects of non-belonging and without legal rights. Gay and lesbian, but also transgender, rights are among the many leftovers of the unfinished business of modern democracies (Kaplan 1997a:3). However, justice and rights are not only given as positive re-enforcement for finally recognised gay identities: they are, and have historically been, more than a protective shield. Through its legal system and means of social control, the state is also a primary agent in regulation, normalisation, and exclusion. The legal rights won have changed the status of gay men and lesbians in society. However, as demonstrated before, while that may hold true for many gay and lesbian activists, these rights have also been seen by scholars in gay and lesbian and feminist studies as an effective extension of privileges to some – mainly to those who benefit from other racial, class or gender hierarchies – maintaining a heteronormative and binary gender norm(ality).

Critical and feminist jurisprudence has placed race, gender, and sexuality at the centre of defining legal discourses, the constitution of the law, and practices in courtrooms. Adding to this analysis, queer legal theorists have contributed another critical observation: the legal realm has been described as fundamentally heterosexual in that it is based on heteronormative discourses that essentialise sexual identities (Halley 1993:97). According to many queer legal theorists, the legal realm essentialises homosexuality, creates the subjects it needs to govern and is, thus, a major force in maintaining the privilege of heterosexuality (Morgan 1995:10). Nevertheless, while the law plays a role in the regulation of sexuality, the processes of courtrooms can also inadvertently produce ungovernable pluralities (Stychin 1995:140). The legal realm is, thus, not simply seen as the site of dominant and exclusionary regulation, but can potentially produce an entry point of challenge and change.

Thus, the complex political significance of the legal realm as a major site of rights movements needs to be investigated alongside the double-edged possibilities that realm contains. This means that the importance of legal battles is not denied from a queer theoretical perspective, but rather specifically and locally examined for the dilemma legal politics produces: a dilemma whose tensions are simultaneously irresolvable and productive. I will analyse two court cases at the European Court of Justice in order to demonstrate points of collusion between legal rights politics and queer critiques, and probe the consequences of this complicity.

Before the Amsterdam Treaty came into force, a few specific anti-discrimination court cases were heard. Two of them attempted to broaden the then existing anti-discrimination legislation based on sex and gender to cover gender identity and sexual orientation before the European Court of Justice: *P v. S and Cornwall County Council* (C-13/94 ECR (1996)) and *Lisa Grant v. South West Trains Ltd* (C-249/96 ECR (17.2.1998)).[1] Both cases revolve around questions of sex discrimination in employment concerning transsexuals (in *P*) and homosexuals (in *Grant*). As there was no anti-discrimination legislation that explicitly included gender identity or sexual orientation, activists tried to argue protection under the existing EU Directive on sex discrimination – successfully in *P* and unsuccessfully in *Grant*. The arguments employed in both cases unveil and question a distinction commonly unquestioned in European gay and lesbian politics: the distinction between sex and gender and the resulting separation of issues relating to gender identity – transgender – and sexual orientation – homosexuality. However, for queer theoretical purposes a re-connection of these issues is a primary concern. This chapter will, therefore, also focus on a theoretical contribution to the queer claim of fundamental alliances within l/g/b/t movements based on shared political and structural ground.

For the purpose of my analysis of the sex/gender divide I critique a traditional feminist argument in which sex is defined as the biologically fixed and basically value-free difference between men and women, their chromosomal and visible bodily difference. Gender is then used to emphasise the social construct of roles ascribed to men and women, institutionalising a hierarchy that structurally disadvantages women. This distinction has been an important concept of feminist thought prior to the advent of feminist poststructuralism, which has consequently reshaped most feminist scholarship with respect to the gender/sex distinction. This distinction has long moved from feminist thought into different academic fields and is by now also quite commonly found in the legal and political sphere in Europe, both among activists and within political and legal institutions. The distinction has, thus, gained a certain dominance in the perception of sexual difference and often counts as the modern, new approach to gender inequality.[2] This distinction is one of the reasons for the lack of alliances between homosexual and transgender rights movements since the advent of identity-based fights for liberation in Europe in the late 1960s.

The struggles for inclusion of lesbian and gay concerns in the transgender movement and vice versa are bound to the consequences the sex/gender divide bears on the distinctions between gender identity and sexual orientation. Both movements have long struggled to explain that lesbians and gay men are still *real* women and men and that transsexuals are primarily concerned with changing their outer appearance to their *inner true sex*. Matters of sexual object choice are of only secondary concern (Currah 1997a:1380). This explanation is a historical product of the dominant gender order, not an invented choice of the movements. Yet, it does lead once again to the belief in the biological essence of sex and the social construction of gender. This belief, in turn, produced politics based on the fact that sexual orientation and gender identity are two distinct and unconnected issues. Thus, while the separation is not an issue of false consciousness, these politics do continuously veil the intrinsic link between a normalised binary gender system and the exclusion of homosexuality from the pantheon of naturally, socially, and morally promotable choices. These politics also obscure the fundamental connections of transgender and homosexual or bisexual issues which would turn the alliances of those movements into more than a sympathy towards other oppressed people. The division of the apparently clearly distinguishable categories of sexual orientation and gender identity more often than not produces a subordination of one category under the other. According to Antke Engel (2000:157–75;163–5), even recent innovative suggestions for a 'Bill of Gender Rights' do not escape this logic of subordination.

Throughout the following discussion I will focus on both concerns outlined. I illuminate the complex potential of rights struggles in the legal field and argue for the intrinsic connections of transgender and homosexual issues through drawing out the intriguing interrelationship between gender, sexuality, and gay and lesbian rights politics. For this purpose I offer a critical reading of *P v. S* and *Grant v. SWT*. First, the two cases and the responses given to *Grant* by lesbian and gay rights activists are described. This is followed by a brief theorisation of the categories sex, gender, and identity from a queer perspective to illustrate what is at stake in politics based on notions of stable definitions of those concepts. Finally, I will offer a more in-depth analysis of *P* and *Grant* to show how the complexity of legal discourse can be an instrument of normative regulation, while at the same time highlighting the contingency of boundaries and disrupting the seeming coherence of gender and sexuality.

The cases and the responses: fabricating legal politics

Equality of men and women in the workplace is one of the fundamental pillars of the EU. The definition of the parameters of sexual discrimination has been dealt with regularly at the European Court of Justice in Luxembourg. In the second half of the 1990s, sex discrimination parameters have been tested as to their applicability to discrimination on the basis of gender identity and sexual orientation. In both cases, the issue at stake was the compliance with the 1976 Equal Treatment Directive and Article 119 of the Maastricht Treaty.[3]

P v. S and Cornwall County Council involved a male-to-female transsexual, P, who worked as a senior manager in a Cornwall education establishment. On informing her employers that she was undergoing gender re-assignment and wished to come to work as a woman, she was given notice of the termination of her contract. She was not allowed to return to work during the period of her transition, when she was living full time as a woman but had not undergone surgical genital reassignment. Her period of employment terminated without her returning to work. P brought an action before an industrial tribunal, claiming that she had suffered discrimination on the ground of sex. Both S and Cornwall County Council claimed that, on the contrary, she had been dismissed by reason of redundancy. The tribunal referred the case to the European Court of Justice, which decided in favour of the transsexual and found evident discrimination on grounds of Article 5(1) of the 1976 Directive. This decision was undeniably a huge step forward for the transgender movement.[4]

The outcome of the *Lisa Grant* case on 17 February 1998 was less favourable. Lisa Grant, an employee of South West Trains, claimed discrimination on the ground of sex. Travel concessions offered by her employer were granted to the common law opposite-sex spouse of her predecessor in her job – a man – but were denied to her partner – a woman – on the ground that the 'privilege tickets are granted for one common-law opposite sex spouse of staff ... subject to a statutory declaration being made that a meaningful relationship has existed for a period of two years or more' (C-249/96 para. 5). Grant had been living with her partner, Jill Percey, in a long-term relationship that formally fulfilled the requirement South West Trains Ltd set for those employees who lived with an opposite-sex partner. The annual travel pass disputed by Lisa Grant amounted to a substantial pay benefit. Grant's counsel argued along the lines of sex discrimination instead of sexual orientation discrimination, for which the EU had no mandate at the time. They took the sex of Grant's partner as given and argued that if Lisa Grant had been a man, her woman partner would have had access to travel concessions – the 'but for' test[5] (para. 17).

The granting or not granting of the pay benefit depended, thus, on the sexes of the partners. Although the Advocate General, as in *P v. S*, had advised in favour of applying Article 119 of the EC Treaty – equal treatment for women and men – the Court ruled against Grant – and in doing so diverged from its common practice of accepting the opinion of the Advocate General. It denied that there was sex discrimination and it identified sexual orientation discrimination to which a man living with a man would be subjected as well (the 'equal misery' argument). The Court also found that in view of the EU law and the law in most Member States, homosexual couples could not be regarded as equivalent to married or unmarried heterosexual couples (para. 35). Interestingly enough, the Court comes to this conclusion by calling on the decisions of most Member States to grant, if at all, partial rights only and by citing negative decisions of the European Court of Human Rights on Article 14 – Protection of Family Rights. It mainly mentions *X, Y and Z v. United Kingdom* (Case No. 75/1995/581/667) in which a transsexual British man claimed the right to be named as the father of the daughter born to him and his female partner through officially granted AID – as is common for other heterosexual couples in the same situation in Britain. His claim was dismissed. Apart from being the follow-up case to *P v. S*, *Grant* is, thus, also compared with *XYZ* as another transgender case.

Grant was referred to the ECJ, citing the ECJ's decision in *P*, and the comparison of both cases has created a stir in legal academic circles and among activists. The failure of *Grant* then sparked a deep sense of disappointment among activists, who had believed that by virtue of *P* and the opinion of the Advocate General Michael Elmer, *Grant* was virtually already decided. The complications implied in the working of the European legal system concerning the understandings of sex and gender are expressed in those responses in two ways: in the discussions of the merits of sex discrimination being applicable to sexual orientation and in the disappointment about the failure.

Jill Percey, Lisa Grant's partner, stated: 'We are bitterly disappointed by this ruling. It is scandalous that Lisa's employers can discriminate against her just because she is a lesbian. We hope the government will now act to make such discrimination unlawful.' (Stonewall press release, 17 February 1998). Anya Palmer called the judgment a 'blow to lesbians and gay men everywhere in the EC', and Angela Mason – Executive Director of Stonewall – said 'it is unbelievable that in this day and age, we have a judgment that means that lesbians and gays effectively have no rights in the workplace' (Stonewall press release, 17 February 1998). 'All speakers' of the European Parliament Intergroup 'Equal Rights for Gays and Lesbians' 'were unanimous in their disappointment and regret about the decision, some called it a scandal. ... ILGA-Europe representative Kurt Krickler heavily criticised in his statement the arguments and substantiation put forward by the Court in its decision. He stressed that this was clearly a political decision by which the Court sent out the signal that lesbians and gays still are second class citizens in the EU' (EP Intergroup minutes, 18 February 1998).

These responses are interesting on several levels. The decision is portrayed as a 'blow to lesbians and gay men everywhere in the EC' or 'a signal that lesbians and gays still are second class citizens in the EU'. This portrayal implicitly substitutes Lisa Grant's lesbian identity, and the discrimination on grounds of it, with lesbian and gay citizens, and the lack of protection from discrimination suffered by those citizens. There is no distinction made between the failure of a sex discrimination case and the refusal to protect lesbians and gay men *qua* their identity from unjust exclusion of heterosexual pay privileges. Jill Percey's call for the moral responsibility of the Labour government in Britain is a statement in kind. None of the official responses from the gay and lesbian press and political lobby groups made any distinction *after* the judgment. Before the judgment, however, there was also strong criticism of the equation of sexual orientation discrimination and sex discrimination among lesbian and gay EU lobbyists.

Three reasons were mentioned most frequently in my discussions with activists at the EU level: firstly, a fear that mixing issues of gender and sexuality might potentially make it difficult for gay men to claim the same discrimination. Secondly, a fear of aligning the gay and lesbian movement with the transgender cause and thirdly, a fear of inhibiting the proper inclusion of sexual orientation discrimination legislation into forthcoming EU Directives. (EGALITE newsletter issue 22/23, 1998) Politically speaking, for parts of the European lesbian and gay rights movement the case was an attempt to do something now with the existing legislation rather than wait for a possible prohibition of sexual orientation discrimination in the EU later. As such it was a viable goal. Its negative outcome has, however, prompted lobbyists to focus once again on including sexual orientation in the anti-discrimination shopping list of EU law on its own merits, which has since happened.

The Court already referred to Article 13 in its judgment in *Grant*, pointing to the fact that the Council will under certain conditions – such as an unanimous vote on a proposal from the Commission after consulting the European Parliament – be able to take appropriate action to eliminate various forms of discrimination, including discrimination based on sexual orientation (para. 48). This has since then happened. The reference to Article 13 prompted hopeful responses from ILGA-Europe and the European Parliament Intergroup on lesbian and gay issues (ILGA press release, 18 February 1998; minutes of the EP intergroup meeting, 18 February 1998). Although the chances of success in creating a Directive on anti-discrimination seemed slim at the time, activists responded to *Grant* with an increased effort to stabilise a system of anti-discrimination shopping lists that name sexual orientation in its own right. In doing so, gender identity is excluded from the discussion and the strategy of arguing via sex discrimination is entirely abandoned. From a practical perspective, this move might make sense. From a queer theoretical perspective, it gives away important avenues of creating more fundamental change in the epistemological workings of the law.

As I hope to show, the implicit disruption of the separation between lesbian identity and gender identity in *Grant* did not work, for two reasons. On the one hand, the epistemological and ontological gender hierarchy of Western law cannot allow such disruption. On the other hand, the argumentation in *Grant* could simply not go far enough in calling heteronormativity into question. In the following discussion I theorise aspects of the evident connection of lesbian identity and gender identity in the two cases by introducing some fundamental critiques of sex, gender, and identity as foundations of rights battles. Rather than dismissing the argumentation in *P* and *Grant*, I wish to put it on a firmer footing than it was ever placed in the European gay and lesbian rights movement. Connecting gender identity and sexual orientation – or sex discrimination and sexual orientation discrimination – is a vital challenge to identity-based politics from a queer theoretical perspective.

Theorising sex, gender, and identity

In both cases, *P* and *Grant*, the central turning point was officially a definition of sex discrimination. Also in both cases, the opinions of the Advocates General were directed towards a more purposeful interpretation of sex discrimination, and the decisions of the Court focused on a comparison centred test for discrimination (Bell 1999:70). Mark Bell (1999:74) maintains that the legal incoherence of the two cases relates to 'the size of the group concerned; the potential political consequences; and the "moral" dimension'. His argumentation is undoubtedly correct, but there is another set of fundamental parameters at work here. The actual question negotiated in those cases is not, as the Court explicitly said, a definition of sex discrimination, but the question underlying *Grant* is rather: what does the apparently natural fact of two sexes/genders mean for permissible expressions of gender identity and sexual object choice and their protection in the labour market? In other words, what kinds of gender crossing or meaningful sexual relationships are worthy of protection if the natural existence of two clearly distinct sexes is taken for granted?

From the legal perspective, *Grant* could have proven what Robert Wintemute (1997:347) claims to be a tenable argument: 'Once the definitial link between sexual orientation and sex is understood, it should be clear that discrimination based on sexual orientation is *simultaneously* discrimination based on sex as to who may choose a partner of a given sex'. For Wintemute this legal argument does not, in consequence, deny sexual difference, and it does not conflate gender identity and sexual orientation. From a queer theoretical perspective, the dismantling of those distinctions in the analysis of discrimination litigation is, in contrast, of particular interest. The fundamental disturbance of stable, coherent identities is at the centre of queer theoretical attention and the legal and political implications such disturbance produces are significant.

Although the 1976 EC Directive on sex discrimination does not attempt to offer any real definition of sex, man or woman, any effective functioning of the legislation depends on them having a clear meaning. The mapping of the law rests on two assumptions: there are two types of human bodies, and two distinct sets of gendered behaviour – including sexual object choice – follow from this alleged natural fact. The existence of sexual orientation as a marker of difference arises out of the construction of sex and gender as previously described. Any legal proceeding concerned with questions of homosexual, transgender, or women's rights contributes to the definition of the relationship between sex and gender. Through the predominantly heteronormative foundation of Western law, sexual identity becomes the conflation of anatomical sex, socially constructed gender, and sexuality. In that logic, penis equals male and male equals sex with female. This rule has a long historical tradition. According to Ernst van Alphen (1995:3), sexuality used to be understood as derived from the gendered soul: 'first we have a gendered identity, next, in its wake, a sexual orientation. When the gendered mind is incarnated in the corresponding body it results in authentic, that is heterosexual, sexuality'.[6]

At the same time, however, an advanced modern European law insists on being able to distinguish between natural fact and social behaviour. Katherine Franke (1995:2) maintains that 'by accepting these biological differences equality jurisprudence reifies as foundational *fact* that which is really an *effect* of normative gender ideology'. In other words an enlightened post-women's liberation law in Europe rests on an understanding of sex difference – as biological difference – accounting for the social construct of gender. This social construct might at times be acknowledged as discriminatory; but the fact of an existing gender difference that faithfully mirrors sex and biological difference is not really questioned. Within a poststructuralist feminist approach, however, this constitutes an exchange of fact and effect. The social and cultural construct of gender is here proclaimed to be (re)productive of biological difference. This exchange of fact and effect is evident in the activists' responses to *Grant* and in the judgment itself; and it is central to a critique of the conceptualisation of sex and gender as brought forward in queer theory.

Identity politics are embedded in a language of establishing identity as difference from others: as a distinction of presence and absence. Hence, homosexual identity holds a promise of a group unity, solidarity, and universality, which it perpetuates but cannot fully deliver (Butler 1993:188). The performance of homosexual identity as a marker of discrimination rests on the existence of distinguishable genders as its pre-condition. In fact, the discursive establishment of the heterosexual/homosexual divide depends fundamentally on – and is part of – the discursive establishment of the gender binary. What we conceive of as identities, and, thus, make politically and legally intelligible, is constructed within the boundaries of permissible dominant discourses about the so-called fact of two biologically distinct sexes. The discourses on sexuality and gender apparent in the European legal and political contexts always rest on perceived bodily difference between the sexes. This is the case independent of whether the argumentation appropriates, enhances, constructs, or contests the dominant perception of human sexuality as heterosexuality.

The perception of bodily difference – and the subsequent construction of a coherent gender identity that constitutes desire as directed to the opposite sex – is integral to the very (re)production of heterosexuality as the one and only healthy, normal, natural sexuality. As Judith Butler (1990:22) formulates it:

> Gender can denote a *unity* of experience, of sex, of gender, and desire, only when sex can be understood in some sense to necessitate gender – where

gender is a psychic and/or cultural designation of the self – and desire – where desire is heterosexual and therefore differentiates itself through an oppositional relation to that other gender it desires. The internal coherence or unity of either gender, man or woman, thereby requires both a stable and oppositional heterosexuality. That institutional heterosexuality both requires and produces the univocity of each of the gendered terms that constitute the limit of gendered possibilities within an oppositional, binary gender system. This conception of gender presupposes not only a causal relation among sex, gender, and desire, but suggests as well that desire reflects or expresses gender and that gender reflects or expresses desire.

In addition, 'neither sexuality nor social identity is given exclusively through the body' (Poovey 1988:51), and sex – as sexual difference and as sexual act – itself does not '*describe* a prior materiality, but produces and regulates the *intelligibility* of the *materiality* of bodies' (Butler 1992:17). The dividing lines of sex and gender are, thus, disintegrated, for – as Butler (1990:7) writes:

> If the immutable character of sex is contested, perhaps this construct called 'sex' is as culturally constructed as gender; indeed, perhaps it was always already gender, with the consequence that the distinction between sex and gender turns out to be no distinction at all ... This production of sex *as* the prediscursive ought to be understood as the effect of the apparatus of cultural construction designated by gender.

Hence, sexual orientation, or to be more precise the exclusion of homosexuality from definitions of natural human sexuality, is fundamentally a question of gender identity, or indeed sex difference, albeit not always a mere second consequence. Only through the maintenance of two clearly identifiable sexes, which produce coherent *normal* gender identities, can heterosexual object choice be the normalising effect of a regulatory regime that institutes heterosexuality as the foundation of human sexuality. Following this thought to its logical consequence results in an intrinsic connection between homosexuality in its basis and issues of sex discrimination *as well as* of gender identity, and, thus, to transgender politics. The infamous l/g/b/t alliances that combine the sexual politics of gays, lesbians, and bisexuals and the gender politics of the transgender movement, proclaimed by so many involved in queer critical thought, are a necessary consequence of this logic. Paisley Currah (1997a:1385) brings this to a political point: 'In challenging the sex-based classifications so embedded in so much discrimination against gays, lesbians, bisexuals, queer, and transgendered people, it is vital that we get to the root of the problem and challenge the very premises of the classification system itself.' Along with Paisley Currah, most queer critics argue that traditional gay and lesbian rights lobbying never reflects this connection.[7] To some extent, this observation is correct.

For example, ILGA-World and ILGA-Europe include gay men, lesbians, bisexuals, and transgender people in their mandate. The practice of ILGA-Europe's political argumentation shows a clear awareness of gender as an important theme related to sexual orientation, but omits the intrinsic connection of gender identity and sexuality. Homosexuals, while being in solidarity with transsexuals, mostly remain a discrete insular group with specific issues of concern.[8] ILGA-Europe rarely makes gender identity an explicit target of political practice and has never given it much explicit attention until 2003. Where it is mentioned it usually remains separated. One example of a formulation is the convention address and the specific submission of 27 April 2000 towards the EU draft Charter of Fundamental Rights. The submission argues:

> ILGA-Europe submits that the non-discrimination article of the EU Charter should also include the ground 'gender identity' so as to make it clear that people who are transsexual or transgender are protected and in recognition of the particular vulnerability of this group.[9]
>
> Transsexual and transgender people are one of the most vulnerable minorities in Europe. Their relatively small numbers make it extremely difficult for them to obtain any protection against discrimination through new legislation. They face violence, harassment and the denial of jobs or services because their gender identity or expression does not correspond with their recorded birth sex. The discrimination they face can be quite as severe as that faced by other groups who traditionally are accorded specific protection by national and international anti-discrimination legislation.

Here, ILGA-Europe refers to a separation or division into different groups of marginalisation. This is not astonishing given the historical development of identity movements, in fact, it is a common approach taken by NGOs who designate their constituency as consisting of different groups. While it is important that ILGA-Europe finally designates some of its lobby-power to transgender issues, the origin of a separation approach is worrisome. This origin rests on the dominant discourse on gender and sexuality in European societies, which defines homosexual identity as unitary and essential, residing clearly, intelligibly, and unalterably in the body and psyche, fixing desire in a gendered direction. The 'coming out' rhetoric and a clear segregation of lesbians, gays, bisexuals, and transgender people into four distinct groups becomes a way of healing proper male or female gender identity which was historically damaged by homosexuality or the transition phase of transsexuals. Anything that opens this old wound seems at best too theoretical and away from political practices and at worst too dangerous to be entertained.[10]

Underneath this fear is the presentation of rights as rights of individuals who are conceptually and ontologically prior to society. In consequence, this presentation makes it possible to pursue rights as if equality for lesbians and gays could be accommodated within the existing social gender order without significantly undermining heterosexual privilege (Rahman and Jackson 1997:118). In principle, the segregation of sex and gender – and the disconnection of gender identity and sexual orientation – is theoretically and politically dissolvable at this point in time. Yet, it does involve a disclaiming of historically developed positions that more often than not appear to be the only positions that can be occupied with regards to justice and equality.

The practices of politics are, though, never one-sided and simple whatever position they occupy. For example, through the reference to *P* in the referral of *Grant* to the ECJ and in the *Grant* judgment itself, as well as through the proceedings of both cases, the implications of the homosexual and transgender alliances favoured by a queer theoretical approach have already gained entry into the world of large-scale European legal politics in an interesting and complex way. *P v. S and Cornwall County Council* and *Grant v. South West Trains Ltd* can indeed both be read to re-inscribe and disrupt discourses of sexual and gender difference simultaneously. Further, while both cases create a logic of sexual difference, *Grant*, in particular, additionally produces a site of ontological contestation.

Reading *P v. S* and *Grant v. SWT*: re-inscribing and contesting binary divisions

The discourses underpinning the Court's decision in *Grant* re-create, maintain, and defend the exclusion of gay men and lesbians as non-normal and not worthy of protection. However, *Grant* also contains a contestation of precisely that exclusion through implicitly exposing the contingency of the binary gender system. *Grant*, therefore, involves a two-fold logic.

Four aspects of the proceedings of *Grant* and *P* illustrate this two-fold logic and the connection of gender identity and sexual orientation. Firstly, the meanings of gender and sexuality are individualised *and* totalised. Although the sex of Lisa Grant is argued by her counsel as the grounds of discrimination (paras 16–18), her gender identity remains non-conforming for the Court, in that her sexual object choice is non-conforming: a real woman chooses a man, not another woman. Thus, for the Court the discrimination has to be because of her lesbian identity, not her woman identity. Secondly, in order to stand any chance of winning this case, the apparent disruption of the connection between gender norms and sexuality evident in Lisa Grant's argument had to remain on the surface; the argument could not disrupt biology, i.e. the body as the fundamental, transparent marker of difference.

Thirdly, the law needs that marker to order and create the possibility of equality, which is in itself a critical goal of gay and lesbian politics. Finally, allowing a conflation of sex discrimination and sexual orientation discrimination could render same-sex desire and other-sex desire an intrinsic possibility of all gender identities. The excluded homosexual would, thus, be allowed to return and disrupt the claim of two coherent heterosexual genders. To my mind it is at this last level that one finds the site of contestation in *Grant*, in that gender potentially ceases to be recognisable as a cultural inscription on a prior essential set of differences.

Wayne Morgan (1995:22), a queer legal theorist, identifies simultaneous individualisation and totalisation of the subject as a fundamental procedure of disciplinary power of modern states. *P* and *Grant*, and their comparison, perpetuate a simultaneous individualisation and totalisation of the meaning of gender and sexuality. On the one hand, identifying individuals as part of either one sex or the other, and subsequently of clear gender categories – even if those categories can be change – is part of exercising power in the direction of ordering and defining. Gender is acknowledged as changeable; sex – as biological and chromosomal foundation – is not.[11] The individual subject can only ever be part of one or the other gender; a transition period is only temporarily acceptable and often constitutes the fundamental problem for the social and employment environment of individuals. The law cannot know its subject if it cannot define it clearly in mutually dependent gender and sex categories.

In fact, from a queer theoretical point of view the law produces the subject *as individual* it claims to govern. On the basis of intrinsic signs of individuality and personhood, the legal procedures play with a clear unrelatedness of sex and sexual orientation, rendering permissible those gender identities that do not pervert themselves through the false sexual object choice. On the other hand, the applicability of sex discrimination to lesbians, gay men, and bisexuals as it was argued in *Grant* still totalises the definition of identities into a belief in a rigid biological system of two sexes. There is still a sense of normality, a total and complete identity, which is not transgendered or homosexual. In consequence, the embodied difference of those who are granted protection from discrimination must be retained. The discriminated subject can only remain discriminated. The opinion of the Advocate General in *P* (I-2154-5) illustrates the double bind of individualisation and totalisation:

> I believe that the principle of non-discrimination on grounds of sex permits only those exceptions which, because they aim at attaining *substantive* equality, are justified by the objective of ensuring actual equality between persons ... I must add that, for the purpose of this case, sex is important as a convention, a social parameter. The discrimination of which women are frequently the victims is not of course due to their physical characteristics, but rather to their role, to the image which society has of women. Hence the *rationale* for less favourable treatment is the social role which women are supposed to play and certainly not their physical characteristics.

Tesauro's fairly progressive approach in fact re-inscribes the individualisation of gender identity and the clear-cut distinction between sex and gender, although he does not distinguish the terms. When he maintains that 'any connotations relating to sex and/or sexual identity cannot be in any way relevant' (para. 2154), he dispels the equal misery argument, which would argue that female-to-male transsexuals would have suffered the same discrimination. He does this by invoking the notion of equality encapsulated in the Directive, claiming that it required sex to be rendered a legally irrelevant criterion. He also claims that it is not the physical constituency of men and women *per se* that is the cause of the discrimination. It is rather the erroneous gender stereotyping that places the value of one sex over that of the other. His more dynamic, responsive interpretation of the Directive is welcomed and progressive in comparison with the pure comparator-based approach

(Skidmore 1997:107). It manifests and re-creates, however, the existence of two distinct sexes: only the content of gender and its meanings are up for discussion in relation to the situation in which one individual finds herself.

That argumentation works when approaching the case of gender reassignment, and could have worked in *P* – although the Court in the end did decide on the basis of comparing the pre-operative person with the post-operative person. As soon as sexual orientation enters the stage, though, the sex/gender divide becomes more problematic through its maintenance of gender identity as distinct from sexual orientation. Subsequently, in *Grant* (para. 42) the Court promptly draws the line exactly at a distinction between gender identity and sexual orientation, and rules against Lisa Grant:

> The Court (in *P*) considered that such discrimination was in fact based, essentially if not exclusively, on the sex of the person concerned. That reasoning, which leads to the conclusion that such discrimination is to be prohibited just as is discrimination based on the fact that a person belongs to a particular sex, is limited to the case of a worker's gender reassignment and does not therefore apply to differences of treatment based on a person's sexual orientation.

At first sight the negotiation of sexual orientation discrimination as pertaining to forms of sex discrimination in Grant's argumentation could be a way out of rigid gender norms. Indeed, Grant's argument conflates sex and gender and, therefore, potentially makes the connection between gender identity and sexual orientation:

> Ms Grant contends, next, that such a refusal constitutes discrimination based on sexual orientation, which is included in the concept of 'discrimination based on sex' in Article 119 of the Treaty. In her opinion, differences in treatment based on sexual orientation originate in prejudices regarding the sexual and emotional behaviour of persons of a particular sex, and are in fact based on those persons' sex. She submits that such an interpretation follows from the judgment in *P v. S* and corresponds both to the resolutions and commendations adopted by the Community institutions and to the development of international human rights standards and national rules on equal treatment. (para. 18)

Grant's argument maintains that the discrimination on grounds of sexual orientation is part of discrimination based on sex. She claims the fact that only men are allowed to have female spouses creates a prohibition of homosexual relationships. Inherent in this argument is already a critique of the regulatory regime of sex and gender that binds the essence of real womanhood or manhood to heterosexual desire. Upon closer examination, however, this argument cannot disrupt the fixity of biology behind gender, i.e. the belief in the body as the objective marker of difference, whatever that difference means.

Gay men and lesbians in the excerpt quoted above still belong to a clear sex; it is their sexual and emotional behaviour that differs. Keeping in mind that Lisa Grant was trying to win a case within the limitations of existing anti-discrimination legislation in the EU, the limitations of legally arguable disruptions of a fixed biology become also very clear. In the end, it is the latter limitations that made the Court decide against Lisa Grant's case. Thus, the law cannot undo markers of difference such as biology since it depends on them in its very existence. Lisa Grant's argument could not have gone much further and still remain legal. The belief in a fixed biology remains at the heart of the problem. This belief is a major justifier for institutionalising difference as the fundamental marker of social order and justice, against which the comparators of the judgments and the principle of equality are measured. Law, thus, needs this marker to purport any concept of equality at all. In short – to state the obvious again – difference is needed to conceptualise equality.

Equality looms large in the argumentation brought to the European Courts on matters of transgender and homosexuality. The press follow-ups to *Grant* quoted above identify the lost legal battle as a setback for progress towards equality for all lesbians and gay men in the EU. Yet, what equality is sought here? Which norm(ality) is the equaliser? Who compares what to whom? The Advocate General in *P* (para. 2155) dispels the equal misery argument of the UK – no discrimination evident because female-to-male transsexuals are treated equally badly – by arguing that:

> to maintain that the unfavourable treatment suffered by P was not on grounds of sex because it was due to her sex change or else because it is not possible to speak of discrimination between the two sexes would be a quibbling formalistic interpretation and a betrayal of that fundamental and inalienable value which is equality.

The Court in *P* reaffirmed the principle of equality as a fundamental principle in Community Law. It held that the scope of the Directive had to be interpreted wider than discrimination 'based on the fact that the person is of one or other sex' (para. 20) to include discrimination arising from gender reassignment. However, it located this again within a comparative approach. The appropriate comparator is not a female-to-male transsexual but the previous persona: had P continued to belong to the male sex and gender, she would not have been discriminated against (para. 21).

The appeal by the Court to higher values of equality, dignity, and autonomy masks the difficulty of manipulating sex discrimination concepts to accommodate transsexuals: there cannot be any sex discrimination legislation without clear categorisation into man and woman (Skidmore 1997:108–9). Sex needs to remain highly relevant in order to reach the goal of legislation in rendering sex irrelevant. There is a strong need in this to exclude the transition phase there is no third sex in law. Tesauro is happy to treat P as a woman without regard to her chromosomes, gonads, or genitalia, but she needs to be treated as either man or woman, a woman who has concluded the transition. She has concluded the transition and can now be compared by the court to her former complete and clear status as a member of the male sex. Gender identities are not questioned. The legal imagination is limited to binary poles with nothing outside them and a middle ground that can be crossed quickly in a state of sickness, but that cannot become a space of occupied identity.

The type of equality achieved for transsexuals is, thus, a system-intrinsic equality within a rigid binary gender system. The equality granted in *P* is surely highly welcome. If nothing else, the implementation of a universal right to equality reduces the salience of the binary divide between normal women and men and transsexuals in employment. However, it does not call the apparent nature of sex and the mutually dependent category of gender into question. It does not threaten privileges that come with conforming to one's apparently true sex in expressing the appropriate gender identity.

While the 'equal misery' argument was dispelled in *P*, the equal misery of gay men was the deciding factor for the Court in *Grant* to justify its negative ruling (para. 27). The argued comparison with a heterosexual man, who is allowed to choose a female partner, is denied. Equality – on a par with the fundamental human rights dimension – is a right that is taken as evident; it is not reasoned. It rests on the presumption that sex is an objective, coherent, and stable difference, while the law has now reached the point of allowing gender to be a changeable concept. All comparison is ultimately comparison with a norm(ality). When Lisa Grant's counsel compares her situation with that of unmarried heterosexual couples then all the Court does, and not unexpectedly, is to throw marriage into the discussion. It necessarily comes to the conclusion that gay and lesbian relationships are pretended relationships in comparison with real marriages or stable heterosexual relationships and can, thus, not be regarded as legally equal.[12]

> It follows that, in the present state of the law within the Community, stable relationships between two persons of the same sex are not regarded as equivalent to marriages or stable relationships outside marriage between persons of opposite sex. Consequently, an employer is not required by Community law to treat the situation of a person who has a stable relationship with a partner of the same sex as equivalent to that of a person who is married to or has a stable relationship outside marriage with a partner of the opposite sex. (*Grant* para. 35)

As *Grant* proves once again, the campaign for equality in courtrooms on the basis of two distinct sexes and a permanent homosexual minority remains somewhat misguided. The hope of equality litigation is that sex/gender and sexual orientation will one day be no more significant than being left handed. The significance of discrimination against gays, lesbians, bisexuals, and transgender people is reduced to the belief that an irrational prejudice must simply be abolished. However, neither gender nor sexuality is a natural difference that can be treated by equality; each remain inevitably a discourse with a history of subordination, norms, and hierarchies.

Having said this, it has to be noted that in *Grant* the implementation of a universalistic right of equality can be seen as progressive: in certain aspects it makes sexuality irrelevant in employment opportunities, reducing the salience of the binary divide between gay and straight. In practice, though, such a right need not call the culturally compulsory element of heterosexuality into question; it does not threaten the maintenance of heterosexual privileges. Claiming legal equality remains, therefore, a strategy that can be successful from a practical perspective, reducing the everyday hardship and cruelty many lesbians, gay men, bisexuals, and transgender people experience. Yet, it will not actually deliver what it promises, namely fundamental equality and social justice. As soon as rights are demanded in areas that are central to the institutionalisation of heterosexuality, mainly the family, political practices in legal equality will necessarily fail. The explicit exclusion of adoption and custody of children in almost all gay and lesbian partnership legislation in Europe – apart from the Netherlands – is a good example in this respect.[13]

In summary, *Grant* is another instance in which homosexual identity is simultaneously inscribed, made intelligible, and excluded. These effects occur as the coherence of sex, and possible sex discrimination, comes to depend on the denial of any intervention that exposes the contingency of *natural* sex, gender identities, and sexuality. The Court cannot deal with a multiplicity of identities, sexualities, and discriminations that do not fit into neat categories. The specificity of Lisa Grant's lesbian identity can only be demarcated by exclusion; it cannot be allowed to enter the definition of sex discrimination, as that would be a disruption of a culturally dominant belief system. There are two natural and coherent sexes that result in the desire to have a normal heterosexual gender identity. So re-considered from this perspective, sexual orientation discrimination argued as sex discrimination produces indeed a site of ontological contestation.

The intersections of sex, gender identity, and sexual orientation that surface in parts of the *Grant* argumentation begin to disintegrate the boundedness of the category of the homosexual, whose anti-discrimination rights were then not covered by Community legislation. Gender thereby ceases to be recognisable as a cultural inscription on a prior essential set of sex difference, to which compulsory heterosexuality is intrinsically bound. Thus, one could argue that what made *Grant* fail while *P* succeeded is more than the issues Mark Bell (1999:74) identified, namely the size of the group, the political consequence, and morality. Underlying this case is the urge to maintain homosexual identity separate from the definitions of gender identity, whose normality needs to remain heterosexual to continue serving as the comparator to which discrimination litigation adheres.

Grant and *P* have, hence, done more than participate in a legal discussion on the definition of sex discrimination. Potentially, their argumentation opens up a debate on the meanings of sex, gender identity, and sexual orientation. Surely, all rights claims and all political practices in that respect participate inadvertently in this debate, even if they do not challenge, but rather re-affirm, hegemonic orders. *Grant* and *P*, though, carry the additional potential to render the intrinsic connections of those identity categories visible. The return to a shopping list that includes separate categories of discrimination, as in the Amsterdam Treaty, will ultimately not deliver the justice and equality gay men, lesbians, bisexuals, and transgender people hope for. It will not challenge any of the fundamental cultural markers of difference that produce the discrimination suffered in the first place. In fact, the law cannot undo these markers at all, since it is ontologically bound to them. At certain instances these cultural markers of difference can become visible and may be turned into the target of debate. The aim can, thus, not be a call for a resignation from litigation or legal rights. Yet, a heightened awareness and constructive use of the inevitably produced dilemma of legal politics called for.

Conclusion

For many writers in queer theory the legal arena is one of the places where deviant subjects are produced. This is indeed a process to which we should turn our analytical attention. The legal arena cannot operate without the logic of identity, yet subjects of the law do not exist prior to their negotiation in the legal processes. The power of the law lies in representing something as real, as the only possible representation of the real. So while subjects in courtrooms are real people, they can only ever be represented partially in their diversities. The legal subject can only present itself *as subject* in the discursive logic of the juridical. Other possible truths and realities are existent, but the reality that can be heard by the legal interpretation is hegemonic and dominant. Thus, the power of law is its acclamation of one reality as the most true reality, the most important reality (Herman 1994:6).

This approach de-mythologises legal rights and destroys the sometimes illusionary hope for true justice. At the same time it acknowledges the epistemological authority of the law: not as an all-powerful discourse, but as an important site for the constitution, consolidation, and regulation of sexuality (Stychin 1995:156). Certain activist discourses on legal rights as fulfilment of equality are surely ripe for ontological and epistemological doubt. However emancipatory the political and legal actors, texts, and regulations try to be, they somehow remain within the logic of a heteronormative binary gender system. This makes the whole process of staging l/g/b/t legal politics at least a complicated and at times a very critical project. The rhetoric of the liberated future whose approach we are apparently witnessing is marked by a romanticised fascination with equality before the law while gayness, bisexuality, and transgenderism continue to cross boundaries of cultural norms. This rhetoric, which remains the dominant rhetoric of gay and lesbian rights lobbying, does not always recognise the pre-condition of the existence of the legal order: manifesting regimes for normalised governable subjects.[14]

In spite of this, institutionalised legal battles are not only a site of normative regulation and the production of deviant subjects. They can never undo the cultural markers that create, cement, institutionalise, and change the meaning of difference and identity. That can only be done by social movements in a historical process of discursive challenge. Yet, they are potentially a battlefield on which cultural markers could be rendered visible and where human diversity can at least be spoken. The connection of gender identity and sexual orientation, i.e. of what constitutes a real woman and what sexual choices that woman makes – evident in the *Grant* case – is one instance which carries that political potential. The *Grant* case carries a political potential that is, to my mind, reaching further than the separate anti-discrimination shopping lists of the Amsterdam Treaty ever can.

Legal battles are a theatre in which activists try to stage a logic of emancipation while desperately aiming at going beyond that same logic to incorporate the experienced social ruptures of their constituency. This apparent clash needs to be vocalised. The great majority of those involved in fighting for legal rights do surely not pretend that the implications of rights argumentation are entirely unproblematic.[15] Yet, so far the complexities of the discursive spaces available in legal politics have not been turned into a political practice in themselves. Political practices that engage the law frequently invest in a logic that incorporates diversity into the norm(ality), but rarely invest in a logic that questions the gender identities and sexuality of that norm(ality). Much depends on how and where gay men, lesbians, bisexuals, and transgender people want to constitute themselves as governable minorities to claim legal rights and where the coherence of sex, gender identity, and sexuality can be disrupted. It is important to identify how legal arguments can be used to disrupt normative assumptions and how they can re-negotiate the conditions for the constitution of the legal and political subject. Cases like *P* and *Grant* at the ECJ take one step in that direction and participate in the inadvertent production of ungovernable pluralities (Stychin 1995:140). Ungovernable pluralities are also needed to conceptualise citizenship in a way that can be called democratic and that consciously engages in processes of recognition with regard to diversity.

Notes

1. There was a third case still pending after the *Grant* decision, *R v. Secretary of State for Defence, ex parte Perkins* (C-168/97), which was concerned with the same argumentation as *Grant*. This case was, however, never completed since the British Court that referred it to the ECJ withdrew the case a while after the *Grant* decision. On 28 January 1999, the Court of First Instance dismissed another anti-discrimination case concerning employment of gays and lesbians at the EU institutions and the acceptance of Swedish registered partnership for employment purposes at the EU Commission (*D v. Council of the European Union*, T-264/97). The appeal to the ECJ was lost in 2001 (C-122/99P and C-125/99P, *D and Sweden v. Council*).
2. This is even true for language contexts, such as German, that do not know such distinction. In these contexts words like 'gender role' (*Geschlechterrolle*) became the substitute for the English term 'gender' and 'gender' (*Geschlecht*) remained the equivalent of 'sex'.
3. 76/207/EEC, 9.2.76 (OJ 1976 L 39): Council Directive on the Implementation of the Principle of Equal Treatment for Men and Women as Regards Access to Employment, Vocational Training and Promotion and Working conditions. Article 119 of the Maastricht Treaty sets out the basic principle prohibiting discrimination based on sex. It was updated in 2002.

4 For responses from the transgender community to this case see the Press for Change web archive: www.pfc.org.uk (particularly the response by Stephen Whittle and Christine Burns).
5 The discussion around the disaggregation of sex and gender in sexual discrimination litigation is not new within legal scholarship. See, for diverse general discussions, Franke (1995) and Case (1995) and for the specific European context Wintemute (1997).
6 According to Alphen (1995:6–7), the questioning of the relationship between the gendered soul and sexual identity has a long history since Freud's psychoanalytic theory. To open the relation between gender and sexual desire we need not, however, turn to psychoanalysis. The contemporary practices of homosexuality and lesbianism imply that gender identity can no longer be seen as the source of homosexual or heterosexual desire, 'but as an effect of identification, constructed in specific historical and cultural contexts' (1995:7).
7 Some critics maintain, however, that queer theory does not fully take into account the issue of transgenderism either. At worst, queer theory is said to subsume transgender under gay and lesbian issues; at best, it is said to make a spectacle out of transgendered people through its focus on performativity. See, for an elaboration on this, Goldman (1996) and Namaste (1996a; 1996b; 1998).
8 This is an insight gained from practical experience with presenting submissions on gender identity and sexual orientation at the Council of Europe and with pressing the issue of gender identity in the running work of the executive board of ILGA-Europe. That most activists see homosexuality and transgenderism as distinct issues was supported in almost all interviews I conducted and in many discussion during lobby work until about 2000, when the approach to transgender issues changed in ILGA-Europe. Yet, not only gay and lesbian activists separate homosexuality from transgenderism. The UK-based lobby group Press for Change includes some interesting discussion on this matter on its website and had to address issues of homophobia (private e-mail discussion between the co-ordinator of PfC and the author in 1998).
9 ILGA-Europe defines the term 'transgender' to 'include both pre- and post-surgical reassignment transsexual people. It also includes transsexual people who choose not or who, for some other reason, are unable to undergo genital reconstruction. It further includes all persons whose perceived gender or anatomic sex may conflict with their gender expression, such as masculine-appearing women and feminine-appearing men.' This is the first time ILGA-Europe adopted such a broad and pro-active definition taken from the definitions European transgender organisations offer.
10 Individual activists in ILGA-Europe and one of the interviewees (Tatjana Greif), however, see this issue decisively different.
11 Robert Wintemute, for example, painstakingly attempts to delineate a still existent chromosomal sex underneath all gender reassignment, and, thus, shows the deep difficulty some legal analysis has with a collapse or a final deconstruction of the sex/gender divide (1997:335).
12 The concept of heterosexual stability is particularly fraudulent here, considering the high divorce rates in Western Europe. The dream of 'stable marriage forever' is explicitly retained as the marker distinguishing those who deserve to be protected from employment discrimination from those who do not. Stability of relationships is a concept in urgent need of more fundamental challenge from gay and lesbian lobbyists at EU level.
13 The Netherlands is the first country in the world to allow full civil marriages as of 1 April 2001. Custody, artificial insemination, and adoption – but not of children

outside the Netherlands – are allowed. Belgium has followed suit on 16 July 2003, but excluded adoption. Other registered partnership laws Europe allow some custody for daily matters, some make a second parent adoption possible, yet none grants the same rights as for heterosexual parents.
14 See Halley (1993), Morgan (1995 and 1996), Stychin (1995), and Bower (1997) for an explanation of this condition.
15 For example, none of my interviewees saw legal rights as the ultimate solution, but almost all centralised the law in their work for rights.

7 A process of recognition: European citizenship

> The European Union is a product of the history of the Western nation state. Moreover, Europe as a political identity produces its own nationalist discourse through which it differentiates itself from 'other' nations (both within and outside the geography of Europe). But it has also been argued that the new European order might serve as a forum for the reimagining of the nation state, if not to transcend at least reduce the dependence of identity on the construction of the national other.
>
> (Stychin 1998:115)

> the value of rights to gays, lesbians, and others has been made to fluctuate with the politics of sovereignty, and can only be augmented with a renewed attention to the contours of state and economy.
>
> (Jonathan Goldberg-Hiller 1998:520)

> Europe will be a Europe for all, or it will be nothing at all.
>
> (European Commission 1996)

During the press conference after the judgment in the *Grant* case, Kurt Krickler – Co-Chair of ILGA-Europe – stressed that he saw the judgment as a political decision which 'sent out the signal that lesbians and gays are still second class citizens in the EU' (EP Intergroup minutes, 18 February 1998). Tatjana Greif (e-mail interview, January 2000) from Slovenia – member of ILGA-Europe's executive board – also connected rights to second-class citizen status in the EU:

> For me, the civil and consequently the social inequality is the most important case of discrimination of Lesbians and Gays. All citizens should have equal rights, but gay/lesbian citizens are mainly second-grade citizens. The legislation should be the basic field to assure the formal equality for gays and lesbians, and later on their social position could change and public opinion toward homosexuality would change.

To elevate lesbians and gay men into first-class citizenship status – or to abolish all laws that create a first- and second-class citizenship – is a central theme of gay and lesbian rights politics. Citizenship is a crucial concept employed in political practices and it has also sparked a wealth of academic debate in various disciplines. In this chapter I discuss the complex and contradictory implications of citizenship argumentation as a political practice in Europe.

European citizenship is a complicated and hazy concept in political practices. Claims to equal citizenship are most commonly claims to participation rights based on a set of civil rights. Yet the reference to European citizenship is not clear cut and easy to define. I will briefly show some of the complications in the first section of this chapter. On the level of lobby politics discussed in this book, citizenship claims are almost never formulated as participation rights in the definition of citizenship culture and of the principle structure of democracy (Quaestio 2000:21), but rather simplified into legal inclusion. As such they follow certain steps of argumentation to embed themselves within historical themes of citizenship and within previous struggles to recognition. Those themes, in turn, play upon liberal and occasionally republican ideals. After tracing these implications in specific quotations in the second section of this chapter, I go on to discuss other European histories and conditions that are invoked in political practices around citizenship: the construction of Europeanness in its strong bond to the ideology of nation states, transnationalism, and the Eurocentric exclusion of the racially marked outsider. Another central tenet of the history of citizenship in the EU specifically is the economic nature of EU citizenship, which I discuss in the fourth section. These four angles on the concept of citizenship in Europe illuminate the contradictory complexities in the call to citizenship from a political and historical view. Yet, claims to citizenship are also contradictory on a more procedural and philosophical level. They necessarily involve a process of recognition that contains contradictory forces in itself. The fifth section of this chapter offers a different close reading of the quotations used in the second section which exemplifies how the process of recognition becomes the key to understanding the procedural and structural problems of citizenship.

Complications of the term citizenship in a European context

Citizenship in the context of rights politics never just applies to an inhabitant of a geographical unit. In a generalised formulation citizenship is a matter of inclusionary principles. Citizenship is a respectful contractual relationship between autonomous subjects and their state, symbolised and certified in a contemporary sense by passports and an understanding of sharing rights of freedom and equality as fundamental human rights. This sense of citizenship draws on the history of a distinction Hegel described – which was also used in a transformed way by Karl Marx – between a *Bürger* and a citizen (*Staatsbürger*). The first are participants – subjects for Marx – in the economic life of civil society, endowed with rights to participate freely in socio–economic relations. Citizens have a status conferred upon them by the rules of justice and political participation (Binnie 1997:239). The rights of the *Bürger* or the individual – as a human right – can be denied irrespective of the political status. Citizenship rights can also be denied – for example to refugees and asylum seekers – but they cannot be guaranteed except in the context of a state that confers nationality.

'Sexual citizenship' – a term made relevant by David Evans (1993) – describes the relationship between states and sexualised citizens. The term emphasises that sexuality is regulated by the state and plays a role in the definition of what nationality entails. It also emphasises that sexual dissidents do not enjoy what is termed full citizenship in any state of this world. In the claim to change that fact, two aspects of citizenship are commonly implied: citizenship as a right to rights – as access to existing privileges given by legislative institutions to groups and individuals, such as marriage – and, simultaneously, as a claim to rights of full participation in the decision process of how rights are designed and executed. Sexual dissidents have historically been excluded from both forms of participation. Therefore, it makes sense to assume that whenever citizenship is claimed, its historical inheritance of exclusion leaves its traces.

The post-enlightenment norm of the citizen was male, white, and middle class, a rational, wealth maximising, breadwinner as head of a family unit (Flynn 1996:291). By definition citizenship excluded racial, ethnic and sexual minorities, slaves, criminals, the lower classes, women, children, or the elderly (Stychin 1998:15). All of these groups have formed organisations and movements to combat their exclusion at some point in the nineteenth and twentieth centuries. Considering the mixture of all these historical developments makes the concept of citizenship in political practices a very unstable and hazy concept at the best of times.

Taking into account that ILGA-Europe makes a claim to inclusion of sexual and gender minorities into concepts of European citizenship, citizenship rights are complicated even further. It is symptomatic of the European question in general that the name 'Europe' is notoriously vague, malleable to many forms of individual, political, or cultural inscriptions. The term 'Europe' generally implies a lot of different meanings simultaneously: a geographic description – the mainland continent, whose geographical borders at the Urals are an ideological question; political affiliations with the history of parliamentary democracies; cultural heritage – the heirs of Bach, Shakespeare, Kant, and Aristotle; life-style and cosmopolitan identities; national affiliations – the history of nation states that became the world's colonisers; and economical values – free market and reign of the Euro.[1] Generally speaking, post-war E(U)ropean identity is attached to economic freedom and human rights. Wherever Europe is invoked it carries an excess of meaning that can never be fully captured in any one deployment, although every deployment moulds itself into a chain of citations of all those elements of meaning about Europe.

In the specific case of EU citizenship, there is a strong connection to the existence of a communal order of states. The EU lacks definite joint conceptions of its own principal polity structure that would make it possible to conceive of it like a proper state in itself. It connects, according to Jachtenfuchs, Diez, and Jung (1998:419), four polity ideas: intergovernmental co-operation, federal state, economic community, and network approaches. The term 'federalism', subsequently, became a problematic debate in the Convention on the Future of Europe, which ended up not including it in the draft constitutional text in 2003.

Reference to the principle debate of what the EU is in terms of its polity structure is generally carefully avoided by most NGOs, since the different national backgrounds of their member organisations would comprise differential national opinions or party alliances with different European models. Gay and lesbian citizenship claims, as non-governmental forces that shape forms of European constitutionalism, have strings attached to this debate. ILGA-Europe's documents implicitly suggest a wide array of ideas and ideologies about the EU and being European. They depend, in effect, little on a coherent policy idea about the EU and more on the common practice of arguing sexual rights into any polity-idea that seems opportune at any one moment or towards any one political actor. ILGA-Europe participates in building European communities in a very diffuse, decentralised, and fragmented way. Although this is a non-essentialist move, it further complicates an analysis of the stakes of citizenship.

Given the exclusionary history of citizenship and the complications of meaning any European citizenship implies, it is surprising how strongly the concept of citizenship features in rights argumentation, and it is not surprising how strongly it features in critical political theory.[2] Citizenship discourse remains important in almost all discussion about rights. This speaks to the paucity of alternative languages about rights and civic participation. Citizenship discourse in the specific context of gay and lesbian rights campaigns towards the European institutions, therefore, warrants critical investigation in the context of this book. To this end, I will offer several close readings of two official ILGA-Europe statements on citizenship and of two quotations from the interviews conducted with active members of the executive board to trace the argumentative strategies employed and the historical roots drawn upon.

Implications of the claim to citizenship: arguments and histories

Two different kinds of citizens are called upon through the portrayal of gay men and lesbians as second-class citizens in political rights practices: the sexual citizen emerging from gay and lesbian lobby politics, and the transnational European citizen of the European Union or of the human rights conception of the Council of Europe. Both kinds mould themselves into a chain of citations of the history of both the idea of Europe and the concept of citizenship.

This combination is visible in a speech made during the expert hearing for the anti-discrimination report of the Council of Europe and in the anti-discrimination report ILGA-Europe published in February 2000.[3] Carlos Hernandez – co-ordinator of the youth work in the Spanish rights organisation Fundación Triángulo – expressed the hope that institutions such as the Council of Europe and the EU, 'established to defend and promote fundamental rights, will have the courage to lead the way to progress and full citizenship for all Europeans without discrimination based on sexual orientation'. ILGA-Europe, in fact, places citizenship as an indivisible concept alongside human rights:

> Lesbians, gays and bisexuals seek nothing more than this. They do not seek special privileges. They do not just seek tolerance, valuable though this quality is. They seek equal citizenship, an equal opportunity to live openly and freely, and to contribute equally in every area of their lives. Citizenship, like freedom, is not divisible. (Discrimination Report to the Council of Europe, February 2000)[4]

The claim to 'live openly and freely and to contribute equally' places sexuality in the public sphere through the assertion of participation rights while also implicitly cultivating and maintaining the right to separate subcultural spaces. Steffen Jensen (e-mail interview February 1998) – Danish member of ILGA-Europe's executive board – formulated these connections astutely.

> What I mean is that we are ordinary citizens in our societies taking part in mainstream politics, culture etc., BUT we are also lesbians and gay men with the right to live our lives our way. We demand the right to have other 'family' relations than father–mother–children, to have our own 'subculture' parallel to the other things we also take part in.

Jensen develops a sense of sexual citizenship in which gay men and lesbians have a right to their own culture and to non-normative family relations while fully taking part in all other areas of citizens' participation in the social, political, and economic world. Sexual citizenship here highlights the relevance of sexuality beyond the private sphere and beyond subcultural semi-publics to the public political domain. At the same time it creates the conditions for a normalisation of homosexual identities by claiming equal value participation in the public sphere through the claim to citizenship (Stychin 2001:8).

Additionally, sexual citizenship is combined with a sense of Europeanness. Hernandez's reference to a European tradition of fundamental rights highlights the relevance of sexuality to the question of historical exclusion from the national imaginary that fuels the idea of citizenship. It is this imaginary that subsequently defines the transnational solidarity among the excluded strongly evident in the European minority rights movements. Claiming European citizenship, not surprisingly, seeks inclusion into the imaginary of Europe and argues that deviance from the heterosexual norm should not be a bar to full citizenship in Europe and specifically in the EU. Thus, ILGA-Europe attempts in various ways to construct their constituency as good citizens – or 'ordinary citizens' as Jensen calls it – for example, good taxpayers and equal participants in all areas of life. European sexual citizenship, thus, highlights something beyond the relevance of sexuality to the public political sphere. It highlights the pretended irrelevance of sexuality to the imagery of Europe: the difference of sexual orientation is not supposed to matter with regards to an Europeanness based on human rights. Thus, the historical roots of the imagery of Europe are highly relevant to any understanding of European citizenship or of any rights claims to European sexual citizenship. Sexual citizenship and European citizenship bond in the history of the concept of citizenship.

Bryan Turner (1992a) gives an account of this history. He argues (1992a:47) that citizenship is bound up with the development of the city-state in the classical world of Rome and Greece, and in the course of European history became an important element of rationalism. In his essay, a comparative analysis of the different developments of the concept in France and Germany in the nineteenth century as well as a consideration of citizenship in Hegel, Marx, and Gramsci leads to two historical dimensions implied in the concept of citizenship: the passive–active contrast depending on whether citizenship grew from above or below, and the tension between a private realm of the individual and the family in relationship to the public arena of political action (1992a:52). The political negotiation of those dimensions – the transfer of sovereignty from the body of the king to the body politic of citizens – was, thus, a major turning point in the history of Western democracies. It indicated a considerable expansion of political space, indeed the creation of political space (1992a:57). Turner (1992a:39) concludes:

> Citizenship is, as it were, pushed along by the development of social conflicts and social struggles within such a political and cultural arena, as social groups compete with each other over access to resources. Such a theory of citizenship also requires a notion of the state as that institution which is caught in the contradictions between property rights and political freedoms. Finally, the possibilities of citizenship in contemporary society are, or have been, enhanced by the problems of war-time conditions in which subordinate groups can make more effective claims against the state.

Turner's summary of the outcome of a history of citizenship affirms the sovereign subject as a privileged political agent. The history of the concept of citizenship also affirms the sovereign state as a primary site of political struggle. The state is the principal and privileged location for the recognition, validation, and enforcement of rights claims on the part of those sovereign subjects, understood as members of a particular society (McClure 1992:110). After Kant and Rousseau, European citizenship, thus, changed from a historical pact between king and subject to an abstract model of how political authority and the nation-state were constituted and legitimated. Nation was no longer designated a pre-political entity, but something that defined the political identity of a citizen belonging to that nation (Habermas 1992:3-4). The consensus achieved among citizens nominally conceived of as free and equal became bound to a set of rules based on democratic constitutions and law as well as on one dominant morality and ethic, identically applied to all in the same procedures.

Citizenship – as well as the French concept of *citoyenneté* and the German *Staatsbürgerschaft* – was historically seen as analogue to membership in a nation, which secures the legal status of a person as citizen, expressed in the right to vote and passports. Parallel to that conception, a model of achieved membership in a self-determining ethical community also developed (Habermas 1992:2). As passport holders individuals remain external to the state, while in an ethical community they are integrated like parts of a whole. The latter conception also involves an extension into the realm of civil rights, a move that has only recently been the focus of critical theories of citizenship.[5]

In summary, what makes people fellow citizens in the dominant discourse of European liberal democratic regimes is a set of political principles specific to the tradition of citizenship: the ideological principles of freedom and equality and the membership in a nation-state. To be a good citizen is to recognise the authority of those principles and the rules in which they are embodied. Thus, citizenship implies legal status as well as a form of identification, in this case a type of European political identity. ILGA-Europe's political practices enter the circle of citizenship at precisely this point. They are constructing a sense of European citizenship that includes sexual minorities. The quotations from ILGA-Europe activists and documents above place sexual citizenship in an intricate relationship to both the idea of Europe and the history of the concept of citizenship. Eight elements can be traced in the quotations that shed light on how this intricate relationship between sexual citizenship and European citizenship is argued. I will trace these elements in two steps of four[6] and additionally trace the implicit argumentative reference to liberal and republican models of citizenship.

The first element generally argued is the need for recognition of all individual sovereign members of a society and an enumeration of their rights, duties, and powers. This element becomes evident in the argument that gay men and lesbians are already contributing equally to their societies and should, thus, in return have equal rights, as Steffen Jensen emphasised. A second element of citizenship claims stipulate the relation of governance, the rules and procedures that guide the conduct of members in a fair system of social co-operation. Asserting that gay men and lesbians are still second-class citizens calls into question the fairness of the rules applied in the EU, as Tatjana Greif stated: 'All citizens should have equal rights, but gay/lesbian citizens are mainly second-grade citizens.'

In a third move, citizenship claims generally lay out a set of procedures and institutions for discussion and alteration of prevailing relations of governance among members of a society. ILGA-Europe addresses the European institutions as committed to the ideal of citizenship, as having an interest in changing the second-class status and in extending prevailing rules of governance to include people with same-sex relationships. The fourth element includes an emphasis on the principles, values, and goods of European democratic constitutions that are brought to bear on the identification of members, the relations among them and the discussion or alteration of their identities and relations over time. Hence, for the call on European citizenship to be fully applicable to sexual minorities, sexual orientation must be connected to the values and goods expressed in the treaties of the European institutions as political communities. For the EU this means equality and freedom for all as well as access to full participation in at least all economic relations, but also in social and political ones. This aspect fuels the statement of the anti-discrimination report denying the claim for special privileges and insisting on equal citizenship. Equality becomes the key principle to ensure the end of persistent discrimination of some citizens, as Tatjana Greif also asserted in the quote at the beginning of this chapter.

These four elements of argumentation set out the apparent principles of democratic citizenship procedures in European tradition as a reference point for the political context in which citizenship claims are made. On their heels follow another four argumentational elements that relate to the struggle over recognition. First, in the claim to recognition the present is portrayed as a non-fulfilment of the ideal of equality. Kurt Krickler accuses the European Court of Justice of sending out the signal that 'lesbians and gays still are second-class citizens in the EU'. This constitutes, second, a severe injustice, as Tatjana Greif asserted: 'For me, the civil and consequently the social inequality is the most important case of discrimination of Lesbians and Gays. All citizens should have equal rights, but gay/lesbian citizens are mainly second-grade citizens.' Third, the rights of inclusion wanted are portrayed as just and well supported when ILGA-Europe affirms that lesbians and gay men do not seek special privileges, but simple equal citizenship. And, fourth, recognition by the other members of society would render the overall European identity a just and stable system of social co-operation that adheres to its own ideals, as Carlos Hernandez envisages for the Council of Europe.

Thus, the demand for recognition as full citizens implicitly problematises not only the present status of those demanding recognition, but of all members of European societies and the relations among them as far as these are regulated by European law and moral ideology. Unwittingly and mostly unnoticed, citizenship claims as a set of civil rights reach far beyond minority groups into a negotiation about the nature of European culture, political history, and ideology.

Besides the argumentational steps I just traced, claims to European (sexual) citizenship adhere to a specific historical argumentation that references a specific political context: the idea of Europe and the concept of European citizenship historically has had strong bonds with liberal, humanist understandings of citizenship. Again, these bonds are well visible in citizenship claims made by ILGA-Europe documents and activists. Liberal citizenship designs human beings as autonomous, rational agents whose interests are ontologically prior to the society they belong to qua their citizenship (Dietz 1992:64). Society – and the state as its representative – should ensure the freedom of all its members to realise their capabilities equally (1992:64). The historical development of this definition was prominently summarised by John Rawls who viewed citizenship as the capacity for each person to form, revise, and rationally pursue his or her conception of the good. Citizens are seen as using their rights to promote their self-interest with certain constraints imposed by the exigency to respect the rights of others (Mouffe 1992b:226). In this liberal conception the differentiation between Karl Marx's *Bürger* – who has economic property rights and exercises his [sic] economic freedom – and the citizen as member in a national value community is erased. In liberalism, citizenship and rights with respect to capitalist economy are intrinsically connected.

The argument that gay men and lesbians cannot utilise all their capabilities in the economic sphere because of (partnership) discrimination, for example, attaches itself to a liberal concept of freedom as the possibility to realise all capabilities of the individual. ILGA-Europe portrays non-normative sexual orientation as a perfectly natural way of being and equal rights with regard to the freedom of movement in the EU are a rational economic self-interest that does not constrain the rights of others. ILGA-Europe asserts that 'citizenship, like freedom, is not divisible' (Discrimination Report, February 2000). Thus, if citizenship rights – such as freedom of movement – are granted then the differentiation on grounds of sexual orientation hinders the freedom to exercise work-related choices.

Liberal citizenship speaks to individuals as averaged or normalised political persons, as individual bearers of the exact same formal rights designed to protect her or him – though the her was conveniently forgotten for centuries – from the infringement or interference of others and to guarantee him or her the same opportunities or equal access as others (Dietz 1992:65). Becoming European citizens against the background of this liberal history implies the need to be a good citizen: a good worker or taxpayer who fits into the norm of those for whom citizen status was originally designed. Thus, ILGA-Europe does not ask for special rights, just for those rights that apparently apply to everybody. There is emphasis on lesbians and gay men being part of all mainstream society.

Moreover, as Carl Stychin (2001:1) among others convincingly argues, liberalism has constitutively connected the concept of citizenship to a number of binary constructs: public versus private, active versus passive, and body versus liberal-subject.[7] Through the deployment of these, subjects could be not only included as citizens within the broader polity, but also excluded as non-citizens (2001:2). The tradition of locating rights discourse on the private side of the public/private dichotomy and the existence of an active state that gives rights to passive citizens cannot be so easily traced in current claims to lesbian and gay citizenship. While the enjoyment of rights, such as partnership rights, may be centred in private, de-politicised spheres, the pursuit of rights – i.e. the political practices that form the rights campaign and the life of the subculture – are an active and public endeavour. As Stychin maintains, there may well be radical potential in ILGA-Europe's claim to citizenship (2001:2). Claims to citizenship even in a liberal discourse can correct the historical limitations and constitutive exclusions of liberal citizenship if the distinctions between public and private spaces and active and passive citizens are disrupted. While I agree that this potential is real and important, what remains problematic – for reasons of historical developments that I addressed in previous chapters – is the structural exclusion of the maintained dominant liberal concepts of equality, of freedom, of the nature of human beings and of autonomous, sovereign subjects of the law.

Liberalism is not the only reference point for present citizenship claims. Activists' approaches as well as mainstream EU definitions of citizenship also have roots in other historical models, such as social citizenship or the republican model. For reasons of brevity, I will only briefly trace some aspects of the latter. When ILGA-Europe calls citizenship a 'non-divisible' concept and addresses the European institutions as 'established to defend and promote fundamental rights', it deploys a belief in a true and natural polity encompassing human rights. Yet, the claim to be citizens of equal worth that participate equally in all areas of society while simultaneously maintaining a distinct historical difference that necessitates and justifies separate subcultural spaces could be read to also refer to civic republican thought. ILGA-Europe participates in the definition of citizenship by independently defining the status of lesbians and gay men in Europe as second class. This is an active demand to insert a historically excluded group into political communities that negotiate the definitions of citizenship. As a political goal the re-definition of citizenship through a claim to inclusion is also close to a republican ideal.[8]

Civic republicanism emphasises the value of political participation and attributes a central role to individuals' and groups' insertion into a political community (Mouffe 1992b:227). Richard Bellamy and Dario Castiglione (1999), for example, present a recent and advanced republican model in which fixed constitutions cease to be a precondition for politics and political debate. Instead debate becomes the medium through which a polity constitutes itself. Justice, then, is identified with the process of politics and *audit alteram partem* – hear the other side – forms the watchword of legal fairness (Bellamy and Castiglione 1999:11). As a result, conflicts of values and interests can be confronted as problems to be resolved rather than as threats and a rationale is provided for creating multiple sites for decision-making that reflect the plurality of political identities and the complexity and diversity of the problems requiring regulation (Bellamy and Castiglione 1999:17). In consequence, the polity is seen as constituted in the processes of political debate and can, thus, never be constituted as true, natural and encompassing of human rights in advance.

While these efforts of circumventing liberal assumptions provide a potential for political intervention into the history of liberal exclusions, the principle of *audit alterem partem* does not address the question who can speak and who is heard in relation to definitions of citizenship in the EU. For example, it usually takes an organised transnational NGO structured around traditional forms of representation of a constituency to participate in any lobby spaces opened at decision-making institutions. Additionally, the normatising effect of the idea of good, normal citizens, for example, those living in long-term monogamous relationships, is perpetuated through the citation of European values embedded in civic republican morality. Bellamy and Castiglione's (1999:12) recourse to 'moral resources of deliberative democracy' will continue the invocation of a troubling sense of Europeanness. While liberalism has its well-argued exclusions, such as gender, the civic republican ideal has been documented as not necessarily any more inclusive (Stychin 2001:2), and any process of defining Europeanness is prone to exclusion. Beyond the implications of citizenship claims I traced in this part of the chapter – the sexual citizen emerging from gay and lesbian lobby politics in her/his intricate relationship with the history of Europe and European concepts of citizenship – has particularly strong ties to nationalism and European cultural dominance that need further elaboration.

National legacies and the idea of Europe

Etienne Tassin (1992) argued that the idea of Europe evident in the EU Treaty and political structures is not exhausted simply in the common affirmation by Member States of a political will to defend the principles of democracy, human rights and social justice. He states (1992:171) that 'if there is to be a political community, presumably it should be rooted in a common experience and a tradition of thought and history that reside equally in all the peoples of Europe'. Tassin (1992:172) concludes that the political Europe – as a political community with a possible future citizenship identity – saw the light of day as the Europe of the mind was collapsing. What he implies is that the shock of World War II and the Holocaust turned the cultural idea of joint European humanism into a philosophical farce: Western metaphysics had been shaken to the bone and the idea of a historically superior European mind had been invalidated factually and conceptually. The idea of an European political community drew its meaning from an armed struggle and a humanitarian disaster. Thus, it broke to some extent both with the philosophical humanist idea of Europe and with a political tradition of purely sovereign and antagonistic nation states. This break led to a remodelled set of values, 'ousting at a political level the traditional framework within which the history of Europe had developed over six previous centuries' (1992:178).[9]

After 1945 the idea of a political Europe featured two elements in response to the total disaster: the federalist principle – a Europe of regions – and the national principle – a European community. Both ideas became elements present in the structure of the EU, which developed a very particular combination of a supranational composition with clear community powers, but also equally clear restrictions to preserve national sovereignty. This complicated balance and the ideological differences around its development resurfaced strongly in the debate on the Future of Europe conducted by the Convention in 2002–03, which in the end could not include the word federal or a 'Union of ever closer States' in the draft Constitution.

The idea of Europe expressed in the political community of the EU is both dependent on, yet also seeks in some sense to transcend, the historical construction of the European nation states. According to Stychin (1998:115), this tension proves to be at the heart of the newly emerging political and legal order. The European Union produces its own nationalist discourse through which it differentiates itself from other nations, both within and outside the geography of Europe. Stychin (1998:116) adds that originally the history of the European Community has been characterised by a highly market-oriented conception of citizenship, but increasingly the carving out of an identity also meant an extension to a more political and social concept of citizenship. However, the belief in the promise of this extension – expressed in calling on an indivisible concept of European citizenship and in calling to end the second class citizen status accorded to sexual minorities – often conveniently forgets a central historical legacy of Europe: a deeply gendered and racialised nationalism embedded in the very idea of Europe and expressed in the imperialist history of Europe's relation to the world.

The historical constitution of European identities was closely tied up with both Christianity and the Enlightenment. Through their metaphorical, ideological, and literal principles, borders and boundaries were created within which national identities could be consolidated.[10] Gender, race, and sexuality coalesced and justified a European colonialism by virtue of the idea that femininity and sodomy were associated with other races that were, as a consequence, naturally inferior. This was a process that generated intricate bodies of discourses around gender inequality, class priorities, sexual privilege, and racial superiority that became the markers of national and European identities (1998:119). Feminist theorists maintain that nationality depends on an obsessive representation of the nation as community up and against the difference of those excluded. Additionally, nationality depends on the only secondary subsumation of women into the nation and on homosocial bonding between men (Parker *et al.* 1992:5–6).

In the founding of the EU, the historical dominance of the imperialist nation state was left ideologically unchallenged. To this day, the concept of nation-states provides the central locus of citizens' identity and rights in the EU as well as within the Council of Europe, although by now the EU discourse features some postnational elesments.[11] The philosophical and political principles of the concept of citizenship in Europe are placed against the background of the historical development of nations and the idea of Europe. Claims to sexual citizenship, therefore, involve recourse to the membership of a group in the national community and to re-defining the parameters of this community to include previously excluded groups. Gay men and lesbians are members of a group that is a legitimate and important part of national and European communities. To achieve that goal, several political communities need to be re-defined: that of gay men and lesbians in Europe, that of Europeans, that of citizens, and that of nation-states.

ILGA-Europe strongly emphasises that the importance of equality discourse around rights and participation stems from the interrelationship of the social, political, and economical environment of which gay men and lesbians are a part (ILGA-Europe, Equality Report 1998:15). Different kinds of discrimination are, therefore, interrelated.[12] However, the meaningfulness of sexual identity is nevertheless asserted. A seemingly natural sexual identity traverses Europe – despite acknowledged differences according to race, age, gender, ability, and class – and this identity simultaneously invokes a natural state of Europeanness. The EU is sometimes implicitly addressed as a form of embodiment of Europeanness, the locus at which political communities are negotiated and at which identities gain rights. European citizenship for gay men and lesbians implies the assumption that cultural diversity can be suspended for the moment while at the same time national difference functions as a prominent justification of the argumentation.

The argument advanced runs approximately like this: by virtue of being European, all gay and lesbian citizens across Europe want the same rights as some citizens of the EU – for example, the Dutch, the Danish, or the Swedish – already have. In consequence, Europe becomes a project comprised of national achievements of rights and compromises between national differences. Transnational politics of citizenship reflect the idea of simultaneously merging and differentiating national differences. They usually accept national boundaries as decisive markers of culture and of analytical units, for example, as far as the description of discrimination is concerned. The claim to citizenship is, in summary, equally bound to discourses of national difference and achievement while at the same time claiming and enacting transnational politics that call on an Europeanness.[13]

It is a political practice locked in the need to still become citizens *as* Europeans and *as* gay men and lesbians, while claiming at the same time to already *be* citizens in the fulfilment of all other aspects of their lives. Some of the interviews explain this logic.

Understandably enough for the context of equal citizen rights, national achievements in legal rights are re-iterated in the attempt to export best practice to Europe as a whole. Steffen Jensen (e-mail interview, February 1998) from Denmark gave a good example again: 'ILGA's main goals on the European level must be to create equality before the law and in everyday life for lesbians and gay men. I would not say to export the Scandinavian/Dutch way of life to the rest of the world – but something like that!' Here, Jensen clearly conveys several things: first, an insistence on legal rights as the centre of his conception of ILGA-Europe's mission; second, a sense of achievement in Scandinavia and the Netherlands which figures as the example to strive towards; and third, he expresses a hope for progress within the European institutions which will eventually come to their senses and generalise the Scandinavian or Dutch model of equality all over Europe. Certainly Jensen does not display any easy sense of nationalism. Yet, he is proud that rights of partnership for homosexuals are part of what he can identify as Danishness.[14] He explicitly does not want to export a way of life, just the legal recognition into an assumed common European legal order.

Nevertheless, it is clear to see that the combination of both – national difference and transnational political goal – creates the very spirit of a European political community. Hannele Lehtikuusi (e-mail interview, July 1998) similarly reasserts the benefit of international co-operation in the learning procedures for the fight at home: 'My hopes are in co-operation in lobbying and pressure – when they are needed. The international "example" seems to be very often effective and as well co-operation with other organisations clarifies a bit the goals/aims we are in different countries really heading for.' For Lehtikuusi, the decisive point is not to export to Europe, but to import from Europe, leaving the focus of rights claims in the nation-state. The difference is typical for activists from countries that do not have as many rights. It is partnership rights that are taken as the measure for what constitutes the have and have-not countries.

The importance of nationality and of import or export of rights was evident in all interviews I conducted, whether the interviewees were personally strongly in favour of European integration or rather critical of the EU in principle.[15] What nearly all interviews illustrate is a simultaneous appreciation of transnationality while focusing on national impact and success.[16] On the one hand, the theme of transnationality evident in European citizenship claims creates an assumed commonality between all gay men and lesbians in Europe, ultimately regardless of their diversity. On the other hand, the language of citizenship never overcomes its own recourse to and constant re-iteration of nation-states as the basis of rights *and* of gay and lesbian culture, which infuses every concept of European citizens with nationalist traits.[17] The intricate connection between the possibilities of rights as membership and the ideology of nation-states becomes a political tool with little to no capacity of interrogating itself. Steffen Jensen (e-mail interview, February 1998), yet again, provides a very insightful summary:

> The impact of the EU, I think, can been seen in two different ways: a) Through EU-legislation and through the Court [European Court of Justice] ... b) Political pressure. The fact that it is not accepted any more in most parts of the EU to discriminate g/l's, creates in the long run a political pressure on other parts of Europe to do likewise. *You have to behave to be of the family!* (emphasis added)

Indeed, the Directives following Article 13 are one way to apply family pressure. However, l/g/b/t and feminist histories have surely proven that any family consensus needs a definition of 'family' and will also apply to those children who do not fit its concept. In exchange for rights, gays, lesbians, bisexuals, and transgender people will have to learn how to behave to be of the family, too. Whether this normalisation is nation wide or Europe wide does not affect its potential for exclusion, marginalisation and maintenance of privilege for some: namely those who live the life of – polemically speaking – the good consumer and obedient citizen in stable, long-term relationships. The family pressure, so to speak, is a move of divide and conquer.

While it will eventually provide the inclusion for some into existing citizenship orders, it is likely to split the gay and lesbian movement into those who fit in – who can successfully participate in the economic project of Europe as regulated workers moving across nation states – and those who do not. As an historical event, the split of former allies is nothing to be bemoaned since it has happened many times before and will simply result in shifting solidarities and movements, of which the political movement queer is one already. The exclusion of non-normative sexual life-styles in the concept of European sexual citizenship is problematic for lesbians, bisexuals, gay men, and transgender people in Europe, but even more so is the racial and cultural exclusion this citizenship also implies.

ILGA-Europe most certainly insists on being an organisation of and for all l/g/b/t groups and people living in Europe who wish to be part of the umbrella organisation ILGA. It also insists on integration, diversity, and a very broad concept of Europe. Its working efforts are significantly focused on Eastern and Central Europe. However, ILGA-Europe to some extent privileges the EU as the political community in which Europeanness is negotiated. The EU is in the day-to-day work for ILGA-Europe the location at which rights will be achieved first. This is a realistic and sensible approach and it is in no way particular to lobbying for gay and lesbian rights. In fact, it is clear that if the EU changes its rules the accession process has and will in the future ensure change in other non-EU countries.

However, this practicality does more than participate in the possibilities of gaining rights from a transnational institution: it creates specific meanings of Europeanness and potentially inadvertently substitutes Europe with the EU.[18] In this respect Europe as ideological concept and concrete institution could become more an addiction than a model for critical activism. Thus, becoming European on the basis and virtue of national citizenship is potentially a replica of the old constructions of national self and other in their deeply gendered and sexualised fashion rather than a re-imagining of new spaces (Stychin 1998:116). This affects not only Eastern Europe, but has a severe impact on all those people in Europe who are not citizens of the EU, so-called third-country nationals – a revealing terminology to say the least.

Sexuality across Western Europe is by no means as nationalised as it is, for example, in the US.[19] In fact, the national discourses of we and them in most Member States of the EU are not sexualised at all, but rather racialised. This racialisation is affirmed through the bulwark ideology of the EU at its outside borders, as well as through the severe restrictions on citizenship rights. In some Western European states, for example in Germany and France, xenophobia is, in fact, the most central turning point of national discourse and politics, the issue along which all parties rally and along which society is the most divided. In the debate on the future Constitution of the EU, it was Germany which succeeded at the last moment in preserving unanimity for immigration and no competence of the EU in matters of access to the labour market for third-country nationals.

While ILGA-Europe explicitly and very vocally supports citizenship rights for third-country nationals, this aim is hard to achieve within the language of European citizenship. The EU is itself a polity in the making without precedent and the process of the Convention on the Future of Europe illustrated this vividly once more. In theory, it is a polity, which does not have an *a priori demos*, conceived of as a complete, self-reproducing and non-contestable body, one that views national boundaries as crossing points not as barriers as long as they are within the Union. Yet, in order to transcend the problem of severely racialised barriers within and outside the Union two aspects of European citizenship need to be dislodged.[20]

On the one hand, without a politically sound excavation of the past of the idea of Europe and of European citizenship, the production of a *we* in citizenship is inevitably placed against a *them* along lines of race and ethnicity rather than along lines of subscription to democratic principles. The test of the European integrative project is neither the establishment of an area of freedom, security and justice – such as the freedom of movement – nor the acceptance of the abstract legitimacy of political values – such as equal citizen status. Rather, it is the determination to build a heterogeneous polity in which the marker 'European' is either an explicit and precise political value or only a geographic description. The marker 'citizen' is consequently openly sexualised, gendered, and racialised to an extent that addresses the diversity of lives in Europe. Considering the history of both terms – 'European' and 'citizenship' – however, this will be hard to achieve.

On the other hand, the borders of citizenship in a political community need to be defined beyond a functional meaning. Beyond passports they regulate one's belonging to a historical community united by a perceived common fate and political life from which the identity of its citizens takes its meaning. As such, those borders are permanent political capital, neither finite nor finished. However, the concept of citizenship in Europe has historically not developed as permeable political entity at all, but is, at least as far as the EU is concerned, firmly rooted in the logic of a capitalist market citizenship. The economic citizen of the EU is a crucial part of understanding the historical implications of European sexual citizenship.

Economic citizens

The Maastricht Treaty of 1993 established the concept of EU citizenship, with every national of an EU Member State becoming a citizen of the Union. This was of greater symbolic than real significance, as the status of Union citizens would only apply to the limited civil and political rights defined in the Treaty. These included – *inter alia* – the right to live and work anywhere in the EU, and the right to vote and stand as candidates in European Parliament and local elections, both subject to certain limitations. Maastricht also coined the term 'the peoples of Europe'. It raised the question of European identity but never went beyond the nation-state as the basis for citizenship. Maastricht, thus, missed a historic chance. Instead of designing a pluralistic and heterogeneous political community that would then issue disturbing calls to national constituencies to redefine themselves in a pluralistic way, European citizenship made national citizenship more valuable. The implications of this for the values underpinning the EU and its legitimacy were not seriously considered.

The result of Maastricht had an impact on sexual citizenship. The free movement has facilitated the ability to move between geographically distinct gay and lesbian spaces, to create connections between them, and to re-imagine their relationship to European space and national restrictions (Stychin 2001:8). For single gay and lesbian EU nationals and for those in a relationship with EU nationals who have jobs in high-demand areas, the freedom of movement has created a new right. In terms of European lesbian and particularly gay history, high mobility is nothing new.

Gay men and lesbians privately consumed services created for them and developed distinct life-styles, albeit in monitored secondary markets and subcultural community territories (Evans 2000:5). These spaces and markets – often called villages – are to be found in large urban territories, such as London, Paris, Amsterdam, and Berlin. Mobility has been a strong feature of European gay and lesbian history and, according to David Bell and Gill Valentine (1995:1), one can today literally 'map desire' in any European metropolis. Many gay men and perhaps fewer lesbians have embraced a consumer citizenship in a fetishisation of subculture commodity as identification – at least, we shop and are recognised as consumers.

As David Evans (2000:1) elaborately explains, the so-called homosexual liberation in Europe was and is a history of the 'moral state' allowing 'amoral consumption'. Post-war European states first legalised previously illegal and thus non-consuming sexual status groups, most spectacularly, male homosexuals. Thus, they released considerable specific minority commodity markets. Yet, the state had to safeguard absolute moral sexual standards. Manoeuvring between sexualised consumerism and state-managed morality, the market was deregulated whilst the state secured fetishised moral authority by granting only those legal rights which made consumption possible (Evans 1993:52). According to Evans, degrees of citizenship or non-citizenship in Europe incite the fragmentation of communities with sectionalised access and specialised markets, degree and forms of consumer status and lifestyle (1993:6 and 44). To him (2000:1), consumerist leisure markets and the heterosexual principle of moral sexuality are dialectically interrelated through the practices and ideologies of sexual citizenship. Thus, every claim to citizenship incorporates the wish to maintain rights to lesbian and gay services and subcultural spaces, which Steffen Jensen expressed so aptly in his demand to have 'other family relations' and our own subculture accepted.

Subcultural space is a decisive feature of the enactment of sexual citizenship and it plays on the tradition of public versus private distinctions. The EU has traditionally refrained from regulating private gender and sexual relations since the rule of subsidarity has left all family issues to the power of nation-states. The freedom of movement is tied to a promotion of the economic integration of the Union, and the creation of a transnational capitalist society. Citizenship rights are geared towards economic integration not the ideal of equality *qua* equality. It is, therefore, not surprising that the first anti-discrimination directive that covers many grounds of discrimination is an employment directive.

The issue of gender equality is another good example: the justification for gender equality – equal pay for equal work – early on in the European Economic Community was not concerned with women's equal access to the economic sphere. The reasoning behind it was concerned with levelling the cost factors of production, particularly between France and the Federal Republic of Germany, to ensure equal market competition between the Member States. The rights of gay and lesbian citizens are the rights of economic actors that move production freely across national boundaries of EU Member States, providing they are EU nationals and are gainfully employed. It is the employed citizen in a transnational marketplace that is the focus of much official rights discourse in the EU. Although the idea of citizenship in the EU has been overwhelmingly rights based, with little official conception of duty, the rights articulated have been primarily socio–economic market rights, market mobility is the liveliest construction of a European, or EU citizens' identity (Stychin 2001:6).[21]

The discovery of the so-called 'pink pound' has surely created market visibility for a certain section of gay men and occasionally some lesbians, which increased the range of economic argumentation that political organisations could use.[22] Therefore, gay men and lesbians as a group have long been entangled in a contradictory relationship with capitalism. Open homosexuals face occupational segregation and discrimination, but they also owe much of their new-found freedom to economic trends. Gay commodity culture makes clear that heterosexism in the economic system is not a seamless web either. Visibility and a sense of a community of sameness – not to mention a long list of specific products and services – are a strong attraction of the more open consumer citizenship available in the Europe of the 1990s. As much as the Pride Parades in Europe have become a largely de-politicised event of fun, games, and shopping, which many criticise, for most they are nevertheless an extremely important outlet of visibility, community, and friendship

It is, therefore, not astonishing that despite its clear critique of economic exclusion ILGA-Europe occasionally deploys economic arguments in relation to equal citizenship. The Equality Report on the EU from 1998 (p. 19) states, for example: 'There is already a degree of recognition that discrimination and harassment adversely affects [sic] the efficiency and performance of public and private sector organisations, through a climate which precludes employees individually or collectively from developing to, or operating at, their maximum potential.' Similar argumentation appears regularly when partnership rights and freedom of movement are defended. There is surely success attached to economic reasoning within the climate of the EU. However, this argumentation also translates the discrimination against lesbians and gay men into a disturbance of the smooth running of the market, whose welfare should be at the heart of all EU citizens. The need to participate in this European logic sheds light on the intricate complexity of an EU-based European citizenship. There is a connection of Europeanness to the EU and to the logic of capitalist market economy, and, in turn, that chain of logic becomes connected to sexuality, sexual citizenship, and nation-states.[23]

Claims to equal citizenship for sexual minorities in Europe focus on a set of rights and not on re-negotiating the principles of democratic participation. Through this focus citizenship claims reify certain interconnected histories of the idea of Europe, of nationalism, of liberalism, of racism, of capitalism, of citizenship, and surely some other histories I did not touch upon in this chapter. The historical exclusions those claims revive are problematic on ideological and political levels, as I have shown. However, even this rather long consideration of only some of the intricate complications of European sexual citizenship has as of yet not shed light on the problematic procedural aspect of citizenship claims that has also not received much attention in the literature on sexual rights: European sexual citizenship necessarily involves a contradictory process of recognition.[24] The recognition that is sought remains contradictory because, on the one hand, the claim to become first-class or simply equal European citizens is connected to a problematic history of European citizenship, and, on the other hand, this claim simultaneously maintains a distinct sexual form of citizenship fitted with identities and specific markets that already exists. The contradiction of this claim to *become* something rests in the assertion to already *be* full citizens.

The process of recognition

The process of recognition implied in citizenship claims can be untangled through yet another reading of two excerpts analysed above:

> Lesbians, gays and bisexuals seek nothing more than this. They do not seek special privileges. They do not just seek tolerance, valuable though this quality is. They seek equal citizenship, an equal opportunity to live openly and

freely, and to contribute equally in every area of their lives. (Discrimination report, February 2000)

What I mean is that we are ordinary citizens in our societies taking part in mainstream politics, culture etc., BUT we are also lesbians and gay men with the right to live our lives our way. (Steffen Jensen, e-mail interview, February 1998)

The phrase 'they seek' clearly refers to a quest for acknowledgement and for recognition in the legal, social, and economic realm. Citizenship claims – like rights claims in general – are built on the quest to become visible and recognised. That quest is necessarily followed by the quest to have inhuman conditions revoked through a second move of recognition that results in legal, economic, and social change. This logic contains four elements that are characteristic of a process of recognition in rights claims.

First, the equal contribution 'in every area of their lives' implies that the recognition sought only acknowledges what is already there: gay men and lesbians contribute to social and economical relations on all levels. Steffen Jensen's words are even more explicit in this respect. The 'we' he implies is already there, recognised as ordinary citizens, taking part in ordinary relations, *and* living a life that is particular to a sexual identity in certain respects. He directs his statement to heterosexual society, the state, and the law, which according to him do not acknowledge the fact that gay men and lesbians contribute equally to society. The claim is based on the vision that recognition of already existent facts will lead to incorporation as well as to maintenance of the separation in specific life-style.

Therefore, second, seeking recognition will result in a situation in which lesbians and gay men can 'live openly and freely', which is presumably not fully realised yet. There is a clear before and after in these claims to citizenship. Now, before the change towards inclusion, there is discrimination and second-class citizen status evident in all European societies, although the excluded group has existed for a long time and contributed to society. Through this argument society becomes a unity that grants rights of inclusion if they are deserved. Afterwards there is the recognition of same, equal rights, while the distinct life of the group is maintained and given acknowledged specificity although – presumably – the need for that specificity has ceased to exist.

Third, the existing excluded group is seeking inclusion into another existing group, in this case society, which in turn needs to first realise and ultimately judge the valuable existence and contribution of the group that seeks inclusion. Once that inclusion has taken place, there is no more need for two groups; the principal relation of the groups as oppositional fades.

Finally, fourth, the fight of those agents is concerned with an *as*. They seek to be recognised as something, namely *as* European and simultaneously *as* sexual citizens; two things shall become one and remain nevertheless separate. These four elements of the process of recognition highlight the contradictory nature of citizenship claims on yet another, theoretical, level. Alexander Garcia Düttmann's philosophical investigation of recognition in his book *Zwischen den Kulturen. Spannungen im Kampf um Anerkennung*[25] is helpful in this respect.

For what I have so far termed recognition, Düttmann uses mainly the German terms *anerkennen* or *Anerkennung*, but also *erkennen* and *wiedererkennen*. These terms, taken from Hegel, imply a range of meanings in English: recognition, acknowledgement, appreciation, tribute, legitimisation, legalisation, or approval, and in a philosophical sense identification of something as such and an identifying act through which one finds oneself in the other. I will follow through here with the term 'recognition', which has also been used by Düttmann's translator, while emphasising that the processes involved indeed incorporate aspects of all those meanings.[26]

In a nutshell, Düttmann (1997:110,118,122) argues that any political practice which calls on an already existent *we* – a given, definable group with shared experiences that constitute identities – crosses out the process of recognition as a process of interpretation and labelling, which it necessarily is. If the 'we' in a right claim is already there contributing to society and maintaining historically specific identities and spaces then there is no real recognition of that fact necessary – besides, maybe, an issue of broad social awareness and visibility. The process of recognition sparks a continuity between three identities: between the not yet recognised identity – the identity that is in the process of formation through the struggle for recognition; the identity that is self-recognised in the struggle as a free and self-confident pre-existing subjectivity; and the discriminated identity, which needs the recognition that significantly results from the struggle (1997:182).

Therefore, there is no recognition possible without a group or a self that seeks to fulfil her or his wish, but that wish can never be completely fulfilled. The process of recognition makes citizenship claims deeply contradictory. The claims to citizenship simultaneously include an already existent group and a group in the making, namely the equal European sexual citizen. Düttmann asserts that recognition is necessarily an act of interpretation. To him the claimed category – in this case the equal European sexual citizen – is open for political negotiation. He (2000:120) concludes: 'The struggle for recognition turns into a struggle of the subject which attempts either to include otherness within itself, or else to exclude it from itself. The politics of recognition becomes a fundamentalist and immanentist politics, regardless of the intentions and instruments with which it operates.'

Düttmann (1997:53) comes to this conclusion by identifying in detail that recognition reproduces the connection or the relation of the person who recognises towards the one who grants recognition.[27] What is to be certified is at the same time that which is produced by the claim to recognition. Recognition is the pre-condition of acknowledgement: in order to attain a right, a group needs to be recognisable as deserving that right. The dilemma of acknowledgement for citizenship as participation right, thus, rests in a dilution of the difference between being acknowledged as deserving a right and being acknowledged as different. As such it rests between an *Anerkennen* and a *Wiedererkennen* – recognition and repeated re-cognition. The group to be recognised by the recognising majority is also already a recogniser of the authority of those set up to decide and judge whether the demanded recognition is justifiable and legitimate. Therefore, whenever we want to speak about recognition or acknowledgement we need to speak about a fight – a principled and never-ending fight – about the conditions of recognition and about the interpretation and maintenance of difference (1997:54).

What Düttmann (1997:66–7) implies here is that any simple understanding of the process of recognition ignores the circular erasure of recognition through its own processes. Or to explain it more concretely: if recognition is defined as purely a relation of inequality – excluded citizens demand recognition of their second-class status – we would have no answer to the question of how a society can relate to this inequality without adhering to the illusion of equality. Thus, despite its exclusionary history, the illusion about an equal concept of European citizenship is re-iterated. If recognition is defined as purely a relation of equality – the already equal participation in society as tax payers is asserted – we would again have no answer to the question of how one can relate to equality without re-asserting existing inequality. We lack an explanation of the fact that equality is not realised for all European citizens, although the ideal of equality is nailed into all democratic constitutions.

If we are, then, to define recognition as a dialectic relation of equality and inequality, this would give no answer to the question of what differentiates a form of recognition that results in the destruction of inequality, from a form of recognition that eventually destroys the specific identities and their subcultures forcing gay men, bisexuals, lesbians, and transgender people into sameness and normativity. Recognition as the functional process of citizenship claims illustrates that these rights are neither a state nor a result nor, in fact, a solution. Struggles for recognition do not come from outside; they live within the processes of recognition and are self-perpetuating.[28] No recognition is conceivable which sets an end to the struggle around it. Or, as Johannes Fabian (1999:66) puts it in the context of anthropology: recognition 'is an agonistic relationship; it involves participants in confrontation and struggle ... it is achieved through exchanges that have startling, upsetting, sometimes profoundly disturbing consequences for all participants'. The struggle is not ended through the inclusion into an exclusionary European citizenship. The result of that recognition is not a lasting state of *being recognised*.

I would argue that fundamental rights claims could not be made if they were easy to recognise in European democratic societies and were truly achieved by brief legal amendments. The hope to end a second-class citizen status once and for all intrinsically locks itself to the wish for an end to the culturally meaningful historical prohibition of homosexuality. This claim contains something immeasurable, something excessive and boundless: it calls for an end to a fundamental prohibition, which forms a pre-condition of European political thought, of the very epistemology of Europeanness.

In the struggle between majorities that grant rights and excluded minorities that seek them, the excessive immeasurable factor needs to be countered by a measure, a quantitative factor (Düttman 1997:122). ILGA-Europe demands no special rights, but the institutions are held up against their own fraught ideology of measurable equality. This potentially disruptive and anarchic quality of claims to European citizenship as homosexual citizenship is the blind spot of the process of political recognition. The after remains bound to the before; there is no after that erases the before, what is actually claimed cannot be achieved without dislodging Europe's epistemological and ontological history. Yet, that is, indeed, an entirely unachievable aim. Not because the heterosexual majority does not want to be challenged, but because the actual fulfilment of an end of discrimination against sexual minorities is also the end of homosexual identities as the deviation from the norm (Scott 1997:21).

If we nevertheless engage in struggles over recognition, which are nominally one of the more successful political practices concerning rights, then these struggles ought to focus on the *as*: the meaning production of what it is one wants to be recognised *as* and the structure of this *as*. This focus is indeed the most interesting aspect of the process of recognition in political practices. Any absolute recognition contains an annihilation of the difference that led to it[29] (Düttmann 1997:124). Yet, since that is not achievable, the best result of citizenship claims remain in principle preliminary (1997:192). The recognition possibly achieved – for example partnership rights as a preliminary end to a certain struggle – remains unequal, unfinished and one-sided for all its obvious exclusions, continually falling short of its own equality aims. However, if we politically emphasise the process not the result, recognition as acknowledgement, re-recognition, and repeated recognition – *Anerkennen*, *Erkennen*, and *Wiedererkennen* – can become a mobilisation of difference with a chance of producing different knowledge and identifications (Fabian 1999:68). Citizenship claims are, therefore, not wasted at all, but could be seen as the first step towards a different set of political aims and practices. They are a necessary part of politics today and they necessarily involve processes of recognition, which are, in turn, fundamentally connected to any perception of the personal and the political.

Conclusion

So far I have presented a theoretical analysis of the argumentational strategies used and the histories cited in political practices concerning citizenship, as well a detailed problematisation of the process of recognition involved in these practices. Beyond critical analysis I have not offered a thorough re-conceptualisation of citizenship capable of circumventing at least some of those problems. I have not done so for two reasons.

Firstly, I am not sure a re-definition of the concept of citizenship in the specific context of lobby politics would be a tenable escape from the contradictions analysed. As a claim to a set of civil rights, citizenship is too intricately enmeshed in historical relations of exclusion. I would rather suggest that the theoretical concept of recognition as the principle formation process of social and legal relations – critically separated from its positivistic and universalising philosophical tendencies (Fabian 1999:67) – has to become the future focus of political re-conceptualisation. Thus, the nature or target of citizenship claims would change away from asking for inclusion rights to a struggle about the possibilities of social and political participation and the very nature of democracy. Yet, once that change has occurred, the kind of political practices I investigate would not be the same anymore either.

Secondly, the existing literature offers quite a few elaborate re-conceptualisations already. These include a wide array of approaches from re-definitions of citizenship as simple participation rights in social and political relations,[30] to the focus on legal and rights definitions,[31] or a conceptualisation of citizenship with regard to space.[32] I will briefly summarise a few of those re-conceptualisations that, taken together with my foregoing claim, offer at least a creative starting point to re-thinking sexual citizenship.

Within the attempts to re-define citizenship conceptually Chantal Mouffe and Bryan Turner are two of the best-known theorists. While Mouffe (1992b:13) postulates the impossibility of a final realisation of her radical democracy, she also re-introduces the principles of freedom and equality as concepts in tension. To be a citizen is to recognise the authority of those principles and the rules in which they are embodied; to have them informing our political judgment and our actions. This implies seeing citizenship not as a legal status but as a form of identification, a type of political identity: something to be constructed, not empirically given (1992b:231). Turner (1992b:2) defines citizenship as: 'that set of social practices (juridical, political, economic and cultural) which define a person as a competent member of society, and which as a consequence shape the flow of resources to persons and social groups'.

Both Turner and Mouffe offer a non-static and non-empirical concept of citizenship capable of acknowledging historical exclusions. Turner's emphasis on citizenship as practice comes close to my own understanding of politics as practices: a social, economic, and historical construct that involves many levels of engagement beyond the juridical definition of citizenship and that defines competent members with a view to specific social structures and political movements. Citizenship, thus, becomes a meaning-creating act of participation.

Considering the question of European citizenship, Etienne Tassin (1992:189) insists that citizenship ought to lose any reference to general will or supranational identity, as well as to individualised European bodies and minds. The political ambiguity of Europe can, then, be resolved through the development of a European fellow-citizenship broken away from nationality. Whatever the citizen's cultural or national identity, his or her insertion in public political space needs to become elective and not native. It derives from a political choice and not from birth or from an identity passed on by history. This replaces the idea of a European fatherland with that of a public space of disparate communities.

With particular respect to sexuality Stychin (1998; 2001) and Evans (1993; 2000) have taken the concept to the test of recycling after analysing many of its problems in their field of interest. Stychin (2001:10) underscores how political activism around citizenship is not a lost cause, and argues that 'actors within civil society can always, through the language of rights *and* participation, breathe active life into what may appear to be static citizenship constructs'. To him (1998:17) the power of rights discourses lie in their claim to universality – as contentious as that might be – with no inherent limits on who can make those rights claims, potentially broadening the horizon of citizenship in the process. Stychin's model of citizenship recognises communities characterised by rights. Yet, the boundaries of those communities are sites of contestation in which the disciplining force of the history of European citizenship is resisted while recognising democratic politics as vital: 'The possibilities of European citizenship lie in the potential to synthesize rights and belonging, in the creation of opportunities for democratic contestation in the interstices between liberal rights, the disciplinarity of the free market, and across the differences between and within national identifications' (Stychin 2001:12). This concept challenges the historical construction of public and private and problematises the distinction between active and passive citizenship, all of which have been crucial elements of the exclusionary history of citizenship. Stychin's (2001:10) approach is a balanced appraisal of the indeterminacy of citizenship and rights, close to Shane Phelan's (1995:345) model of coalition and affinity, rather than identity.

David Evans's concept of sexual citizenship – mainly employed to critique forms of commodification of identities and rights – adds another relevant point to Stychin's re-appraisal. The way to resist economic organisation and control of sexualities through political and economic citizenship institutions and practice, is not only to question the dominant assumptions of what citizenship as participation rights have meant historically. It is rather to deeply trouble the exclusionary citizenship culture practised in the gay villages and to defy the claim of fundamental cultural and identity difference. Evans calls this project to 'queer the queer'. He (2000:7–8) identifies three linked political fetishes that are equally troublesome for his definition of citizenship: the essential gay individual, equal rights, and the gay community. In conclusion, as Cooper (1993:168) emphasises, citizenship has a multiplicity of valences. It contains 'different traces of meaning', including both duty and empowerment, and it always has the potential to be re-articulated, depending 'upon the precise historical circumstances' in which it is voiced.

Stychin and Evans are two of the many theorists who point to possible political and theoretical ways out of the impasse brought about by the critical deconstruction of citizenship concepts. However, with respect to the kinds of mainstream lobby politics that are the object of my investigation, those re-conceptualisations are to some extent unrealisable. Up until now it has been the lived crisis of sexualised identities in national locations that continues to mobilise citizenship rights claims. This crisis certainly also fuels the resistance against heteronormativity and binary gender regulation among gays and lesbians. Yet, the former is not exactly the same project as the latter. Collapsing one into the other – even if desired from a queer perspective – is not likely to happen in the current political climate. And maybe this is not even necessary.

The rights claims staged by NGOs such as ILGA-Europe will most likely – in due course – be successful unless Europe returns in its majority of countries to a period of extreme right-wing governments. Yet, the movements behind rights claims will just as probably collapse the moment after the big pride party to celebrate those rights has ended. Gay and lesbian identity will be less meaningful to most after that point, while the actual hierarchical conditions of why they became meaningful in the beginning remain in place. As a matter of political and theoretical practicality this will potentially be the point at which critical citizenship concepts gather around them larger movements that work together according to identifications different from gay and lesbian identities. The decisive political move will be a move of content with respect to struggles around citizenship. Understood 'as the way in which a society thinks and organises social membership, political participation, and social design' (Quaestio 2000:22, translation mine), citizenship becomes a conceptual framework that problematises social relations and historical conditions and re-thinks the nature of democratic participation.

Partly, activists position themselves clearly in relation to this dissolving of rights movements through their claim to end a second-class citizenship status. They want to become and be recognised as part of the family and to some extent they are explicitly aware about the reformation of solidarities and identities this move implies. It is part of their agentic choices to pursue certain forms of citizenship and not others and, it is to be hoped, to deal more explicitly to the exclusionary aspects of those models that are currently on offer in Europe. Yet, predictably, potential new solidarities will, in turn, produce another set of problems of exclusion that become the objects of future critical analysis.

Notes

1 There is ample academic work on the creation of the idea of Europe and its connection to the justification of colonialism, othering and social stratification. See, for example, Delanty (1995), Stychin (1998), Tassin (1992), and Zizek (1992).
2 Citizenship has in fact become one of the central conepts through which the conflict between sets of civil rights and the way a society thinks and organises membership, political participation, and social relations is analysed (Quaestio 2000:16–22).
3 Human Rights Sub-Committee of the Parliamentary Assembly of the Council of Europe, 14 October 1999.
4 This excerpt is drawn from ILGA-Europe's demands for recognition of partnership and custody of children. It continues: 'It makes no sense to acknowledge the case for equality under the criminal law, but to deny recognition and protection to same-sex partners and their children.'
5 Hannah Arendt was probably the first philosopher to establish that direction of thought. Recently this re-articulation has been developed particularly within feminist, gay and lesbian, and postcolonial studies.
6 These eight elements of argumentation were suggested to me by James Tully in a workshop on citizenship theory in 1999. He named them in the context of the Quebec issue in Canada and argues that if these eight steps are followed, problems of democratic

participation for minorities can be solved (1999:4–6). I do not agree with his conclusion, in fact these arguments are precisely part of the problematic I analyse here.

7   What Stychin means here is the denial of bodily needs as relevant to the public political sphere in liberal thought. The right-wing argument that gay rights are solely concerned with gay nature, whereas liberal development is the historic victory of reason over nature, implies that gays are incapable of being fully reasonable subjects (Goldberg-Hiller 1998:532). As Didi Herman argues, liberal thought is open for Christian right-wing arguments about the overconcern of gays and lesbians with their own bodies, a hyperindividualised identity that runs contrary to social and familial responsibilities and makes homosexuals undeserving of rights (Herman 1997:82/115/128-31). This is an argument that potentially holds within liberal thought since liberalism maintains a dichotomy of body versus liberal subject of reason (Stychin 2001:3).

8   It is actually close to a model of radical democracy based on republican ideas that Chantal Mouffe (1992b:227) favours.

9   Tassin (1992:179) explains how this historical framework had its beginning in an Europe of Christendom, replacing the juridical bonds of the Roman Empire with religious bonds. This was succeeded by a Europe of sovereigns and the slow birth of nation-states grounded on the cultural and ideological cement of humanism. The Europe of sovereigns eventually replaced the principle of a Christian imperium with the principle of a community of nations. The peace of Westphalia in 1648 wiped the last idea of a Europe of Christendom in favour of ensuring a fairly peaceful equilibrium among slowly evolving nations. The French Revolution and the Napoleonic Wars then turned Europe into a Europe of nationalities, which was cemented by the ideology of the Treaty of Vienna 1815. The idea of a united political Europe became a contradiction to the concept of nation-states. Napoleon's conquest was, thus, not a uniting move but the first expression of the imperialist dimension of nation-states. In this sense the wars of 1870-71 and World War I were national wars and it was the nationality principle that dominated the Treaty of Versailles. Following this logic, German Fascism was then one way of taking the ideology of essential national values to a perverse extreme.

10 See Stychin (1998) for an elaborate discussion of this feature in Europe and in other Western cultures.

11 See, for an elaboration on these opportunities, Shaw (1999). The debate in the Convention on the Future of Europe also often featured elements of such an argument.

12 This was further elaborated by ILGA-Europe in its Project Proposal for 'Road Blocks and Stepping Stones' to the EU commission, a project that was funded by the EU and conducted during 2000 together with other large European NGOs through seminars and a report on the connection between racial, sexual orientation, and disability discrimination. The report can be found on ILGA-Europe's website.

13 The reports on discrimination are often structured according to nation-states. If they are structured according to issues of discrimination, they obviously always have to refer to legal and cultural difference among nation-states to argue their point. There are many academic examples of this too. Berry Adam, Jan Willem Duyvendak, and André Krouwel's 1999 collection *The Global Emergence of Gay and Lesbian Politics. National Imprints of a World Wide Movement* presents a good example of the dangers entailed in an unreflected ordering of analysis within national boundaries. Although they acknowledge the reproduction of dominant discourses through gay and lesbian political practices (1999:9), overall their anthology does not reflect on this critically. They (1999:8) justify their project on national gay and lesbian contexts through defying

queer critiques and questioning the applicability of these critiques for third world national contexts. Yet, the anthology itself sadly misses the chance to discuss an unproblematised nationalism – almost a kind of nationalist imperialism of European colour – in the description of world-wide gay and lesbian culture and politics. Political practices are described in terms of nation-states only. In the face of this lack of problematisation their conclusion about the absolute impossibility of describing one world wide, or even an European, form of gay and lesbian politics, almost becomes a truism.

14 Interestingly enough Flynn (1997:503–6), for example, offers an analysis of how a concept of Irishness became the decisive motor of the homosexual law reform in Ireland. National discourses are not necessarily always simply reactionary when it comes to minority rights. Their workings occasionally can be more complicated in this respect.

15 The critical ones were not only those that have rights and feared to lose them through EU compromises. Activists form the 'have-not' countries were also occasionally very EU critical. The hope of export or import was expressed by eight of the interviewees. However the specificity of this hope depended on personal political affiliation and, particularly, on national EU perception.

16 This is a common attitude. In their analysis of transnational policy networks Keck and Sikkink (1998:202) state that 'for almost all transnational campaigns, how the issue of nationalism is engaged is crucial to achieving issue resonance'.

17 The Gay Games are another example of this kind of move. Becoming the largest gay, lesbian, and bisexual event in the world, they happily incorporate the idea of national sports competition while they challenge the general assumptions about the sexual orientation of athletes world-wide.

18 See Einhorn and Gregory (1998:293) for an analysis of the fortress of Europe with regards to Eastern Europe and women, and Slavoj Zizek (1992) for an analysis of the othering of Eastern Europe and re-emerging nationalism.

19 This was illustrated again through the prominence of the Monika Lewinsky affair. In EU countries such an affair could never have had the political impact it had in the US.

20 Severely racialised since the situation is not the same for all third-country nationals. In all EU states white immigrants from North America or Australia and Aotearoa/New Zealand are in practice treated very differently from non-white people of other origin.

21 See also Shaw (1998), Evans (1993, 2000) and Stychin (2000) on this matter.

22 Interestingly enough, research has shown that gay men are not as rich and middle class as they are made out to be. In fact, as Gluckman and Reed's (1997) collection shows, there is a disproportionate percentage of poverty evident in gay and lesbian communities in North America. Similar research has been done for some European contexts (Binnie 1995:199). Economic arguments in relation to rights campaigns are always fraught with problems, they easily fuel an anti-gay agenda (Herman 1997:120–8).

23 Hennessy (1995:51) has analysed a similar effect in the US context. According to her, there are invisible links between nationhood and public sexual discourse as well as the public spaces in which a (hetero)-sexualised national imaginary is constructed in people's everyday lives.

24 The understanding of recognition as a process, not a property or state of legal rights, is an idea that Johannes Fabian advanced for anthropology (1999:68).

25 There exists an English edition of the book called *Between Cultures. Tensions in the Struggle for Recognition*, published in 2000, which I used for the direct quotes and for clarification of the German terminology in English. The page references in the rest of the text, however, refer to the original German edition.

26 In his translation Kenneth B. Woodgate distinguishes the German terms through using the terms 'recognition', 're-cognition' and 'repeated re-cognition' (Düttmann 2000:ix).

The concept of recognition is not new, nor is it reduced to one discipline or one theorist such as Düttmann. The concept has been deployed in feminist analysis, anthropology, postcolonial studies, and certainly philosophy. It has been inspired by Hegel and Fichte and extended by Frantz Fanon and Jean-Paul Sartre. My deployment of the concept is admittedly limited. See Johannes Fabian for an overview of the utilisation and discussions of the concept in philosophy and its possibilities in anthropology (1999:63–9). Fabian particularly emphasises the distinction between the German terms '*anerkennen*', '*erkennen*', and '*wiedererkennen*' as an important entry point into utilising the concept of (re)-recognition (1999:53 and 68).

27 Düttmann's analysis could easily incorporate the concept of the performative here. Since he does not use this concept I will also refrain from incorporating it here. It could, however, serve the analysis well if not located on the side of the subject nor on the side of language, but on the interconnection between them, as in Judith Butler's work.

28 Düttmann (1997:183) calls any struggle for recognition a fight that is necessarily about life and death. I do not think this logic is applicable to citizenship and I will, therefore, not elaborate on this point.

29 Politically Düttmann (1997:212) concludes that the contradictions of recognition can only be followed by a politics of rescue, since one has to rescue that which is not yet existing and which is, therefore, particularly present. He terms politics then an irony of rescue and a rescue of irony. However, I prefer Fabian's (1999:67) response of emphasising the 're' in 'recognition' and concentrating on recognition as an epistemological problem to avoid certain positivist problems of recognition.

30 See, for example, Duggan (2000), Smith (2000), Stein (2000), and Kupp and Taylor (1999).

31 See, for example Shaw (1998), Kaplan (1997a), and Flynn (1997).

32 This approach stems mainly from critical and feminist geography. See, for example, Binnie (1995 and 1997), Bell and Valentine (1995), and Kofman (1995).

8 Framing the debate: kinship

> A constitutional right for the care of the community is granted to mothers in our constitution, the importation of catamites, for example, is not mentioned.
> (Catholic Bishop Johannes Dyba on the plans of the German government to introduce registered partnership, July 2000)

> to the extent that norms operate as psychic phenomena, restricting and producing desire, they also govern the formation of the subject and circumscribe the domain of a livable sociality.
> (Butler 1997b:21)

The demand for equal citizenship is commonly assessed against the legal and social recognition gay and lesbian partnerships receive. In fact, marriage and the right to adoption, custody, or artificial insemination – in short the right to be recognised as a family – are the central rallying point of European gay and lesbian rights struggles and also the greatest stumbling block. In this chapter I will focus on the conditions of the political debate on kinship in Europe.

The possibility of legal partnership recognition for gays and lesbians comes at a time when capitalism can quite happily accommodate a group of independent producers and consumers operating outside the constraints of the traditional nuclear family, while historically the development of capitalism has depended upon the nuclear family as principal unit (Pateman 1988; Stychin 2000). At a time when the ideal of the nuclear family is being eroded, gay men and lesbians have adopted kinship ideologies that use uncommon categories of friendship, networking, and community to generate common meanings of love, endurance and commitment (Weston 1991; 1998). What was hardly a political goal in the 1970s and early 1980s, namely access to marriage, gained an overarching dominance among gay and lesbian rights advocates and in the general political debate in the 1990s (Warner 1999:122–3). A number of European countries now have partnership laws that either recognise homosexual couples as equivalent to non-married heterosexual couples or give them some, or most, of the same rights as granted in marriage through a registered partnership.[1]

However, throughout all European countries – with the exception of the Netherlands, where adoption is allowed – the relation of homosexuals to children is portrayed as a political and a social threat. Debates over same-sex marriage are always connected to parenting. While most opinion polls in Western Europe show a great deal of support for limited partnership rights, two elements are always strongly emphasised in the political debates: the maintenance of a certain privileged status for heterosexuals as part of the founding unit of society and the strict exclusion of parenting rights for homosexuals. Both elements retain the discursive exclusion of lesbians and gay men from what counts as authentic kinship. The best summary of what is at stake anti-gay/lesbian agenda can be found in the Vatican's lengthy call to Catholic politicians on 31 July 2003 to oppose all forms of homosexual partnership rights, which openly incites hatred and calls gay/lesbian parenting violence against children.

Lesbians and gay men face extensive discrimination in relation to parenting. They are commonly denied custody and access. They are refused the ability to adopt as a second parent or as a couple, as well as the right to artificial insemination.[2] Such discrimination is usually based on the view that to be brought up by lesbian or gay parents is in some way damaging for a child. It is assumed that gay and lesbian parenting may lead to confusion over gender roles, or sexual identity, or to maladjustment in social relationships. Another concern frequently expressed is that children brought up by lesbian and gay parents are themselves likely to develop a homosexual orientation. Polemically speaking, all tolerance ends when it comes to the care for children.

This line of argument was partly deployed in the negative 2002 judgment by the ECHR in *Frette* v. *France*, where a single gay man in France was denied adoption solely on the ground of his sexual orientation. While the judgment recognised sexual orientation as clearly falling under anti-discrimination in Article 14, it nevertheless stated that there was not enough common understanding among Member States on homosexual parenting, that science was still divided over the consequences of homosexual parenting for the child and the child's interest had to be safeguarded until proof of non-harm can be established.

Consequently, on the one hand, the language of partnership and family is employed to establish that gay men and lesbians are just like heterosexuals – loving and caring partners and parents – while, on the other hand, the same language serves the opponents of rights for sexual minorities. The reason why the definitions of kinship relations are at the heart of almost all political debates about human rights, anti-discrimination, citizenship, or legal recognition, rests in the establishment of kinship as the politically, socially, historically and psychologically most basic human need and condition.

Gay and lesbian theorists themselves often re-assert kinship's role as a basic human need. Morris B. Kaplan (Kaplan 1997b:206), for example, states that:

> By turning to marriage, partnership, and family rights, the movement for lesbian and gay rights and liberation affirms deeply felt human needs to establish intimate relationships as part of the ongoing conduct of life, culminating for many in the desire to bear and raise children of their own or otherwise to share in the care of others.

Kaplan's (1997b:218–21) argument asserts, furthermore, that the existence of different sexualities with their own modes of intimacy is itself a contribution to human flourishing and that to claim a right to marry justifiably derives its ethical and political force from appealing to ideals of equal citizenship. Kaplan precisely formulates what is at stake in the political practices around kinship: kinship is seen as a basic human need, something all people want to establish, because it is part of their human nature. Taking this as a given, kinship occupies an important political position: it forms a continuous pre-sphere to the political, it is its playground and, in turn, its outcome.

In the following I argue that kinship is the frame upon and in which the social being that forms the basis for the political sphere in European culture is created, shaped, and enacted. Full participation in the political sphere presumes an adult citizen who, in principle, moves among equals that – en masse as the general public – can exert authority through their free will. Citizenship is, thus, distinguished from the kinship relations that are meant to produce, harbour and educate such adult citizens. The participation of an adult in the formation of political will in a democratic society is a result of enlightened developments in European culture, while kinship is regarded as the primitive natural realm deriving from our natural biological condition. Tamed and civilised, but still representing the authentic human nature, the family remains the natural unit that produces sociability.

Kinship regulates not only partnership and procreation, but also the fundamental meanings of gender and sex as well as the move from childhood to adulthood. To evaluate policy questions of partnership laws and access to parenting is therefore to evaluate what sex is – what counts as human sexual acts – whether states can and should regulate it, and how the intimate life of pleasure and of parenting does or does not matter publicly. In fact, it is to evaluate how, when, and where the future citizen and the rules of social and civic participation are decided upon.

Yet, kinship is not as value free a condition of human nature as it seems. Kinship has a context, or better a frame, outside of which it cannot exist and enjoy its claim to authenticity. This frame is heteronormative. Using two specific examples, this chapter begins with an analysis of what kinship is presumed to be when discussed in the institutional political sphere. This analysis leads to the conclusion that heteronormativity frames the kinship debate which, in turn, led to vehement critiques of activism aimed at registered partnership or marriage. A second section will summarise those important critiques before proceeding to my own contribution towards a critical analysis of the conditions of European political kinship debates, which are the focus of the third section. I will argue that the theoretical concept of framing can increase our understanding of the relationship between political kinship debates and heteronormativity without ever reducing the one to the other. This understanding is achieved through the introduction of a web of interrelating frames that surround kinship, but are not reducible to the supra-frame heteronormativity: love, authenticity, desire, and subjection.

Kinship in official political discourse

At first glance 'kinship' is one of the most innocent descriptive terms imaginable. Yet, as anthropology has shown over decades, kinship is fraught with temporal connotations (Weston 1991; Fabian 1991). Kinship connotes something like primordial ties and origins and, thus, has a persistent strength and meaning attributed to it. The meaning of 'kinship', in principle, is actually rarely debated or questioned in political practices, while most other categories associated with it do receive revision and debate. It is as if kinship – particularly the dimension of parenting – somehow remains authentic, no matter what changes time has brought about.

Thus, when advocacy organisations such as ILGA-Europe call for partnership and parenting recognition, this demand has to be seen in the context of the primordial functioning of kinship in the political sphere in Europe. The statements and claims of the rights activists are made in a very factual manner, similar to the human rights debate and discrimination reports. However, since acknowledgement of kinship is the most contentious issue in rights struggles, the apparent factuality has a distinct quality: it consistently refers to what is portrayed to be a truism – namely that kinship ties are formed by every human being as a matter of biological need, just as everybody has a sexuality and a gender identity. In spite of the strangeness generally attached to the image of homosexual families, the rights claims with regard to marriage and parenting re-enforce kinship's primordial character.

The way kinship is re-played as pre-political sphere, as a basic unit of society, and as biological necessity can be traced in the official debates on gay and lesbian rights at the European institutions. I will quote two longer excerpts as examples to argue this point. One example is taken from the address by ILGA-Europe to the Drafting Convention on the Charter of Fundamental Rights of the European Union on 27 April 2000. This excerpt exemplifies well the kind of rhetoric commonly employed throughout Europe either towards the European institutions or towards national governments. The second example is a speech made by a Conservative Norwegian MP, Ms Annelise Høegh, delivered in the debate on 30 June 2000 in the Parliamentary Assembly of the Council of Europe about the situation of lesbians and gay men throughout Europe.

This debate is particularly interesting, because it was overwhelmingly positive as far as legalisation, equal age of consent, hate crimes, employment discrimination and, to some extent, partnership rights were concerned. Only one Polish contribution placed homosexuality into the context of paedophilia and portrayed it as a threat to Christianity and the Enlightenment. Yet, as I explained in Chapter 1, the reference to adoption in the report of the Subcommittee of Human Rights and Legal Affairs created debate and eventual rejection. This PACE debate is a good example of the overall character of European kinship debates that attract different national opinions on the topic, yet also display the commonality of the rhetoric. The Høegh speech displays an exemplary connection of conservatism with homosexual rights that calls upon a sense of European values. It is a supportive speech, whereas explicit support from conservative parties is very rare in the European institutions. Høegh, therefore, made an extraordinary contribution that highlights astutely what is at stake in the European debate on kinship.

Address by ILGA-Europe to the Drafting Convention on the Charter of Fundamental Rights of the European Union on 27 April 2000

Turning now to the question of partnerships and family life: some of the realities of life in Europe today are:

- that millions of people are living together as same-sex partners;
- that in many cases children are being brought up by these couples, or indeed by single people who are lesbian, gay, bisexual or transgendered.

To repeat: these are realities. They cannot be wished away or ignored.

The qualities which go to make up a good partnership and a good family – for example, love, mutual respect, commitment, equality – are in no sense dependent on the sex of the members. The desire to be a parent, and the qualities that make a good parent, are also unrelated to the sexual orientation or gender identity of the individual.

These partners, these children, these parents, these families, deserve the protection and support of society just as much as any others. This protection and support can come only with proper and full legal recognition. We urge therefore that the articles of the Charter dealing with these issues be drafted in a manner that is inclusive rather than exclusive, acknowledging that a variety of forms of family exists in today's society.

We have emphasised the need for the new Charter both to signal the unacceptability of discrimination based on sexual orientation or gender identity, and to foster a vision of family life, which is humane, inclusive, and grounded in reality. We have highlighted the progress made in recent years, but also shown how far there is still to go. Europe will be a better, freer, and more accepting place for all its citizens when those who are lesbian, gay, bisexual and transgendered can be themselves, openly and without fear. We believe that if our suggestions are taken up in the Charter, that Europe will be one step closer to becoming a reality.

The Høegh speech

THE PRESIDENT. – Thank you, Mrs Faldet. I call Ms Høegh. I hope that I have pronounced your name correctly.

Ms HØEGH (Norway).– No, that was not the right pronunciation, but I understood who you meant.

As a Conservative, I feel that it is natural to support this excellent report. I concur entirely with all the recommendations in the report on the situation of lesbians and gays in Council of Europe Member States, apart from the section in paragraph 9 of the draft recommendation about the right to adopt children, because in my view no adult has the right to adopt. Children have certain rights, and I am glad that the Committee accept the revised Amendment No. 7.[3]

I should like to comment on paragraph 11.iii.h, which deals with a registered partnership.

In my country, Norway, we have had such legislation since 1993. I was my party's spokesman on the subject, although my positive view represented a minority position. However, I hasten to add that, seven years later, the overwhelming majority of the Norwegian Conservative Party supports registered partnership. As politicians, we have an obligation to make it possible for all citizens to take responsibility for themselves and for their families. People should enjoy equal rights, but also equal duties. Unfortunately, that is not the case as most European countries deny homosexuals the right to register their partnerships. Consequently, they are left to live without the security and the confidence that legal recognition of partnership would provide. How, then, can we be surprised that many lesbians and gays find it difficult to be self-reliant and proud citizens who try to be true to one partner? That is difficult enough for the rest of us; how much more difficult must it be for them?

Registered partnership is the tool that homosexuals need to be [sic] enable them to live in stable and binding relationships. That is all the more important from the AIDS perspective. Registered partnership is modelled on the institution of marriage, and instead of seeing it as a threat to marriage, which it is not, we should regard it as a token of the strength of matrimony, which is what it really is. It should be considered to be a model.

I remind possible sceptics of some examples from history. Some of our forefathers opposed universal suffrage, not only for men, but for women. Others opposed equal rights for children born out of wedlock. None of us is very proud of those examples today, but I have mentioned them because once in a while I have found it useful to think about whether some of my own hesitations about granting someone a right or supporting new legislation are perhaps founded on old habits, or even prejudice, rather than on true reflection. We should not retain old habits if they stand in the way of enlarging the scope of human rights.

As a Conservative, I want to emphasise that Conservatism is not about keeping everything as it always has been. Such an attitude is reactionary – nothing more, nothing less. True Conservatism is about creating a society that acknowledges and respects the individual and the individual's right to be different. Fortunately, most homosexuals today do not hide their sexual orientation, so would it not be sensible and responsible to create institutions whereby they can take responsibility not only for themselves but for their partners?

As I have said, my view was not shared by the majority of my party, but it is today. The legislation has had no negative effects in Norway – indeed, the contrary is true – and it has functioned positively in the homosexual community. That is why I urge the few sceptics in the Assembly to think about the reports and to accept them so that tomorrow they do not have to regret rejecting them.

THE PRESIDENT. – Thank you, dear lady. I call Mr Jaskiernia from Poland, of the Socialist Group. ...

Overall, Høegh's speech clearly indicates the direction of the debate about kinship and sexual orientation in Europe: partnership yes, but parenting no. The adopted amendment No. 7 she welcomes in the beginning of her speech is an amendment that sought to cut the reference to adoption and artificial insemination originally part of the draft recommendations of the PACE report. For Høegh, amendment 7 is a question of children's rights, which implies that the question remains open whether gay fathers or lesbian mothers are detrimental to children's rights. That lesbian and gay parents are at least potentially negative for children is so obvious to Høegh that she offers no elaboration on this point, but simple states the disparity between gay and lesbian parenting rights and children's rights before elaborating at length on partnership rights. While partnership rights are arguable from a conservative view, gay and lesbian parenting is so far removed from any reasonable consideration that the denial of such a right needs no further explanation.

Both excerpts clarify once more from different perspectives that any analysis of sexual minorities always requires to be thought of in relation to an analysis of kinship. Gay men and lesbians are often not considered human or worthy of protection because they are regarded as estranged from what counts as the kinship figuration through which the human becomes recognisable (Butler 1994:15). Sexuality in this context need not even be thought of in terms of reproduction only for the conclusion to be drawn that it obviously cannot be thought of outside of kinship. Although gay men and lesbians are not born into their identities by virtue of their parents' identities, kinship matters distinctively.

It is kinship – even if not their kinship to their original families – that configures the identities of sexual minority groups: their gender performance and their sexual practices define their forms of partnerships and their efforts at parenting as illegal, as pretended or at best as tolerable, but always as an imitation of the real thing.[4] This principle is substantiated through at least four aspects of argumentation that can be identified in the excerpts quoted: first, the definition of marriage or partnership as simultaneously a contract and a status; second, the prolongation of the split between the private and public sphere, politically distinct, but mutually dependent; third, the link between partnership regulations and questions of gender and of gender identity; and fourth, the naturalness of kinship and its connection to biological parenting, which re-asserts the claim to human authenticity in partnership and parenting. I will trace and analyse these four aspects in the excerpts cited.

Status and contract are rhetorically entangled in both texts, simultaneously invoked and equally valorised. ILGA-Europe's claim for recognition of all families already existent in Europe portrays partnerships as involving a contract between equals. Those elements, which define the good family – namely love, mutual respect, commitment, and equality – are elements that point to possibilities of contractual relations between partners and between parents and children. The discourse of contract implies that the rational will of the individual makes it possible to take on social obligations and responsibility within autonomous intentional arrangements made between equal people. However, the right to live a publicly and legally recognised family life, claimed by ILGA-Europe in the same breath, is not a question of contract but of status. Status can be defined as denoting 'persons bound into a social order, their obligations and legal duties constricted by their position within familial, occupational, and religious institutions' (Goldberg-Hiller 2000:7).

Høegh's speech also displays a modernist assumption about the ability to form contractual relationships. She propagates registered partnership as an arrangement based upon mutual understanding and as a tool that enables homosexuals to live in stable and binding relationships. A concept of free choice underlies both her argument as well as that of ILGA-Europe. Yet, she simultaneously plays on status. The status of marriage is maintained in that registered partnership is a token of the strength of matrimony, marriage remains the model, its status is neither threatened nor questioned. The reference to historical change in conservative attitudes, for example with regard to suffrage, retains marriage as an important status signal with the capacity for change. Høegh seems to appreciate the advanced forms of marriage existent in Europe today in comparison to their earlier incarnations. However while deeply supportive, Høegh also exhibits a growing anxiety about the maintenance of that status as is evident in most debates about homosexual marriage. This anxiety stems from the inevitable need to assert some authority and legitimacy over *who is what* amid the rapid social change in Europe.

The entanglement of status and contract is not only evident in supportive statements, but in virtually all contributions to the kinship debate. This fact makes 'the very categories of the legal form discursively unstable and increasingly mutually interdependent' (Goldberg-Hiller 2000:10). The reference to a *contractual* relationship features an abstract identity of each person involved in the partnership, no matter what gendered or racial self, for example, is involved. Any identity either one of the partners might have beyond sexual orientation is imagined to be in parity with the identities of the other. Legal recognition of these partnerships is intended to encourage negotiated and egalitarian family relations. The *status* implied in claiming the right to legal recognition and equality, in contrast, interpellates the society as a whole: the status of registered partnership will make possible for them what is already difficult for us – the us being the heterosexual majority in Høegh's terms.

According to ILGA-Europe, the contracts gay men, lesbians, bisexuals and transgendered people, together with their children, have already entered into provide the democratic legitimacy for legal recognition. The status of marriage and its imitation registered partnership can, then, be interpreted as finally turning gay men and lesbians – bisexuals and transgender people are not mentioned in any European extra-marital partnership laws – into respectable citizens imbued with human values above simple legal rights. Thus, when registered partnership is argued to be a fair source of protection for those who lack the benefit of marriage, the language of contract depicts the material consequences of social obligations and claims political space to constitute an authentic kinship contract. Simultaneously, when registered partnership is argued for as a stepping-stone to full participation in citizenship for gays and lesbians and as a final recognition of their status as equal contributors, the new status is depicted as cost free to society as a whole. Nothing changes in the principal social web.

Jonathan Goldberg-Hiller (2000:26) has summarised the effect of this mixture astutely:

> That domestic partnership can be portrayed as a compromise, one able to preserve the status of traditional marriage while providing 'equal rights for everyone' suggests the cultural interplay of contract and status will continue to define a political space in which the denial of citizenship for a few can be made in the name of citizenship for all.

In consequence, the diffuse mixture of both arguments leaves kinship regulations within the domain of a pre-set norm that is deeply heterosexual and that presumes, in principle, the gender of the two contractors to be opposite. While kinship offers a rhetoric of rights, it also continues to offer an argument for the legitimacy to deny those rights for the sake of all.

Second, a similar effect can be witnessed in the maintenance of the distinction between public and private in the language of kinship recognition. Høegh provides a particularly clear example of this distinction in which mutual dependency is asserted through kinship ties. For Høegh the opportunity to achieve private happiness through the security and confidence that legal recognition of partnership provides creates self-reliant citizens capable of taking on responsibilities for themselves and their partners. Private stability, or better the opportunity to create that stability through being granted legal recognition, leads to the possibility of becoming or being recognised as a good public citizen. This connection is also evident in the rights rhetoric of ILGA-Europe: partners, children, parents, families deserve protection and support for their private lives and that can only come about with proper and full legal and public recognition. Both excerpts imply a duty of the public to protect the private. The private is portrayed to some extent as pre-condition of the public. Only a functioning private realm makes the democratic public realm a possibility, secures its functioning and secures the reproduction of public and private future players.

The maintenance of the distinction between public and private spheres in which kinship is traditionally relegated to the private and citizenship to the public has a historical tradition from Aristotle to Hegel (Phelan 2000:2). That both are mutually dependent for the (re)creation of the originally male citizen who can participate in the public sphere, is another of kinship's historical features. As a haven in a heartless world, the family, according to Wendy Brown (1995:161), 'functions discursively as the background of the socially male individual. While the individual is understood to be made possible through the family – harbored, grounded, and nourished there – all cannot be individuals or there would be no family, no "it" that harbors, grounds and nourishes'. Brown takes this as a historical fact from Hegel and Rousseau, who relegated the substantial vocation of women to the family and asserted that it takes two – a man and a woman – to make one – a new male citizen.

It is crucial to note here how Høegh works with the pre-condition of private happiness for the creation of responsible public citizens, while simultaneously asserting a decisive heterosexual privilege with respect to parenting a young citizen. Høegh concurs

> entirely with all the recommendations in the report on the situation of lesbians and gays in Council of Europe Member States, apart from the section in paragraph 9 of the draft recommendation about the right to adopt children, because in my view no adult has the right to adopt. Children have certain rights, and I am glad that the Committee accept the revised Amendment No. 7.

While she is correct in asserting that children have rights to good parenting, her juxtaposition of gay and lesbian parenting rights with children's rights indicate that these rights are somehow in opposition to each other. Behind her formulation stands the opinion that the responsibilities she refers to shall not cover parenting since children have the right to heterosexual parents and should, thus, not be raised by homosexuals. Apart from suggesting that Høegh's speech could be read as homophobic in this respect, I rather want to suggest that it is the ideological tradition of the split between the public and the private which makes the exclusion of gay and lesbian parenting rights necessary and justifiable. Two aspects of this tradition are relevant in this respect.

Firstly, through the split between public and private the family retains a symbolic opposition to work and business, in other words to the domain of capitalism (Lehr 1999:19). In consequence, as Shane Phelan asserts (2000:12–13), kinship and citizenship cannot be thought of independently of each other in discourses on rights. Any play on the dualism of public and private invokes meanings of both kinship and citizenship and their relationship to the functioning of democratic and capitalist European societies. The dualist split evident in the texts blurs the fact that the so-called public sphere of responsibility in partnership actually conflates three things: the relation of the individual to the state, the relationship of marriage to the official economy of paid employment and the relationship of sexuality to the arenas of public discourse. For the politically significant meanings of kinship, all of these relations are important. Secondly, the role of these relations is made invisible by the gender-neutrality displayed in arguments for partnership and family legislation that retain a strict separation of public and private.

This seeming gender-neutrality is itself the third of the four problematic aspects of the political kinship debate I want to identify. To define the qualities that make up a good partnership and a good family as including love, mutual respect, commitment and equality is certainly a legitimate political argument. As argumentational strategy it tries to go beyond the normativity of family definitions that relate only to heterosexuals and make heterosexuality the only defining element of family. ILGA-Europe's argument, therefore, aims at dislodging a certain historical condition of kinship regulations. What this argument misses, however, is that families have never only been about love, mutual respect, commitment, and equality as long as gender has had any meaning in social relations.

Partnership and the desire to parent cannot be thought of independently of gender and gender identity, while sexual orientation might possibly be regarded as sometimes irrelevant, although even this is questionable. As political practice this claimed irrelevancy makes sense, but the implications are potentially dangerous. Høegh's speech illustrates some of these dangers. Her sense of contractual choice and responsibility appears to be gender neutral. Yet, through distinguishing marriage proper as the status model and through the exclusion of rights to adoption her conception becomes highly gendered. While she tries to disconnect partnership from procreation, the intrinsic, natural connection of both in marriage is re-asserted. Gender and gender identity are the most relevant markers of how human relations are defined by either marriage or registered partnership. One is allowed to procreate; the other is not. Høegh's argument centres on responsibility for oneself and for one's family. Whereas that should be made accessible to lesbians and gay men, the true model – heterosexual marriage – has a historical legacy with respect to responsibility: the male breadwinner is historically the legal and public body of both man and woman.[5]

The contractual ideas of a gender-blind partnership legislation will continue to be problematic for women in heterosexual relationships and for men and women in gay and lesbian relationships who, for one reason or another, are placed in roles or aspects of roles traditionally assigned to the female domain. Carole Pateman's (1988:231) well-known analysis of the sexual contract shows that what appears as a free partnership contract actually centres on the regulation of sexual intercourse. This means that marriage is less a contract between equals and more a means of defining the status of men and women in a non-equal relation to each other, particularly with respect to parenting and childcare. The fact that the overarching majority of nuclear family units throughout Europe today re-create and maintain certain forms of gender relations and gendered work is uncritically continued in the family rhetoric employed for rights. This reality is not only a heterosexual one, for gender structures and their unequal consequences are also at work just as readily in many gay and lesbian parenting relationships.[6]

Gender roles and their ways of organising social relations such as work, citizenship, reproduction, ownership, pleasure, and identity have a persistent effect on structures of dominance in all forms of families. As Shane Phelan (2000:5) puts it, lesbian and gay families are 'not created from a cultural vacuum, but are bricolages of existing elements from both sexual subcultures and heterosexual family cultures'. At the same time, these cultures and gendered structures vary and are sites of social struggle in both heterosexual relationships and homosexual ones. The failure to address the deeply gendered realities and ideological conditions of kinship masks one of the very conditions that have historically made possible the exclusion of gay men, lesbians, and transgender people from certain forms of recognised kinship.

Fourthly and finally, the central factor in the justification of this exclusion rests on the seeming naturalness of heterosexual marriage as the starting point for parenting relations. This naturalness is rooted in an ideology of human need for sexual relations that are stable and enduring and provide a context for the role of sexuality as procreation. While advocacy of gay and lesbian partnership recognition usually questions the natural need for heterosexual sexual relations, the principal need is commonly asserted. This naturalness of sexual relations is connected to a claim of authenticity. Love and the free choice of a sexual partner as an authentic expression of one's essential self is a prominent part of kinship arguments.

The vision of a Europe that is humane and acknowledges the human realities of homosexual families expressed by ILGA-Europe connects the definition of a true family as encompassing love, mutual respect, commitment, and equality to a sense of basic humanity and of human rights. Categories such as love are employed to assert a claim to authenticity. According to the advocates, the reality is that lesbians, gay men, bisexuals, and transgender people are human, they love and live in partnerships and they raise children according to their natural desire. While Høegh excludes the last mentioned aspect as inappropriate, the first one – love – is nevertheless the marker of authenticity for her as well. It is the category that renders everyone human and that must be acknowledged through equality and respect even according to a conservative world-view.

Yet, Høegh also points to the need to civilise and tame nature; stable, binding relationships are for her the answer to problems such as AIDS. Traditionally, this aspect of taming was assigned to male sexuality that could only be controlled when confronted with the social responsibility of fatherhood (Lehr 1999:115–18). This discourse of 'wild male sexuality' is one of the reasons why gay male sexuality is often portrayed as threatening: gay men are said to be obsessed with sexual pleasure only and not capable of the responsibility needed for fathering. It is reasonable to assume that Høegh – as usual – was visualising gay male couples rather than lesbian couples while speaking. Høegh's argument is highly conservative – which she explicitly intends it to be – and, therefore, depends on the need to order kinship to promote responsible citizenship in a functioning sociality and market economy.

Thus, one important aspect of the debates about the cultural and legal status of homosexual partnerships is that the social advantages which accrue to heterosexual married couples are portrayed as doing so because heterosexuality represents an authentic form of true human need and sexual desire. Claiming equal rights to form kinship ties according to one's sexual desire plugs into the same discourse of authenticity while trying to disconnect this authenticity from heterosexuality. It is the very idea of status relationships as true and biologically authentic expressions of human nature that provides the basis for the official political debate about gay and lesbian partnership laws on both sides. All alternative suggestions in this debate remain limited by the need to adhere to the norms of kinship as natural and authentic biological expressions of human nature.

In summary, similar to citizenship claims, advocacy of kinship rights presents a rhetorical inversion in reference to the discursive construction of partnership rights. This inversion is invoked when the law is called upon to substantiate a claim for equal status, while this status itself is fetishised as already existent and as the central proof for rights of equality. The rhetoric of kinship evident in both ILGA-Europe's approach and Høegh's speech involves the same contradictory process of recognition I have analysed with regard to citizenship. The claim for kinship recognition crosses out its own process since it implies a recurrent inversion of the before and the after.

Høegh's speech exemplifies this circularity. It proclaims a form of equality that is not only gender- and race-blind, but also very explicit about its active reconstruction of a norm. While being supportive of registered partnership Høegh categorises some forms of kinship as model and others as imitation. The conservative rejection usually goes one step further in declaring this imitation fictive kinship. Yet, whether it is fictive or imitative is a matter of terminology, since the presumption is that blood relations formed by procreative heterosexuality constitute actual true kinship and provide the only model for all derivative forms of families. Therefore, ILGA-Europe's insistence that what makes a true family is love, mutual respect, commitment and equality maybe directed against heterosexuality as the only valid marker, but it, too, models itself according to values that are said to underlie the definition of family. It sounds like a truism, then, to state that all kinship regulations and almost all public political discourse about them are involved in a 'catch 22' situation: either way they cannot escape the heteronormative structure of kinship. The right to liberation and recognition in and of itself re-affirms the normative frame that is the source of the state of rightlessness. It is this insight that for many years has fuelled a vehement and vocal opposition among many gay, lesbian, bisexual, and transgender activists and academics against partnership laws or gay marriage.

Families of our own making: critiquing partnership laws

Those countries that have introduced partnership legislation are faced with an interesting trend: together with marriage, registered partnership is generally on the decline, but in proportion to the assumed gay and lesbian population and the number of marriages, partnership regulations are rarely used. In Denmark, less than 1 per cent of all ceremonies are registered partnerships. 1999 figures show that 0.8 per cent of all ceremonies in Sweden and 0.7 per cent in Norway were registered partnerships. 2000 figures show that 0.8 per cent of all ceremonies in Iceland were registered partnerships and only in the Netherlands – where both mixed-sex couples and same-sex couples could enter registered partnership since before marriage proper was opened on 1 April 2001 – were the figures as high as 1.9 per cent (Hinzpeter 2000:13). Why is this form of marriage, which was so heavily fought for, not used more?

Many critics would ascribe this to the fact that marriage is in decline as an antiquated institution in most western European countries and, more importantly, it is also in opposition to gay, lesbian, and bisexual cultures and, thus, not actually wanted by the majority of the sexual minority population. This view has been elaborated on from many angles: from the perspective of critical law, from a case study perspective, from a political (science) perspective, and from a philosophical critique.

Heather Brook (1998:10–11) explains the historically problematic transformation in the marriage ceremony from individuals to a complex conjugal body:

husband and wife become one person in law, not only through the state act, but more importantly through consummation, which is defined as proper heterosexual intercourse and the only real sexual act. For Brook (1998:11), the 'notion of consummation, then, is a corporeal yoke linking law and marriage'. Tracing the conjugal performance in the now more advanced partnership laws of Australia, Brook (1998:20) comes to the conclusion that:

> If same-sex marriage were to be recognised as marriage, the heterosexual logic of the conjugal body politic might be shaken, but perhaps only as it risks reinforcing sex – or certain sorts of sex – as performatives inscribing the governmental regulation of bodies. Whether the potential benefits render the risk worthwhile must remain, at least for the time being, something of a moot point.

Brook's conclusion is comparatively careful, whereas much of queer literature is more radical in concluding that gay marriage not only consolidates the primacy of heterosexual monogamy but also the interrelated systems of power of gender, race, and class.

Valerie Lehr (1999:62), for example, explains with respect to the US American context how the rise of companionate marriage and the institutionalisation of the nuclear family required a re-definition of femininity and masculinity that provided altered but clearly gendered hierarchies. At the same time, the racial binarism – white versus black – and the class binarism – poor versus middle class – were constructed in relation to a particular understanding of family life (1999:63). According to her, gay and lesbian marriage cannot escape these historical legacies. This radical queer critique is countered by Morris Kaplan (1997b:221) as both understating and exaggerating the importance of formal legal rights. To him, this critique underestimates the practical and material consequences of partnership laws as form of empowerment. Yet, it also exaggerates the extent to which individuals are deprived of the capacity to shape and revise the institutions they voluntarily create. He taps into the hope that the opening of marriage to lesbians and gay men will actually change the deeply oppressive history of marriage as an institution.

Kaplan finds himself in good critical company with this argument. Kaplan's defence of gay marriage gave new fuel to an already heated debate. Rune Halverson's (1998:210–11) examination of the Norwegian Registered Partnership Act as a case study, for example, answers to Kaplan's claim that even the symbolic effect of the Act has been less than either opponents or proponents expected. Nothing has changed the institution itself; heterosexual marriage remains at the peak of kinship hierarchies. Mainstream political discourse in Norway still draws contrast between couples and families. The selfish sexuality of those who do not raise children – lesbians or gays are not allowed to adopt or receive artificial insemination – is contrasted with those who are heads of families.

Michael Warner (1999:147) and Shane Phelan (2000:9) address Kaplan's argument directly on a political level. They argue against the split between citizenship and kinship by means of which individuals are disconnected from the heteronormative working of the law that regulates all forms of belonging from citizenship to kinship. Yet, the problem lies not in married lesbians and gay men imitating heterosexuals. According to Michael Warner (1999:142), this would be a naive understanding of how norms work. What the individual does or does not do, in fact, has little to do with the ramifications of the act of marriage. It is this act that always needs the recognition of a third party, the state with its interest in maintaining the naturalness and the biological essentialism of heterosexual procreation. Hence, the sudden change in the focus of gay, lesbian politics away from the system critique of the 1970s to the emphasis on marriage and families in the 1990s presents, on the one hand, a hierarchical exclusion of certain more radical forms of struggle (Ohms 2000:24). On the other hand this move presents a new kind of coming out that is different from coming out in the 1970s. Whereas, at the time, coming out implied impropriety because it broke the rules of what should go without saying, marriage embraces this saying as propriety, promising not to say too much and live in a regulated order (Warner 1999:148; Weston 1998:90). In more polemical writings, registered partnership is called a placebo, while the real thing, marriage, remains a privilege of real people. Lobby activists are accused of not realising that they are not accepted as serious political players by politicians but are, at the best of times, pink clowns in the corridors of high power who will be satisfied with little pieces of the cake. They apparently do not realise that what they are aiming at is much worse than the status quo[7] (Stedefeldt 2000:68).

Another approach takes up the critique from a philosophical point of view by criticising liberalism as the dominant ideology of kinship. Linda Nicholson's (1986) feminist analysis was one of the first to assert that liberal theory naturalises a particular version of the family and reifies a distinctly modern and ideological division between family, civil society, and state. Wendy Brown (1995:152–65), consequently, offered an elaborate critique of the common dualisms of liberalism and their impact on family values.[8] This analysis forms the background to her (1995:134) conclusion that when rights are articulated as material necessities, 'when they are "brought into discourse", rights are more likely to become sites of the production and regulation of identity as injury than vehicles of emancipation'. Marriage does not deliver equality and liberty, but inscribes certain identities for those who need protection. Marriage continuously excludes certain relations from what counts as real families.

Generally, queer critique maintains that – despite some restricted potential to destabilise the traditional notion of the family through gay marriage – uncoupled lesbians and gay men, or those whose manifold relationships do not fulfil the norm of monogamous coupledom, are excluded from the group seeking inclusion. As long as heterosexuals marry, the state will disregard the sexual lives of those who do not or cannot marry. The eventual validation of gay marriage will invalidate, delegitimise, and stigmatise other relations, needs, and desires (Warner 1999:133). The need to prove that homosexual relationships are familial in a heteronormative sense again and again gives power to judges to issue authoritative definitions of what constitutes the family. Politically speaking, the entitlement to social benefits should, therefore, not be based on the degree of intimacy attained with only one partner. Rights need to be de-familialised.[9]

In fact, according to Valerie Lehr (1999:138), the political kinship strategy needs to change fundamentally:

> The goal of articulation of a new narrative means that each of the separate groups currently harmed needs to move away from trying to gain resources and power by proving that they can enact current norms. It also requires that these groups move beyond fixed understanding of identity and group, recognizing instead that the identity itself only exists through exclusion, generally of those who are least able or willing to conform to the dominant constructions of society that in other ways oppress the group as a whole.

Lehr's conclusion is based on some additional claims about l/g/b/t subcultures. Gay, lesbian, bisexual, and transgender cultures are said to have strong links with non-monogamous sex. This image appears in homophobic and transphobic discourses, but also in proud self-depictions of the l/g/b/t scene. The slogan 'We are your worst nightmare. We are your best fantasy' plays with the double-bind of sex as definitional marker of a minority identity and of what apparently constitutes a biologically essential and natural need to form stable partnership attachments. The liberty of sex without procreation remains an underlying threat to the responsibility the good citizen has to take according to Høegh and that, according to ILGA-Europe, gay men, lesbians, bisexuals, and transgender people throughout Europe are already taking.

However, in spite of all the critique, there is a disposition towards romance in many gay, lesbian, bisexual, and transgender cultures. This disposition is a powerful temptation with regard to marriage. According to Kath Weston (1998:64), even if friendships are constructed as the most reliable and enduring form of kinship – a discourse common for l/g/b/t scenes – this alternative discourse can be radically innovative and thoroughly assimilationist at the same time. Weston (1998:84) shows that gay and lesbian kinship ties are described according to standardised categories such as shared experience, love, and closeness and 'there are reasons other than caprice to explain why, when it comes time to enumerate family relationships, Einstein the cat is in, but Angela the goldfish is out'. Weston (1998:87) concludes, therefore, that in practice chosen families do not disrupt the type of family mostly referenced in political debate. According to her, something is changing, but it is nothing so monolithic as *the family*.

The evident desire to marry or live in publicly acknowledged long-term relationships, clearly says nothing about whether pursuing legal marriage is a good political strategy. The existence of this desire in the everyday life of many also says nothing about what partnership rights do to the normativity of marriage and public control of sexual acts. Yet, this desire is a present and crucial feature in all alternative kinship designs and cannot be disregarded in any analysis of the political kinship debate. In fact, desire is an important means through which heteronormativity frames kinship and asserts authentic definitions. However, desire is not the only element in this intricate process. For all its obviousness and its long tradition in feminist and queer theory, the term 'heteronormativity' should not be taken as self-explanatory in relation to kinship. In what follows, I want to suggest that the concept of framing as an analytical tool can advance our understanding of the interrelated workings of specific political kinship debates in Europe. Kinship debates are interrelated both with heteronormativity and with other central ideological concepts such as love, authenticity, desire and subjection, concepts that support but also exceed the system of heteronormativity.

Framing kinship

Jürgen Habermas (1999:236) – who can scarcely be described as a queer thinker with feminist affiliations – admits that through the democratic procedures of political decision-making, mainstream morality asserts a place for itself in the justification of norms. This mainstream morality has been identified by many feminist writers as gendered and sexualised. Consequently, queer theory has made heteronormativity the central concept in analysing the workings of such mainstream morality. In a nutshell, queer theory asserts that heterosexuality is functionalised in a heteronormative way to occupy the centre of human sexuality, gender relations and indeed the political order and the conditions of social existence itself. Corinna Genschel (1996:528) summarises queer theory's stake in the term 'heteronormativity' as follows:

> In that heteronormativity is thematised, and not only heterosexuality, the institutional power of certain sets of discourses becomes visible. Heteronormativity organises more than just the sexual. It organises what is described as sexuality and many of the societal norms, values, and structures that seem so natural. To question heterosexuality as given by nature makes it possible to uncover different seemingly 'sexuality-free' ideologies and institutions. (translation mine)

According to Genschel (1996:529), queer analysis is directed against those systems of thought and those institutions which insist on the naturalness, the binding nature, and the pre-condition of heterosexuality, just as feminists have shown how gendered terms such as 'morality', 'rationality' or the 'public sphere' are deeply dependent on gender.

The power of heteronormativity is secured by material consequences that are accorded to those who by virtue of their heterosexual relations are considered kin. In fact, the regulation of kinship relations is probably the most powerful arm of any heteronormative order. Within kinship, it is not necessarily the genitals of certain bodies that define acts as heterosexual and consequently wield definitional power over what counts as a true, authentic relationship. It is rather the relationship between these activities and the heterosexual drama of clearly gendered roles that receives public recognition through a third witness to the marriage ceremony – the state and public interest. Gender and heteronormativity provide the historical context for all intimate interactions and this has different consequences when those interacting are two women or two men, or indeed two or more people whose gender identity cannot so easily be determined.

However, having asserted the centrality of heteronormativity, there is no precise answer to the question of how different political practices around kinship claims interact with concrete legal regulations of everyday life or with the desire for official recognition. Nor can heteronormativity alone sufficiently explain the political and legal centrality of certain sexual acts and how that centrality interacts with concepts such as desire, authenticity, or love. I want to suggest that the working of kinship norms in the context of political practices can only be understood when heteronormativity is not left on its own as the 'big dark and horrible coat' that eventually smothers all attempts of finding alternative means of political kinship recognition. Understood as a frame, however, the powerful workings of heteronormativity can be analysed more forcefully.

The political practices around kinship can be thought of as a text on which many different parties work, fighting about which word fits where. Yet, nobody argues about the need for a context, whereas all parts of the text reference this context. As my examples of the political debate on marriage and families in Europe show, the only narrative context that makes kinship politically intelligible is based on heterosexuality as norm. Yet, heteronormativity is more than just a context. The confining nature of such a force is better understood as a frame. This is more than a simple matter of terminology. According to Jonathan Culler (1988:xiv), context creates an opposition between an act – in this case a political practice in which kinship recognition is demanded – and its context, which presumes that the context is given and determines the meaning of the act. Not every meaning that can be read into the excerpts I analysed above is entirely or only determined by heteronormativity. This would oversimplify the workings of heteronormativity and other thought structures in the passages I quoted .

Framing, on the contrary, in Culler's words, is something we *do*. According to Mieke Bal (1996:32–3), the concept of framing is crucial to understanding any process of reading, in fact, 'framing is a constant semiotic activity, without which no cultural life can function'. There exists an intrinsic need to read, i.e. interpret, what one sees, experiences or does. This need implicates a necessary designation of a frame – consciously or unconsciously. To talk, for example, about our alternative families which already exist all over Europe, one needs a narrative frame in which this form of talk makes sense, in this case the frame of arguing against heterosexuality as the only existent form of family ties. In fact, as Ernst van Alphen (1999:34) argues, without a frame, no narrative makes sense. To him, no experience is experiencable outside a narrative frame to which its narrative refers and which grants a subjectivity capable of speech.[10] Centralising framing in cultural intelligibility in this way – as Bal and van Alphen do in the context of art and history respectively – is a move to substitute a problematic concept of context by the concept of frame or, better, framing. (Bryson 1994) The current interest in framing has emerged with Jacques Derrida's (1982) reading of Kant in *The Truth in Painting*. Just as the frame of a painting had to protect the purity of art and connect it to the world outside the picture, framing as an analytical concept produces meaning, but, more importantly, has a capacity to limit meaning while making the limitations visible, hence, open for scrutiny.[11] Conceptualising heteronormativity as a frame to the political debate on kinship allows one to go beyond the queer conclusion that heteronormativity produces meaning about seemingly real kinship ties.

The concept of framing allows one to see the limitations of meaning heteronormativity is capable of producing through its intersection with other frames, as well as making those limitations open for scrutiny. No political debate can occur outside of a frame: 'trying to eliminate the activity of framing is futile' (Bal 1996:33). Yet, it makes sense to hold participants in that debate accountable for their active reference to a frame (1996:33). Not in the sense of autonomous choice, but in the sense of creating a need for justification that allows questions about the constant re-applicability of a certain frame. Participants in the official European kinship debate feel the need to present their evidence up and against a frame they perceive as decisive, which, in turn, actively frames the debate and gives the frame authority of meaning. This circular process is crucial and it is the only entry point for a possible future accountability.

It is obvious that Høegh creates – probably quite consciously – a liberal setting for what counts as partnership, namely endurance, responsibility for the other partner, and monogamy. She refers to these ideologies actively. After all, she expresses an explicitly conservative view in terms of which she understandably defends the naturalness of heterosexuality. Her heteronormative frame is a conscious act of framing her political argument about kinship. In the case of ILGA-Europe's claim the same active framing is not as explicit. The address insists: 'To repeat: these are realities. They cannot be wished away or ignored.' This rhetoric of repetition and insistence alludes to the idea that same-sex or transgender headed households are commonly seen as strange, outside the norm, but since they are an existing reality ILGA-Europe re-iterates their existence.

This is a semiotic functioning of heteronormativity, which firmly determines the object – marriage and family – separating it off as different from the frame itself as if it could exist without it. Yet, through this separation, the frame as the only authoritative frame is asserted once again. What follows is then a metaleptic substitution of cause and effect on a rhetorical level. Whether the heteronormative was there before the political argument – pro or contra – or whether the political argument creates the frame through its reference to it remains a moot point. For such circularity is characteristic of the concept of frame.

Heteronormativity as a frame for the political kinship debate passes on its norms to the debate in a transfer that has elements of substitution: the terms of the debate articulated in political practices need to reference the frame, thus supporting it, while picturing themselves as a strategy that aims to become a new frame. However, not only the legal and moral institution of marriage and the nuclear family are framed by heteronormativity, but, more interestingly, so too are categories such as love, desire, or intimacy as well as the wish to care for children. Hence, attempts to redefine the family in terms of love and not heterosexual procreation imply the wish to replace a heteronormative frame with another frame, namely love. Yet, actively framing the debate with love is, in fact, also a reference to kinship discourses that are bound to heteronormativity. Thus, ILGA-Europe's reframing cannot escape the fact that no political meaning of kinship can be established outside of its heteronormative frame. In other words, there is a certain pre-determination of meaning at work.

Gay and lesbian rights claims necessarily argue with the real. In this case the real or original is said to be a family comprising of mother, father – at best married and monogamous – with one or two children. However much activists and parliamentary supporters are personally convinced of the propriety of homosexual partnership and parenting, their words always reflect the impropriety of their claim. 'Homosexual families' is an improper name for the proper thing, even if gay men and lesbians love the same way and their parenting is proven to be just as good as heterosexual parenting. The question of pre-determination is not how the heteronormative frame became so overarchingly powerful that it can maintain the power of the ultimate referent. While no political practice employed in kinship debates at the European institutions can exist outside the circumstances of the historically heteronormative framing of kinship, there is nothing heteronormativity can do to fix all outcomes of the debate in all future settings. It is, thus, more important to ask about the political conditions that make it necessary to always refer to a frame. Judith Butler's concept of performative reiterability can be of help here.

As I argued in Chapter 2, all political practices must be understood as meaning-producing in a performative manner. A performative manner is not understood 'as a singular or deliberate "act", but, rather, as the reiterative and citational practice by which discourse produces the effects that it names' (Butler 1993:2). Hence, the fixing of the referent in claims to rights is always 'a 'citation' of an original fixing, a reiteration of the divine process of naming', something like the 'primal baptism' (1993:212). For Butler, hierarchical gender orders and normative heterosexuality are an intrinsic part of any 'primal baptism'. However, the referent is only secured on condition that a differentiation is made between proper and improper definitions of family, which means, in Butler's argument, that the referent is produced in consequence of that distinction.

The term 'referent' here is not used in its proper Saussurean linguistic sense as the thing that is referred to. It is used in Butler's sense as a frame of reference that emphasises the process of how dominant discourses establish definitional power. In this sense, frame and referent are similar concepts, in the context here even interchangeable. This referent or frame depends essentially on precisely those acts of speech that fail to refer, or that refer in the wrong way (1993:217). Homosexual parenting, for example, necessarily fails for reasons of an apparent biological misfit the lack of procreation. Hence, the performative aspect of ILGA-Europe's political practices – their claim to authentic speech about rights and equality – only works insofar as it '*raws on and covers over* the constitutive conventions by which it is mobilized' (1993:227).

As I argued above, kinship ties as family relations are generally portrayed as a basic and biological human need. Kinship as basic human need is the implicit mobilising force of the political kinship debate. This mobilising force remains strong through kinship's implication of basic human traits, such as love and desire. Heteronormativity as the frame is not made explicit in the political debate. Yet, it appears under the name of substitutes, of categories that are intrinsically bound to it. There are many important sub-frames involved in the exhibition of kinship as the seemingly most natural human art. These sub-frames are, however, not simply subordinate to or dependent on the overarching frame of heteronormativity. They assert a discursive power on their own terms that, at times, utilises heteronormative arguments to support their own authority. The sub-frames relevant in the mainstream political debate on kinship are love, authenticity, desire, and subjectivity/subjection.

The sentence 'love makes a family – nothing more and nothing less' is a well-known political assertion employed in kinship debates by activists in Europe. Love in this sentence functions as self-validating; it seems to be beyond ideology, beyond mediation, beyond contestation. It seems to dissolve contradiction and dissent about what constitutes a real family into a basic, but also higher, truth. Love is much more tricky to theorise than sexuality. Despite love's large role in human culture, and subsequently in the political culture of rights, it is often relegated so far into the intimate sphere that it becomes virtually untouchable, too mysterious to be theorisable in social and political science.[12] Love validates human beings as human morally and emotionally. For many love is incompatible with those considered sexual perverts, homosexuals or, more recently, S/M practitioners. In that sense the image of two leather men gently kissing is much more troubling than the image of them engaged in rough sex.

The recourse to love in political practices around kinship is an attempt at treating the wounds of discrimination with the same discourses that insist on a proper and an improper meaning of love. The fact that gay and lesbian families are loving families is constantly set up to be proven in and through political statements or through the appeal to allegedly objective research, in which sexual orientation is deemed to have no influence on the child's development. Through this need of proof, love's higher truth is re-connected to one proper setting where it does not need to prove itself. Heterosexuality frames proper love, while love, as a category in rights claims, mobilises the political attempt to overcome that frame. The circularity of framing is at play within the frame of love, and it connects love to the frame of heteronormativity again. The mobilising force of circularity in love, in turn, rests partly in the claim to authenticity.

Political kinship debates in the European institutions are fundamentally aiming at separating the genuine from the imitative by linking authenticity not only to the biology of procreation, but also to the duration of partnership commitment. Høegh's speech – with its exclusion of adoption and its insistence on long-term commitment – provides an excellent example of this link. Similar to other normative categories such as nationality and ethnicity, kinship is naturalised through an attribution acquired at birth and then fixed as referring to biological ties conceived of as immutable. The two most inevitable events in human life, birth and death, are the elements that grant certain forms of kinship an authentic and authoritative status.

Kath Weston (1998:78) proclaims birth and death to be the two foundational episodes that establish kinship. For her, birth is the focal point of alliance and blood, and only a biological process – death – as opposed to a social process – rejection or neglect – is capable of sundering blood ties. Death, then, is the terminus that marks the attainment of forever in a relationship (1998:79). This attainment of forever is expressed in the traditional sentence 'till death do us part' and reflected in the ideology of endurance and responsibility. Birth and death establish a permanence presumed to grant a form of authenticity which confers the authority to act, speak, order, and control in relation to those linked through birth and death to oneself. Birth and death as fixed designators turn kinship debates into a quest for an origin and an original, which are miraculously found again and again in biology's authenticity. Hence, if authenticity were to be removed as a frame from the political debate about kinship, the question of the true origin of kinship might become meaningless. Kinship retains its centrality because it orders and institutionalises a fundamental human sentiment in an apparently authentic way: desire.

If 'love makes a family, nothing more and nothing less', then true families are implicitly loving, mutually respectful, and equal in short there is a cohesiveness and peacefulness that is presented as natural to families. While this claim makes sense in the political climate of the European institutions, it is also potentially preposterous in the face of the abuse that happens in families throughout Europe. The family functions as the haven in a heartless world, the private harbour in which true nurturing and support are possible. This familial rhetoric depends on a liberal conception according to which everybody involved in this private unit desires it equally and is equally able to enact her or his desire. Love and desire are close together in the political practices of debating kinship rights. It is inappropriate sexual desire that places gay men, lesbians, and bisexuals outside of normative kinship rules. Yet, their desire for public recognition – or for what I have previously termed (Chapter 3) the desire for rights – is just another side of the same coin that declared their sexual desire an improper form of love. The desire to marry is itself, therefore, an aspect of the normativity of marriage.

While homosexual desire can be said to transform the definition of legitimate marriage to some extent, sexual desire and the desire for public acknowledgement are only intelligible with reference to a norm that precedes kinship definitions. In principle, this says nothing about how transformable marriage is. What it does indicate, however, is that although heterosexual, monogamous, and procreative coupledom does not smother all attempts at forming significantly different family ties, it remains the frame thereof. It remains a definite referent for all the desire that is at work in speaking about homosexual families, and for the right to have that desire publicly acknowledged through a performative legal act with substantial material consequences.

To some extent this also means that certain social norms about appropriate desire have become internalised, not only as a psychic process in the individual, but as something like a psychic process underlying the political debate. In the process of incorporation or internalisation into a framework of political struggle, a norm becomes part and parcel of that political struggle. Judith Butler (1997b:21) describes norms as operating as psychic phenomena, restricting and producing desire, while also governing the formation of the subject and circumscribing the domain of liveable sociality. She is clearly speaking about the psychic realities of individuals. However, her conclusions make this process transferable to processes of political struggle.

For Butler (1997b:21), there is no normativity that can be internalised prior to the social: 'Just as the subject is derived from conditions of power that precede it, so is the psychic operation of the norm derived, though not mechanically or predictably, from prior social operations.'[13] Applied to ILGA-Europe's rhetoric of rights, this means that whatever language is employed will, on the one hand, reference a normative frame of kinship, since this frame precedes the formation of any political kinship debate on the matter of sexual rights. On the other hand, the difference in sexual desire, which sparks the desire for rights in the first place, is itself derived from normative processes in the same political struggles that seem to be their expression. When ILGA-Europe fights the discrimination and subjection of its constituency, it needs to assert that discrimination as subjection in the first place in order to re-iterate those realities that 'cannot be wished away or ignored'. Subjection therefore becomes another sub-frame that frames the European kinship debate.

Butler (1997b:2) defines subjection as the process of becoming subordinated by power as well as the process of becoming a subject. If there is no formation of the subject without a passionate attachment to those by whom she or he is subordinated – in the first instance the parents – then subordination proves central to the becoming of the subject (1997b:7). This means that one is dependent on power for one's very formation and that the story by which subjection is told is inevitably circular (1997b:9-11). Power acts on the subject in at least two ways: first, as what makes the subject possible, and second, as what is taken up and reiterated in the subject's own acting, but power is both external to the subject and the very venue of the subject (1997b:14). According to Butler (1997b:27), the subject cannot be reduced to power nor power to the subject's formation. She concludes that '[o]n this understanding, subjection is the paradoxical effect of a regime of power in which the very "conditions of existence", the possibility of continuing as a recognizable social being, requires the formation and maintenance of the subject in subordination'. Transferring Butler's argument to issues of the kinship debate involves a leap Butler does not make herself: a leap from individual subject formation to the processes of political struggle analysed within a concept of framing.[14] What is relevant for political struggles around kinship is not how rights claims reproduce individual discriminated subjectivities. It is, rather, relevant to trace a connection between the referential frames of a political debate and the political claim to represent subjugated, discriminated, or marginalised people who are materially disadvantaged.

I would suggest that the link between subjection and the political struggle for minority rights is the attachment to subjugation that kinship relations produce. Love and family – and their intrinsic connection to parenting or the much-proclaimed rights of children – can to some extent only be thought of as a reference to the necessary protection of those most vulnerable insofar as they are dependent in a subordinated manner for their own survival. The relationship of parents and children is, discursively and legally, a relationship of subordination expressed in care, love, and protection. Kinship as fundamentally connected to parenting, therefore, is also fundamentally connected to subjugation as the means through which a child becomes a subject and, later, a responsible citizen capable of taking on heterosexual procreative responsibilities. This is one of the hidden reasons why parenting, adoption, custody, or artificial insemination are still perceived as threatening in relation to homosexuality and transgender.

To permit an identity excluded and subjugated by heteronormativity to procreate or significantly relate to children could unfix the naturalness of the heteronormative referent. It is feared that children who grow up with lesbian, gay, bisexual, or transgender parents might in the course of time not be psychologically subjugated to the naturalness of binary genders and heterosexuality. In fact, the consequence of this connection between subjugation, heteronormativity, and parenting is particularly violent for transgender people. Most European countries do not allow full legal gender re-assignment without proof of surgical, permanent, and irreversible infertility of the person. This policy can only be described as fascist, a violation of physical integrity, and a violent form of control over who is allowed to procreate biologically and in what gender role. The thought of a transgender man, who enjoys social privileges of masculinity, actually giving birth obviously severely unhinges the frame of the heteronormative painting.

In conclusion, although kinship laws and regulations are contested within the political domain, kinship is actually set up as the pre-political domain, the domain that, in fact, enables the political. As shown above, for Butler, children come to their subjectivities through the workings of power which subjugate them to the rules of gender, sexuality, class, and race in their attachment to those who subjugate them – in the first instance the parents. Thus, kinship enables speech as the precondition for social intelligibility or subject status that is, in turn, never entirely separated from the social and the political. Within a heteronormative frame, it is the rhetoric of kinship as heterosexual parenting that assures the continuous reference to the frame and maintains its definitional power. In order also to maintain heteronormativity's self-evident naturalness as a frame, the choice and the desire for heterosexual parenting is understood as an authentic expression of love for another adult and for children based on the biological meanings of two distinct sexes and genders.

All the frames involved in the political kinship debate form an intricate web that secures citizenship as the expression of participation in the political at the price of keeping kinship out of the political. Kinship is the realm women dominate prior to the male order of citizenship, morality, and public political participation, a conclusion much feminist analysis has drawn. The state therefore needs to presume kinship and kinship presumes the state. Citizenship and the state need to control kinship to produce male citizens capable of political and economical action (Brown 1995:150). The performative acts enacted in the name of one are enacted within the framework of the other.

Love as authentic biological expression should not need a performative act of marriage that incorporates the condition of a state and the law. Marriage, therefore, veils the difference between state and kinship on a rhetorical level while at the same time it secures the stability of the terminological difference between the two in a moment of crisis. The demands on parenting made by lesbians, bisexuals, gay men, and transgender people are such a crisis that conflates kinship and citizenship in their claim for citizenship rights that enable kinship relations. Within a heteronormative frame kinship relations are the place that make politics possible without ever entering the political stage as such, which is originally a Hegelian thought. Thus, political intelligibility is to a large extent based on the pre-political nature of kinship relations as an authentic expression of human biology superseding culture and civilisation. The challenge of political practices to do with kinship rights, then, lies precisely in their effort to drag kinship out of the pre-political into the political frame. And drag, here, is best framed as a pun.

Conclusion

Through my act of framing kinship heteronormatively, I have once again asserted the analytical importance of heteronormativity. The issue I could not analyse here concerns how theorists, in turn, have to question the role of heteronormativity as supra-frame in the future: is this concept an almost physical object, an idea that already exists prior to political debates on kinship and that just awaits reference there? Or is it only the political debate that by a performative act of speech 'enacts or produces that which it names' (Butler 1993:13)? In fact, it is both, in an interrelated process. Theorists ought to consider heteronormativity, over all, as a rhetorical strategy of signification that can be subverted and displaced through counter strategies and simultaneously as a near-inescapable and permanent consequence of European histories. Without critically addressing the active framing theorists undertake, heteronormativity as a master category of queer and feminist theory might run the danger of becoming a fetish rather than a precise concept of analysis.

The nature of heteronormativity needs to remain closely scrutinised wherever it is employed as an analytical concept, carefully delineating the difference between the liberal and strictly gendered tales of Rousseau, Hobbes, and Hegel and the processes of referentiality in political practices in Europe today. In the effort to problematise what seems so unproblematic and in the effort to re-evaluate the potentials of what many queer critiques discard as hopelessly normative lobby politics, I have deployed heteronormativity as a frame for political debates at several points in this book.

When I nevertheless urge to consider the meanings of this act of framing carefully in every particular analysis, this move stems from the worry that queer theory and heteronormativity have been sleeping together a lot lately and that as with all intercourse too much closeness in everyday life destroys the exciting edge. One of the exciting edges of rights politics is the agency that activists assert for themselves in the achievement of change, of whatever quality that change might be in relation to the dominance of heteronormative thinking within Europe. Therefore, I will in the last part turn away from the structural level of political practices to the individual agents of change and agency as a re-visited political concept.

Notes

1 Countries that grant forms of registered partnership in Europe include Denmark, Sweden, Norway, Iceland, France, and Germany. The Netherlands and Belgium are the only countries in the world that allow access to marriage proper. Countries that grant some rights include Hungary, the Czech Republic, Belgium, Spain, the UK, and Switzerland.
2 However, in 1999 the ECHR in *Salgueiro Da Silva Mouta C v. Portugal* concluded that the denial of access to a biological child after divorce could not be denied solely on the grounds of sexual orientation, whereas adoption rights of a single gay man were not consider valid in *Frette v. France* (2002). ILGA-Europe officially acted as *amicus curiae* to this latter case.
3 Høegh here refers to the amendment that restricts access to adoption, which I discussed in Chapter 1.
4 'Pretended families' is the infamous phrase of Margaret Thatcher about homosexual partnerships and families, given in support of Section 28. Section 28 is a UK law that prohibits cities, among other things, from 'intentionally promot[ing] homosexuality' or teaching 'the acceptability of homosexuality as a pretended family relationship' in schools. Scotland repealed this law on 21 June 2000 the Labour government in London has finally announced the repeal in July 2003.
5 See Brook (1998), Brown (1995), Pateman (1988), and Fraser (1990) for further elaboration on the historical development of this model.
6 The studies of Reimann (1997) and Sullivan (1996) provide very interesting results with regard to gender and lesbian parenting. Through extensive research they have found that where couples divide housework and childcare according to a traditional breadwinner model, the same inequalities and lack of self-worth on the part of the care givers, who subsequently feel like 'women', occur as in heterosexual families structured similarly. The decisive factor was unequal work divisions according to gender traditions, not the biological difference of the partners. See also Tasker and Golombok (1998).
7 Occasionally the harsh words used against gay and lesbian partnership laws from a queer perspective – as they were voiced, for example, in Germany during 2000 – go as far as stating that no discrimination on the grounds of sexual orientation exists at all and that any political claim that refers to this discrimination is ridiculous (Klauda

2000:54). I find this line of argument the only one in the queer perspective on kinship that is entirely unconvincing and ridiculous itself.
8 Brown analyses dualisms such as equality/difference, liberty/necessity, autonomy/dependence, rights/needs or duties, individual/family, self-interest/selflessness, public/private, and contract/consent for their deeply masculinist nature.
9 To some extent the French law, PACS (*Pacte Civiles de Solidarité*), is seen by many as a move in the right direction. Since 9 November 1999 it has provided for different forms of contracts that are not bound to the existence of a sexual relationship between the signatories. The German Socialist Party PDS has also suggested a Bill that follows a non-sexual principle, where different degrees of kinship can be assigned to different people. Despite the advantages, there is a catch to these measures: these ideas do not deal with the necessary protection of heterosexual women who live their lives in unpaid domestic labour. Their security from abandonment after years of labour outside the wage market would have to be assured through extra laws once marriage is entirely de-privileged.
10 Van Alphen exemplifies this convincingly with reference to the testimonies about the Holocaust.
11 This line of thought was suggested to me by Mieke Bal.
12 One of the very few sociologists who has thoroughly covered love is Giddens (1992). However, there exists a substantial body of literature on love in feminist psychoanalytic thought. See, for example, Lauretis (1994) and Silverman (1996).
13 Butler explicitly distances herself from the Lacanian concept of a pre-existing and fixed symbolic order here.
14 Michael Warner (1999:154–57) has argued against the possibility of transferring Butler's thought to the politics of gay marriage by arguing that her explanation of normalisation is similar to her theory of performativity. He interprets her argument as implying that queerness is an inevitable principle of heteronormativity and successful normalisation an impossibility. To him this makes judgement on the political usefulness of gay marriage impossible. While Warner's argument is logical, I do not agree with his conclusion and still find the appropriation of Butler's theory of subjection useful for the question of kinship politics.

Part III
Activists

9 The political activist: agency

> The homosexual is a kind of time bomb, encoded with its own explosion. Or perhaps rather its own discreet disappearance. (Henning Bech 1997:195)

> Finally, thinking about norms in relation to practices eliminates the duality between principled and strategic actions. Practices do not simply echo norms – they make them real. Without the disruptive activity of these actors neither normative change nor change in practices is likely to occur.
> (Margaret Keck and Kathryn Sikkink 1998:35)

> How is it that we can think we have, and act as if we have (and can be required by law to have), a sense of agency, and recognise at the same time that it is in the constitutive force of discourse that agency lies?
> (Bronwyn Davies 1997:272)

In the previous chapters the analysis focused on the structural and organisational level of political practices and on the theoretical concepts behind those practices. The level of individual subjectivity has occasionally been touched upon, but the individual activist as an agent in political practices has not been discussed. This concluding chapter approaches the important other side of political practices – the individual and her or his activism – with regard to the implications of agency as the theoretical and political concept behind individuals' engagement in bringing about change. Broadly speaking, agency in the political field is defined as connoting the will, desire, and power to act physically, intellectually, or emotionally in order to maintain or change rules and structures within society and between society and state.

Gay and lesbian politics are obviously geared towards change on a normative, structural, or practical level. Be they volunteers or professionals in organisations and institutions, the people involved in gay and lesbian politics usually bring with them a vision and an ideal about change; they perceive themselves as influencing change on different levels. Activists 'identify a problem, specify a cause, and propose a solution, all with an eye toward producing procedural, substantive, and normative change in their area of concern' (Keck and Sikkink 1998:8). In short, political activists are commonly understood as agents of change. Agency and the individual activist on the European stage would warrant a whole study on their own. However, this concluding chapter, which also forms the third part of this book, only seeks to offer an entrance point into this different level of analysis and an entrance point into the many other areas of European political practices still to be investigated.

During the interviews I asked the activists about their motivations for their involvement in gay and lesbian politics, what type of actions they had been involved in over the years, how they measured success, and whether they thought their own sexual identity mattered in this respect. Answers to these questions were also included in some responses to other issues, for example, in the area of how important identity and minority politics were to them. The way agency is addressed by the activists is not simple and straightforward. It rather highlights contradictions and complexities which can only be grasped if the theory of agency is re-thought and moved away from its connection to the independent, free will of autonomous and coherent humanist subjects.

How activists describe the relevance of identity for aspects of their activism strongly suggests that drawing on identity as a source of agency does not mean telling a fixed truth either about themselves or about how gayness and lesbianism is defined in essence. What seems to be obvious at first glance, namely that activists in the field of sexual orientation are motivated by their own identities and claim to represent a coherent group, is clearly more complicated. That identity is a complicated and contradictory feature of the possibility of agency highlights the fact that agency is not simply an expression of autonomous, independently acting individuals, but is discursive in its dependency on how individuals position themselves with regard to specific actions to promote change. In the wake of that insight, I argue that, although the framework in which most activists locate their agency seems to be a liberal humanist framework, the way they actually express their agency already includes a re-thinking of that framework. Aspects of interviewees' talk that relate to agency suggest a tension between activism as contingent – the interviewees were aware of the need for coherent political action – and an identity in flux – they acknowledged the complicated way in which identity is relevant in political action.

To understand the ways activists locate agency, it is important to introduce different conceptions of agency available in the academic debate.[1] After briefly sketching available models, I will proceed to analysing the way the interviewees locate their agency. Successfully bringing about change is a major theme of activism, yet the way success and change become the measure of activism is neither clear cut nor measurable, but depends on the framework activists adopt. Gay and lesbian identities, as personal subjectivities, as minority identity, and as personal enjoyment, feature significantly in this referential framework, but do not in themselves explain how important identity and personal enjoyment are/and how the different aspects of identity are differentiated. In a last step the chapter will draw out the importance of a differentiated sense of identity for conceptualising agency. I will also discuss how a contradictory and complicated view of identity enables activists to establish authority to agency.

Differences in the approach to political agency

Political scientists Margaret Keck and Kathryn Sikkink's (1998) book *Activists beyond Borders* is one of the very few academic analyses of the influence of transnational activist networks in relation to international politics that takes the agency of individual activists into account. In the beginning of their book, they emphasise that transnational networks multiply the voices that are heard in international and domestic policies. According to them (1998:x)

> these voices argue, persuade, strategize, document, lobby, pressure, and complain. The multiplication of voices is imperfect and selective – for every voice that is amplified, many others are ignored – but in a world where the voices of states have predominated, networks open channels for bringing alternative visions and information into international debate.

To them (1998:5–14), advocacy networks embody elements of agency and structure simultaneously and their activists are people who care enough about the issue that they are prepared to incur significant personal costs and act to achieve their goals. Activists are defined as agents of change. At the end of their introduction Keck and Sikkink (1998:35) state:

> What distinguishes principled activists of the kind we discuss in this volume is the intensely self-conscious and self-reflective nature of their normative awareness. No mere automatic 'enactors', these are people who seek to amplify the generative power of norms, broaden the scope of practices those norms engender, and sometimes even renegotiate or transform the norms themselves. They do this in an intersubjective context with a wide range of interlocutors, both individual and corporate. Finally, thinking about norms in relation to practices eliminates the duality between principled and strategic actions. Practices do not simply echo norms – they make them real. Without the disruptive activity of these actors neither normative change nor change in practices is likely to occur. States and other targets of network activity resist making explicit definitions of 'right' and 'wrong', and overcoming this resistance is central to network strategies.

Keck and Sikkink clearly define political practices as strategic tools that participate in norms, by reiterating or disrupting them, making something real and, in consequence, potentially introducing change. Activists are context dependent, but they are also free to choose in a self-conscious and self-reflective manner and utilise the generative power of norms for their end and purpose. What makes activists successful is the way they frame debates and get issues on the agenda, the way they encourage discursive commitments from states and other policy actors, the way they cause procedural changes, and the way they affect policy and the behaviour of target actors (1998:201). In their conclusion, Keck and Sikkink (1998:214) propose a concept of the activist that is explicitly not liberal, in that activists are more than self-interested and risk-averse individuals who calculate benefit and success with regards to context only. This distancing from liberalism has an implication for the concept of agency they propose. It touches upon an academic controversy they do not explicitly mention since they are writing within the context of political science only. In the predominant liberal humanist discourse that prevails in the social sciences and humanities, the coherent rational character of personhood is assumed to be a constitutive part of what enables agency in a person. Therefore, being a person in the liberal humanist sense is a pre-condition for agency. According to Bronwyn Davies (1991:42–3), the individual in a liberal humanist framework is antagonistic to society. Individual choices are considered to be based on rational thought, seen as coherent and autonomous from the social, which is external to the selfhood of the individual. Identity and selfhood are continuous and stable. Individuals can speak for themselves as well as accepting full moral responsibility for their action.

Traces of this liberal humanist model of agency can often be found in books and reports about the history of gay and lesbian activism that celebrate individuals who stand out from the collective and shape or change the world around them on their own merits.[2] This model is most commonly found in the traditional descriptions of political history where the 'men who make history' – from kings to modern presidents and prime ministers – are not understood as being discursively produced by their times, but as the heroes who manage their times. It is this liberal humanist framework of agency that dominates in the everyday work of institutional and parliamentary political work. It presents the framework that most activists refer to in the conceptualisation of their agency, whether they adopt it or distance themselves from it to some extent.

By contrast, within a poststructuralist feminist or queer thinking the concept of a coherent rational liberal humanist personhood is deconstructed. Subsequently agency is not bound to a notion of autonomous, coherent, unified, essential personhood. Agency is still motivated by a desire to change or give meaning. Yet, the will, desire, or power to act and speak is always constituted within discourses, not generated by the core of a human essence. It is constituted within discourses that we actively create, maintain, and change. Those discourses, in turn, give authority to attribute meaning to actions and, thus, give actions the potential for recognition, resistance, change, and re-location of subjectivities. As such, the availability of discursive spaces is a pre-condition for the meaning of actions, while we can also simultaneously engage in creating discursive spaces.

Keck and Sikkink (1998:214) implicitly touch upon this controversy and locate themselves somewhere in the middle ground. They share the liberal assumption that governments represent a society – even if imperfectly – and that individuals influence governments through political institutions and social practices linking state and society. Yet, they pose an important question that, in their opinion, liberalism cannot answer: how individuals and groups, through their interactions, might constitute new actors and transform understandings of interests and identities. Their (1998:214–15) answer to this problem is a network theory that links 'the constructivist belief that international identities are constructed to the empirical research tracing the paths through which the process occurs, and identifying the material and ideological limits to such construction in particular historical and political settings'.

While this proposal is new for political science and allows the reader to understand intricate complexities, it is also located at the end of the conclusion of Keck and Sikkink's book and, thus, has not been fully worked through theoretically or analytically. The way they conceptualise activists could be applied in an analysis of gay and lesbian activism on the European stage. However, the network approach they postulate lacks a more detailed definition of what they call the constructivist side. Their model could be advanced by additionally understanding agency as discursive, or, in Scott's (1990:851) words, as 'discursive effect'. With this formulation, Scott implies that certain dominant discourses assign the power to contextualise oneself as agentic. Only in effect then does one become agentic. Although mostly located in a humanist framework, the notion of agency 'my' interviewed activists express alludes to agency as a discursive effect that does not drain a sense of choice, desire, will, purpose, or resistance that is indeed part of the reality of European activism. Hence, political agency is located at neither end of the academic controversy: it incorporates and exceeds both poles.

The kind of agency that activists can and want to take up depends on the political discourse in which they locate their actions. Most commonly that discourse provides for a sense of achieving change based on political negotiation. The state and its citizens can exchange opinions and successfully alter the conditions of social relations. Here agency moves within the realm of liberal humanism. Yet, just as importantly, the agency of activists depends on a personal motivation for the job and on diverse understandings of sexual identity as a personal and representational factor that grants an authority to speak on behalf of a group. Here agency can become highly contingent: it is put in relation to the many divergent social relations in which an individual locates herself or himself. Thus, agency explicitly depends on the context in which it is voiced. The will, desire, and power to act physically, intellectually, and emotionally is situated in very different approaches to what counts as change, to what sexuality as an identity means, and to how an authority to speak is acquired.

Successfully bringing about change

Agency is context-specific to the conceptual language available to agents. Joan Scott (1988:42) defines agency as 'the attempt (at least partially rational) to construct an identity, a life, a set of relationships, a society within certain limits and with language – conceptual language that at once sets boundaries and contains the possibility for negation, resistance, reinterpretation, the play of metaphoric invention and imagination.' Scott's location of agency in language demonstrates that there is a will to agency within the individual. However, this will is neither directly nor necessarily connected to an autonomous, coherent choice; will and autonomy are not necessary for each other. This means that activists' agency is not determined by only one discourse (for example the discourse on citizens' equality in Europe) activists can in fact always choose between several available discourses. Nevertheless, their agency within the European institutional framework is never outside the conceptual language of rights available at the time. Activists act within the framework of discourses that assign them the possibilities to act or resist. Their agency is, therefore, an effect of intersections between politically dominant discourses that make certain actions available to individuals speaking for a recognised NGO. Political agency is not a trait of autonomous, coherent individuals, yet their personal involvement is not pre-determined.

While the activists I interviewed did not formulate their agency in these words, their own descriptions feature traces of agency as discursive. The meaning of success is one area in which this tracing is possible. Even though all interviewees found it relatively easy to identify their goals – for example equality or protection from discrimination – they all found it difficult to measure how successful their personal involvement or ILGA-Europe's involvement is or was in relation to the ideal goal. Success was identified as change on one of the many levels of political concern such as legal changes or changes in attitude towards homosexuality in society, access to goods and services, change in publicity or changes in the norms perpetuated around what human sexuality is. Marion Oprel (March 1998) – Co-President of EGALITE – gives one example for a version of success:

> Well, I measure it in the sense that things are published, the debate keeps on expanding. After the intergroup [Equal rights for lesbians and gay men] meeting in December for example ... Cyprus was discussed in the press conference and the next day it was all over the papers in Bulgaria, in Hungary, in Holland and in the UK, the fact that countries such as Cyprus need to respect gay and lesbian rights if they want to become members of the European Union ... It is an old thing and then you mention it here and it is all over the papers and on the internet. It becomes part of the debate from then on. So awareness, presence, and debate are very important to me to measure success

In identifying success, Marion Oprel sees her role as an activist, not as a leader of an organisation, but as a member of a network that disseminates information. It is fulfilling to her 'to be able to put people into contact with each other and to be able to bridge somewhere between organisations that need each other' – in her case the European Parliament and NGOs such as ILGA-Europe – 'and it is good to get to know so many people that approach this issue from many different angles'. Thus, she positions herself clearly as someone who has an effect on awareness, presence, and debate. Successful change to her is reached by disseminating information about discrimination and about good practices to combat discrimination. Her activism could be called information work from an explicit ideological perspective – namely that discrimination on grounds of sexual orientation is a violation of human rights. This information work influences change on the level of debate and knowledge, with very practical consequences through the specific political discourses of human rights and membership to the EU. In order to understand the type of agency Oprel claims here, one has to understand that success and change do not operate on a clearly identifiable level where input equals output. Success and change operate within an intricate web of what information can be placed where, when, and how, which incorporates the awareness that different structural or organisational situations need different sets of arguments and allow different levels of influence.

Every point of change is, therefore, context-specific. Hannele Lehtikuusi (e-mail interview July 1998) – Finnish activist and former member of the executive board of ILGA-Europe – expressed this need for context specificity when asked after the definitions of identities in a political context and the problem of representation:

> Maybe not definable but how can you define Afro–American? I believe that most of the minorities have diversity and multiplicity inside of them. I find this defining politics a bit academic and after doing lobbying work I have dropped the whole idea. It does not work so simply. The world is not changed by the fashions/modes of thinking – it is changed by making a point so clear that it makes a difference.

Apart from a certain opposition to academic enquiries – obviously including mine – Lehtikuusi acknowledges to some extent the undefinability of homosexual identity, i.e. of the total sameness of all people in that group, while she simultaneously uses identity politically. Lehtikuusi sees the fashion of critiquing as counterproductive to deploying what is deemed successful in politics, even if homosexual identity is not definable. In order to make a political point clear and achieve success through actively working for change, in her opinion one has to be persuasive and legible within the discourse on rights that dominates the field the action takes place in. This legibility – making the point clear – achieves rights and progress and nothing else can do the same. Lehtikuusi, thus, propagates a strategic essentialism.

While I find this view problematic from a queer theoretical standpoint, with regard to agency it offers an interesting insight. Making a point so clear that it makes a difference defines change as situative: specific to the context in which it is argued. To make a point clear means to enssure that all actors participating in the debate understand the referential framework in which a claim is voiced. If clarity according to Lehtikuusi cannot be reached by a critical academic analysis of identity but only on a practical political level, then what makes political sense – and in consequence brings about political change – defines the possibility of agency. Change is not tangible in any easy form that is valid in all situations, times, and places, but is acknowledged by all interviewees to be dependent on its own location in activist discourses and strategies. Yet, even within those discourses and strategies, it is not easy to define what has been influenced or changed through which action.

Kurt Krickler – long-term Austrian activist and Co-Chair of ILGA-Europe – acknowledges the difficulty of identifying change and success in relation to his own active involvement in different sorts of gay and lesbian political actions over twenty years. During his narrative on the kinds of activism in which he has been involved, he touched upon many themes relevant to understanding the possibility of agency. Here, he (February 1998) is reporting on his outing actions against the homophobia of the Catholic Church in Austria whose anti-gay lobby he wished to counter.[3]

I have collected a huge amount of newspaper clippings ... 100 people came to the press conference, six camera teams from major European broadcasters, even the Vatican reported ...

Nico: Were you alone?

Yes, only me ... It was great fun. Mind you, I thought back then already that, you know, you are already too old for these actions, the younger ones should do this. But it is as usual in Austria, you have to do everything yourself. I have constantly participated in these actions since 1980 ... Really lustful actions ... At the same time we did lobby work and talked insistently to generations of politicians whose names are not known to anybody anymore ... I started in '79 ... and at some point I came to the conclusion that this is actually crazy, that you work for something for that long and actually have no success and result with regard to, for example, the legal situation ... Looking back on it, I am pretty disappointed, because actually this is outrageous. The only comforting thing is that the societal situation has totally changed; homosexuality, to be lesbian or gay, has not got such a stigma attached to it anymore and it is present in the media. I remember that twenty years ago we were totally excited about every mentioning of homosexuality and that was collected and archived and it became a big sensation. Nowadays you could not manage to do that anymore ... Things have changed and that has an impact on society, the questions that were relevant twenty years ago do not exist anymore and that is comforting because you see that it was not all for nothing. But the question certainly remains: what is societal development and what have you really influenced through your work? That is difficult to assign ... I just thought that it could function in Austria the same way it functioned in Scandinavia that an NGO, a citizens' movement, could fight for their rights and actually participate in politics. And that is the disappointment of my life. In Scandinavia this worked much better. But the level on which politics function in Austria is different; it is not the factual questions of evidence and rationality that count, but ideology and in this case Christian conservative fanatic ideology in which lesbians and gay men are second class in the consciousness of politicians ... (translation mine)

Asked what types of activism he found more successful, Krickler explained that direct actions, such as the outing of the bishops, do not directly work towards his goal of change. Yet, they create publicity, are funny, and do not harm the cause, although some politicians pretend that the public scandals he regularly causes are detrimental to getting rid of the discriminatory laws still existing in Austria. Actually to achieve political success through pressure at the EU is an excellent place of political work for him despite his personal dislike of European centralism. Krickler's story explains his take on his own active involvement through his belief in the influence his actions should have. As much as the other interviewees, he defines himself as an active agent, free to identify a problem, pick his strategies, and decide when and where to enact them. He believes in the possibility of a direct effect of his actions.

However, Krickler clearly touches upon several complications in his opportunities to define himself as agentic in the sense of achieving change. For him, change is not directly measurable as an outcome of activism, but depends on historic and social developments as well. He situates the possibility of change in a political context, in this case a specific national context. He believes that both forms of politics in which he is involved – direct action and lobbying – can achieve explicit aims to different degrees. It is the great disappointment of his life that they did not, while in other places the goals were achieved. Rational arguments and evidence are the bench markers for his argumentation. The reason for this rests in what he calls a Christian conservative fanatic ideology that reduces gay men and lesbians to second-class citizens. He implies that, in consequence, the dominant heteronormativity in Austria denies a certain group agency in that it prevents their fight for rights from reaching successful completion.

Beyond this implication his account reflects on his sexuality as the motivating factor in the work for rights. There is a group that is jointly interested in change; there are generations to follow him in activism even if he bemoans a lack of brave and forthcoming involvement among the younger ones. Sexual orientation fuels political agency and the belief in an ideal goal of equality is a feature in his account as well as his very personal enjoyment in activism. Since both these last aspects intersect in almost all interviews, they appear to be crucial for an understanding of political agency as discursive agency.

All interviewees connected their activism to their personal enjoyment, their personal anger, or their personal needs, as well as to shared identifications with the group of homosexuals in Europe. However, personal motivation was never simply a logical consequence of shared identification. For the interviewees, identity seems not necessarily to pre-condition what a person gets out of her or his activism nor does it necessitate shared goals. Yet, the concept of identity was alluded to in the understanding of agency in political practices voiced by them. Most interviewees acknowledge a significant personal gain through learning the technicalities of political activism, but to what extent the ideal changes mattered personally varied to a great degree. Different frames of reference become evident in the way the interviewees conceptualise their motivation for activism as well as the importance of identity as a shared feature that entitles them to speak on behalf of a group.

Steffen Jensen (e-mail interview, February 1998) – Danish activist and board member of ILGA-Europe – stated that

> the discrimination of g/ls is important for my way, it makes me angry and I want to change it, but it does not mean anything for my own identity, I have never been discriminated myself, and the discrimination in itself does not mean that I feel more in common with other g/ls.

Roy Dickinson (May 1998) – Co-President of EGALITE – similarly disclaims personal relevance in envisaging that 'were we to achieve our aims at this moment it would make no difference for me personally, only it would be deeply satisfactory in principle, the symbol, the political significance of achieving your goal'. Steffen

Jensen and Roy Dickinson, thus, do not occupy a position of personal suffering as motivation for their immensely time-consuming involvement. They claim not to be active out of personal necessity to fight unbearable discrimination in their own life or out of the need to find a group to identify with or indeed because they thought they were sharing something significant, but out of anger with regard to others and out of political principle. Their activism surely connects to their personal identities, but the intent, will, and power to achieve change is for them not pre-conditioned by their sexual orientation, but rather by reference to a more general framework of agency: one that grants freedom of speech and action to equal citizens endowed with the human capacities to execute will and carry the responsibility for actions. With reference to this framework, the discourse of equality becomes the means by which an agentic position is taken up and by which the power to change is claimed.

Gay and lesbian identities, as personal subjectivities and as group identity, feature significantly in this referential framework, but do not in themselves explain why activists become active and what their agency means to them. Michiel Odijk – Dutch Parliamentarian and long-term ILGA activist – and Jan Willem de Jong (February 1998) – Dutch and long-term ILGA activist – add to their political tactics, their own personal hesitation about the existence of a clear gay identity:

> For practical purposes it is sometimes quite useful to say I am gay, I do that myself as well. Sometimes you need so much explanation for people, so to be short let's define it in this way ... OK, I am gay and this is what I want. But if you have some more access to the EU, if you have talked to people more extensively then you can make it clear that it is not so clear ... (Michiel Odijk)

> One of the beautiful things of being involved in ILGA is, then you can see how other concepts are, you get an awareness of other cultural definitions of identity. Homosexuality in the Netherlands is different from the US or South Africa ... (Jan Willem de Jong)

Michiel Odijk strategically utilises identity, but only to a certain degree; there comes a clear point at which he feels his firm critique of essentialist gayness can and does enter the way he works for change. Jan Willem de Jong directly added that this belief, for both of them, stems from an intercultural experience they gained in the decades of their ILGA involvement. While there is a clear political task that Odijk identifies, essentially shared identifications are not the motivating factor for formulating and enacting those politics. De Jong and Odijk's sense of agency does not depend on personal identification and sameness with a minority group, while they also do not deny that they use a sense of shared group identity for certain political purposes.

Identity nevertheless matters significantly for political agency. It is not disclaimed by the interviewees but is, instead, re-instated. Roy Dickinson (May 1998), for example, re-introduces the significance of his sexual orientation with regard to changes he can achieve within settings that are based on the notion of out and closeted gays in the workplace. His political agency has various, and according to him distinct, features in which the notion of identity carries a different political relevancy.

> Well there are distinct levels. I mean there is the sort of traditional political lobbying formal bureaucratic stuff of being an activist, in terms of writing letters, having meetings, doing concrete things to try and achieve results ... Then there is a second political level. I mean the fact that I was an out gay man at work, everybody knew I was gay ... is itself a bit political, it really does influence how people think about lesbians and gays and in the sense of changing individuals' perceptions probably that is more successful than having meetings and writing letters ... just being open does make you feel more politically significant ... . Being out at work is a political statement in a broad sense.

Dickinson changed his mind in the course of the interview. In the end, he does insist that there is a shared identity based on the shared experience of coming out and that this aspect did produce a group that had to endure a certain pressure and, thus, gained authority to act on its own behalf.

Marion Oprel (March 1998) also re-instates identity in her argument of how she gains access to making a difference while insisting that sexual orientation is not very decisive for her personal identity. While identity does not matter too much in her daily life, she comes back to group identity as the factor that grants the position and authority to speak about human rights and discrimination:

> If you want to stop discrimination you ought not to pay too much attention to differences yourself, you ought not to judge, you ought not to put people in different boxes or subsections of society. The fact that we are discriminated against on grounds of our sexual orientation, which shows itself in our identity and in our longing to be recognised as such, makes us work in EGALITE and for changes. It is not my primary political, personal occupation and worry in life ... We have bisexual and straight members too and all these people want to see discrimination end, they want the institutions to grant us legally recognised space ... but we are the only ones who have the logical reason to organise ourselves, because heterosexuals who opt not to marry but to live together don't have this steady ground we are standing on ... . It is a question of principle, we have a stronger ground than they have, and we are fighting their fight too ...

Oprel insists on a shared group identification and solidarity as a motivating factor for activism, claiming the prerogative to speak up politically and to influence the debate successfully, while at the same time disclaiming sexual orientation – or her lesbian identity – as a decisive marker of the self, envisaging a future in which categorising people will not be necessary any longer.

She and Roy Dickinson obviously make a distinction between different ways to interpret identity in response to my question about the significance of sexual identity to their political work. This was also made explicit by Maren Wuch (March 1998) – a German activist and member of the board of ILGA-Europe at the time of the interview. The idea of a fixed identity in content sits uneasily with her. She

THE POLITICAL ACTIVIST: AGENCY 213

elaborates at length about the fact that she does not believe she shares much with all lesbians and gays, that, in fact, she does not assume homosexuality alone would make another person her ally or somebody she would want to align herself with. Yet, she definitely denies that successful political practice – defined by her as a practice that brings about change – can do without speaking for a group, and, thus, arguing for a minority.

> I think one can only argue with the minority concept ... It is a critical concept one should think about, but it is politically useful ... I mean, one cannot say this for ILGA, there are a thousand member groups who have an opinion, and every member of a member organisation has an opinion ... But I think it [ILGA] is a politics for a minority ... ILGA-Europe can display an opinion, do its job well, and can raise its voice in Europe, which is, I think, important for lesbians and gays in Europe ... but I need something on which I can in this moment fix my personality, characterise it, connect to the circumstance out of which I speak, so it is important ... This is difficult, when you speak about gays and lesbians. There are opinions of lesbians I cannot do anything with and it gets even harder with gay men. There are a good amount of them who are highly misogynist, so it is difficult to speak in an entirely positive fashion, but at the moment of politics you do not think whether you just yesterday had a stupid argument with a stupid gay man in the pub, you speak of a general minority which claims its rights ...
>
> Nico: Would you say, then, that your politics and ILGA politics are based on an idea of identity?
>
> Yes ... but that can change in content ... I have to admit I have never occupied myself with these things ... [laughter] Hanno say something [that is the dog] ... if there wasn't any identity there wouldn't be any ILGA work ... most others have not thought about this question either, but we wouldn't connect if we did not think we shared something. (translation mine)

Wuch describes a minority or a group one speaks for as the only way to gain rights, create change, make the political goal representable, and render homosexual life-style choices intelligible, and, thus, give her agency. She also uses identity as the marker for solidarity that grants a sense of self as an activist. Yet, quite importantly, my question about identity was also something she did not consider before and it made her uncomfortable to be asked to voice a clear opinion on it – my dog, who was present at the interview, was rendered part of the discussion by her at this point. Yet, in fact, her opinion is not entirely clear-cut in the end. Her reference to difference in opinion and attitude about what it means to be gay or lesbian ruptures her later assertion that identity is the only successful way to argue politics.

All quoted accounts utilise the term 'identity' in various interpretations of its meaning. The interviewees all implied manifold concepts of identity such as an emphasis on individualisation or on a sense of being and simultaneously on a sense of doing. Identity functions as subjectivity, as a referent to commonalties between people, or as a marker of their group status. The all-encompassing and hazy understanding of identity explains the necessity for an implicit distinction between personal identification, personal motivation for activism, and the authority to speak on a certain issue. Since identity can mean so many things, activists use the single term to conceptualise different aspects of their lives and work, but still clearly differentiate those uses. This differentiation is more than a confusion of various aspects under the one concept of identity. Understood as a discursive subject position, the implicit differentiation among definitions of identity actually enables activists to adopt a critical concept of political agency.

Identity and the authority to agency

Judith Butler (1997a:14) wonders 'whether the subject is the condition or the impasse of agency'. She goes on to suggest that it is both (1997a:14–15). The subject is itself a site of ambivalence, emerging as the effect of a power that forms the basis for a radically conditioned form of agency. A subject is, therefore, subject in both senses of the word – a subject who determines and is determined or subjected. The subject as an individual whole that consciously attributes meaning to objects is replaced 'by a conception of the subject as a position, a place where different systems intersect' (Bal 1991:156). This implies that a politically deployed sexual identity depends on the conditions in which the homosexual subject is determined, subjected, as well as determines itself.

An analysis of the agency taken up by activists in transnational networks needs to take this ambiguity into account. Such an analysis has to take into account that the politically predominant liberal humanist sense of a person as continuous is created through discourses on essential selves. A consistent positioning within a frequently used dominant discourse comes to be regarded as a feature of the person rather than the discourse (Davies 1991:49). This involves a process of taking on, as our own, discursive practices that in fact do not originate in us but constitute us. We claim authorship to characteristics that seem to locate us, subsequently, within categories of collectives (Davies 1990b:506). According to Bal (1991:46), the traditional split between the individual and the social is an ideological construction to subject us to a system, while at the same time making us believe in our own personal autonomy.[4] This view is relevant with regard to homosexuality in the political field. Homosexual identity is exposed to the process of subjugating powers of discourse to create a sense of continuity. In Bronwyn Davies and Rom Harré's (1990:46) words the individual activist[5] could be said to emerge 'through the processes of social interaction, not as a relatively fixed end product but as one who is constituted and reconstituted through the various discursive practices in which they participate'. Therefore, persons as speakers or agents acquire beliefs about themselves that are shifting with the discourses in which they are positioned and with the story lines they take up (1990:58), and which, in turn, position them as members of certain identificatory collectives. To remain within possibilities of communication, a subject needs public language to understand itself and be understood as a social agent (Bal 1991:36). The 'I' of the activist – her or his personal identification – is spoken into existence through taking up story lines that characterise the activist's identity as a part of collective discourses that provide the rules of political practices.

The constitutive forces of each political practice, then, lie in its potential to open up possible subject positions. The subject positions available to an activist with regard to utilising identity as personal or group incentive for action are never disconnected from existing collective political practices. Yet, they are not connected in a simple one-way road from collective practices to individual subject positions; their interrelation is, rather, a process of mutual influence that makes the creation of new or different subject positions possible. Power here becomes a decisive element of the conditions in which sexual identity can become politically meaningful in the first place. Butler (1997a:14) points out that the power to act or the agency of the subject is located in time and I would add also in space, place, and political system. For power to act, there must be a subject, but that necessity does not turn the subject into the origin of power. Power makes the subject possible. The subject's power to act refers to both the subject's power to incorporate as well as to resist the norms of how rights and equality are distributed. As Bal (1991:38) summarises: 'Since social interaction goes on at the level of signs, the more substantial struggle is the struggle for power over signs, because possession of signs makes possible the representation of authority, and assures the possessor a place in the ideology under formation.'

If the substantial struggle is the struggle for power over signs, then the substantial political struggle is a struggle for the power to designate various subject positions as true subjectivities. Taking up those positions is occupying a place as well as actively doing something (1991:45). Yet, according to Bal (1991:45), the positions made available in political practices are pre-positions – established in advance – and sub-positions – insinuated from the actors and from social reality itself. Both aspects of positioning serve as the basis from which one acts individually and as a stage on which one plays a specific attributed role. What Bal terms 'subjectivity' and 'subject position' are usually incorporated in the term 'identity' in the political realm. On the one hand, activists use the term 'identity' to describe their subject positions with respect to their activism. On the other hand, the discussion of agency is most commonly bound to the question of identity and so-called identity politics. While 'subjectivity' is the theoretically more precise term, identity keeps visible the complexity and contradictions that are implied whenever sexual identity or sexual orientation is used to describe a group that has authority to politically represent its experience. How the contradictions of identity enable agency becomes apparent on three levels.

Firstly, the differentiation Odijk, de Jong, Oprel, and Dickinson make with regard to identity is, in fact, the complex relation among sexual subjectivity, group identities, and the possibilities of agency for individual activists and NGOs to participate in debates on rights and equality. As a political activist, Oprel asserts a subjectivity that enables her to speak. She, thus, implicitly acknowledges that 'each person can only speak from the positions made available within those collectives through the recognised discursive practices used by each collective' (Davies 1990a:343). Hence, the will, desire, and power of gay and lesbian activists to speak and act was never independent from the processes in which gender identities and sexuality were made desirable and wanted within any particular collective. Nor were acts ever independent of the processes in which personhood and the interrelation between group and individual are constituted. Yet, being dependent on political rules that foreground identities and give them authority does not determine action fully since every political strategy excludes possible interpretations and remains incomplete or fragmented, and as such, contradictory. Partly, those contradictions are expressed in the contradictory ways the interviewees related to their own motivations of involvement with regard to identity.

Secondly, the contradictory accounts of identity mirror activists' proficiency in the rules of the political debate in which they intervene and in the rules of the political collectives to which they belong as individuals. Political discourses provide contradictory and changing positions with regard to how much influence the individual activist has on change. Thus, activists' agency becomes a process of weaving together social, cultural, and political meanings of available positions. This process attaches meaning to certain actions that can result from personal experiences, from relating to others in the same positions, from the discourses that legitimate democratic change and equality, and from the cultural moral system that links and legitimates choices (Davies and Harré 1990:59). Yet, most importantly, the language of identity makes available a very crucial subject position: it grants access to the authority to speak and be respected as an agent in a political setting.

Thus, thirdly, the authority to speak and be an agent has a significant connection to identity in the political field. Adrian Coman (e-mail interview, June 1999) addressed that connection explicitly:

> Sometimes I am sorry for having a career that has to do with my sexual orientation. I wonder, if I had been straight, would I still have been a good human rights activist? Isn't everything too personal? I know there are some advantages. I am probably more credible this way in gay circles. Or less credible, in straight circles. Or, it depends on the approached issue rather than on the environment.

His identity as a gay man makes him credible – or incredible, depending on the situation in which he speaks. The issue and the environment define the connection between his identity and the possibilities of creating change. This once again, highlights the discursivity of agency. Who has what authority to speak when and where are extremely important to the assessment of possible change, while that authority is recognised by Coman as fluid and contestable. Authority depends on the referential framework in which action is located by the activists or by the political institutions or indeed by hegemonic discourses on human gender and sexuality.

Thus, authority depends on the access to subject positions that include the right to speak and be heard, that constitute a person as the author of meanings and desires, and gives a sense of the possibilities to combine discourses that compete and that provide an imagination of what could be (Davies 1991:51). Authority to agency might, therefore, not always be available to marginalised groups in institutionalised contexts, although discursive opportunities exist, through which such groups may claim an authority to agency. More often than not this claim is built upon the connection of personal experience to group identifications and generalised ideals of equality. Such connection is the background to a common story line of activists' argumentation in politics. The story line runs approximately like this: because I am a man and sleep with men I am gay, which means I have a specific experience of discrimination that I share with the group of all gay men and we all want to be treated as equal to heterosexuals. Yet, this chain of logic could be interrupted at any point in institutional contexts to deny that such an act is legitimate, that such an identity exists, that there is any discrimination that is not in the healthy defence of morals. The language of rights claims often utilises this logic in defence against the historical denial of agency. This double-bind of the language of minority politics is clearly identified by Tatjana Greif (e-mail interview, January 2000) – Slovenian activist and member of the board of ILGA-Europe:

> If a certain human praxis is not transparent, it doesn't mean it does not exist or that it exists as a minority. I'm not trying to say, that g/l are a majority, I simply think that the self-definition of a minority is not always productive or positive (it might be understand as victimisation etc.), but in some case it may be. Depends on the situation.

For Greif, the authority to speak is not only relevant on a political level. It is also relevant for the connection between activism and personal motivation. She takes up discrimination and the invisibility of her lesbian identity in general – as well as within the gay and lesbian movement – as the personal motor for her involvement that caused significant trouble in her life.

> In a way it sure gives me a form of my personal satisfaction. The fact that g/l are discriminated against is one of the basic grounds, which motivate me to keep working. Sometimes I also feel that I simply have to deal with the invisibility of lesbian women in g/l movement and the society as such. That's why I decided to live and work as an open lesbian in a small country such as Slovenia. This caused a lot of problems with my family, relatives etc., but I feel there is no way back. Pretending not to be gay is a way of self-destruction, I guess.

Nigel Warner (February 1998) also emphasised personal satisfaction and said that twenty years ago, activism meant acquiring an identity for him, which was more necessary then than it is now.

> I have always said for the first ten or fifteen years that activism is like a therapy [laughter], to shake off all the horrors of oppression and all those sorts of things. So I must say it has been a wonderful therapy, a really good one. I have always done activism because I enjoyed it because it was good for me, not only

for anyone else ... I suppressed myself from my mid-teens to my mid-twenties ... I had not got an identity, I was a vacuum ... So for a few years going around talking to people helped a lot, I felt more professional about what I was doing ... And today, I feel that very strongly now too, but not quite so as I did before, with last year retiring and people saying 'What are you going to do, you are fifty and have all this time and energy?' and 'Are you going to work?'. Well, [laughter] I said I am going to be a gay activist and get back to doing what I really like doing best ... It is not about a power trip ... I am more happy in the background ... I want the organisation that I work for to be successful and respected ... I am very much an organisational person.

For both Warner and Greif, the personal gain of identification is decisive for what they define as successful political engagement *as well as* access to the opportunities to speak up about issues that concern them and others. As with most of the others, they both re-iterate the need for personal and group identification as a strategic tool in different political settings and for different political aims. They create a referential framework – from personal experience to anger about the lack of equality for others – which is quoted as motivation and justification for an involvement in an organisation, in this case a large and officially recognised NGO that represents the authority to stipulate changes on institutional levels.

How the interviewed activists formulate the relevance of identity with regard to various aspects of their activism suggests that, in drawing on identity as agency, they do not claim to tell a fixed truth about themselves or about how gayness and lesbianism is defined in essence. What seems to be obvious at first glance, namely that activists in the field of sexual orientation are motivated by their own identities and claim to represent a coherent group, is clearly more complicated. I have shown identity to be a relevant, but complex and contradictory feature of the possibility of agency. Activists do not only conceptualise their personal motivation and their power to achieve change as a simple expression of their own coherence and independence from the constricting forces of a marginalised sexuality. Implicitly, they position themselves in relation to their actions for change and those relations are discursively determined through the rules of political participation and the historical ideal of equality and justice. This assertion seems to contradict the common understanding in most queer theoretical writing of what agency in mainstream lobby activism entails. The activist as an agent of change is relevant and real in the transnational political sphere. From a queer point of view, her or his existing role should not be abandoned, but critically re-considered.

Conclusion

Activists are aware of the tensions between activism as contingent and the sense of a sexual identity that is not fixed in essence. This tension carries implications for the agency activists can take up. Political agency involves an immense discursive, political, and individual complexity that does not entirely escape those who believe they are successfully bringing about change. Yet, there is still no politically intelligible and applicable explanation of how it is 'that we can think we have, and act as if we have, (and can be required by law to have) a sense of agency, and recognize at the same time that it is in the constitutive force of discourse that agency lies' (Davies 1997:272). While precise answers to this question are still lacking, the tension within the concept of political agency is a significant aspect of the fundamental tensions that characterise all struggles for sexual minority rights. The individual level of activists' agency analysed in this chapter connects to the structural and organisational level discussed via political and theoretical concepts in the previous chapters.

When Hannele Lehtikuusi (e-mail interview, July 1998) asserts 'that most of the minorities have diversity and multiplicity inside of them' and that 'the world is not changed by the fashions/modes of thinking – it is changed by making a point so clear that it makes a difference', she explicitly brings an old conflict between theory and practice to the fore. Yet, the way she positions herself in this conflict includes the assertion that she is able to make a point so clear that it makes a difference. Obviously, for her the line between normative and non-normative has ceased to simply run along the heterosexual–homosexual divide and that the breakdown of that divide is possibly the greatest success of the gay and lesbian movements in obtaining visibility, acceptance, and tolerance. Although theory is often too academic for Lehtikuusi to make practical sense, queer theory need not pose a threat to those interested in political change. It does not deny political agency. Nor does the theory–practice gap need to be sharpened. Queer theory simply foretells the breaking apart of what was formerly a group characterised by solidarity, into new affiliations around different rally-points than homosexual identity. Most importantly, the queer critiques put desire back on the agenda, centralising it by understanding the formative power it wields over the claim to rights and over the subject formation of activists as agents of change. The interrelation between desire and agency is fundamental for an assessment of all sexual and gender politics.

The interrelation between desire and agency also partly accounts for the trouble that sexual rights as human rights produce. The concept of humanity has a history that is not positively inclined towards non-normative expressions of sexual and gender desires. When those who live non-normative sexualities claim agency to change, it is their desires that ground both their capacity to change and the denial of the right to enact and deserve change. While the discourse of human rights is a powerful tool, human identity and its heteronormative sexuality ought to remain a temporary political strategy that is intelligible in institutional political discourse, and that is a means to an end. Adrian Coman (e-mail interview, June 1999) suggests human identity is a means to dissolve problematic group identifications: 'I think that the concept of a "human identity" should first be brought into both politics and in our lives with less hypocrisy. If that works, we may NOT need to refer to particular groups.' Coman makes explicit rather than implicit the reliance on the problematic history of humanity, which is a history of hypocrisy. He positions himself in relation to a history of humanity that does not liberate, but burdens those who are designated as a minority group. The way activists position themselves in relation to this territory of humanity is already differentiated, but ought to be made more explicit. For as long as the stakes of humanity are not openly designated as the territory of negotiation, human rights will continue to burden those they actually seek to liberate.

As we have seen, a crucial part of human rights is the right to freedom from discrimination. Like human rights, anti-discrimination rights are set up as indivisible and as means to ensure diversity rather than normatising sameness. The category discrimination is a strong factor in forming an identity that becomes politically deployable and presents the motivation to take up agency. As Marion Oprel formulated so succinctly: 'the fact that we are discriminated against on grounds of our sexual orientation, which shows itself in our identity and in our longing to be recognised as such, makes us work in EGALITE and for changes'. While Oprel clearly acknowledges the connection among discrimination, identity, and an authority to speak politically, the implications of this connection are not made explicit. Activists insert themselves and their agency into the theme of discrimination to an extent that raises problems with regard to the normatising effect of remaining a discriminated, clearly identifiable group subjected to the hegemony of the juridical that only assigns certain kinds of agentic roles. Yet, the response to this problem cannot be to discard legal measures in the future. The problems of anti-discrimination draw different responses on a theoretical and a practical level, which Tatjana Greif (e-mail interview, January 2000) acknowledges:

> Politics around g/l issues should do both, I guess, defining and redefining these identities. In the situation where there is the problem of social invisibility of g/l, for example, you should define l/g/b/t identities in order to make them visible. In more developed situation, or on the level of theory, art etc. you should try to deconstruct and redefine them in order to get rid of the stereotypes, negative meanings etc.

All political practices – in one way or the other – already engage in a negotiation about the pre-conditions of what can be conceptualised and granted as rights, although there is much scope for development in this respect. The law as a whole, therefore, is not to be disregarded in relation to how activists take up agency for change. Steffen Jensen (e-mail interview, February 1998) explains his actions for legal change as one way actively to position himself against the injustice that concerns him most. His motivation for his activism has a strong connection to a specific belief in the law:

> The most difficult discrimination to fight is not the legal one but the day-to-day discrimination in the society. But legal equality and the introduction of formal rights are important in the fight against the day-to-day discrimination. Formal rights will eventually lead to changes in the opinion of ordinary people. When legislators go ahead others will follow!

In a way his discourse on legal rights as a fulfilment of equality is surely ripe for ontological and epistemological doubt. The rhetoric of the liberated future whose approach we are apparently witnessing is marked by a certain romanticised fascination with equality before the law while gayness and transgenderism continue to cross boundaries of cultural norms. In spite of this, Jensen's hope of leadership of the law is not only a site of normative regulation. He does not believe that the law can undo the cultural markers that create, cement, institutionalise, and change the meaning of difference and identity. Yet, legal cases are potentially a battlefield on which cultural markers – Jensen's day-to-day discrimination – could be rendered visible and where human diversity can at least be spoken. Both contradictory aspects are present in the ways activists take up agency with regard to the law.

The rights claims staged by NGOs such as ILGA-Europe will most probably in due course be successful in Europe. The freedom European economic citizenship offers will eventually be applied to gay men and lesbians as long as they fit the bill in other aspects of the order. At the point of full citizenship in the European order, gay and lesbian identity movements will probably dissolve politically, while the hierarchical conditions of why they became meaningful remain in place. Partly, activists already position themselves in relation to this dissolution through their claim to end a second-class citizenship status. They want to become and be recognised as part of the family and to some extent they are explicitly aware of the potential reformation of solidarities and identities this move implies. It is part of their agentic choice to pursue certain forms of citizenship and not others and to hopefully deal more explicitly with the exclusionary aspects of those models that are currently on offer in Europe. The motivations for involving oneself in activism have already changed significantly with the move towards more citizenship rights. Yet, the agency citizenship rights accrue is bought at the price of segregating public citizenship from private kinship, while rights of kinship are simultaneously the most decisive stumbling blocks for rights and the motivation to seek a home in activism. Political groups used to and function still today as a family substitute for those abandoned by their families of origin and for those not admitted to the legal and social recognition of their chosen kin.

Nigel Warner, as the oldest activist of ILGA, succinctly puts his motivation for activism in the quote above into a context of finding a new family, a group of people who affirm him in his position as an agent of change. To some extent Warner, thus, explicitly connected his activism and his activist group with his former lack of self-worth and of recognition for the intimate attachment he actually wished to form since his teenage years. His gay kinship relations became the place that made politics possible without ever entering the political stage as such. The challenge to kinship rights that l/g/b/t activism poses, then, lies in a hopefully more explicit future effort to drag kinship out of the pre-political into the political frame. Activists as agents of change are entangled in the heteronormativity of European kinship rules, but the way they position themselves agentically with regard to kinship complicates the tensions already apparent in kinship rights.

In summary, political agency is not independently available to everybody irrespective of their positioning in relation to an authority to speak and create change in a certain setting. Political action is not purely creative; even the most obviously innovative practice pre-supposes an incorporation of the rules of the political routine and pre-reflexive forms of behaviour in activism. Yet, creativity remains a concept of importance with regard to realising norms and values in concrete practices, 'the existence of values also presupposes a creative process by which values are fashioned and transmitted' (McNay 1999:189).

Creativity and agency need to be explored further to enhance an understanding of how it is that psychic anger or subjection is channelled into activism. While I have shown that activists' individual involvement and their concept of agency is not a straightforward humanist conceptualisation, it remains to be clarified how the interface between the social and the psyche work here. It also remains to be clarified how the interface between psyche and the social relate to institutional and non-institutional politics and how creative action detaches itself from its original conditions of enactment, thus, giving rise to a set of new values which become resources for further action (McNay 1999:189).

Struggles for sexual minority rights primarily produce tensions, since they are to some extent necessarily hybrid. They are hybrid not only with respect to agency, but also with respect to all other conceptual frames of political practices – from human rights to anti-discrimination and the law, from citizenship to kinship and the possibilities of agency. All political practices engage, in one way or another, in a hybrid negotiation of these tensions.

Notes

1. Some of my summaries in this chapter with regard to poststructuralist understandings of agency have been elaborated at length with respect to historiography in Beger (1997).
2. In general terms, the autonomous, rational, unified individual is the individual of modernity and of economic utility necessary to the development of capitalism.
3. A few years ago he announced a press conference to occur in two months in which he would identify gay bishops in Austria. To his amusement, all the outing work was done before the set date by journalists who researched the matter and published articles in which certain bishops were not named but were identifiable. On 1 August 1995 he then held the announced press conference, which became a major media event. In consequence the Austrian Catholic Church took Kurt Krickler to court with charges of libel. He lost in all instances. He was sentenced to disclaim his action in the leading newspapers and to pay the legal costs since, according to the court, stating that a person is gay causes severe stigma and career disadvantages for this person. Since he lives on social benefits, he wrote a letter to the Church, claiming not to have the financial means to enable him to pay for the space in the newspapers and for the legal costs. He offered to collect the money in front of the Cathedral in Vienna. Faced with the prospect of another public action on this matter, the Church backtracked, accepting the loss of a large amount of money in the legal procedures. Krickler then brought this case to the European Court of Human Rights under the head of freedom of speech, where it was

disallowed in October 2000, although similar earlier Austrian cases on freedom of speech have been successful in Strasbourg. During the interview Kurt Krickler reported about many other equally inventive and funny actions he has been involved in over the years besides his strong role in lobby politics in Austria and on the European level.

4 Kurt Krickler used the German term 'lustvolle Aktionen', which incorporates the English 'lusty' and 'pleasurable', as well as the sexual tinge of 'lustful', yet not as strongly.

5 See Davies (1991:47–8) and Bal (1991:41–6) for further discussion on the subjugating character of discourses.

6 Davies and Harré work within the field of education and agency in classrooms. They do not actually write about political activists.

Afterword: tensions in the struggle for sexual minority rights

My quest to que(e)ry political practices in Europe for the underlying centrality of gender and sexuality as epistemological ordering principles set out in the introduction has initially led me from working definitions of queer theory and of political practices to investigating a form of tension that accompanied the years of this research: the conflict between politics – or what can be called *Realpolitik* – and queer theory. I analysed the implications of this tension in my own work and attempted to fertilise the relations between critical theoretical inquiries and political practices around sexual minority rights through a deployment of the concept of hybridity in its relation to antagonism, desire, and dialogism. Consequently, dissolving practice-theory tensions as insurmountable gaps gave way to a critical reading of the conditions of struggles for sexual minority rights in Europe.

The fact that queer approaches to politics have had little resonance among European activists led me to think about the difference between the European transnational context and the mainly US-based theoretical critique. The most decisive difference is the centrality of human rights discourses. However, while I followed the logic of human rights argumentation in Europe, the concepts underpinning human rights, such as freedom, equality, integrity, and respectability, turned out to be very perceptible to a critical queer investigation. The concept of humanity produces tensions that cannot be reduced to the seeming objectivity and universal applicability of the human rights discourse. Struggles for sexual rights as human rights are different from civil rights strategies, albeit no less problematic.

Even within the realm of anti-discrimination legislation – which so far has never been critically deconstructed – a careful exploration of the concrete implications of the discourse of discrimination illuminates tensions in a struggle for rights and those tensions are only apparently academic. The way activists speak about discrimination and, thus, politically materialise and utilise the situation of lesbians and gay men in Europe, incorporates themes and concepts – such as material change, ideological rewards, diversity, liberal legal equality and the hegemony of the juridical – which can be read as problematic from a philosophical and a practical political view.

A similarly precise analysis must be conducted on European courtrooms as spaces of political action for change. The tension between the hegemony enshrined in the binary gender system – including the consequences that system bears on questions of sexuality – and the law as a decisive actor in maintaining that very hegemony is not as severe as might be assumed. The theoretical interconnection of gender and sexuality, gender identity and sexual orientation, and, subsequently, homosexual and transgender politics necessitates a critical reflection on the realm of the law as allegedly the most important guarantors of rights, justice, and equality. Yet, paradoxically, specific legal arguments and procedures already in use can be deployed to disrupt the epistemological authority of the law as a crucial site for the constitution, consolidation, and regulation of sexuality.

The lack of legal rights is often criticised as indicating a second-class citizen status for lesbians and gay men. Citizenship is a particularly important and complex issue in European politics, since it is the indicator of European integration in general. For sexual rights the historical, political, and economical legacies implied in the concept of European citizenship once again illuminate intricate complexities and tensions in the call to citizenship. Unravelled as a contradictory process of recognition, these complexities become interpretable. Claims to citizenship involve the production of meanings of what it is one wants to be recognised *as* and of the structure of this *as*. While citizenship claims cannot fulfil their goal of equality, they can clear the view to shifting solidarities and political group-making.

In European political and philosophical history, the concept of citizenship has strong connections to kinship. The role of the economically active citizen depends on kinship ties that create a private haven in which the active citizen is created and nurtured. In struggles for sexual minority rights the demand for equal citizenship is commonly assessed against the legal and social recognition gay and lesbian partnerships receive. In fact, the right to be recognised as a family constitutes the most central rallying point in European gay and lesbian rights struggles but also their greatest stumbling block. The language of kinship centrally serves both sides of the argument – those for and those against gender and sexual orientation equality – and has its origin in the centrality of kinship for all political formation in European capitalist democratic societies. An analysis of the official kinship debate illustrated how kinship is the frame upon and in which the social being that forms the basis for the political sphere in European culture is created, shaped, and enacted. This analysis highlighted the role heteronormativity plays in the framing of kinship. The theoretical concept of framing can increase our understanding of the relationship between political kinship debates and heteronormativity without reducing the one to the other. This understanding is achieved through the introduction of a web of interrelating frames that surround kinship. Framing kinship makes explicit once more the tension between justified claims to family recognition and the problem that these claims contribute to re-instating heteronormativity as the overarching frame of any kinship debate.

While tensions are clearly apparent on the structural level of struggles for sexual minority rights, there are also tensions that arise from the way individual activists locate themselves as agents of change. Activists do not only conceptualise their personal motivation and their power to achieve change as a simple expression of their own coherence and independence from the constricting forces of a marginalised sexuality. They also explicitly deal with the contradictions agency produces with regard to actively seeking change in the order of gender and sexual relations. The concept of political agency positions activists in relation to their actions and those relations are discursively determined through the rules of political participation and the historical ideal of equality and justice. Political agency is inevitably marked by contradictions.

In conclusion to my initial quest, I maintain that tensions in the struggle for sexual minority rights are neither a purely academic concern nor a political hindrance. Theory cannot predict all political necessities and incorporate all aspects of politics' contingency. Yet, it can become a technique of reading that finds and explains tensions that are already apparent to those working for change in the political field. Thus, I have to resist the temptation to end this investigation with 'here are my ten prescriptions to better it all' or to write the last chapter under the theme of 'what is to be done' for such a move pre-empts the whole point that political decision are invariably connected to frame and contingency. It remains an ongoing political and theoretical task to find those instances in the present political practices that actually touch upon the fundamental, underlying conditions of discrimination, marginalisation, and violation. To analyse whether certain political practices are of help in actually breaking present exclusionary regimes and presenting radical ruptures or whether they have within them traces of the very regimes they want to expose is a specific task which this research adds to future what-to-do lists in many disciplines. However, any theory needs to remain alert to the ironies possibly involved: what seems radical might not turn out to achieve radical change and aspects of practices that seem almost reactionary turn out to unwittingly leave a trail of radical impact. This is where the process of history permeates all theory.

Even if no such what-to-do list on the political level is attached to this conclusion, there remains a rather large agenda for research in the field of European politics. For one, my limitation to traditional lobby politics as the political practices investigated must be supplemented. What are the implications of political practices on other levels and how do different forms of conceptualising the political intersect with each other? At another level, the academic debate on activism and political change warrants more scrutiny from a transdisciplinary approach that interrogates the assumptions underpinning the difference among approaches in political science, legal studies, sociology, and philosophy. Additionally, the intersecting lines of various forms of marginalisation beyond gender and sexuality – such as race, ethnicity, disability, or age – need to be incorporated into a larger picture of political rights practices in Europe.

These and other problems remain to be addressed in further research within the field. Emphasising existing tensions with regard to the political practices analysed and with regard to the reductions and limitations one has to impose to make writing manageable is a conclusion that remains faithful to both theory and political practice. It promises further work and gives access to many more important questions to be asked. Thus, the only tenable characteristic of que(e)rying political practices in Europe is to continuously illuminate, materialise, and analyse the manifold tensions in the struggle for rights and to emphasise the central role gender and sexuality play in all political discourses on rights.

Appendix

The interviewees

Peter Ashman, human rights lawyer, head of the European Human Rights Foundation, founding member of ILGA. Now works for the European Commission.

Adrian Coman, full-time employee of ACCEPT, the Romanian lesbian and gay organisation, member of the executive board of ILGA-Europe from 1997–2002. Now works for OSI New York.

Roy Dickinson, civil servant in the EU Commission, Co-President of EGALITE until 1998.

Tatjana Greif, academic, activist in the Slovenian gay/lesbian and women's movement, member of the executive board of ILGA-Europe since 1998.

Steffen Jensen, head of a department in the Danish Ministry of Education, long-standing ILGA activist, member of the executive board of ILGA-Europe from its establishment in 1996 until 2000.

Thomas F. Kramer, political scientist, works for an internet company, founding member of EGALITE, activist in North-Rhine-Westphalia.

Kurt Krickler, translator, full-time ILGA-Europe and HOSI Wien activist (Homosexuelle Initiative, Austria), Co-Chair of the executive board of ILGA-Europe since 1996.

Hannele Lehtikuusi, Secretary for Organisational Affairs (The Green Party of Finland), activist in Finnish Rainbow Families, Chairperson of the national lesbian and gay organisation SETA 1993–96, member of the executive board of ILGA-Europe 1996–97.

Michiel Odijk and Jan Willem De Jong, Michiel works for the Dutch Commission for Environmental Impact Assessment and is a member of the Utrecht Provincial Parliament. Jan Willem is a psychiatric nurse. Both have long been involved in the COC, belong to the oldest members of ILGA, and are active members of RozeLinks (platform for sexual diversity of the Dutch Green Left Party).

Outi Ojala, MEP (Member of the European Parliament), head of the intergroup 'Equal rights for lesbians and gay men' until May 1999, Member of the Finnish Parliament since 1999.

Marion Oprel, interpreter, civil servant for the European Parliament, Co-President, later President, of EGALITE until 1998.

Rebecca Sevilla, Director of the Homosexual Movement of Lima (Peru 1988–92), ILGA-World Co-Secretary General 1992–95, Get Organized Co-ordinator, 1997–2000. Now works for Education International.

Hein Verkerk, assistant to the Dutch Green MEP group, veteran of ILGA and COC.

Nigel Warner, accountant, founding member of ILGA, full-time ILGA-Europe activist since 1998, co-representative to the Council of Europe for ILGA-Europe, member and Treasurer of the executive board of ILGA-Europe since 2000.

Maren Wuch, journalist, activist in the lglf in Cologne, member of the executive board of ILGA-Europe 1997–98.

Interview questions

This list of questions was a guide for my interviewing. Not all questions have been asked in this formulation nor in this order. In the interviews with EU officials I did not refer to ILGA and also shortened the list of questions for reasons of time constraint. Yet, every area of concern was covered.

1. What types of political activism in relation to gay and lesbian issues were/are you involved in? What are the most important dates, events, and goals of ILGA for you, particularly in relation to the European context?
2. What kind of hope do you connect to the EU as an international political stage for gay/lesbian political activism? How can your goals be achieved there? Why not just lobby nationally?
3. What forms of discrimination against gay/lesbian people are of main concern to you? What is the relative importance of partnership regulations and formal/legal rights in comparison to other areas of discrimination? How can ILGA argue that sexual rights are human rights?
4. Is the concept of minority an important strategy for gay/lesbian politics in the EU, e.g. is it important to argue that gays/lesbians in the EU are a discriminated minority group and, therefore, either need to gain access to rights or obtain anti-discrimination protection? Are your – or ILGA's – politics, therefore, politics for a certain group, or for freedom of sexuality as a concept for all people, or even against the concept of normative heterosexuality in general?
5. How does ILGA negotiate its politics of representation, i.e. speaking for l/g/b/t people? Can that be problematic? If yes, could ILGA pursue non-representational politics at all, or is speaking for a group simply the most effective and pragmatic way to reach political goals? Is the concept of identity important for politics? How definable are sexual identities for specific political purposes? Do you think politics around gay/lesbian issues take part in defining, or re-defining, what gay and lesbian identities are?
6. How important is gender to your and ILGA's political work? Is the dominant definition in our culture of two clearly distinct genders – assumed to be heterosexual – the main 'enemy' which, for example, gays, lesbians, and bisexuals share with transsexual/transgender people or should sexual orientation be regarded as a different issue from gender identity?
7. Is race/ethnicity important for your work on the European stage?
8. How do you measure success? What kinds of standards are implicitly/explicitly implied? How does that influence the planning of further political action?

9 What do you get out of your activism personally? Does it give you a form of professional identity? Does your possible position of relative power and influence within the gay and lesbian community, or other communities, help fuel your continuing activism? Is the fact that gays and lesbians are discriminated important for the formation of your own identity? Do we share a sense of community, of somehow belonging together, because we experience similar discrimination?
10 Is there any other issue that is important to you in European gay and lesbian politics that you think my research should cover?

Glossary

Civil Society Contact Group: Largest NGO alliance in Europe, bringing together four large NGO sectors – social (Social Platform), environment (Green8), development (CONCORD), human rights (EHRDN) – plus the ETUC (European Trade Union Confederation). It ran a large NGO campaign around the Convention on the Future of Europe called 'act4europe'.

Committee of Ministers: Meetings of the Foreign Ministers of the 45 member states of the *Council of Europe*. It is the legal decision-making body of the *Council of Europe*.

Convention on the Future of Europe: Body called by the Council of Ministers to draft a Constitution for the EU that would prepare it for enlargement and bring it closer to its citizens. It was comprised of Members of the European Parliament and all national Parliaments, as well as government and commission representatives, both from Member States and accession countries. Finished its work in July 2003.

Council of Europe: 45 member states that have signed the *European Convention on Human Rights*. Its bodies are the *Parliamentary Assembly*, the *Committee of Ministers*, and the *European Court of Human Rights*. The flag of the Council of Europe is blue with a ring of yellow stars and a capital C in the middle. Its seat is in Strasbourg, France.

Council of Ministers: The *European Union*'s main decision making body, consisting of the ministers of the 15 member states in charge of the topic to be decided. The meeting of the heads of state is called the *European Council*. Meetings held in view to amend or change treaties are called *Summits*.

EGALITE: Gay and lesbian staff organisation of the European institutions (EU and Council of Europe). Mainly concerned with issues relating to employment in the European institutions and with social reunions, but also an excellent source of information on political lobbying, EU law and upcoming EU programmes.

European Charter on Fundamental Rights and Freedoms: New fundamental rights charter of the *European Union*, declared in December 2000. It has no legal status or binding nature until the Constitution comes into force. It contains the fundamental Rights and Freedoms of the *European Conventions of Human Rights* and certain social rights, which pertain to *EU* citizens specifically as far as *EU* law is concerned. The Charter has the furthest reaching anti-discrimination article of an international charter in the world (art. 21). Art. 21 refers to sexual orientation, but not to gender identity.

European Commission: Executive organ of the *European Union*. Its civil servants draft all legislation, administer finances and control execution of *EU* legislation in member states. The Commission has its seat in Brussels.

GLOSSARY 233

European Communities: Contain the European Economic Community (EEC often called the EC), a treaty on anatomic energy (Euratom), and the European Coal and Steel Community (ECSC). Were extended and followed by the *European Union.*

European Convention on Human Rights (ECHR): International human rights treaty signed by 45 European countries since 1949, extending from Vladivostok to Lisbon and from Istanbul to Helsinki. It is enforced through the *European Court of Human Rights.*

European Court of Human Rights (ECHR): Court of the *Council of Europe.* Can be approached by individuals in relation to human rights violations, provided they have exhausted the legal possibilities in their countries. Approximately 800 million people are eligible to appeal to the *European Court of Human Rights.* The ECHR has its seat in Strasbourg. It judgments are binding on the member states, but it cannot enforce them through penalties.

European Court of Justice (ECJ): Court of the *European Union.* Has among others two principal functions: to check whether instruments of the European institutions and of governments are compatible with the treaties and, at the request of national courts, to pronounce on the interpretation or validity of *EU* law. The ECJ has its seat in Luxembourg.

European Parliament (EP): Parliament of the *European Union.* Directly elected by the citizens in the 15 member states. It is divided into party groupings not nationalities. The EP has its seat in Brussels, but assembles in Strasbourg for one week every month. The EP is not as powerful as national legislative bodies, yet through is agreement to the budget of the EU it can issue considerable pressure. It also has co-decision rights for most EU laws passed. Since 2000 it has its own building in Strasbourg. It used to share the building of the *PACE.*

European Union (EU): Founded in 1992 in the Treaty of Maastricht as a broadened successor and addition to the European Communities. By 2001, the EU has 15 Member States, by 2004 it will have 25. It is primarily an economic union. Its main bodies are the *European Parliament,* the *European Commission,* the *Council of Ministers,* and the *European Court of Justice.* The flag of the EU is blue with a ring of yellow stars.

European Union Law: Three main types of binding legislation exist: *Regulations, Directives,* and *Decisions.* Regulations have direct effect and apply in all Member States. Directives are binding but must be enacted in national law, form and method is left to the decision of the member states. Decisions are legally binding for those to whom they are addressed. The names will be changed in the future Constitution.

ILGA: The International Lesbian and Gay Association, largest umbrella organisation for l/g/b/t groups throughout the world. Its European branch – *ILGA-Europe* – is the major lobbyist at the European institutions with official consultative status to the *Council of Europe.*

Intergovernmental Conference: Preparatory group for the *Summits* of the *European Council*, the meetings at which new *EU* treaties are decided.

PACE: Parliamentary Assembly of the *Council of Europe*. MPs are sent by national parliaments, the composition of each national delegation reflects that of its parliament of origin. Parliamentarians meet in political groups and forms committees on certain issue such as, for example, the Committee on Human Rights and Legal Affairs. PACE issues reports, recommendations, and opinions, which are published and sent to the *Committee of Ministers*. It assesses the application of new member states and can suspend the voting rights of member states if their human rights record is not satisfying (recent example: Russia). The Assembly has its seat in Strasbourg and meets four times a year.

Social Platform: The Platform of European Social NGOs was established in 1995, and now regroups 39 European non-governmental organisations, federations and networks working in the social sector and promoting the interest of a wide spectrum of European civil society. ILGA-Europe is a member of the Social Platform.

Summit: Meeting of the heads of member states of the *European Union* with the aim to amend or decide new treaties.

Treaty of Amsterdam: Amending the Treaty of the *European Union*, the treaties establishing the European Communities, and certain related acts. Came into force on 1 May 1999. It adds an anti-discrimination article, Article 13, which led to a new *European Union* law (directive) in 2000 with respect to anti-discrimination.

Treaty of Nice: Amending the Treaty of the *European Union*, the treaties establishing the European Communities, and certain related acts. It came into force on 1 February 2003.

Bibliography

Relevant websites

The following websites contain information about the European institutions, NGOs, and political or legal documents used or referred to in this research. All ILGA-Europe documents can be found on the ILGA-Europe web page. Legal text are generally available on the websites of the European Court of Justice and the European Court of Human Rights, yet some full texts can only be accessed in legal library connections.

European Union

Committee of the Regions: www.cor.eu.int
Convention: http://european-convention.eu.int
Council of the European Union: http://ue.eu.int/index.htm
Court of Auditors: www.eca.eu.int
Economic and Social Committee: www.ces.eu.int
EU Citizens' Rights: europa.eu.int/abc/cit1-en.htm
EU Social Policy News:
    http://europa.eu.int/comm/employment_social/general/news/001221_1_en.htm
European Commission: www.europa.eu.int
European Court of Justice: http://curia.eu.int
European Ombudsman: http://www.euro-ombudsman.eu.int
European Parliament: www.europarl.eu.int
European Union website on Fundamental Rights: http://db.consilium.eu.int
Treaty of Amsterdam: http://europa.eu.int/abc/obj/amst/en/index.htm

Council of Europe

Cases of the ECHR: www.echr.coe.int/Eng/Judgment.htm
Commissioner for Human Rights: www.commissioner.coe.int/include
Committee of Ministers: http://cm.coe.int
Council of Europe Youth Directorate: www.coe.fr/youth
European Court of Human Rights: www.echr.coe.int
News from the Council of Europe: http://press.coe.int
Parliamentary Assembly: http://stars.coe.fr
Parliamentary Assembly Debate on Draft Protocol 12: http://stars.coe.int/verbatim/20001/E/0001261500E.htm
Parliamentary Assembly Debates on both Reports on the Situation of Lesbians and Gays
    http://stars.coe.int/verbatim/20003/E/0003301000E.htm
Parliamentary Assembly Opinion on Draft Protocol 12:
    http://stars.coe.fr/doc/doc00/edoc8614.htm
Presentation of the CoE: www.coe.fr/eng/present/index.htm
Report and Recommendations on the Situation of Lesbian/Gay Couples with Regard to
    Asylum and Migration: http://stars.coe.int/doc/doc00/edoc8654.htm

Report and Recommendations on the Situation of Lesbians and Gays in Council of
 Europe Member States: http://stars.coe.int/doc/doc00/edoc8755.htm
Signatories to Protocol 12 of the ECHR: http://conventions.coe.int
Treaties of the Council of Europe: http://www.coe.fr/eng/legaltxt/treaties.htm

NGOs

ACCEPT (Romania): http://accept.ong.ro
AGE: www.age.org
Civil Society Contact Group: http://act4europe.org
Euroletter (political and legal newsletter of ILGA-Europe): www.steff.suite.dk/eurolet.htm
European Anti-Poverty Network: http://eapn.org
European Disability Forum: www.edf-feph.org
European Network Against Racism: www.enar.org
ILGA-Europe: www.ilga-europe.org
ILGA-World: www.ilga.org
Mobility International: http://mobility-international.org
Press for Change: www.pfc.org.uk
Social Platform: www.socialplatform.org
Solidar: www.solidar.org
United for Intercultural Action: www.united.non-profit.nl

E-mail information and news lists

Euroletter (published on behalf of ILGA-Europe)
Euroqueer
Rex Wockner International News

Court cases cited

European Court of Justice

D v. Council of the European Union (T-264/97)
Grant v. South West Trains Ltd (C-249/96 ECR)
KB v. National Health Service Pension Agency and the Secretary of State for Health (C-117/01)
P v. S and Cornwall County Council (C-13/94 ECR)
R v. Secretary of State for Defence, ex parte Perkins (C-168/97)

European Court of Human Rights

ADT v. United Kingdom 2000 (No. 35765/97)
B v. France 1992 (No.13343/87)
Dudgeon v. UK 1981 (Ser. A, No. 255-C)
Frette v. France 2002 (No. 36515/97)
Goodwin v. United Kingdom 2002 (No. 28957/95)
Karner v. Austria 2003 (No. 40016/98)
van Kück v. Germany (No. 35968/97)
L and V v. Austria 2003 (No. 39392/98 and 39829/98)
Lustig-Prean and Beckett v. United Kingdom, 1999 (No. 31417/96; 32377/96)
Modinos v. Cyprus, 1993 (Ser. A, No. 259)

Norris v. Ireland, 1988 (Ser. A, No. 142)
SL v. Austria 2003 (No. 45330/99)
Salgueiro Da Silva Mouta C v. Portugal, 1999 (No. 33290/96)
Sheffield and Horsham v. United Kingdom 1998 (No. 31-32/1997/815-816/1018–1019)
Smith and Grady v. United Kingdom, 1999 (No. 33985/96; 33986/96)
Sutherland (Euan) v. UK, 1997 (No. 25186/94)
XYZ v. United Kingdom 1997 (No. 75/1995/581/667)

United Nations

Toonen v. Australia (UNHR Committee Doc. No. CCPR/C/50/D/488/1992)

References

Abelove, Henry. (1995). 'The queering of lesbian–gay history: an examination of the emergence of gay identity, community, and culture in modern English literature since the 1960s.' *Radical History Review* 62:44–57

Abelove, Henry, Barale, Michèle A. and Halperin, David (eds). (1993). *The Lesbian and Gay Studies Reader.* New York and London: Routledge

Adam, Barry D., Duyvendak, Jan Willem and Krouwel, André (eds). (1999). *The Global Emergence of Gay and Lesbian Politics: National Imprints of a Worldwide Movement.* Philadelphia: Temple University Press

Adams, Hazard and Searle, Leroy (eds). (1986). *Critical Theory Since 1965.* Tallahassee: University Presses of Florida

Alphen, Ernst van. (1995). 'Introduction. The gender of homosexuality.' Thamyris 2(1):3–10

Alphen, Ernst van. (1999). 'Symptons of discursivity: experience, memory, trauma.' In Bal *et al.* (eds), 27–38

Altman, Dennis. (1997). 'Global gaze/global gays'. *A Journal of Gay and Lesbian Studies* 3(4):417–36

Amnesty International. (1997). *Breaking the Silence: Human Rights Violations Based on Sexual Orientation.* London: Ennisfield Print

Amnesty International. (1998). *Indonesia: An Agenda for Human Rights Reform.* London: International Secretariat

Annets, Jason and Thompson, Bill. (1992). 'Dangerous activism?'. In Plummer, Ken (ed.), 227–36

Armstrong, Nicola. (1992). 'Handling the hydra: feminist analyses of the state'. In DuPlessis (ed.), 224–38

Bakhtin, Mikhail M. (1986). 'Discourse in the novel'. In Adams and Searle. (eds), 664–78

Bal, Mieke. (1991). *On Story-Telling: Essays in Narratology.* Sonoma, California: Polebridge Press

Bal, Mieke. (1996). 'Reading art?' In Pollock (ed.), 25–41

Bal, Mieke. (2001). 'Introduction: travelling concepts and cultural analysis'. In Goggin and Neef (eds), 7–26

Bal, Mieke and Boer, Inge E. (1994). *The Point of Theory: Practices of Cultural Analysis.* Amsterdam: Amsterdam University Press

Bal, Mieke, Crewe, Jonathan and Spitzer, Leo. (1999). *Acts of Memory: Cultural Recall in the Present.* Hanover: The University Press of New England

Banakar, Reza and Travers, Max (eds). (2002). *An Introduction to Law and Social Theory.* Oxford: Hart Publishing

Barett, Michel and Philips, Ann (eds). (1992). *Destabilizing Theory. Contemporary Feminist Debates.* Cambridge: Polity Press

Barthes, Roland. (1986). *The Rustle of Language.* New York: Hill and Wang

Baumann, Zygmunt. (1996). 'Morality in the age of contingency.' In Lash *et al.* (eds), 32–56

Bech, Henning. (1997). *When Men Meet: Homosexuality and Modernity.* Chicago: University of Chicago Press

Becquer, Marcos and Gatti, Jose. (1991). 'Elements of vogue'. *Third Text* 16(17):65–81

Beemyn, Brett and Eliason, Mickey (eds). (1996). *Queer Studies: A Lesbian, Gay, Bisexual, and Transgender Anthology.* New York, London: New York University Press

Beger, Nico J. (1996) 'Culture shaping gender relations: Polish–Jewish women in the nineteenth century'. *History Now 'Te Pae Tawhito O Te Wa'* 2(1):24–30

Beger, Nico J. (1997). *Present Theories, Past Realities: Feminist Historiography meets 'Poststructuralisms'.* Frankfurt(O.): Viademica

Beger, Nico J. (1999). 'Gay and lesbian rights are human rights! Que(e)rying a political practice in Europe'. Amsterdam School of Cultural Analysis *Privacies. Yearbook 1999*, Amsterdam: ASCA Press, 159–68

Beger, Nico J. (2000a). 'Queer readings of Europe: gender identity, sexual orientation and the (im)potency of rights politics at the European Court of Justice'. *Social & Legal Studies* 9(2):251–72

Beger, Nico J. (2000b). 'Wider lokale Scheuklappen'. In Quaestio (Beger *et al.*) (eds), 63–66

Beger, Nico J. (2001). 'Mind the gap: hybridity and the antagonistic relations of queer theory and gay/lesbian political practice'. In Neef and Goggin (eds), 145–58

Beger, Nico J. (2002). 'Putting gender and sexuality on the agenda: queer theory and legal politics'. In Banakar and Travers (eds), 173–88

Beger, Nico J., Baer, Susanne and de Silva, Angela. (2000). 'Recht und Rechte: Zwischen legaler Anerkennung/Anti-diskriminierungsgesetzen und kultureller "Revolution". Ein Podiumsgespräch'. In Quaestio (Beger, *et al.*) (eds), 182–208

Bell, David. (1995). 'Perverse dynamics, sexual citizenship and the transformation of intimacy'. In Bell and Valentine (eds), 304–17

Bell, David and Valentine, Gill (eds). (1995). *Mapping Desire: Geographies of Sexualities.* London, New York: Routledge

Bell, Mark. (1999). 'Shifting conceptions of sexual discrimination at the Court of Justice: from *P* v. *S* to *Grant* v. *SWT'. European Law Journal* 5(1):63–81

Bell, Mark. (2001). 'Sexual orientation discrimination in employment: an evolving role for the European Union'. Draft provided by the author, in Wintemute and Andenaes (eds).

Bell, Mark, Waddington, Lisa. (1996). 'The 1996 Intergovernmental Conference and the prospects of a non-discrimination Treaty Article'. *Industrial Law Journal* 25(4): 320–36

Bellamy, Richard and Castiglione, Dario. (1999). '"A republic, if you can keep it": the democratic constitution of the Europe Union'. Paper given at the UACES workshop 'Rights, Identities and Communities of the European Union', Leeds University, UK, 30 April 1999 (script provided by the author)

Berlant, Lauren and Freeman, Elizabeth. (1992). 'Queer nationality'. *Boundary* 2:150–80

Berlant, Lauren and Warner, Michael. (1995). 'What does queer theory teach us about X?' *Publications of the Modern Languages Association of America (PMLA)* 110(3):343–9

Berube, Allan and Escoffier, Jeffrey. (1991). 'Queer/Nation'. *Out/Look* 11 winter 1991
Bhaba, Homi. (1984). 'Of mimicry and man: the ambivalence of colonial discourse'. *October* 28:125–33
Binnie, Jon. (1995). 'Trading places: consumption, sexuality, and the production of queer space'. In Bell and Valentine (eds), 182–99
Binnie, Jon. (1997). 'Invisible Europeans: sexual citizenship in the new Europe'. *Environment and Planning* A(29): 237–48
Bischoff, Hans Helmut. (1994). *Europarecht für Anfänger*. München: C. H. Beck
Blasius, Mark. (1998). 'Contemporary lesbian, gay, bisexual, transgender, queer theories, and their politics'. *Journal of the History of Sexuality* 8(4):642–74
Boswell, John. (1990). 'Sexual and ethical categories in premodern Europe'. In McWhirter et al. (eds). 15–28
Bottomley, A. (ed.). (1996). *Feminist Perspectives on the Foundational Subjects of Law*. London: Cavendish
Boutros-Ghali, Boutros. (1994). 'Human rights: the common language of humanity. Opening statement of the United Nations Secretary General.' In *World Conference on Human Rights*. New York: United Nations Department of Public Information:5–29
Bower, Lisa. (1997). 'Queer problems/straight solutions: the limits of a politics of "official recognition"'. In Phelan (ed.), 267–91
Bredbeck, Gregory W. (1993). 'The postmodernist and the homosexual'. In Readings and Schaber (eds), 254–60
Bristow, Joseph. (1997). *Sexuality*. London/New York: Routledge
Brook, Heather. (1998). 'How to do things with sex'. Paper given at the conference 'Gender, Sexuality, and Law', Keele, UK, June 1998 (script provided by the author)
Brown, Wendy. (1995). *States of Injury: Power and Freedom in Late Modernity*. Princeton: Princeton Paperbacks
Bruner, Jerome. (1990). *Acts of Meaning*. Cambridge MA: Harvard University Press
Bryson, Norman. (1994). 'Art in context'. In Bal and Boer (eds), 66–78
Bubeck, Ilona (ed.). (2000). *Unser Stück vom Kuchen? Zehn Positionen gegen die Homoehe*. Berlin: Querverlag
Bullough, Vern. (1990). 'The Kinsey Scale in historical perspective'. In McWhirter et al. (eds), 3–14
Bunch, Charlotte. (1995). 'Transforming human rights from a feminist perspective'. In Peters and Wolpers (eds), 10–19
Bunch, Charlotte and Fried, Susan. (1996). 'Beijing '95: moving women's Rights from margin to center'. *Signs* 22(1):222–6
Butler, Judith. (1990). *Gender Trouble: Feminism and the Subversion of Identity*. New York: Routledge
Butler, Judith. (1992). 'Contingent foundation: feminism and the question of "postmodernism"'. In Butler and Scott (eds). 3–21
Butler, Judith. (1993). *Bodies that Matter*. New York: Routledge
Butler, Judith. (1994). 'Against proper objects'. *Differences* 6(2–3):1–26
Butler, Judith. (1997a). *Excitable Speech: A Politics of the Performative*. London, New York: Routledge
Butler, Judith. (1997b). *The Psychic Power: Essays in Subjection*. Stanford: Stanford University Press
Butler, Judith and Scott, Joan (eds). (1992). *Feminists Theorize the Political*. New York: Routledge

Callari, Antonio, Cullenberg, Stephen and Beweiner, Carole (eds). (1994). *Marxism in the Postmodern Age*. New York: Guilford

Case, Mary Ann C. (1995). 'Disaggregating gender from sex and sexual srientation: the effeminate man in the law and feminist jurisprudence'. *The Yale Law Journal* 105(1):1–100

Cohen, Cathy J. (1997). 'Punks, bulldagger, and welfare queens: the radical potential of queer politics?'. *A Journal of Lesbian and Gay Studies* 3(4):437–66

Cooper, Davina. (1993). 'The Citizen's Charter and radical democracy: empowerment and exclusion within citizenship discourse'. *Social and Legal Studies* 2(2):149–71

Cover, Robert. (1986). 'Violence and the word'. *The Yale Law Journal* 95:1595; 1986:1601–29

Culler, Jonathan (ed.). (1988). *Framing the Sign: Criticism and Its Institutions*. Norman, London: University of Oklahoma Press

Currah, Paisley. (1997a). 'Defending genders: sex and gender non-conformity in the civil rights strategies of sexual minorities'. *Hastings Law Journal* 48(6):1363–85

Currah, Paisley. (1997b). 'Politics, practices, publics: identity and queer rights'. In Phelan, Shane (ed.). 231–66

Darnovsky, Marcy, Epstein, Barbara and Flacks, Richard (eds). (1995). *Cultural Politics and Social Movements. Introduction*: vii–xxiii. Philadelphia: Temple University Press

Davies, Bronwyn. (1990a). 'Agency as a form of discursive practice: a classroom scene observed'. *British Journal of Sociology of Education* 11(3):341–61

Davies, Bronwyn. (1990b). 'The problem of desire'. *Social Problems* 37(4):501–16

Davies, Bronwyn. (1991). 'The concept of agency: a feminist poststructuralist analysis'. *Social Analysis* 30:42–53

Davies, Bronwyn. (1997). 'The subject of post-structuralism: a reply to Alison Jones'. *Gender and Education* 9(3):271–83

Davies, Bronwyn and Harré, Rom. (1990). 'Positioning: the discursive production of selves'. *A Journal for the Theory of Social Behaviour* 20(1):43–63

de Lauretis, Teresa. (1991). 'Queer theory: lesbian and gay sexualities. An introduction'. *Differences: Journal of Feminist Cultural Studies* 3(2):iv–xvii

de Lauretis, Teresa. (1994). *The Practice of Love: Lesbian Sexuality and Perverse Desire*. Bloomington: Indiana University Press

Delanty, George. (1995). *Inventing Europe: Idea, Identity, Reality*. London: Macmillan

D'Emilio, John. (1983). (1998 2nd edn). *Sexual Politics. Sexual Communities. The Making of a Homosexual Minority in the United States, 1940 – 1970*. Chicago/London: University of Chicago Press

Derbyshire, Philip. (1994). 'A measure of queer. Queer-theory and homosexual identities in Britain'. *Critical Quarterly* 36(1):39–45

Derrida, Jacques. (1982). *The Truth in Painting*. Translated by Geoff Bennington. Chicago: The University of Chicago Press

Dietz, Mary. (1992). 'Context is all: feminism and theories of citizenship'. In Mouffe (ed.), 63–88

Donelly, Jack. (1984). 'Cultural relativism and universal human rights'. *Human Rights Quarterly* 6:410–19

Dowell, L. and Pringle, R. (eds). (1992). *Defining Women: Social Institutions and Gender Divisions*. Cambridge: Polity Press

Duggan, Lisa. (1992). 'Making it perfectly queer'. *Socialist Review* 22(1):11–31

Duggan, Lisa. (2000). 'The incredible shrinking public'. In Quaestio (Beger, *et al.*) (eds), 87–95

Duggan, Lisa and Hunter, Nan D. (1995). *Sex Wars: Sexual Dissent and Political Culture.* London, New York: Routledge
DuPlessis, Rosemary. (1992). 'Stating the contradictions. the case of women's employment'. In DuPlessis (ed.), 209–23
DuPlessis, Rosemary (ed.). (1992). *Feminist Voices: Women's Studies Texts for Aotearoa/New Zealand.* Auckland: Oxford University Press
Düttmann, Alexander Garcia. (1997). *Zwischen den Kulturen: Spannungen im Kampf um Anerkennung.* Frankfurt am Main: Suhrkamp
Düttmann, Alexander Garcia. (2000). *Between Cultures: Tensions in the Struggle for Recognition.* Translated by Kenneth B. Woodgate. London, New York: Verso
Duyvendak, Jan Willem. (1996). 'The depoliticization of the Dutch gay identity, or why Dutch gays aren't queer'. In Seidman (ed.), 421–38
Dynes, Wayne R. (1992). *Homosexuality: Discrimination, Criminology, and the Law.* New York, London: Garland
Eco, Umberto. (1976). *A Theory of Semiotics.* Bloomington: Indiana University Press.
Eemeren, Frans van. Grootendorst, Rob, Jackson, Sally and Jacobs, Scott. (1993). *Reconstructing Argumentative Discourse.* Tuscaloosa, Alabama: University of Alabama Press
Einhorn, Barbara and Gregory, Jeanne. (1998). 'Introduction: the idea of Europe'. Special Issue of *The European Journal of Women's Studies* 5:293–96
Engel, Antke. (2000). 'Differenz (der) Rechte-Sexuelle Politiken und der Menschenrechtsdiskur'. In Quaestio (Began et al.) (ed.), 157–74
Engel, Antke. (2001). 'Die VerUneindeutigung der Geschlechter. Eine queere Strategie zur Veränderung gesellschaftlicher Machtverhältnisse'. In Heidel, et al. (eds), 346–64
Engel, Antke. (2002). *Wider die Eindeutigkeit: Sexualität und Geschlecht im Fokus queerer Politik der Repräsentation.* Frankfurt am Maine: Campus
Epstein, Steven. (1999). 'Gay and lesbian movements in the United States: dilemmas of identity, diversity, and political strategy'. In Adam et al. (eds), 30–90
European Commission. (1996). Commission Conference on proposed anti-discrimination Directives, Vienna, December 1998
Evans, David T. (1993). *Sexual Citizenship: the Material Construction of Sexualities.* London, New York: Routledge
Evans, David T. (2000). 'Between "moral" state and "amoral" market: the material dimensions and political dilemmas of homosexual citizenship in late modernity'. In Quaestio (Beger et al.) (eds), 67–82 (quoted from English original)
Evans, Tony. (1998). 'Introduction: power, hegemony and the universalization of human rights'. In Evans (ed.). (1998). *Human Rights Fifty Years On.* New York: Routledge
Eyerman, Ron and Jamison, Andrew. (1991). *Social Movements: A Cognitive Approach.* State College, Penn: Pennsylvania State University Press
Fabian, Johannes. (1991). *Time and the Work of Anthropology: Critical Essays, 1971–1991.* Chur: Harwood Academic Publishers
Fabian, Johannes. (1999). 'Remembering the other: knowledge and recognition in the exploration of central Africa'. *Critical Inquiry* 26(1):49–69
Fields, A. Belden and Narr, Wolf-Dieter. (1992). 'Human rights as a holistic concept'. *Human Rights Quarterly* 14:1–20
Fillieule, Olivier and Duyvendak, Jan Willem. (1999). 'Gay and lesbian activism in France: between integration and community-oriented movements'. In Adam et al. (eds), 184–213

Flick, Uwe. (1998). *Qualitative Forschung: Theorie, Methoden, Anwendung in Psychologie und Sozialwissenschaften*. Reinbek: Rowohlt

Flynn, Leo. (1996). 'The internal market and the European Union: some feminists notes'. In Bottomley (ed.), 286–308

Flynn, Leo. (1997). '"Cherishing all her children equally": the law and politics of Irish lesbian and gay citizenship'. *Social & Legal Studies* 6(4):493–512

Flynn, Leo. (1999). 'The implications of Article 13 EC–after Amsterdam, will some forms of discrimination be more equal than others?'. *Common Market Law Review* 36:1127

Foucault, Michel. (1972). *The Archeology of Knowledge*. London: Tavistock

Foucault, Michel. (1977). *Language, Countermemory, Practice: Selected Essays and Interviews*. Edited by Donald F. Bouchard. Ithaca, New York: Cornell University Press

Foucault, Michel. (1979). *Discipline and Punishment*. New York: Penguin

Foucault, Michel. (1980). *The History of Sexuality Vol. I: An Introduction*. Translated by Robert Hurley. New York: Vintage

Franke, Katherine. (1995). 'The central mistake of sex discrimination law: the disaggregation of sex from gender'. *University of Pennsylvania Law Review*. 144(1):1–99

Fraser, Nancy. (1990). 'Rethinking the public space: a contribution to the critique of actually existing democracy'. *Social Texts* 25/26:56–80

Fraser, Nancy. (1997). *Justice Interruptus*. New York: Routledge

Gamson, Joshua. (1996). 'Must identity movements self-destruct? A queer dilemma'. In Seidman (ed.), 395–420

Garkawe, Sam. (1997). 'International human rights and the law regarding sexual orientation: two book reviews and more'. *Australian Gay and Lesbian Law Journal* 7:69–92

Genschel, Corinna. (1996). 'Fear of a Queer Planet: Dimensionen lesbisch-schwuler Gesellschaftskritik'. *Das Argument* 216:525–38

Genschel, Corinna. (1997). 'Umkämpfte sexualpolitische Räume: Queer als Symptom'. In Hark and Etgeton (eds), 77–98

Giddens, Anthony. (1992). *The Transformation of Intimacy: Sexuality, Love and Eroticism in Modern Societies*. Cambridge: Polity Press

Gluck, Sherna and Patai, Daphne. (1991). *Women's Words: The Feminist Practice of Oral History*. New York, London: Routledge

Gluckman, Amy and Reed, Betsy (eds). (1997). *Homo Economics: Capitalism, Community, and Lesbian and Gay Life*. New York, London: Routledge

Goggin, Joyce and Neef, Sonja (eds). (2001). *Travelling Concepts: Text, Subjectivity, and Hybridity*. Amsterdam: University of Amsterdam Press

Goldberg-Hiller, Jonathan. (1998). 'Entitled to be hostile: narrating the political economy of civil rights'. *Social & Legal Studies* 7(4): 517–38

Goldberg-Hiller, Jonathan. (2000). 'Making a mockery of marriage'. In Herman and Stychin (eds) (paper provided by author)

Goldman, Ruth. (1996). 'Who is that queer queer? Exploring norms around sexuality, race, and class in queer theory'. In Beemyn and Eliason (eds), 169–82

Guess, Carol. (1995). 'Que(e)rying lesbian identity'. *Journal of the Midwest Modern Language Association* 28(1):19–37

Habermas, Jürgen. (1992). 'Citizenship and national identity: some reflections on the future of Europe'. *Praxis International* 12(1):1–19

Habermas, Jürgen. (1999). *Die Einbeziehung des Anderen: Studien zur Politischen Theorie*. Frankfurt am Main: Suhrkamp

Hagland, Paul Eenam Park. (1997). 'International theory and LGBT politics: testing the limits of a human rights-based strategy'. *A Journal of Lesbian and Gay Studies* 3(4):357–84

Halley, Janet. E. (1993). 'The construction of heterosexuality.' In Warner (ed.), 82–104

Halperin, David. (1995). *Saint Foucault: Towards a Gay Hagiography*. New York: Oxford University Press

Halverson, Rune. (1998). 'The ambiguity of lesbian and gay marriages: change and continuity in the symbolic order.' *Journal of Homosexuality* 35(3–4):207–31

Hark, Sabine. (1996). *Deviante Subjekte : die paradoxe Politk der Identität*. Opladen: Leske und Budrich

Hark, Sabine. (1998). 'Acting without a hand rail – paradoxes of civil rights' policies'. Keynote lecture held at the conference 'Queering Democracy: Gender, Sexuality, and Citizenship', Berlin 9–10 October 1998, (script provided by the author)

Hark, Sabine and Etgeton, Stefan (eds). (1997). *Freundschaft unter Vorbehalt: Chancen und Grenzen lesbisch-schwuler Bündnisse*. Berlin: Queerverlag

Heidel, Ulf (ed.). (2001). Jenseits der Geschlechtergrenzen. Sexualitäten, Identitäten und Körper in Perspektiven von Queer Studies. Hamburg: Männerschwarmskript

Heinze, Eric. (1995). *Sexual Orientation and Human Rights*. Dordrecht: Martinus Nijhoff

Hekma, Gert, Oosterhuis, Harry and Steakley, James. (1995). 'Leftist sexual politics and homosexuality – A historical overview'. *Journal of Homosexuality* 29(2–3):1–40

Hennessy, Rosemary. (1994). 'Incorporating queer theory on the left'. In Callari *et al.* (eds), 266–75

Hennessy, Rosemary. (1995). 'Queer visibility in commodity culture'. *Cultural Critique* 94/95:31–76

Herman, Didi. (1994). *Rights of Passage: Struggles for Lesbian and Gay Legal Equality*. Toronto, London: University of Toronto Press

Herman, Didi. (1997). *The Antigay Agenda: Orthodox Vision and the Christian Right*. London: University of Chicago Press

Herman, Didi and Stychin, Carl (eds). (2000). *Sexuality in the Legal Arena* London: Athlone Press

Hinzpeter, Werner. (2000). 'Aktion Sandmännchen'. In Bubeck (ed.), 11–18

Hirschkop, Ken and Shepherd, David (eds). (1989). *Bakhtin and Cultural Theory*. Manchester/New York: Manchester University Press

Hunter, Nan D. (1991). 'Marriage, law, and gender: a feminist inquiry'. In Duggan and Hunter (eds), 107–22

ILGA-Europe. (1998). Equality for lesbians and gay men. A relevant issue in the civil and social dialogue. Brussels: ILGA-Europe

International Lesbian and Gay Association. (1998). *Third ILGA Human Rights Annual Report 1997/1998*

International Lesbian and Gay Human Rights Commission. (1995). *Unspoken Rules: Sexual Orientation and Women's Human Rights*. San Francisco: IGLHRC

Jachtenfuchs, Markus, Diez, Thomas and Jung, Sabine. (1998). 'Which Europe? Conflicting models of a legitimate European political order'. *European Journal of International Relations* 4(4):409–45

Jackson, P. and Sullivan, G. (eds). (1999). *Multicultural Queer: Australian Narratives*. New York: Haworth Press

Jacobs, Francis, Corbett, Richard and Shackleton, Michael. (1992). *The European Parliament*. London: Longman

Jagose, Annamarie. (1996). *Queer Theory: An Introduction*. New York, London: Routledge
Kane, Daniel J. (1992). 'Homosexuality and the European Convention on Human Rights: what rights?'. In Dynes (ed.), 447–86
Kaplan, Morris. (1997a). *Sexual Justice: Democratic Citizenship and the Politics of Desire*. London: Routledge
Kaplan, Morris. (1997b). 'Intimacy and equality: The question of lesbian and gay marriage'. In Phelan (ed.), 201–30
Keck, Margaret E. and Sikkink, Kathryn. (1998). *Activists Beyond Borders: Advocacy Networks in International Politics*. Ithaca, London: Cornell University Press
Kimble, Jennifer. (1992). 'A comparative analysis of *Dudgeon v. United Kingdom* and *Bowers v. Hardwick*'. In Dynes (ed.), 200–11
Klauda, Georg. (2000). 'Vernunft und Libertinage'. In Bubeck (ed.), 43–56
Kofman, Eleonore. (1995). 'Citizenship for some but not for others: spaces of citizenship in contemporary Europe'. *Political Geography* 14(2):121–37
Kramer, Thomas F. (1997). *Die politische Debatte um Gleichberechtigung von Schwulen und Lesben und die Rolle des Europäischen Parlaments*. Unpublished MA thesis, University of Cologne (script provided by the author)
Kupp, Leila J and Taylor, Verta. (1999). 'Forging feminist identity in an international movement: a collective identity approach to twentieth-century feminism'. *Signs: Journal of Women in Culture and Society* 24(2):363–86
Lash, Scott *et al.* (1996). *Risk, Environment, Modernity: Towards a New Ecology*. London: Sage Publications
LaViolette, Nicole. (1997). 'The immutable refugees: sexual orientation in *Canada (A.G.) v. Ward*'. *University of Toronto Faculty of Law Review* 55(1):1–41
LaViolette, Nicole and Whitworth, Sandra. (1994). 'No safe haven: sexuality as a universal human right and gay and lesbian activism in international politics'. *Journal of International Studies* 23(3):563–688
Lehr, Valerie. (1999). *Queer Family Values: Debunking the Myth of the Nuclear Family*. Philadelphia: Temple University Press
Llamas, Ricardo and Vila, Fefa. (1999). 'Passion for life: a history of the lesbian and gay movement in spain'. In Adam *et al.* (eds), 214–41
Long, Scott. (1999). 'Gay and lesbian movements in Eastern Europe: Romania, Hungary, and the Czech Republic'. In Adam *et al.* (eds), 242–65
Martin, Biddy. (1994). 'Sexualities without genders and other queer utopias'. *Diacritics* 24(2–3):104–21
Marx, Karl. ([1969]1843): 'Zur Judenfrage'. In: Marx und Engels Werke 1, S. 347–77, Dietz Verlag: Berlin
McClure, Kirstie. (1992). 'On the subject of rights: pluralism, plurality and political identity'. In Mouffe (ed.), 108–27
McNay, Lois. (1999). 'Subject, psyche and agency: the work of Judith Butler'. *Theory, Culture & Society*. 16(2):175–93
McWhirter, David, Sanders, Stephanie and Machover Reinisch, June (eds)., (1990). *Homosexuality/Heterosexuality: Concepts of Sexual Orientation*. New York, Oxford: Oxford University Press
Morgan, Wayne. (1995). 'Queer law: identity, culture, diversity, law'. *Australian Gay and Lesbian Law Journal* 5:1–41
Morgan, Wayne. (1996). 'Still in the closet: the heterosexism of equal opportunity law'. *Critical InQueeries* 1(2):119–46

Mouffe, Chantal. (1992a). 'Preface. Democratic politics today'. In Mouffe (ed.), 1–16
Mouffe, Chantal. (1992b). 'Democratic citizenship and the political community'. In Mouffe (ed.), 225–39
Mouffe, Chantal (ed.). (1992c). *Dimensions of Radical Democracy. Pluralism, Citizenship, Community.* London, New York: Verso
Namaste, Ki. (1996a). 'The politics of inside/out: queer theory, poststructuralism, and a sociological approach to sexuality. In Seidman (ed.), 194–212
Namaste, Ki. (1996b). 'Tragic misreadings: queer theory's erasure of transgender subjectivity'. In Beemyn and Eliason (eds), 183–203
Namaste, Ki. (1998). 'The everyday bisexual as problematic: research methods beyond monosexism'. In Ristock and Taylor (eds), 111–36
Nicholson, Linda J. (1986). *Gender and History: The Limits of Social Theory in the Age of the Family.* New York: Columbia University Press
Nicholson, Linda and Seidman, Steven (eds). (1995). *Social Postmodernism: Beyond Identity Politics.* Cambridge: Cambridge University Press
O'Driscoll, Sally. (1996). 'Outlaw readings: beyond queer theory'. *Signs* 22(1):30–51
Offord, Baden. (1997). 'Some observations on homosexual rights and sexual identity in the Asia/Pacific'. Unpublished paper delivered at the 13th World Congress of Sexology, Spain, July 1997 (script provided by the author)
Offord, Baden. (1999a). 'Interrogating the (Homo)sexual Activist and Human Rights in Indonesia, Singapore and Australia'. Unpublished Ph.D dissertation, Southern Cross University, Lismore, New South Wales, Australia
Offord, Baden. (1999b). 'The burden of (homo)sexual identity in Singapore'. *Social Semiotics* 9(3):301–16
Offord, Baden and Cantrell, Leon. (1999). 'Unfixed in a fixated world'. In Jackson and Sullivan (ed.), 207–22
Ohms, Constanze. (2000). 'Die Sehnsucht nach Normalität'. In Bubeck (ed.), 23–42
Parker, Andrew, Russo, Mary, Summer, Doris and Yaeger, Patricia (eds). (1992). *Nationalisms and Sexualities.* New, York, London: Routledge
Pateman, Carole. (1988). *The Sexual Contract.* Stanford: Stanford University Press
Patton, Cindy. (1993). 'Tremble, hetero swine!'. In Warner (ed.), 143–77
Patton, Cindy. (1995). 'Refiguring the social space'. In Nicholson and Seidman (eds), 31–48
Pechy, Graham. (1989). 'On the borders of bakhtin: dialogisation, decolonalisation'. In Hirschkop and Shepherd (eds), 48–62
Penn, Donna. (1995). 'Queer-theorizing politics and history: political, theoretical and contextual applications of 20th-century gay–lesbian culture, and analytical organization of so-called queer theory'. *Radical History Review* 62:24–42
Peters, J. and Wolpers, A. (1995). *Women's Rights, Human Rights: International Feminist Perspectives.* London, New York: Routledge
Peterson, Spike V. and Parisi, Laura. (1998). 'Are women human? It's not an academic question'. In Evans (ed.), 132–60
Phelan, Shane. (1994). *Getting Specific: Postmodern Lesbian Politics.* London, Minnesota: University of Minnesota Press
Phelan, Shane. (1995). 'A space for justice: lesbians and democratic politics'. In Nicholson and Seidman (eds), 332–56
Phelan, Shane (ed.). (1997). *Playing with Fire: Queer Politics, Queer Theories.* London: Routledge
Phelan, Shane. (2000). 'Kinship and citizenship: new inclusions, new margins'. In Quaestio (Beger *et al.* (eds), 130–42 (quoted from English original)

Plummer, Ken (ed.). (1992). *Modern Homosexualitie:. Fragments of Lesbian and Gay Experience*. London, New York: Routledge
Plummer, Ken. (1995). *Telling Sexual Stories*. London: Routledge
Pollock, Griselda (ed.). (1996). *Generations and Geographies in the Visual Arts*. London: Routledge
Poovey, Mary. (1988). 'Feminism and deconstruction'. *Feminist Studies* 14(1):51–65
Poovey, Mary. (1992). 'The abortion question and the death of man'. In Butler and Scott (eds), 239–56
Pringle, Rosemary and Watson, Sophie. (1992). 'Women's interest and the poststructuralist state'. In Barett and Philips (eds), 86–107
Quan, Andy. (1994). "The International Lesbian and Gay Movement: ILGA, NAMBLA and the Imagined Future'. Unpublished MA thesis, Department of Political Science, York University, Canada (script provided by the author)
Quaestio (Nico J. Beger, Antke Engel, Corinna Genschel, Sabine Hark and Eva Schäfer) (eds). (2000). 'Sexuelle Politiken : politische Rechte und gesellschaftliche Teilhabe', 9–27. In *Queering Demokratie: sexuelle Politiken*. Berlin: Querverlag
Rahman, Momin and Jackson, Stevi. (1997). 'Liberty, equality and sexuality: essentialism and the discourse of rights'. *Journal of Gender Studies* 6(2):117–29
Readings, Bill and Schaber, Bennet (eds). (1993). *Postmodernism Across the Ages*. Syracuse, New York: Syracuse University Press
Reimann, Renate. (1997). 'Does biology matter? Lesbian couples' transition to parenthood and their division of labour'. *Qualitative Sociology* 20(2):153–85
Richards, David A. J. (1988). 'Human rights, public health and the idea of moral plague'. *Social Research* 55(3):491–528
Ristock, Janice L. and Taylor, Catherine G. (eds). (1998). *Inside the Academy and Out*. Toronto/Buffalo/London: University of Toronto Press
Salecl, Renata. (1993). 'The gender of rights'. *Zeitschrift für philosophischen Ost-West-Dialog*. 3:447–67
Sanders, Douglas. (1993). 'Getting Lesbian and Gay Rights on the International Human Rights Agenda'. Unpublished paper for the Vienna World Conference on Human Rights 1993 (script provided by the author)
Sarup, Madan. (1996). *Identity, Culture and the Postmodern World*. Edinburgh: Edinburgh University Press
Savoy, Eric. (1994). 'You can't go homo again: queer theory and the foreclosing of gay studies'. *English Studies in Canada* 20(2):129–44
Schuyf, Judith and Krouwel, André. (1999). 'The Dutch lesbian and gay movement: the politics of accommodation'. In Adam *et al.* (eds), 158–83
Scott, Joan W. (1988). *Gender and the Politics of History*. New York: Columbia University Press
Scott, Joan W. (1990). 'Review of *Heroes of Their Own Lives: The Politics and History of Family Violence* by Linda Gordon'. *Signs* 15(4):848–52
Scott, Joan W. (1991). 'The evidence of experience'. *Critical Inquiry* 17(4):773–93
Scott, Joan W. (1997). 'Nach der Geschichte'. *Werkstatt Geschichte* 17:5–23, (quoted from English original 'After History' provided by the author)
Sedgwick, Eve K. (1990). *Epistemology of the Closet*. Berkeley: University of California Press
Sedgwick, Eve K. (1993). *Tendencies*. Durham, NC: Duke University Press
Seidman, Steven. (1993). 'Identity and politics in a "postmodern" gay culture: some historical and conceptual notes'. In Warner (ed.), 105–42

Seidman, Steven. (1995). 'Deconstructing queer theory or the under-theorization of the social and the ethical'. In Nicholson and Seidman. (eds), 116–41
Seidman, Steven. (ed.). (1996). 'Introduction'. In *Queer Theory/Sociology*. Cambridge, MA: Blackwell, 1–30
Shaw, Jo. (1998). 'The interpretation of European Union citizenship'. *Modern Law Review*, 61(3):293–317
Shaw, Jo. (1999). 'The emergence of postnational constitutionalism in the European Union'. *Journal of European Public Policy* 6(3):579–97
Silverman, Kay. (1996). *The Threshold of the Visible World*. New York: Routledge
Sinfield, Alan. (1998). *Gay and After*. London: Serpent's Tail
Skidmore, Paul. (1997). 'Can transsexuals suffer sex discrimination?'. *Journal of Social Welfare and Family Law* 19(1):105–14
Skidmore, Paul. (1999). 'Dress to impress: employer regulation of gay and lesbian appearance'. *Social & Legal Studies* 8(4):509–29
Smith, Anna-Marie. (2000). 'Resisting the de-politicizing effects of liberal democratic pluralism: taking lesbian and gay rights beyond the single-issue politics model'. In Quaestio (Beger *et al.*) (eds), 45–62 (quoted from English original)
Smith, Dorothy E. (1987). *The Everyday World as Problematic: A Feminist Sociology*. Boston: Northeastern University Press
Stanley, Liz. (1990). 'A referral was made: behind the scenes during the creation of a social services department "elderly" statistic". In *Feminist Praxis: Research, Theory, and Epistemology in Feminist Sociology*. London: Routledge
Stanton, Donna C. (ed.). (1992). *Discourses of Sexuality: From Aristotle to AIDS*. Ann Arbor: University of Michigan Press
Stedefeldt, Eike. (2000). 'Triumph der Dummheit'. In Bubeck (ed.), 63–80
Stein, Arlene. (2000). 'Citizenship or transgression? Dilemmas of the U.S. movement for lesbian/gay rights'. In Quaestio (Beger *et al.*) (eds), 143–56 (quoted from English original)
Strobl, Rainer and Böttger, Andreas (eds). (1996). *Wahre Geschichten? Zu Theorie und Praxis qualitativer Interviews*. Baden-Baden: Nomos Verlagsgesellschaft
Stümke, Hans-Georg. (1989). *Homosexuelle in Deutschland : eine politische Geschichte*. München: C. H. Beck
Stychin, Carl. (1995). *Law's Desire: Sexuality and the Limits of Justice*. New York, London: Routledge
Stychin, Carl. (1998). *A Nation by Rights*. Philadelphia: Temple University Press
Stychin, Carl. (2000). 'Grant-ing rights: the politics of rights, sexuality and European Union'. *Northern Ireland Legal Quarterly* 51(2):281–302
Stychin, Carl. (2001). 'Disintegrating sexuality: citizenship and the European Union'. (script provided by the author)
Sullivan, Maureen. (1996). 'Rozzie and Harriet? Gender and family patterns of lesbian coparents'. *Gender & Society* 10(6):747–67
Tasker, Fiona and Golombok, Susan. (1998). 'The role of co-mothers in planned lesbian-led families'. *Journal of Lesbian Studies* 2(4):49–68
Tassin, Etienne. (1992). 'Europe: a political community?'. In Mouffe (ed.), 169–92
Tully, James. (1999). 'Justice and Stability in Multicultural Societies: Freedom and Disclosure in Multicultural Societies'. Paper given at the UACES workshop 'Rights, Identities and Communities of the European Union', Leeds University, UK, 30 April 1999 (script provided by the author)

Turner, Bryan. (1992a). 'Outline of a theory of citizenship'. In Mouffe (ed.), 33–62
Turner, Bryan. (1992b). 'Contemporary problems in the theory of citizenship'. In Turner. (ed.) *Citizenship and Social Theory*. London, Newbury: Sage Publications
Vaid, Urvashi. (1995). *Virtual Equality: The Mainstreaming of Gay and Lesbian Liberation*. New York: Anchor
Vicinus, Martha. (1993). '"They wonder to which sex I belong": the historical roots of modern lesbian identity'. In Abelove *et al.* (eds), 432–52
Vicinus, Martha. (1994). 'Lesbian history – All theory and no facts or all facts and no theory?'. *Radical History Review* 60:57–75
Waddington, Lisa. (1999). 'Testing the limits of the EC Treaty Article on non-discrimination'. *Industrial Law Journal* 28:133
Walkowitz, Judith, Jehlen, Myra and Chevigny, Bell. (1989). 'Patrolling the borders: feminist historiography and the new historicism'. *Radical History Review* 43:23–43
Walters, Suzanna Danuta. (1996). 'From here to queer: radical feminism, postmodernism, and the lesbian menace. Or, why can't a woman be more like a fag?'. *Signs* 21(4):830–67
Warner, Michael. (1992). 'From queer to eternity: an army of theorists cannot fail'. *The Village Voice Literary Supplement* 106 June 1992:18–19
Warner, Michael. (1993). 'Introduction'. In Wamer (ed.), *Fear of a Queer Planet: Queer Politics and Social Theory*. Minneapolis: University of Minnesota Press, vii–xxxi
Warner, Michael. (1999). 'Normal and normaller: beyond gay mariage'. *GLQ. Journal of Lesbian and Gay Studies* 5(2):119–72
Warner, Michael and Berlant, Lauren. (1995). 'What does queer theory teach us about X?' (*PMLA*): *Publications of the Modern Language Association of America*. 110(3):343–9
Weedon, Chris. (1987). *Feminist Practice and Poststructuralist Theory* Oxford: Blackwell
Weidenfeld, Werner (ed.). (1994). *Maastricht in der Analyse*. Gütersloh: Bertelsmann Stiftung, 11–54
Weidenfeld, Werner and Jung, Christian. (1994). 'Das Entscheidungsgefüge der Europäischen Union: Institutionen, Prozesse und Verfahren'. In Weidenfeld (ed.), 11–54
Weston, Kath. (1991). *Families We Choose: Lesbians, Gays, Kinship*. New York: Columbia University Press
Weston, Kath. (1998). *Longslowburn: Sexuality and Social Science*. New York/London: Routledge
Wintemute, Robert. (1996). *Sexual Orientation and Human Rights: The United States Constitution, the European Convention, and the Canadian Charter*. Oxford: Clarendon Press
Wintemute, Robert. (1997). 'Recognising new kinds of direct sex discrimination: transsexualism, sexual orientation and dress codes'. *The Modern Law Review* 60(3):334–59
Wintemute, Robert and Andenaes, M. (eds). (2001). *Legal Recognition of Same Sex Partnerships: A Study of National, European and International Law*. London: Hart Publishing
Witzel, Andreas. (1996). 'Auswertung problemzentrierter Interviews: Grundlagen und Erfahrungen'. In Strobl and Böttger (eds), 49–75
Young, Robert J. C. (1995). *Colonial Desire: Hybridity in Theory, Culture, Race*. London, New York: Routledge
Zizek, Slavoj. (1992). 'Eastern Europe's republics of Gilead'. In Mouffe (ed.), 193–210

Index

Note: 'n' after a page reference indicates a note number on that page.

activist(s) 6, 7, 11–14, 19, 37, 111, 125, 193, 202–23, 226
adoption 29, 143n.13, 173–89, 196
age 10, 53, 102, 103, 122n.11, 156, 227
age of consent 1, 29, 33, 39n.16, 80, 90–1, 176
agency 7, 56, 72, 88, 118, 120, 202–23, 226
    authority to 45, 203, 205, 206, 214–18, 222, 226
AIDS 1, 48, 57n.1, 58n.12
Alphen, Ernst van 132, 143n.6, 190, 199n.10
anti-discrimination 6, 8, 23–7, 30, 101–22, 125, 130, 151, 161, 174, 220, 225
argumentation 54–6, 146
authenticity/authentic 175, 176, 184, 191, 192–7

Bakhtin, Mikhail 69–70
Bal, Mieke 8–9, 14n.14, 49–50, 190, 191, 199n.11, 214, 215, 223n.5
Becquer, Marcos 68–9, 71, 76n.10
Bell, Mark 106, 122n.8, 131, 140
bisexual/bisexuality 4–5, 34, 71, 81, 88, 105, 107, 108, 111, 112, 119, 127, 133, 136, 139, 140, 142, 148, 158, 163, 165, 169, 177, 180, 184, 185, 188, 194, 196, 212
black civil rights movement 47
Blasisus, Mark 46
body 133, 134, 183, 186
Bredbeck, Gregory 59
Brown, Wendy 89–90, 94, 101, 109, 119, 120, 181, 187, 197, 199n.8
Bruner, Jerome 52
Butler, Judith 14n.3, 14n.4, 42, 51, 58n.15, 70, 73, 76n.8, 88, 123n.24, 132, 133, 179, 192, 193, 195, 196, 197, 199n.13, 214, 215

children 158, 173–89, 192, 196
    adoption 173–5, 180–9, 194, 198n.2
    custody 173–5, 196
citationality 51
citizen 73, 113, 145–69, 175, 177, 193, 226
    economic 155, 160–2, 221
citizenship 3, 6, 8, 89, 93, 117, 145–69, 174, 197, 221, 222, 226
    European 6, 20, 71, 147–62
    liberal 153
    sexual 146, 148–62
civic republicanism 153–4
class 41, 53, 90, 125, 186, 227
concepts 5, 7–9
    political 3, 5, 8, 9
    theoretical 5, 8, 9
consumerism 160–2
Council of Europe 1, 18–20, 27–33, 79–81, 106, 144, 169n.3, 182
Cover, Robert 109–10
Currah, Paisley 14n.3, 133

Davies, Bronwyn 72, 123n.25, 202, 205, 214–17, 219, 223n.5, 223n.6
decriminalisation of homosexuality 1, 18, 28, 125
democracy 82, 93, 109, 110
democratic 72, 101, 120
Derrida, Jacques 191
desire 70–5, 88, 117, 182, 192, 193–7, 202, 205, 219, 225
dialogism 60, 69–70, 225
disability 87, 102, 103, 122n.11, 227
discourse 37, 42–7, 50–7, 68–75, 155, 184, 207, 219, 225
    human rights 54, 79–100, 102, 184, 207, 219, 225
    legal 110–14, 127, 131–42, 168, 221

discrimination 6, 83, 86, 91, 96, 99n.4, 101, 104–22, 128–31, 136–41, 145–9, 152, 193, 207, 210, 222
discursive practices 72–3
diversity 9, 97, 141
Donnelly, Jack 84
Duggan, Lisa 14n.3, 44, 59
Düttman, Alexander 164–6, 171–2n.26, 172n.29

Eemeren, Frans van 54–6
Engel, Antke 73, 89, 127
equality 5, 8, 22, 37, 47, 71, 79, 86, 93–4, 98, 111, 128, 135, 138–9, 140, 145–9, 151, 156–7, 165, 187, 207, 221, 225, 227
European Convention on Human Rights 25, 27–9, 38n.9, 100n.20, 107, 109
European Court of Human Rights 28–30, 31, 91, 123n.21, 129, 174, 198n.2
European Union 1, 18–27, 37n.1, 79–81, 102–6, 113, 146–9, 151, 159, 160
   Article 13 23, 102, 103–6, 114
   Charter of Fundamental Rights 25–6, 34, 102, 134
   Constitution 21, 25–6, 102, 147, 150, 151, 154, 155, 159, 165
   Commission 3, 21–2, 103, 122n.9, 130
   Council 20–1, 103, 104, 130, 173, 177
   Court of Justice 6, 21–2, 27, 122, 123n.21, 126, 128, 129, 135, 151, 158
   Parliament 21, 23, 24, 25, 37–8n.2, 103, 130
   Treaty of Amsterdam 20, 23, 25, 102, 103–6, 126, 140
Europeanness 145–62, 165
Evans David 44, 146, 160–1, 167–9, 171n.21
exclusion 6, 125, 140
experience 64, 71, 115–16, 215

Fabian, Johannes 165, 166, 167, 171n.24, 176
family 7, 29, 89, 158, 173–89, 192, 194, 221
   see also kinship

feminism/feminist 8, 10, 50, 59, 74, 88, 93, 94, 100n.19, 116, 123n.26, 125, 126–7, 132, 156, 158, 169n.5, 171n.26, 172n.32, 187, 189, 197, 199n.12, 205
   methodology 12
   theory 8, 82–3
Foucault, Michel 3, 14n.4, 44–5, 89
frame 7, 190–8, 226
framing 7, 175, 190–9, 226
freedom 5, 30, 79, 83, 86, 91–3, 98, 152, 187, 220, 221
freedom of movement 27, 155–60

Gamson, Joshua 66
gap between theory and politics 5, 59–67, 71, 225
Garkawi, Sam 99n.5, 99n.19
Gatti, Jose 68–9, 71, 76n.10
gender 3, 6–8, 45, 87, 90, 125, 126, 131–42, 147, 155, 156, 161, 182–3, 185, 186, 189, 226
   binary 42, 66, 73, 88–9, 117, 118, 122, 127, 131–42, 192, 196, 225
   and biological sex 136, 138, 188
   equality 10, 161, 129–31
   identity 6, 25–7, 30, 34, 38n.6, 39n.20, 45, 102, 116, 123n.15, 127–35, 136–42, 175–7, 179, 182–3, 216, 225
   and sexuality 6, 42–7, 118, 126–7, 131–42, 182–3, 186–8, 216, 225
genealogy 3
Genschel, Corinna 45, 48, 189
Giddens, Anthony 199n.12
Goldberg-Hiller, Jonathan 110, 170n.7, 180, 181

Habermas, Jürgen 80, 101, 150, 189
Halperin, David 41
harassment 1, 105–6, 107, 114
Hark, Sabine 50, 61, 120
hegemony 69–70, 140, 225
   of the juridical 71, 109–14, 115, 121, 125, 220, 225
Hennessy, Rosemary 45, 75n.1, 171n.23
Hermann, Didi 108, 111, 118, 121, 170n.23
heteroglossia 69–70

INDEX

heteronormativity/heteronormative 7, 45, 117, 120, 126, 130, 131, 175, 185, 187, 189–98, 219, 221
heterosexuality/heteorsexual 45–6, 91, 117–18, 126, 130, 132, 133, 139–40, 143n.12, 173–5, 183, 185–6, 189, 190, 192–8
homophobia 104, 111, 117, 118, 120
humanism 87, 155
  humanist subject 88, 193, 203
  liberal 7, 88–9, 152, 203–6, 214
humanness 3, 5, 79, 84, 90, 92, 98
human rights 8, 28, 53, 78–100, 175, 207, 219, 222, 225
hybridity 5, 8, 60, 67–75, 222, 225

identity 41–7, 53–4, 79, 96, 115, 118, 120, 125, 130, 156, 174, 180, 203, 205, 208, 218
  homosexual 10, 42, 73, 132, 133–4, 149, 166, 208, 210, 214–19
  politics 1, 13, 42–56, 62–7, 69–70, 97, 132, 208, 212, 213
ideology 108, 119
ILGA-Europe 3, 14n.5, 18–19, 21, 23, 25, 31, 33–7, 38, 53, 62–7, 81, 91, 102, 107, 111–13, 129, 133, 147–8, 151–62, 176–89, 191, 192, 195, 207, 221
integrity 5, 79, 83, 95, 96–8
intelligibility 51, 73, 196, 197
interdisciplinarity/transdisciplinarity 8, 14–15n.14
interviews 7, 11–13

Jagose, Annamarie 14n.3, 66
justice 7, 8, 47, 125, 135, 138, 140, 154

Kaplan, Morris 108–9, 124n.30, 125, 174, 186
Keck, Margaret 1, 18, 36–7, 171n.17, 202, 203–6
kinship 3, 6–7, 173–98, 221, 226
knowledge production 71–2

language 42–4, 67–70
Lauretis, Teresa de 41, 76n.14, 99n.12

law 3, 6, 8, 109–14, 118, 119, 123n.17, 125, 130, 135–42, 153, 207–14, 220, 222
  legal discourse 108–14, 125–42
  legal politics 6, 109–14, 125–42
  queer 141–2
lesbian activism 5, 47, 122, 126
liberalism/liberal 89–90, 108, 113, 151, 153, 154, 187, 203
lobbying 3, 4, 5, 18, 19, 21, 25, 26, 29, 30, 32–5, 70, 86, 96, 102, 106, 133, 141, 208, 209, 210
  lobby politics 1, 2, 4, 35, 36, 45, 51, 53, 54, 70, 95, 114, 123n.20, 146, 148, 154, 158, 167, 168, 198, 222n.3
love 182, 184, 188, 192, 193–8

marriage 139, 173–89, 190, 193–8
  see also kinship
meaning 8–9, 40, 42–6, 49, 69, 80, 87, 98, 115, 121, 125, 131, 135, 136–7, 140, 141, 147, 148, 158, 159, 164, 173, 175, 176, 182, 190–4, 196, 198, 205, 207, 213, 214, 216, 221, 226
  production 50–7, 69–75, 116, 166
minority 47–50, 72, 102, 139, 147, 151, 213–20, 226
Morgan, Wayne 126, 135
Mouffe, Chantal 152, 154, 167, 170n.7

Narr, Wolf–Dieter 82–3
nation state 6, 19, 147, 155–6
nationalism 80, 147, 154, 155
NGO 21–7, 33–7, 103, 106, 147, 207, 215, 218, 221
norm/normal 42–7, 96, 121, 136, 139, 141–2, 204
  regime of the 46, 121, 127, 190–8, 220
normalisation 25, 136, 158, 190–8

Offord, Baden 54, 78, 82, 86, 87, 89, 99n.12, 100n.25
order
  political 155
  social 179–90

paedophilia 104, 122n.10, 176
parenting 29, 174–9, 192
  see also kinship

251

Parisi, Laura 88–9
partnership 6, 29, 38n.16, 47, 80, 173–89, 192
  see also kinship
Patton, Cindy 65
performative/performativity 50–7, 171, 192, 197, 199n.14
Peterson, Spike 88–9
Phelan, Shane 168, 181, 182, 183, 186
political practice 9, 49, 50–7, 90, 111, 116, 153, 167, 202, 215, 225, 227
Poovey, Mary 88, 133
poststructuralism/poststructuralist 2, 9, 13, 14n.13, 42–7, 74, 88, 117, 126, 132, 205, 222n.1
power 42–7, 89
progress 82, 83, 85, 86, 108–9, 112, 208
prohibition 23, 26, 57, 73, 75, 102, 109, 117, 130, 137, 165
psychoanalysis 8, 115–18, 123n.17
public and private 153, 162, 168, 180–2

queer theory 2, 40–50, 59–69, 111, 132, 141, 187, 189, 197, 219, 225

race 41, 53, 67–71, 87–8, 90, 98, 102, 103, 125, 155, 156, 189, 185, 186, 227
racism 10, 24, 71, 112, 118, 155, 159
recognition 6, 8, 79, 94–6, 98, 146, 151, 152, 162–6, 173, 176, 181, 190, 226
  process of 6, 146, 162–6
religion 28
respectability 5, 79, 83, 86, 94–6, 98, 225
rights 2, 3, 8, 37, 62, 70–5, 114–22, 125, 134, 135–42, 145–62, 168, 173–9, 193, 220, 225, 227
  civil 93, 101, 145, 225
  desire for 52, 70–5, 193, 195, 214
  homosexual 2, 79–87
  individual 87
  legal 6, 110–14, 125–42, 157, 168, 220, 207–14
  liberal 89–90, 108, 111, 153
  rhetoric 83

Salecl, Renata 116–17, 118–19, 123n.27
Sarup, Madan 43
Scott, Joan 43, 115, 118, 120, 166, 206
Seidman, Steven 14n.3, 42, 45, 62
sexism 62, 118
sexual orientation 23–7, 63–5, 96, 102–6, 122n.14, 127, 128–31, 132–42, 148, 149, 151, 170n.70, 174, 177, 179, 180, 182, 193, 198n.2, 203, 207, 210, 211, 212, 215, 216, 218, 220, 225, 226
Sikkink, Kathryn 1, 18, 36–7, 171n.16, 202, 203–6
Sinfield, Alan 67–8
Stychin, Carl 100n.18, 121, 125, 126, 141, 142, 145, 153–5, 159, 160, 161, 167–9, 169n.1, 170n.7, 173
subject 43–7, 73, 114, 115–18, 123n.25, 141, 153, 194, 214, 215
subjection 193–7, 214, 222
subjectivity 43–7, 53–4, 115–18, 123n.25, 164, 190, 193–7, 213, 215

Tassin, Etienne 154–5, 167, 169n.1, 170n.7
transgender/transsexuality 4, 5, 14n.7, 27, 30, 34, 38n.20, 41, 71, 81, 88, 108, 111, 112, 119, 122, 125–7, 128–42, 143n.4, 143n.8, 143n.9, 148, 158, 165, 169, 177, 180, 184, 185, 188, 191, 194, 195, 196, 212, 221, 225
Turner, Bryan 149, 167
Tutu, Desmond 78

Vaid, Urvashi 62, 123n.20

Warner, Michael 14n.3, 14n.4, 41, 46, 173, 186, 187, 199n.14
women 88–9, 93, 126, 131, 132, 135, 147, 161, 181
Weston, Kath 50, 173, 176, 187, 188, 194
Wintemute, Robert 86, 99n.15, 131, 143n.11

xenophobia 48, 58n.13, 112, 159

EU authorised representative for GPSR:
Easy Access System Europe, Mustamäe tee 50,
10621 Tallinn, Estonia
gpsr.requests@easproject.com

www.ingramcontent.com/pod-product-compliance
Ingram Content Group UK Ltd.
Pitfield, Milton Keynes, MK11 3LW, UK
UKHW021835140426
5217IPUK00021B/1472